Fodors89

New York City

FODOR'S TRAVEL PUBLICATIONS, INC.
New York & London

Fodor's New York City

Editor: Andrew Beresky
Assistant Editor: Staci Capobianco
Editorial Contributors: Jane Hershey, Nan and Ivan Lyons, J. P. MacBean, Melanie Menagh, David P. Schulz
Illustrations: Brian Callanan, Sandra Lang
Maps and Plans: Pictograph
Cover Photograph: Craig Aurness/West Light

Cover Design: Vignelli Associates

MANUFACTURED IN THE UNITED STATES OF AMERICA
10 9 8 7 6 5 4 3 2 1

Contents

FOREWORD   v

PREFACE   vi

NEW YORK CITY'S ETHNIC MAKE-UP   vii

FACTS AT YOUR FINGERTIPS   1

When to Go, 1; Planning Your Trip, 1; Tips for British Travelers, 2; Tourist Information, 3; Packing, 3; What to Do with the Pets, 4; What It Will Cost, 4; Hints to the Motorist, 5; Drinking Laws, 6; Smoking Laws, 6; Religious Worship, 6; Business Hours, Holidays, and Local Time, 6; Postage, 7; Tipping, 7; Senior Citizen and Student Discounts, 8; Hints to the Disabled, 8; Emergency Telephone Numbers, 8; Metric Conversion, 9

INTRODUCTION TO NEW YORK CITY   11
    Map of Manhattan Points of Interest, 24–25

NEW YORK CITY: A CONGREGATION OF NEIGHBORHOODS   28
    Orientation map of Manhattan, 30–31
    Map of Lower Manhattan, 41
    Map of SoHo—Chinatown—Little Italy, 49
    Map of Greenwich Village, 54–55
    Map of Midtown Manhattan, 64–65
    Plan of the United Nations, 74
    Plan of Lincoln Center, 78
    Map of the Upper West Side, 79
    Map of the Upper East Side, 83

SIGHTSEEING CHECKLIST   100

PRACTICAL INFORMATION FOR NEW YORK CITY   104

    How to Get There, 104
    Telephones, 105
    Hotels and Motels, 105
    How to Get Around, 116
    Tourist and General Information Services, 124
    Recommended Reading, 125
    Seasonal Events, 126
    Free Events, 129
    Tours and Special-Interest Sightseeing, 131
    Parks, 133
        Map of Central Park, 134
    Zoos, 137
    Gardens, 137
    Beaches, 139
    Babysitting Services, 140
    Children's Activities, 141
    Participant Sports, 144
    Spectator Sports, 148
    Lotteries, 151
    Historic Sites, 151

CONTENTS

Libraries, 156
  Plan of the 42nd Street Library, 157
Museums, 159
  Plan of the American Museum of Natural History, 160–161
  Plan of the Brooklyn Museum, 164–165
  Plan of the Cloisters, 167
  Plan of the Frick Collection, 169
  Plan of the Metropolitan Museum of Art, 174–177
  Plan of the Museum of Modern Art, 180–181
Movies, 189
Music, 190
Dance, 194
Stage, 196
Shopping, 200
  Map of Midtown Shopping, 206–207
  Map of Manhattan Shopping, 216–217
Restaurants, 229
Desserts, 282
Coffeehouses (Cafés), 283
Nightlife, 284
Bars, 295
  Map of Areas Active at Night, 300–301

INDEX   305

FOREWORD

Of all the wonders of New York, the greatest is its status as an open city. It has no boundaries, no frontiers, no lines of demarcation. So you want to be a New Yorker? Consider yourself one and you are one.

Because New York is a city-state of mind, its possibilities are infinite. Creativity, in the arts, in business, in virtually every field of human endeavor, flows from this openness. Nothing surprises us here. Everything changes. Some people have pictured New York as harsh and callous. Not true. It is clear-eyed and tolerant.

The bigness and business of all the world's diversity compressed in one place can be unnerving. There are even natives who venture into unfamiliar precincts with a sense of trepidation. This is a shame, and an unnecessary shame. New York is meant to awaken the sense of adventure in every heart.

Take art. No visitor should miss the encyclopedic marvels of the Metropolitian Museum of Art and the breathtaking pleasures of the Museum of Modern Art (MOMA to you and me). But is there a better way to feel at home with the beauty of great art than getting to know the mansion that houses the Frick Collection? And what about the exotic rewards of the sumptuous collection of Tibetan art found in a modest house and garden on Staten Island?

Take music. Of course, there is the grandest of grand opera. And a dizzying array of orchestras and groups and performers. But there is also the most modern of modern jazz in this club or that. There are cocktail lounge smoothies. There is a revivified folk music scene in Greenwich Village. There are punks and performance artists and piccolo players. As Leonard Cohen wrote, "There is music on Clinton Street . . ." and, it seems, on every street.

Take theater. Every time somebody starts to write "Broadway is dead," it comes alive with a burst of innovation and high-energy entertainment. But in New York, theater also means revisionist Shakespeare Off-Broadway, the unknown playwright experimenting Off-Off-Broadway, a new combination of music and dance and words and sounds and movement and backdrops in a SoHo loft.

In New York, a painter can experience the frenzy of the New York Stock Exchange trading floor from the viewing gallery. A stockbroker can learn to sculpt at the Art Students League. Both—and everyone else—can stalk birds in the marshlands of the Jamaica Bay Wildlife Refuge in Queens.

Use this guidebook to pick up the trails and open the doors. And then use your senses to discover the rest. Walk streets that are unlike any other streets in the world. Absorb the energy.

Visit George Washington's pew at St. Paul's Chapel and reflect on New York's role as the nation's first capital. Admire the Statue of Liberty, but don't forget Ellis Island, gateway to the future for most of our forebears. Gaze on the mighty Palisades of the Hudson River from the bluffs of Riverdale in the Bronx. Savor harbor and skyline from the Brooklyn Heights Promenade. Is there a greater urban view anywhere?

There is too much to do and too much to take in. It is a life's work. That's why there's no such thing as staying too long in New York. You simply move faster, talk quicker, and speed up your way of thinking.

It may seem daunting at first, but remember the saving grace: Wherever you come from, you are home in New York.

MAYOR EDWARD I. KOCH

PREFACE

Whatever New York City is—and we won't try to summarize it here, while so many fine writers have fallen short at it—it is the *ne plus ultra* of its type, the ultimate megalopolis. Visitors and residents alike feel this even when coming in on any of its majestic bridges at night or when flying over the city. The city holds forth both the excitement and promise of human achievement.

While every care has been taken to assure the accuracy of the information in this guide, the passage of time will always bring change, and consequently the publisher cannot accept responsibility for errors that may occur.

All prices and opening times quoted here are based on information available to us at press time. Hours and admission fees may change, however, and the prudent traveler will avoid inconvenience by calling ahead.

Fodor's wants to hear about your travel experiences, both pleasant and unpleasant. When a hotel or restaurant fails to live up to its billing, let us know and we will investigate the complaint and revise our entries where the facts warrant it.

Send your letters to the editors of Fodor's Travel Publications, 201 E. 50th Street, New York, NY 10022, or 30–32 Bedford Square, London WC1B 3SG, England.

NEW YORK CITY'S ETHNIC MAKE-UP

New York City must be considered in the context of the urban, suburban, and so-called exurban areas that surround it and of which it is the working center; this area has an estimated population of about 17,000,000 people, and is the most populous urban area in the world. (Mexico City is second and Tokyo third.)

The population of the five boroughs of the city itself is a little over 7,100,000 at the most recent reliable count (1980). Of these, 0.9 million are Jewish (not an ethnic category, to be sure), and about 1.8 million black. The figure for blacks includes those with heritages from Haiti, Trinidad, and other places in the Caribbean area. There are about 1.4 million Hispanic-Americans (Puerto Rico, Cuba, Dominican Republic, South America, Mexico). It is now difficult to estimate the Italian-American population, but it is presumed to be something less than a million, as is the Irish-American community here, many having moved out to the suburbs. The figure for Asians (including Chinese, Japanese, and Korean) is 250,000. Other noticeable ethnic presences are Greek, Indian, German, Hungarian, and Russian.

Here are selected figures for registered *aliens* resident in the city:

Dominican Republic	88,000
China	45,000
Italy	43,000
Jamaica	38,000
USSR	32,000
Korea	20,000
India	15,000
England	11,000
Poland	9,000

The total of registered (legal) aliens is 600,000, but the N.Y. City Planning Commission estimates that there are about 750,000 undocumented (illegal) aliens here, most of whom have not been included in any of the official population figures given above. There are 35,000 members of the foreign diplomatic community in the city.

FACTS AT YOUR FINGERTIPS

WHEN TO GO. Ultimately, the answer to that question is "anytime." Whatever your interests—from grand opera to horseback riding, modern art to sea lore, the stock exchanges to the Statue of Liberty—there'll be more than you can possibly take in during any one visit, no matter what time of year you decide to go or how long you stay. In New York, even the natives (especially the natives, some might say) never see it all!

At one time, it seemed as though New York's cultural life was limited to the months between October and May, when the new Broadway shows opened, and during which span the Metropolitan Opera, the New York Philharmonic, and the Brooklyn Academy of Music's Next Wave Festival held their formal seasons. Today, there are Broadway openings in mid-July, while the hits of past seasons continue to run; the Met and the Philharmonic take to the city's parks for free live performances, and the number of visiting orchestras and opera and ballet companies can be staggering.

With the exception of a handful of holidays such as Christmas, New Years, and Thanksgiving, the city's museums are open year-round (they do have their regular day off during the week, of course), as are the parks for bicycling or cross-country skiing or viewing the fall foliage (in Central Park) or the springtime cherry blossoms (in Brooklyn's Botanic Gardens).

One word of caution, however: The weather in New York can go to extremes. Winter will be marked by a few sub-zero degree days, and summers find the temperature skyrocketing into the 90s (with humidity to match); spring and fall tend to be beautifully mild and dry—but then these seasons seem to be getting shorter every year, as blizzards blow in mid-April and Indian summers run into October. The best advice to a visitor: No matter how warm you expect it to be, carry an extra sweater (you may need it in air-conditioned places even if it's sweltering outside or in the evening for outdoor dining or concerts). Conversely, no matter how cold you fear it will get, bring something lightweight.

PLANNING YOUR TRIP. We urge you to make your basic travel arrangements in advance, whenever possible. It is best to arrive in New York with hotel or motel reservations in hand, lest you find yourself competing with half a dozen major conventions that have booked up most of the rooms available throughout the city or having to pay for accommodations well beyond your needs or anticipated budget.

We also strongly recommend consulting a travel agent. There are numerous "package tours" for New York that provide air travel from your city of origin combined with hotel arrangements and sometimes with meals and theater tickets, and such packages tend to be far more reasonable than you could obtain booking on your own. An agent will be familiar with the latest offerings and should be able to help you find one to suit your interests—whether you simply want air and hotel or whether you want some meals, or theater tickets, or a car as part of the deal. There is no fee for a travel agent's services beyond extraordinary telephone or Telex charges.

As will be explained in further detail later on, having a car in New York City, and in particular in Manhattan, is more of a bother than it is worth. If you insist on driving in New York and do not already belong to an auto club, now is the time to join one. They can be very helpful providing routings and emergency road service (if your car is a rental, the rental company will provide the latter). The most widely recognized is the *American Automobile Association,* 8111 Gatehouse Rd., Falls Church, VA 22047, with many offices around the New York metropolitan area. Members are entitled to free maps, among other publications, which are available at local offices or which may be ordered by mail.

It is a good idea to carry traveler's checks and/or credit cards rather than a large amount of cash, though you may need some form of identification to cash traveler's checks—and traveler's checks are by no means universally accepted. Most major department stores accept one or another major credit card in addition to those they issue themselves. Gas companies, however, increasingly accept only their own cards.

Students and senior citizens will also want to carry suitable identification cards with them at all times, as many museums, some theaters, some hotels, and other institutions offer discounts for those who qualify.

TIPS FOR BRITISH TRAVELERS. Passports and Visas. You will need a valid passport (cost £15) and a U.S. Visitor's Visa that you can get either through your travel agent or by post from the United States Embassy, Visa and Immigration Dept., 5 Upper Grosvenor St., London W1A 2JB, tel. 01/499–3443. The embassy no longer accepts visa applications made by personal callers. No vaccinations are required.

Customs. Visitors 21 or over can take in 200 cigarettes or 50 cigars or 3 pounds of tobacco; 1 U.S. quart of alcohol; duty-free gifts to a value of $100. Be careful not to try to take in meat or meat products, seeds, plants, fruits, etc. Avoid illegal drugs like the plague.

Returning to Britain you may bring home: (1) 200 cigarettes or 100 cigarillos or 50 cigars or 250 grams of tobacco; (2) two liters of table wine with additional allowances for (a) one liter of alcohol over 22% by volume (38.8° proof, most spirits), (b) two liters of alcohol under 22% by volume, or (c) two more liters of table wine; and (3) 50 grams of perfume and ¼ liter of toilet water, and (4) other goods up to a value of £32.

Insurance. We recommend that you insure yourself to cover health and motoring mishaps. *Europ Assistance* (252 High St., Croydon, Surrey CRO 1NF, tel. 01/680–1234).

It is also wise to take out insurance to cover loss of luggage (though check that this isn't already covered in an existing homeowner's policy). Trip-cancellation insurance is another wise buy. *The Association of British Insurers* (Aldermary House, Queen St., London EC4N 1TT, tel. 01/248–4477) will give comprehensive advice on all aspects of vacation insurance.

Tour Operators. The price battle that has raged over transatlantic fares has meant that most tour operators now offer excellent budget packages to the U.S. Among those you might consider as you plan your trip are: *Albany* (Manchester) *Ltd.,* 190 Deansgate, Manchester M3 3WD (tel. 061–833–0202).

American Airplan, Box 267. Walton-on-Thames, Surrey KT12 2TS (tel. 0932–246166).

Thomas Cook Ltd., Box 36, Thorpe Wood, Peterborough, PE 3 6SB (tel. 0733–63200).

Cosmosair plc, Tourama House, 17 Homesdale Rd., Bromley, Kent BR2 9LX (tel. 01–464–3400).

Jetsave, Sussex House, London Rd., East Grinstead RH19 1LD (tel. 0342–312033).

Pan Am/Fly Drive, 193 Piccadilly, London W1V OAD (tel. 01–409–3377).

Speedbird, 152 King St., London W6 OQU (tel. 01–741–8041).

Air Fares. We suggest that you explore the current scene for budget flight possibilities. Unfortunately, there are few standby programs on any of the major airlines, but do check their APEX and other fares, which offer a considerable saving over the full price. Quite frankly, only business travelers who don't have to watch the price of their tickets fly full-price these days—and find themselves sitting right beside an APEX passenger! At press time, an APEX round-trip fare to New York costs from £366. The small daily and Sunday newspaper ads are also a good source of bargain price flights. As we went to press, round-trip flights cost around £235.

Information. One excellent source of information is the *State of New York Division of Tourism,* 25 Bedford Square, London WC1B 3HG (tel. 01–323–0648). Although they are not open for personal callers, they will be happy to let you have brochures and other information to help you plan your trip.

TOURIST INFORMATION. The *New York Convention and Visitors' Bureau,* street level in the modern skyscraper at the south end of Columbus Circle (58th Street and Eighth Avenue), has multilingual aides and several racks full of brochures about the city. You can also obtain bus and subway maps here. The Bureau is open Monday to Friday, 9 A.M. to 6 P.M., weekends and holidays 10 A.M. to 6 P.M. Telephone 212–397–8222.

The *New York State Division of Tourism,* 1 Commerce Plaza, Albany, NY 12245, is an even better staffed office devoted to promoting tourism throughout the Empire State. Among its publications, available free for the asking, are *I Love New York Travel Guide to New York State* and *I Love New York Travel Guide to New York City.* The state's toll-free Vacation Information telephone number is 800–225–5697 or, if calling in the city, 309–0560.

Bus and subway information is available 24 hours a day by calling the Transit Authority Information Bureau at 718–330–1234.

PACKING. The weather in New York City can be surprising, so the trick in packing is to be prepared—without loading yourself down. Common sense is the rule of thumb; a few layers of shirts and sweaters or a down parka will shield you from Wall Street's and midtown's fierce winter winds. In summer you'll want walking shorts. Generally speaking, woolen clothes and an overcoat are what you want in winter (preferably not thermal underwear, as indoor living spaces tend to be overheated); lightweight, wash-and-wear "business" and casual clothes for summer; and medium-weight outer garments plus a raincoat for spring and fall. As you create your checklist prior to packing, be sure to consider the type of trip you're planning. If you intend to dine at the city's four-star restaurants and attend the opera, you'll probably want to dress fairly formally. Otherwise, more casual attire will suffice just about everywhere. Pants suits and leisure suits do not go over big in Manhattan.

For the record keepers, precipitation averages 3.5 inches per month, except in July and August, when frequent thundershowers raise the typical rainfall to 4.25 inches. Snow is likely anytime between November and April. With some rare exceptions, usually as the seasons change, there is not a great variation in temperature in the course of the day. Average highs and lows by month, in degrees Fahrenheit, are as follows:

Jan. 26–39	Jul. 68–85
Feb. 27–40	Aug. 66–83
Mar. 34–48	Sep. 60–77
Apr. 44–61	Oct. 51–67
May 53–71	Nov. 41–54
Jun. 63–81	Dec. 30–41

Rest assured, if you run out of film or toothpaste or other everyday items, there'll be plenty of places to replenish your supply. Discount drug stores selling these and thousands of other items abound, often just around the corner from major hotels—and the discounts will be sizable when compared to what is charged for the same items at hotel counters.

WHAT TO DO WITH THE PETS. If you are going to New York City, leave them at home. The city's dog and littering laws are relatively strictly enforced by special inspectors, with high fines for violators. Moreover, most hotels are less than thrilled by the prospect of putting up pets.

WHAT IT WILL COST. This is perhaps the most difficult question of all to answer, and for most travelers, one of the most important to ask. Throughout this book we try to give you as many guidelines as possible to help you plan out your expenses in advance. But prices for accommodations, for food, for entertainment, and for all manner of services in New York City vary widely; for this reason, the cost estimates given are often for a range. With hotel rooms, for example, the more you plan ahead, the easier it will be to obtain first-class arrangements at the lower end of the spectrum. In contrast, when going to the theater, it's the last-minute tickets picked up at the half-price booths in Times Square, at the World Trade Center, or in Brooklyn that yield the best bargains.

Here, then, are a few general pointers on the two items that will make up the bulk of your budget once in New York—for those keeping an eye on what they plan to spend. More detailed information for budget and non-budget travelers follows in the Practical Information section:

Lodging. A West Side "tourist hotel" (clean but of minimal charm) in the 40s, near the theater district, will charge $75–$90 a night for a double; rates in the 50s for a somewhat classier environment are $25–$50 higher; and for the top Central Park South, Fifth Avenue, or East Side establishments, the rates begin at $160 a night—park views running as high as $250. Again, tour packages can often get much lower rates, even for the top accommodations. Unlike elsewhere throughout the country, only a handful of Manhattan motels have free parking; these are noted in the hotel/motel listings. As most American hotels do not include breakfast as part of the tariff, you are best off going to a neighborhood coffee shop. There the scrambled eggs with bacon, potatoes, toast, and beverage, for which a hotel will charge $12 and up, go for $3 or even quite a bit less. Besides, while business breakfasts are currently in vogue at New York's more fashionable hotels, the food served at them is almost universally scorned.

Food. The best way to eat economically and interestingly in New York City is to partake of the hundreds of small, family-run ethnic restaurants found all over the city. There are also numerous delicatessens and "food boutiques" to be found; at these you can purchase ready-made salads, cheeses, and cold cuts by the pound or by the portion—perfect for summertime lunches *al fresco* in the city's neatly planted "vest pocket parks" or for evening dining during outdoor concerts in the major parks or, for example, at the South Street Seaport. Many bars also serve free hors d'oeuvres from 5 to 7 P.M. weekdays. If you're looking to eat at the city's best restaurants but are still concerned with watching your budget, consider having your main meal at lunch (unlike most Americans), when the prices are lower than in the evening, or seek out those offering *prix fixe* before-or-after-theater dinners. Most establishments post menus in their windows; remember the prices of a few standard items such as coffee, soup, and side dishes with which to make comparisons, and see if complete dinners are offered as well as à la carte selections. Consider sharing appetizers and/or desserts (or sometimes main courses, even if there is a service charge for an extra plate). Insist on no ice in your beverages—you'll get 30–50 percent more to drink. If you enjoy a nightcap, have it at a local neighborhood bar rather than in the hotel bar or from room service; or keep your own bottle in your room. Ice is available for free just about everywhere.

Typical Expenses for Two People in New York City

Room at *budget* hotel or motel	$150
Breakfast	10
Lunch at *inexpensive* restaurant	20
Dinner at *moderate* restaurant	50
Sightseeing tour	20
Evening drinks	10
Museum admission	8
Public transportation	10
	$278

HINTS TO THE MOTORIST. We cannot urge you strongly enough to avoid bringing a car into Manhattan. There is very little street parking available (and violators are towed away literally within minutes), garages can cost as much as $15 for two hours in some neighborhoods, and getting stuck in daytime traffic that simply doesn't move in any direction can only lead to anger and frustration. During the day, subways and foot are unquestionably the most convenient and least time-consuming modes of transportation.

That said, if you still insist on driving in New York City (perhaps you're planning to spend much of your time outside Manhattan or happen to have brought a car as part of a longer trip), keep in mind: The speed limit is 55 miles per hour on highways, lower and as posted elsewhere; you must be able to prove that your vehicle is insured; and you must be over 18 years of age. Motorcyclists and their passengers must wear New York State-approved protective helmets and goggles or face shields. Campers and/or trailers are an even worse idea in Manhattan than are cars. Leaving them unattended on the street even where street parking is available is not advisable and space-conscious garages are frequently not apt to accept them. It is mandatory to wear seat belts and for children under the age of five to ride in car seats.

DRINKING LAWS. Minimum age for the consumption of alcohol is 21. New York City bars may legally stay open until 4 A.M. except Sunday mornings, when they must close at 3 A.M. Some establishments get around this restriction by officially being designated social clubs; these may serve "members" any time. Beer can be purchased at supermarkets anytime except Sunday mornings (until noon). Wine and hard liquor are available at liquor stores only—which are not licensed to operate on Sundays.

SMOKING LAWS. In 1988 some of the nation's toughest antismoking regulations went into effect in New York. The law bans, with certain exceptions, smoking in all public places like stores and areas of restaurants and offices. Fines for violators can be as high as $500, so when in doubt, inquire before lighting up. If you have any questions, call the mayor's office, 566–5700.

RELIGIOUS WORSHIP. A listing of all of New York's religious institutions is subject for a book unto itself. The most comprehensive source of information is the Yellow Pages, which has separate listings for "Religious Organizations," "Churches" (broken down by denomination), "Synagogues," etc. For specific details about services in New York City, consult the Friday *New York Times.*

BUSINESS HOURS, HOLIDAYS, AND LOCAL TIME. New York State, like the rest of America, is on Standard Time from the last Sunday in October until the last Sunday in April. In April the clock is advanced one hour, for Daylight Savings Time, and in October is turned back an hour. The entire state lies within the Eastern Time Zone, which is five hours earlier than Greenwich Mean Time on local standard (winter) time.

Most businesses, banks, and many restaurants will be closed on the following holidays (the dates are for 1989): New Year's Day, Jan. 1; Washington's Birthday (observance), Feb. 20; Easter Sunday, March 26; Memorial Day (observance), May 29; Labor Day, Sept. 4; Thanksgiving Day, Nov. 23; Independence Day, July 4; and Christmas Day, Dec. 25.

In addition, banks and some businesses may be closed on Martin Luther King Jr. Day, Jan. 16; Lincoln's Birthday, Feb. 12; Good Friday (from noon), March 24; Columbus Day (observance), Oct. 9; Election Day (partially), Nov. 7; and Veteran's Day, Nov. 11.

The annual St. Patrick's Day Parade occurs on March 17; this means that Fifth Avenue is closed from 42nd Street to 86th Street, the town may be flooded with mobs of often unruly, drunken, or drugged teenagers, and normal activity in midtown Manhattan all but comes to a halt.

New York City having more Jews than Tel Aviv, it is inevitable that the city slows down considerably on the important Jewish holidays: Passover, starting Apr. 20; Rosh Hashanah on Sept. 30; Yom Kippur on Oct. 9; and Hanukkah starting on Dec. 23.

Subways, buses, and trains provide less service on all official holidays and some of the lesser ones.

POSTAGE. At press time, rates for international mail from the United States are as follows: *Surface* letters to Canada and Mexico are at the U.S. domestic rate: 25¢ for 1 ounce or under, 20¢ for each additional ounce, but these rates actually get airmail carriage to those countries. Surface letters to other foreign destinations are 40¢ for the first ounce and 23¢ for each additional ounce. Airmail letters to foreign destinations other than to Canada, Mexico, and some Caribbean and South American countries are 45¢ per ½ ounce, and 45¢ for each additional ½ ounce. Postcards (except for domestic destinations, Canada and Mexico, which go airmail for 15¢) are 28¢ for surface mail and 36¢ for airmail to any foreign destination. Standard international aerogram letters, good for any foreign destination, are 39¢ but of course nothing may be enclosed in them. Postal rates are no exception in this period of inflation, so check before you mail, in case they have gone up since press time.

TIPPING. Tipping is supposed to be a personal thing, your way of expressing appreciation of someone who has taken pleasure and pride in giving you attentive, efficient, and personal service. Because standards of personal service in the United States are highly uneven, you should, when you get genuinely good service, feel secure in rewarding it, and when you feel that the service you got was slovenly, indifferent, or surly, don't hesitate to show this by the size, or withholding, of your tip. Remember that in many places the help are paid very little and depend on tips for the better part of their income. This is supposed to give them incentive to serve you well. These days, the going rate on *restaurant* service is 15 percent on the amount *before* taxes. Tipping at counters is the same. For *bellboys,* 50 cents per bag is usual. However, if you load him down with all manner of bag, hatboxes, cameras, coats, etc., you might consider giving an extra 50 cents or $1. For one-night stays in most *hotels* and *motels* you leave nothing. If you stay longer, at the end of your stay leave the maid $1-$1.25 per day, or $5 per person per week for multiple occupancy.

For the many other services you may encounter in a big hotel, figure roughly as follows: doorman, 50 cents for taxi handling, $1 for help with baggage; parking attendant, 50 cents; bartender, 15 percent; room service, 10-15 percent of that bill; laundry or valet service, 15 percent; golf caddies, $1-$2 per bag, or 15 percent of the greens fee for an 18-hole course, or $3 on a free course; barbers and hairdressers, 15 percent; shoeshine attendants, 50 cents; manicurists, $1. Masseurs and masseuses in clubs and hotels get 20 percent.

Transportation: Taxi drivers in New York *expect 20 percent.* Limousine service, 20 percent. Car rental agencies, nothing. Bus porters are tipped 25 cents per bag, drivers nothing. On charters and package tours, conductors and drivers usually get $5-$10 per day from the group as a whole, but be sure to ask whether this has already been figured into the package cost. On short local sightseeing runs, the driver-guide may get $1 per per-

son, more if you think he has been especially helpful or personable. Airport
bus drivers, nothing. Tipping at curbside check-in is unofficial, but same
as above. On the plane, no tipping.

SENIOR-CITIZEN AND STUDENT DISCOUNTS. Many attractions
throughout New York City offer considerable discounts to Senior Citizens
and students. Some may require special city-issued Senior-Citizen identification, but in most cases showing a driver's license, passport, or some
other proof of age will suffice—"senior" generally being defined as 65 or
over for men and 62 or over for women. Museums, first-run and neighborhood movie theaters, and even some stores will often post special Senior-
Citizen rates. Those places offering student discounts are generally somewhat more stringent in their proof requirements—a high school or college
ID, international student traveler card, or evidence of age may be requested. Unfortunately, there is no uniformity on these matters.

HINTS TO THE DISABLED. Important sources of information in this
field are: The *Travel Information Center,* Moss Rehabilitation Hospital,
12th St. and Tabor Rd., Philadelphia, PA 19141; *Easter Seal Society for
Crippled Children and Adults,* Director of Education and Information Service, 2023 W. Ogden Ave., Chicago, IL 60612. Other publications giving
valuable information about facilities for the disabled are: the book *Travel
Ability,* by Lois Reamy, published by Macmillan; and the book *Access to
the World,* by Louise Weiss, published by Henry Holt & Co.
   Note. The *Theater Access Project* of the Theater Development Fund offers discount tickets to the disabled (usually half price). In 5 to 7 Broadway
and Off-Broadway shows a month some 30–50 seats in the first 10 rows
of the theaters are set aside for the disabled. For an application form write
Theater Access Program, Theater Development Fund, 1501 Broadway,
New York, NY 10036, or call 212–221–0885. Requests are processed on
a monthly basis. In addition, Theater Access handles requests for one or
two wheelchair locations plus an adjoining seat, for $7.50 each, at all 16
Shubert Organization theaters on Broadway.

EMERGENCY TELEPHONE NUMBERS. For police, fire, or ambulance, dial 911. The Manhattan fire department may also be reached on
628–2900; the fire department also possesses medical emergency equipment.

CONVERTING METRIC TO U.S. MEASUREMENTS

Multiply:	by:	to find:
Length		
millimeters (mm)	.039	inches (in)
meters (m)	3.28	feet (ft)
meters	1.09	yards (yd)
kilometers (km)	.62	miles (mi)
Area		
hectares (ha)	2.47	acres
Capacity		
liters (L)	2.11	pints (pt)
liters	1.06	quarts (qt)
liters	.26	gallons (gal)
Weight		
grams	.04	ounces (oz)
kilograms (kg)	2.20	pounds (lb)
metric tons (MT)	.98	tons (t)
Power		
kilowatts (kw)	1.34	horsepower (hp)
Temperature		
degrees Celsius	9/5 (then add 32)	degrees Fahrenheit

CONVERTING U.S. TO METRIC MEASUREMENTS

Multiply:	by:	to find:
Length		
inches (in)	25.40	millimeters (mm)
feet (ft)	.30	meters (m)
yards (yd)	.91	meters
miles (mi)	1.61	kilometers (km)
Area		
acres	.40	hectares (ha)
Capacity		
pints (pt)	.47	liters (L)
quarts (qt)	.95	liters
gallons (gal)	3.79	liters

Multiply:	by:	to find:
Weight		
ounces (oz)	28.35	grams (g)
pounds (lb)	.45	kilograms (kg)
tons (t)	1.11	metric tons (MT)
Power		
horsepower (hp)	.75	kilowatts
Temperature		
degrees Fahrenheit	5/9 (after subtracting 32)	degrees Celsius

INTRODUCTION TO
NEW YORK CITY

Capital of the World

by
NAN and IVAN LYONS

Nan and Ivan Lyons are native New Yorkers, contributors to Travel &
Leisure, Bon Appetit, *and* Food & Wine, *as well as authors of four novels,
including* Someone Is Killing the Great Chefs of Europe *and* The President Is Coming to Lunch.

New York City is an Oz run by seven and one-quarter million wizards.
The local industry is making dreams come true. Broadway. Fifth Avenue.
Wall Street. Seventh Avenue. No city in the history of the world has been
as hospitable to the yearnings of the human heart. Whatever you want
to find, you can find it in New York. Whatever you want to do, you can
do it in New York. The city is as limitless as your imagination. New York
is a state of mind.
New York is the city against which all others are measured. It is where
cultural and commercial explosions are felt long before shock waves register on local Richter scales. What is whispered today in New York will

11

be talked about weeks later across the globe. Once the nation's first capital, it has become the capital of the world. It is a city of credible fiction, a city of incredible fact. It is Metropolis, Gotham City, Fun City, Fat City, and most of all, the Big Apple.

A Nice Place to Visit

New York City attracts more visitors than any other city in the world. Nearly 18 million strong, they spend over $12 billion annually in New York. And nearly every one of the tourists wonders how New Yorkers can live in a place like New York. It's too crowded and too dirty, they say. Claustrophobic. No blue sky. Not enough trees. Too hurried. Why do people live here? The answer is etched in the Manhattan skyline.

New York at night offers a spectacle rivaled only by the sphinx of ancient Egypt or the splendors of outer space. The illuminated cityscape—as seen by ferry, helicopter, plane, from the top of the World Trade Center, from Brooklyn or Queens or New Jersey—seems impossible to have been divined by mere humans and qualifies as a true wonder of the modern world. It is a symbol of man's desire to reach for the stars.

While looking at the jagged edges of the skyline, one cannot help but soar with admiration, feel energized by the incandescent glow of a city filled with people not only unafraid to dream, but also willing to share their dreams. Don't be misled by the diamond-hard glitz of New York's reflection. That wall of concrete and glass is not meant to keep people out: It is there to keep the dream safe within. New York is a silent partner in the business and personal lives of all who live here. It offers an infinite canvas on which multitudes of people have seen their fantasies come true. For others New York provides an endless panorama that applauds the human spirit.

Living the High Life

The New York skyline reflects the boardrooms of the world's leading corporations, as well as the luxurious apartments that CEOs, financiers, diplomats, and celebrities make their private headquarters. Sandwiched in between are "starter" flats shared by flocks of young executives, aspiring musicians, or flight attendants who have pooled resources to be able to live in the city. Manhattan's rents are astronomical: it's not unusual to pay $1,300 per month for a one-room studio, $500,000 plus monthly maintenance charges to buy a two-bedroom apartment, or a couple of million to rest your weary bones at Trump Tower. But rent isn't the only thing that's expensive. In New York, private-school tuition for kindergarten costs as much as a year in some colleges. Renting a garage parking spot for a car can run more than many people spend on rent.

How, you might ask, do New Yorkers earn the salaries needed to stay in the city? They most often work in the city's leading trades: garment, publishing, finance, export-import, tourism, medicine, insurance, advertising, public relations, printing, broadcasting, and the performing arts. They generate jobs and money for such varied professionals as lawyers, agents, designers, etc., who in turn, depend upon other entrepreneurs to provide messengers, limos, caterers, and exercise classes. A single apartment building in Manhattan may have among its tenants a famous actress, her designer, her psychiatrist, the owner of the chain of studios in which she works out, and—sharing a one-room apartment in the basement—three waiters from the restaurant in which she lunches. Although New York doesn't offer equality, or guarantee the same level of comfort for everyone, most New Yorkers find a way to sink their teeth into the Big Apple and come out chewing.

An Exciting City

The first word to describe New York is "exciting." This is a city in which everyone marches to a different drummer. As a matter of fact, there's probably no place on earth with as many different drummers. From the first immigrant who arrived at Ellis Island to the last young hopeful who stepped off a bus from Des Moines, New York City has always been the official port of entry for the American dream. You won't find the dreams of a two-car garage or a patio barbecue or a gold watch after 25 years in New York. Instead you find waiters who want to be actors, cab drivers who want to be writers, and salesgirls who want to be ballerinas. Few people are what they appear to be in New York. But everyone knows what they *want* to be. New York is a city made up of millions of people whose most priceless possession is themselves. And each person has reserved his or her piece of the skyline.

If you've really got what it takes, the city will welcome you with open arms. No questions asked. It doesn't matter where you came from, who your family was, or what you did yesterday to earn a living. New York is the most socially democratic—but professionally demanding—city in the world. It applauds results. There are no *A*s for effort in this town. Take another look at that glistening skyline. New York wears it as though it were a crown. This is a city for winners.

A Professional City

The next word to describe New York City would have to be "professional." Amateurs to the rear. In a city where time is money, the ordinary is very much out of the ordinary. New York is accustomed to the best. The people who live here expect it. The people who visit expect it, and they are seldom disappointed. With tourism responsible for generating more dollars than any sector other than the garment trades, the care and feeding of visitors is of prime concern.

Whether this is your first or your 50th trip to New York, there are discoveries to be made. There's always a new play, a new restaurant, a new shop. New Yorkers take "new" very seriously. Just as Londoners cherish traditional favorites, New Yorkers thrive on ferreting out the new. Weeks before a new restaurant is reviewed by the press, you'll find it packed with Manhattanites hungry to award their own stars first. Broadway shows that turn out to be turkeys often play to standing-room-only audiences while in previews. There's no audience more eager to be pleased than a New York audience. That's what attracts hundreds of thousands of young hopefuls, from acrobats to zoologists, eager to prove themselves and earn their slice of the Big Apple.

A Big City

Imagine, if you will, the entire populations of Atlanta, Baltimore, Boston, Cincinnati, Cleveland, Dallas, Kansas City, Miami, Minneapolis, New Orleans, Omaha, Pittsburgh, Toledo, and San Francisco living in one city. That's how big New York is. If that doesn't convince you, think of all the people in Amsterdam, Dublin, Edinburgh, Florence, Frankfurt, Geneva, Jerusalem, Oslo, Paris, Quebec, and Zürich wedged into the Big Apple pie. New York may be only the 13th largest city in the world (Mexico City is the first), but it has more than twice as many people as any other city in the United States. (Los Angeles comes in second.)

Of the over 7.25 million people in New York, only 1,478,000 live in Manhattan, the smallest of the city's five boroughs. It is 13.4 miles long and only 2.3 miles across at its widest point. The city's four other boroughs are where you'll find most New Yorkers: Brooklyn has 2,293,000 residents; Queens, 1,923,000; the Bronx, 1,193,000; and Staten Island, has nearly 400,000.

New York experienced its greatest period of growth after the Civil War. Huge waves of immigrants began to sweep in from Europe, and most of the wealth resulting from the winning of the West seemed to flow through the city. This was the era of the great millionaires: J. P. Morgan, the banker; Andrew Carnegie and Henry C. Frick, the steel men; and the transportation magnate, Commodore Cornelius Vanderbilt, whose nautical title derived from his operation of the Staten Island ferry.

New York was a big city even back in the 1890s, with a population of 1,500,000. But it really became a world metropolis on January 1, 1898, when Brooklyn, the Bronx, Queens, and Richmond (Staten Island) were linked with Manhattan to form Greater New York. In 1900, the expanded city's population neared 3,500,000.

In the early years of this century, Manhattanites found a new direction for growth—straight up. The skyscraper became the architectural trademark of New York. It started in 1902 with the 20-story Flatiron Building. In 1913, the 60-story Woolworth Building was the tallest in the world and held its title for 17 years, until it was displaced by the 71-story Chrysler Building. The Chrysler's primacy lasted only one year, until 1931, when the 102-story Empire State Building became king. Even though a television tower brought its height up to 1,694 feet, it was surpassed in 1972 by the twin towers of the 110-story World Trade Center in the downtown financial district. Even though New York lost the world skyscraper championship to the Sears Tower in Chicago, the Big Apple still remains the biggest tourist attraction in the world.

How big? Dust off your calculator and see how these figures add up. New York City has, in its total area of 303 square miles (of which Manhattan contributes a mere 22.7 square miles): 100,000 first-class hotel rooms; 25,000 restaurants; 11,787 licensed taxis (all of which seem to be off-duty or occupied when you need one); 25,000 acres of parks and playgrounds; 780 landmark buildings; 200 skyscrapers; 65 bridges; over 150 museums; 400 art galleries; 30 department stores; thousands of shops and boutiques; nearly 250 Broadway, Off-Broadway, and off-off Broadway theaters; 60 night spots with entertainment, and 50 discos. Should you be in the market for a little urban renewal on a more spiritual level, there are some 3,500 churches and synagogues.

The Melting Pot

The city's reputation as an ethnic stew hasn't changed much, although the pot has overflowed from its epicenter on Manhattan's lower East Side to the other boroughs. The five ethnic groups that make up nearly 80 percent of New York's population are blacks, Irish, Italians, Jewish, and Puerto Ricans. Other large groups include Chinese, Cubans, Germans, Greeks, and Poles.

While Manhattan still has its Chinatown and Little Italy, the Bronx has its own Roman festival on Arthur Avenue. Queens offers a thriving Greek community that would even make Zorba feel at home. Brooklyn boasts Little Odessa, an enclave of Russian émigrés in the Brighton Beach area as well as a Middle Eastern outpost on Atlantic Avenue. There's a lot to be said for Brooklyn, which, if regarded as a city instead of a borough, would be the fourth largest in the country. From the Brooklyn Bridge to Coney Island, you'll find sights and sounds (including "Brooklynese" as still spoken by some of the natives) that have become legendary throughout the world.

The Bronx is named after the Bronx River, which in turn was named after Jonas Bronck, first settler of the region. The Bronx is home to Yankee Stadium as well as the world-famous Bronx Zoo and the New York Botanical Garden. Queens, named to honor Queen Catherine of Braganza, wife of Charles II of England, is New York's biggest borough geographically (118.6 square miles). It houses Shea Stadium, home base for the New York Mets, and Forest Hills Stadium, which is for tennis matches.

Staten Island is where the first European landed in 1524. The name of Giovanni da Verrazano is memorialized in the longest suspension bridge in the country, the Verrazano-Narrows Bridge that ties the Island to Brooklyn. You'll find some of the city's best-preserved "olde New York" settlements here.

Urban Renewal

In any barrel of apples, Big Apples or otherwise, you'll find the entire spectrum of the human condition. New York is no exception. As a matter of fact, the often-reported negatives concerning the poor, the homeless, and the criminal element are perhaps more striking in New York than elsewhere because they exist amid such affluent surroundings.

As a magnet for those seeking fame and fortune, New York attracts social problems the way Capistrano attracts swallows. Not everyone who dreams of striking it rich in New York does. What happens then? The city must provide for those who become hopeless, helpless, or homeless. New York has long been a leader in housing reform. It has the largest public school system of any city in the world. It spends more on welfare programs than any other city in the nation. This is a burden shared by all working New Yorkers who pay among the highest city and state taxes in the country.

New York has been given a bum rap concerning crime. Of course there are people of whom you should be wary. They're basically the same people of whom you'd be wary in Chicago or Nashville or Seattle. But in terms of the annual number of property crimes, New York is ninth in the nation after Detroit, Dallas, San Antonio, Phoenix, Chicago, Los Angeles, Memphis, and Baltimore. In terms of murder, New York has a lower rate than Baltimore, Chicago, Dallas, Detroit, Los Angeles, San Antonio, and Washington, D.C. Contrary to what some people think, New York is not a den of iniquity, and visitors are not moving targets in a shooting gallery. All you have to worry about is observing the same precautions you would in any world capital.

New York's efforts to deal with the urban concerns of air pollution, traffic jams, crime, drugs, race relations, welfare, etc., get space on front pages of newspapers around the world, space that would never be devoted to similar problems in other cities. Everything that happens in NYC is news, but like everywhere else, the news is not always good.

New York Thrives on Deals

All of which brings us to the fact that in this town, everything is a big deal. Everything! It's as big a deal to find the right Chinese restaurant as it is to find a place to live. It's a big deal to wait for a red light to change or to have a baby. The same big deal. For ambitious New Yorkers who orchestrate career moves with the finesse of a Toscanini, everything is important. That's how they keep in training. They don't let their guard down for a moment.

Sounds crazy, but it's actually very democratic. Success in deal-making comes in many guises—from finding a free parking space to floating a million-dollar stock offering. It doesn't matter how many chips you start with, there's always something for somebody to negotiate. Build a better mousetrap in New York and you can bank on someone opening a mouse cemetery. If there's an angle left on the old protractor, the odds are that a New Yorker will find it.

Having traded in the creature comforts and social amenities that still exist in America's heartland, New Yorkers wear inconvenience and hardship like badges of honor. They endure the entire catalog of urban blight, from blackouts to garbage strikes, no less stoically than Londoners faced the Blitz. It's our personal theory that if the city didn't have its share of woes, New Yorkers would invent them. Give them a crisis and it brings out the best in everyone. Next-door neighbors who grudgingly mutter "Good morning" to one another in the elevator, suddenly become the Seven and One-Quarter Million Musketeers. Although notoriously impatient, New Yorkers don't for a moment consider themselves to be unfriendly. And they aren't.

The New Yorker, like the quintessential cowboy, is a loner. He minds his own business, doesn't say too much, and regards strangers warily. The rules of the American frontier apply, anachronistically enough, to its most cosmopolitan city. But so does the code of the Old West about helping people in distress. New Yorkers are proud of their city, and they know there's enough to go around. Ask a question and we think you'll be surprised at how helpful New Yorkers can be.

A City of Critics

As a result of the staggering number of choices available to New Yorkers, this is a city that thrives on critics. The newspapers have people reviewing not only books and movies and plays, but also restaurants, takeout food, markets, computer equipment, and even new buildings. But the most important critics in New York are not paid for their opinions. This is the city that invented "word of mouth"—from kids who argue passionately over which is the perfect chocolate-chip cookie to construction workers who become lunchtime fashion experts as they review the passing parade.

No one in New York is "laid back" about where to spend their money. Prices are generally steep and while they reflect the incredibly high cost of doing business in this city, prices are not always true barometers of quality. The people who pay astronomical rents to live here know that. They want value for their money. "The best," "the most," and "the cheapest" usually find their way into every conversation. Everybody in New York has to be an expert to survive. Everybody is a critic.

Why Is NYC Called the Big Apple?

Ask a New Yorker why and he or she might reply, "Why not?" You'll find that New Yorkers often answer a question with a question. Sometimes they'll even repeat your question, word for word, but with enough added inflection to give Henry Higgins a real run for his money.

The truth is, New Yorkers speak a patois of American-English that is as rich in borrowed phrases from its Jewish, Hispanic, and black heritage as it is in its delivery. What you may notice first is the slurring together or elimination of some vowels and consonants, such as exchanging "d" for "t," and completely dropping the letter "r" at the end of a word, as in asking for a glass of "wawduh." For some reason, the letter "r" enters the diction of most New Yawkuhs only if it's the foist lettuh in a woid. Even transplanted corn-blond Kansans are prey to the joys of Yiddish that have spiced the New York vocabulary since the turn of the century. You'll find the best of the Midwest "schmoozing" at the Oak Bar about some "schlemiel" who had the "chutzpah" to try to beat him out of a parking space.

So ya wanna know why Noo Yawk is called da Big Apple?

The term, The Big Apple, was a favorite of jazz musicians in the 1920s and '30s. If you were playing New York City, you made it to The Big Time. There are lots of apples on the tree, but New York City was—and still is—The Big Apple.

So now ya know, alreddy.

The Sidewalks of New York

New Yorkers are not just street smart, they're street dependent. Everything happens in the streets of New York. Block parties. Parades. Street fairs. This is a city in love with concrete. For many New Yorkers without cars or shopping malls or parks or schoolyards, the street plays a major role in growing up.

Kids play ball, roller skate, play hide-and-seek, and learn how to ride bikes on the street. Tenement dwellers sit on their front steps hoping to catch a breath of fresh air or perhaps the latest gossip. People get into fights, but they also fall in love on the streets. And, sometime or other, everyone eats on the street. You can relax at a sidewalk cafe or line up at one of the carts that sells everything from kosher franks to egg rolls, to tacos, to health salads stuffed into Middle Eastern pita bread. Other street vendors sell old books, magazines, scarves, and sweaters of dubious provenance. We even found a novelist who would write a book for you in 10 minutes. You'll see beggars, mimes, solo trumpeters, and string quartets. Nowhere outside of the Orient is street life as rich and colorful as it is here.

The great democratic experiment that is New York is also evident in the dress of its residents. You'll find everything from jeans to tuxedos—jeans at the Metropolitan Opera, and tuxedos at a local pizza joint. Just as there's no such thing as a typical New Yorker, the only dress code in this city is "come as you are." And, oh, do they ever!

How to Play the Game of New York

One of the true joys of the city is the ease with which a first-time visitor can navigate the streets. Unlike the winding lanes in London, the galaxy of boulevards in Paris, and the sudden piazzas in Rome, New York has a logic to its layout. Patterned on a grid, like a blueprint for success, this most demanding of cities is sometimes easier to get around than to understand.

Here's all you have to remember: Manhattan streets are numbered from 1 to 228 in straight lines running east to west, and the avenues—from First to Twelfth—run north to south. The East River is on the East Side and the Hudson River is on the West Side. A quick glance at the street signs on every block tells you if you're heading uptown or downtown. There are a few exceptions. A sojourn down to SoHo, Wall Street, Greenwich Village, or the Battery is often confusing even for the natives. But relax, it will give you an opportunity to ask someone for help—and dispel the myth about New Yorkers being unfriendly.

The subway system, with none of the ambience of the Underground of London or the Métro of Paris, is still the fastest way to get around town. As you would in any big city, use caution if you're riding off hours. Buses run frequently and their routes anticipate the needs of most visitors. The addition of bus lanes to major streets often allows them to move more rapidly than cars and taxis.

A word about taxis. If ever New Yorkers had a love-hate relationship with anything, it's with taxis. New York cabs are perhaps the world's most uncomfortable as well as the dirtiest. But they are indispensable. As lifesaving as they are infuriating, we cannot imagine doing without them. Be forewarned, however: the worldly wise, lovable New York cabbie of the past has gone the way of the free lunch and shepherds. He doesn't exist anymore. Today's cabbies are rarely garrulous, have little inside information on the city, and as often as not, need *your* help to find any destination beyond midtown.

You've no doubt heard about "gypsy" cabs. Contrary to what their name implies, the driver won't play the violin or tell your fortune. Gypsy cabs are not insured, and if you have a problem with the driver, there's no Taxi Commission to complain to. But, like Mt. Everest, they are there. Real New Yorkers use gypsy cabs all the time. They make certain, if there's no meter, to settle the price in advance. It should be noted, however, that real New Yorkers would hitch rides on a man-eating alligator to get across town.

The best way to negotiate the city, surprisingly, is to walk. If you're staying at a midtown hotel, try to plan your excursions before or after the morning and evening rush hours—or at least bring yourself close enough to home base so that you can walk the last mile if you have to. There's nothing more frustrating than to be stuck in glorious gridlock while the meter ticks away (rates are determined by time as well as distance).

Walking up the Avenue

Put a New Yorker in Los Angeles and the first complaint you hear is that there are no people on the street. Where is everybody? There's no one to push past hurriedly. No one to bump into because they've stopped suddenly to glance in a shop window. Ironically, the New Yorker who guards his privacy as zealously as the Secret Service guards the President is like a fish out of water unless surrounded by a crowd. In this city, walking is more than a means of getting from one place to another. It is a chance for New Yorkers to renew their love affair with the streets.

Each avenue has its own personality and a particular set of landmarks. They are as different in character as the people who walk them daily. Here's a kaleidoscope view of midtown Manhattan's major thoroughfares.

First Avenue is where you'll find two of the most important medical addresses in the city: University Hospital and Bellevue. Heading north toward the forties, First Avenue begins pulsing with the political impact of the United Nations. Past the UN to 59th Street, it becomes a neighborhood street offering shops and services to residents in the posh Sutton Place area. After a short dip under the Queensboro Bridge, First Avenue emerges with the renewed vitality it needs as "the singles highway" of New York. Here's where you'll find the bars, trendy restaurants, and shops frequented by still swinging singles. The avenue ages the higher up it goes and by the time it reaches the mid-80s, it is the address of a downright middle-aged community.

Second Avenue begins at the tip of the tenement-crowded lower East Side. While downtown, Second Avenue refuses to surrender its ethnicity, clinging to remnants of Jewish, Armenian, and Slavic cultures as its security blanket. You'll find antique shops and slowly maturing crafts studios left over from the East Village (East Greenwich Village). But by the time it reaches the forties, Second Avenue has developed total amnesia. All it can think about are restaurants and shops to service the most conspicuous consumption. Second Avenue is a main drag for the yuppies, those upscale, homegrown versions of the early immigrants who also came to seek their fortune.

Third Avenue has more personalities than a schizophrenic chameleon. It begins on the edge of Chinatown as the Bowery, and runs briefly through the thirties as a user-friendly neighborhood artery filled with shops and services. But when Third Avenue crosses 42nd Street, it suddenly becomes the address for some of the world's best-known corporations.

After razing the old Third Avenue Elevated Subway Line (the "El"), property values went up and up and up until finally high enough for Donald Trump. He's made a spectacle of himself again in a dazzling new apartment complex within charging distance of Bloomingdale's. Third Avenue heads straight uptown as a moneyed address for chic East Siders before easing into Spanish Harlem and the *barrio*.

Lexington Avenue, despite being dominated by Grand Central Station at 42nd Street, manages to maintain a neighborhood feeling. Jam-packed with small shops, you can still find family businesses and stores that sell things you can't get anywhere else. You'll also find the fabulous Citicorp Building's enclosed mall on Lexington Avenue.

Park Avenue has all the swank for which New York is famous. The timeless, Park Avenue–style apartment houses were built and have remained untouched since the 1920s because there's simply no way to improve upon them. With its roots in the old Fourth Avenue, now rechristened Park Avenue South, Park Avenue comes into its own at 34th Street. Like the Waldorf-Astoria and the Seagram Building, Park Avenue maintains its identity despite the often banal architecture that sprang up along the avenue in the fifties. Nothing seems to change the personality and the dignity of the avenue. That's old money you hear jingling in the pockets of its residents. Like a pair of sensible shoes, Park Avenue was made to last.

Madison Avenue is elegant, elegant, elegant. The boutique capital of the city, it exudes chic as though chic were going out of style. Despite a rocky start in the twenties, and a blitz of midtown mania that culminates in the AT&T building near 57th Street, Madison makes a quick about-face and becomes—all the way through the eighties—the most European of Manhattan's streets. You can walk for blocks and never hear English spoken.

Fifth Avenue is the most romantic avenue in the city. It borders Central Park from 59th to 110th streets, and lives up to its legendary status as one of the world's most famous thoroughfares. If you only have enough time to see one street while in New York, it should be Fifth Avenue—from the sheer majesty of the Metropolitan Museum of Art to the opulent apartment houses of the rich and famous, to the equally deluxe Pierre, Sherry-Netherland, and Plaza hotels. From 59th Street down, some of New York's most famous landmarks are just blocks from each other: Bergdorf's, Tiffany's, Trump Tower, St. Patrick's Cathedral, Rockefeller Plaza, the New York Public Library, the Empire State Building. Fifth Avenue gets an attack of the tacky below 34th Street, but revives just past 14th Street to make a photo finish at the arch in Washington Square—the official hub of Greenwich Village.

Sixth Avenue may have had its name changed decades ago to Avenue of the Americas, but there isn't one New Yorker worth his bagels who calls it anything but Sixth Avenue. The best thing about Sixth Avenue is its run from Canal Street through the heart of Greenwich Village. After 14th Street, it loses its identity and becomes little more than a bus route along which to gaze up at corporate headquarters for publishers, broadcasters, and insurance companies. One saving grace: you'll find Radio City Music Hall at 50th Street.

Seventh Avenue, like the flip side of a hit record, can't buck its own competition. What it lacks in style, it makes up for with star attractions. Seventh Avenue and 57th Street is where you'll find Carnegie Hall, after which it meets Broadway in the forties and crisscrosses to form Times

Square. Seventh takes you into the heart of the garment center, Macy's, and Pennsylvania Station before easing into Greenwich Village.

Broadway is hot. It's the main stem. It's New York all the way and for more reasons than the fact that it runs the entire length of Manhattan. Everything begins and ends with this most famous street in the world. Once the best and brightest of boulevards, it has weathered the slings and arrows of its outrageous fortune and is being reclaimed. Guilty of everything terrible you've ever heard about it, Broadway in the forties is still worth singing about. It heads up to Lincoln Center in the sixties and then becomes the pulse of the Upper West Side.

Eighth Avenue, in midtown, is seedier than a Burpee catalog. The only exception is in the low thirties where it runs between Madison Square Garden and the truly heroic General Post Office at 34th Street. Otherwise, Eighth Avenue is mostly for traffic until it metamorphoses at Columbus Circle into *Central Park West* at 57th Street. As the mirror image of Fifth Avenue, CPW lacks Fifth Avenue's panache but does have even more extraordinary apartment buildings—including the landmark Dakota on 72nd Street.

Ninth Avenue, despite the onslaught of taxis heading for the Port Authority Bus Terminal and endless caravans of trucks maneuvering toward the Lincoln Tunnel, is a gourmet's delight. It's still got the feel of first-generation ethnicity. Smart New Yorkers shop here for spices, fruits, vegetables, meat, and exotic ingredients they can't find anywhere else. Serving both the wholesale and retail trades, Ninth Avenue is to delicious what Seventh Avenue is to fashion. When Ninth Avenue turns into *Columbus Avenue,* it becomes the official brunch capital of the West Side. From Lincoln Center up to the mid-eighties, Columbus Avenue is the perfect place to discover new boutiques, restaurants, cookie shops, and ice-cream stores. It is the miracle mile of the "Yupper" West Side, filled with more young people than a Billy Joel concert. Don't miss it.

Tenth Avenue is little more than a truck route heading uptown to the Upper West Side, where Tenth Avenue changes from a frog into a prince named Amsterdam Avenue. Once a bastion of mom-and-pop businesses, Amsterdam has been swept up in the massive West Side gentrification that threatens the area with terminal "trendy."

Eleventh Avenue is where you find the stunning new Javits Convention Center and most of the city's car showrooms and garages before it, too, makes a change to become *West End Avenue,* the poor man's Park Avenue. By poor, we mean you can still find a three-bedroom cooperative apartment for under a million dollars. (It takes looking, but you just might find it.)

Twelfth Avenue has been pressed into service as a midtown replacement for the West Side Highway. The good news is that it offers the best view of the Hudson River, and the cruise ships and occasional ocean liner that dock alongside it. Driving down Twelfth Avenue from midtown to the World Trade Center, you're likely to find the *Queen Elizabeth II* competing for your attention with the commanding aircraft carrier-cum-museum, *Intrepid.*

Your Bite of the Big Apple

Whether you're here on business, attending a convention, or in town strictly for pleasure, New York has what it takes to please you. More than what it takes. The joy of New York is that it allows visitors to exercise the widest range of personal choices available in any city.

Unlike many locales where there's *the* hotel and *the* restaurant, *the* City of New York will match your taste, mood, and expense account without sacrificing quality. You can eat better—high or low tab—than you can in other cities. You can see better theater—on Broadway or Off-Broadway—than you can anywhere else in the country. You can do more varied shopping—better selections at better prices—than almost anywhere in the world. (We found that New York's discount camera shops beat the prices being charged in Hong Kong!) All of this is possible because New York does such high-volume business.

Whether it's food or fashion, museums or music, the key to navigating New York's treasure chest is to know what you want. Use the expertise reflected in this book to make your choices before you arrive. Then all you have to do when you get here is enjoy yourself.

Restaurants

New York is the restaurant capital of the world. From sushi to pastrami, haute cuisine to hot dogs, nouvelle to nosh, the Big Apple is in business to satisfy all palates and purses. Even the current vogue for "grazing" (different courses at different restaurants) is raised to new international heights in New York. You can have a dim sum lunch in Chinatown and walk a few blocks to the Italian side of Mulberry Street for cannoli and cappuccino in Little Italy.

In a city where three-digit dinner tabs hardly raise an eyebrow, restaurants have to satisfy more than hunger. New Yorkers "do" lunch and dinner the way other people do their taxes: line by line. Because people frequently eat out, and because there are so many choices, restaurant owners realize they won't get a second chance. Either you like them the first time or you don't come back. (Unfortunately, many restaurants—because of high-traffic locations—survive solely on the inexperienced and unwary. You won't find them listed in this book.)

Let's say you love Italian food and are looking for a place to have dinner. The first question in NYC is "What kind of Italian food?" Are you partial to Southern Italian or Northern? Perhaps you'd prefer a restaurant that specializes in la cucina Romana? Tuscany? How about nouvelle Italian? If you're not prepared for all that, just sit back with an open mouth and sample something new and exciting. Even if it turns out that you're not partial to Tuscan cooking, at least you know that you may have tasted the best Tuscan cooking in the country.

If you're looking for New York cuisine, forget all about Manhattan clam chowder and Long Island duckling. For a true taste of New York, head for a deli. And we don't mean one of those fancy food shops where you buy goat cheese, mineral water, and tricolor pasta salads. We mean the kind of deli they filmed in Woody Allen's movie, *Broadway Danny Rose.* In fact, we mean *that* deli.

Even if the Carnegie Deli, on Seventh Avenue and 55th Street, hadn't been used as a movie set, it would qualify as one. Clearly, it can't be real. No one could make a living by selling sandwiches big enough to feed three hungry people, by giving away seltzer, and by packing customers in at long tables where you learn to love thy neighbor real fast. The Carnegie is noisy, crowded, hilarious, and delicious. It's pure New York. According to one of the owners, the secret to the pastrami and corned beef is found in New York's tap water. The beef steams over boiling water and absorbs minerals.

Now wouldn't you think that people who jam themselves into subway cars, and who dodge one another as they fight for space to cross the street would seek out a cozy little table in the corner to sip their matzoh-ball soup in peace and quiet? Not if you understood New Yorkers, you wouldn't.

Theaters

Broadway, when you talk about theater, is more than the name of a street. It's an internationally recognized code word for the best that professional theater has to offer. Because the whole world is influenced by Broadway, it attracts performers from around the globe. The glamour of Broadway also results in the highest theater-ticket prices anywhere. (The section on *Stage* will tell you how to get around that problem.)

High prices or low prices, on Broadway or Off-Broadway, the theater will always be at the very heart of New York. Wherever you go in the city, there is theater. You'll find it in churches, basements, converted storefronts, in restaurants, lofts, and even in the park. Although Broadway's mega-hits are what draws audiences to New York, you won't have a complete picture of the city's theatrical magic without sampling Off-Broadway as well.

Music and Dance

New York offers the most exciting, most enriching programs to be found anywhere in the world. On a given night, you have the choice of an unparalleled range of artists. In the Lincoln Center complex alone, you'll find the Metropolitan Opera, the New York Philharmonic, and the New York City Ballet all performing within a few hundred feet of one another. A few blocks south is legendary Carnegie Hall and a host of other auditoriums in which singers, dancers, and musicians who have prepared for years are appearing.

Galleries and Museums

New York has art galleries and museums the way other cities have 7-Eleven stores. You could spend weeks going from gallery to gallery, and by the time you'd covered them all, they'd have new shows. One of the city's most elegant spectator sports, gallery-hopping is how New Yorkers discover up-and-coming young artists.

The museums in this city offer an endless array of riches. New York has a museum for everything—fine arts, history, Indians, crafts, transportation, broadcasting, costumes, and there's even one for New York itself. The collections you'll find on permanent display, as well as the visiting exhibitions, represent the ultimate flowering of man's creative genius.

Shopping

There's nothing you can't buy in New York. Even better, there's almost nothing you can't buy wholesale. No matter what your budget or inter-

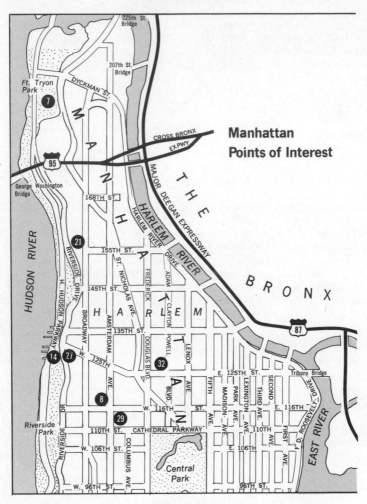

225th St. Bridge
207th St. Bridge
Ft. Tryon Park 7
DYCKMAN ST.
CROSS BRONX EXPWY
Manhattan Points of Interest
95
George Washington Bridge
168TH ST.
HARLEM RIVER
MAJOR DEEGAN EXPRESSWAY
THE BRONX
HUDSON RIVER
21
155TH ST.
RIVERSIDE DRIVE
145TH ST.
ST. NICHOLAS AVE.
FREDRICK DOUGLAS BLVD
ADAM CLAYTON POWELL BLVD.
DRIVE
HARLEM RIVER
87
H A R L E M
BROADWAY
AMSTERDAM
135TH ST.
14 27
W. 125TH
AVE.
32
LENOX AVE.
E. 125TH ST.
Triboro Bridge
M A N H A T T A N
8
W. 116TH ST.
FIFTH AVE.
MADISON AVE.
PARK AVE.
LEXINGTON AVE.
THIRD AVE.
SECOND AVE.
FIRST AVE.
E. 116TH ST.
F. D. ROOSEVELT DRIVE
29
CATHEDRAL PARKWAY
110TH
Riverside Park
RIVERSIDE DR.
110TH ST.
W. 106TH ST.
COLUMBUS AVE.
E. 106TH
EAST RIVER
Central Park
W. 96TH ST.
96TH ST.

Points of Interest

1) American Museum of Natural History
2) Carnegie Hall
3) Central Park Zoo
4) Chinatown
5) Citicorp Center
6) City Hall
7) Cloisters
8) Columbia University
9) Empire State Building
10) Frick Museum
11) Gracie Mansion
12) Gramercy Park
13) Grand Central Station
14) Grant's Tomb
15) Guggenheim Museum
16) Hayden Planetarium
17) Jacob J. Javits Convention Center
18) Lincoln Center
19) Madison Square Garden
20) Metropolitan Museum of Art

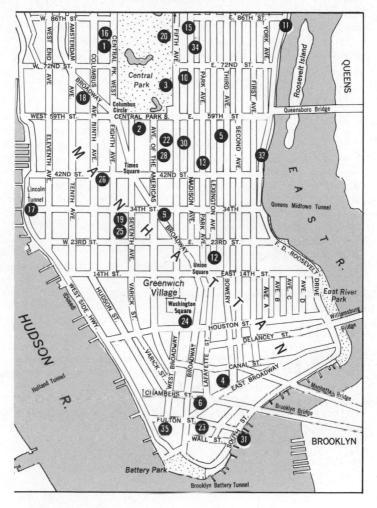

21) Museum of the American Indian; American Numismatic Society; Hispanic Society of America
22) Museum of Modern Art
23) N.Y. Stock Exchange
24) New York University
25) Pennsylvania Station
26) Port Authority Bus Terminal
27) Riverside Church
28) Rockefeller Center
29) St. John's Episcopal
30) St. Patrick's Cathedral
31) South Street Seaport
32) Studio Museum of Harlem
33) United Nations
34) Whitney Museum
35) World Trade Center

est—antiques, jeans, diamonds, rare books, or the latest in cameras—you can buy it here. A single trip to New York puts the bazaars of the world within easy reach. You'll find it all here, designer originals and low-priced rip-offs, often on the same block. Buyer beware! But, most of all, buyer be dazzled!

What to Do First

We've saved the best for last.

It's really quite simple. Go to your hotel, register, and unpack. Then head immediately for the South Ferry. Do not stop to look up at the buildings or down at the litter. Do not attempt any first impressions whatsoever. Don't even grumble about the traffic. Just hop into a cab or take the subway to the very tip of Manhattan. OK, maybe one peek, just one, at the Statue of Liberty.

Plunk down a quarter and board the Staten Island ferry. Now this is the hard part: *Don't look back* (pretend you're Lot's wife). Check out the bridges, the harbor, the seagulls, your shoelaces—anything. Trust us. Once you arrive in Staten Island, get right back on the ferry and this time, go for it! Let the eyes have it. The skyline will embrace you with its magic. It has for everyone willing to see it for what it is.

Once you've docked, head for the World Trade Center. If you've timed it right, it's dusk or early evening by this time. You don't want to reach the observation deck of the city's tallest building until the lights go on all around town.

We don't care who you are, or how old you are, or how much money you have, or how many times you've been to New York before—if the sheer beauty of the city spread out below doesn't take your breath away, return immediately to your hotel. Head for the hills—you're hopeless!

For the rest of us, the millions and millions who have surrendered at least one heartbeat to the city, the excitement of New York is purely visceral. It defies explanation. There is no logic. You don't need a reason to love New York. You need a dream.

NEW YORK CITY

A Congregation of Neighborhoods

by JANE HERSHEY and MICHAEL IACHETTA

Jane Hershey is a New York–based writer whose work has appeared in Good Housekeeping, US, *and* Elle. *She is also a contributor to* Fodor's Selected Resorts and Hotels of the U.S. *Michael Iachetta, a syndicated travel writer with the New York Daily News, is a member of the Society of American Travel Writers.*

Knowing a bit of New York's history will help you to understand the character of the city and its citizens.

Unlike New England whose settlers came to the New World primarily to escape political and religious injustices, Nieuw Amsterdam, as New York was named first, was settled by Dutch families in the employ of the West India Company, a Netherlands trading combine whose sole interest was carrying on a profitable trade with the Indians. From the start, they fared well. In their first year, they realized a profit of 250 guilders from the skins of beavers and otters alone. Considering that their governor, Peter Minuit, paid only sixty guilders, or roughly $24, worth of trinkets to the Indians in exchange for the island of Manhattan, it was an exceptionally good year.

From its earliest days—Giovanni da Verrazano having discovered New York Bay in 1524, landing on Staten Island on April 17—the community welcomed the stranger. It needed the brawn and skill of the newcomer's hands to help build the village, and it cared little about his race, color, or religious beliefs. A French Jesuit who passed through in 1643 reported home that "there may well be four or five hundred men of different sects and nations . . . there are men of eighteen different languages." Eight years later another sect was added when twenty-three Jewish men and women arrived to seek sanctuary. A Virginian, who paused on his way to the English colonies north, also complained: "The people seem not concerned what religion their neighbor is of, or whether he hath any or none." And so it has remained throughout the centuries.

New York's geographic location—an elongated island jutting into a huge protected harbor, with a mighty river at its side coming from deep within the country's interior of untapped riches—foreordained her supremacy as the greatest commercial city in America.

New York also straddled a strategic slice of the Atlantic coastline, separating the English colonies of New England from Virginia and cutting off the westward expansion of Connecticut and Massachusetts. This, plus her commercial enterprise, nettled the British and in 1664, King Charles II presented his brother, the Duke of York, a little gift of "all the land from the west side of the Connecticut River to the east side of the De la Ware Bay," and sent a flotilla of warships to convince the Dutch colony's governor, Peter Stuyvesant, that surrender was preferable to annihilation. The practical, business-as-usual tradespeople urged the governor to surrender "in the speediest, best and most reputable manner." Nieuw Amsterdam passed into the hands of the British, was renamed New York, and the citizens went on about their business of trade and commerce.

The city learned early how to assimilate rather than be devoured. Long after the capitulation to the British, the Dutch clung to their traditions. The character of early New York became a composite of Dutch vigor and English tenacity. Trade remained the city's cachet, and has throughout the centuries. The ramifications of this have not been to everyone's taste; Emerson (from the vantage point of Boston) called New York "a sucked orange."

From the first, New York insisted upon and enjoyed a greater degree of religious liberty and political freedom than did most of the other colonies, and word of these special privileges spread abroad. The city's character reflected one bright new facet after another as wave after wave of political and religious refugees broke over its shores.

French and German Palatinates, fugitives from the religious persecutions of Louis XIV, sought sanctuary here in the early 18th century, followed by settlers from England, Ireland, and Scotland, who fled their homelands as the Stuart cause began to collapse.

Migrations ceased while New York suffered through seven bitter years of siege during the Revolutionary War. Again New Yorkers adjusted themselves to living under the threat of British guns, suffered a disastrous fire which destroyed the heart of the city, and played a waiting game, hoping that come what may, they would retain their individuality. By November, 1783, New York was part of the new Union and served as the nation's capital for the following six years.

"Loud, Fast, and Altogether"

Why didn't New York remain so? Its citizens may have decided that being the home of the national government would divert them from their historic role. A century and a half of history had tempered and forged New York into the nation's greatest city of commerce. Whatever the reason, New York passed the plum on to Philadelphia and got on with the business of becoming the "noisy, roaring, rumbling, tumbling, bustling, stormy, turbulent" city Walt Whitman found so disturbing.

In a way it always had been turbulent. Even in 1774, John Adams complained that "They talk very loud, very fast, and altogether. If they ask you a question before you can utter three words of your answer, they will break out upon you again, and talk away." There are grounds for complaint today in this respect.

It wasn't just rudeness, as John Adams felt, but rather exhilaration. The city has a way of stimulating the mind, crowding it with ideas, opinions, thoughts which refuse to be dammed up for long and come spilling out "loud, fast, and altogether." These are the very forces which have sent New York spiraling upward and outward.

The Erie Canal's completion in 1825 assured New York's monopoly of the nation's rich trade. Building burgeoned and the city's growth reached out to such scattered rural hamlets as Greenwich Village and absorbed them. By 1850 New York's population was well over a half-million and its real estate was valued at $400,000,000. Grand opera, concerts, and legitimate theater productions were adding the needed note of culture. Men were becoming millionaires and their wives were casting eyes abroad for titled mates for their daughters. Fifth Avenue soon would sprout with palatial residences and galas be given for visiting royalty. New York was, if ever there was, the pot of gold at the end of the rainbow.

Once again immigrants came to find it: Russian Jews fleeing the Tsarist pogroms; Italians escaping oppressive poverty; Irish Catholics who had coped with confiscation of their property and denial of religious freedom but could no longer battle starvation after the awful potato famine; and many more.

Their voyage often took ninety or more days. Jammed into the reeking holds of sailing ships with scarcely room enough to lie down, many succumbed to cholera. Those who survived the journey were often so weak they had to be carried off the ship. By the time the last of these "floating coffins" was retired, more than 23,000,000 immigrants had come through this gateway over a 40-year period.

Many headed for neighborhoods where immigrants from their homeland had already settled. Here they were able to buy familiar foods, join their own societies, read the news in their own language. Few ever learned to speak English.

Politicians preyed on their ignorance and poverty, manipulated their votes or, if need be, bought them with picnic excursions and food baskets. They were crowded into slums on the lower East and West sides, not too many cuts above their steerage experiences. Sweatshops paid slave wages for a 60-or-more-hour week. Advertisements for domestic help at one period often read "No Irish need apply."

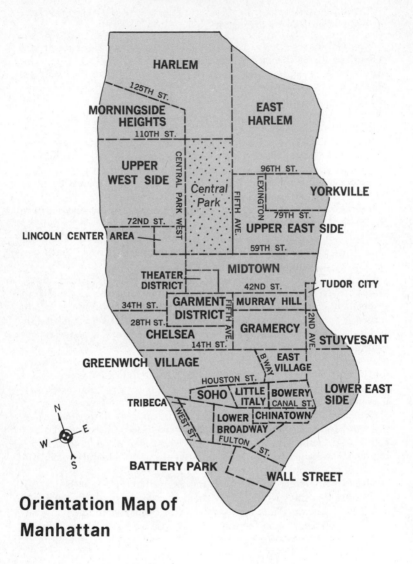

Orientation Map of Manhattan

Lower Broadway, Wall Street area, and **Battery Park** (including Battery Park City) area are what New Yorkers call "downtown," by which they mean the financial district. Almost no residential.

Chinatown: Life out on the streets or in restaurants in full force. Little night life, though, in the bar and night club sense. Heavily residential, but in tenement buildings.

Little Italy: Residential area like no other in city. Restaurants, Italian food shops, cafés, and street life in full measure among shabby tenement buildings.

SoHo: A strange mix of artists-in-residence and trendy shops and restaurants, some quite expensive. **TriBeCa** is similar but with more industry and less street life, fewer residents.

East Village: Mostly lower-income residential in tenements, but mixed with some shops and commerical enterprises. East portion is redolent of Middle-European immigrants who settled here. Hippies were centered here in 60s and 70s. Rapidly growing art community.

Greenwich Village: Primarily residential, and often quite expensive housing. New York University a big presence in central area. Restaurants, bars, night life, and stay-up-late street life as overwhelming as ever. Attractive brownstone buildings, especially in the "West Village." Far west is strongly gay.

Chelsea: An area in transition. Some artists' lofts and good housing, lots of not so good. Street scene is improving, but there are seedy stretches. Developing restaurant district.

Murray Hill: Predominately low-rise buildings, a mix of offices and residential housing, often quite good. The **Gramercy Park** area is similar but with more light manufacturing in loft buildings in the west—and artist and photographer lofts too. Restaurants and street life spotty, especially at night.

Garment District: Fascinating but hectic during the day, but not promising for ordinary visitors. Little residential, so deserted at night.

Theater District: Crowded with restaurants, too. Can be extra sinister late at night. *Avoid* 42nd St. between Broadway and Eighth Ave., even during the daylight hours, but don't miss the Off-Broadway theaters and lively dining on 42nd west of Eighth.

Midtown: *The* business district—but the east side of the area is heavily residential, with high-grade housing. Restaurants, night life, street life abound in spots throughout. Watch out for bicycles during the day. **Tudor City** is almost entirely residential.

Upper East Side: On its west side, the most expensive living space in the country—lawyers, doctors, stockbrokers, bankers. Slick. Mostly cooperative or condominium apartments. Exquisite brownstone buildings on sidestreets. Posh galleries too. Profusion of restaurants and night life is mostly in residential eastern half of area—young executives, singles, relatively few families—where rents are a bit lower, though still high.

Yorkville: Mix of expensive and inexpensive housing. Strong element of German and Central-European heritages.

Lincoln Center Area: Besides the Center, it is middle class residential, with plenty of restaurants and street life revolving around the Center.

Upper West Side: The far west and far east zones are middle- and upper-class residential, good but not quite as high-rent as the Upper East Side. Musicians, dancers, writers, actors, and middle-class families between Broadway and Riverside Drive. Broadway has bag people and looks seedy. Lots of restaurants, night life, street life on the two sides, up Broadway and Columbus Avenue, where the apartment buildings are largely cooperatives or condominiums. The Amsterdam zone in the middle is still mostly low-income tenements, but the area is in the process of being upgraded.

Morningside Heights: Its west side is the Columbia University/Barnard area.

The other areas of Manhattan such as the **Lower East Side** and **The Bowery** offer discount bargains, unusual trendy restaurants, and great buys in lighting and kitchen equipment. However, it's best to avoid them at night. Northern parts of Manhattan, such as **Harlem,** are worth exploring with an organized tour.

Yet the ideal of America never dimmed. The immigrants were free and their children were free. Free to learn, to pull themselves up by their bootstraps and become lawyers, doctors, merchants, financiers, patrons of the arts, and senators. The fabric of New York is shot through with the sparkle, color, and tensile strength of these multitudinous ethnic-religious-political groups. They and their children and grandchildren have helped to make this city great.

In your wanderings throughout the city you will see remnants of these immigrant enclaves and find the imprint of their imagination on the sky-scrapers of lower Manhattan, the elegant shops along Fifth Avenue, the bright lights of Broadway, the opera houses, concert halls, museums, and the home of the United Nations. The imprints of the Dutch and English are there, too. It is this pattern of people and events which has made New York the fascinating, cosmopolitan, polyglot city that it is. New York City has always been the most un-American of American cities—though Miami is now challenging it in this respect.

Sailing Around Manhattan

One of the best introductions to New York City, weather and season permitting, is to take a three-hour Circle Line boat around Manhattan. The Circle Line operates from Pier 83 on the Hudson, at 43rd Street and 12th Avenue, from March 21 to November 15. Boats leave approximately every 30 minutes beginning in mid-morning, less frequently in March, April, October, and November; for specific departure times call 563–3200. The cost for adults in 1988 was $15; children under 12, $7.50.

As the boat pulls out of the dock, heading down the Hudson River, you pass the gleaming new crystal palace—the Jacob K. Javits Convention Center, stretching four blocks long and with 630,000 square feet of exhibition space. Next will be the remains of the 14th Street Meat Market, the far West Village, Manhattan Community College, the World Trade Center, and Battery Park City. The ferry rounds the island's southern tip, giving a superb view of the Statue of Liberty and of the Wall Street skyline. Heading up the East River, you'll pass under three very different spans to Brooklyn: the Brooklyn, Manhattan, and Williamsburg bridges. A glimpse of fashionable Brooklyn Heights is available and you may see, a mile or so upriver, the old Brooklyn Navy Yard.

Looking back to the Manhattan side, you'll have passed Chinatown and the Lower East Side and now be closing in on the United Nations Building at 44th Street and First Avenue. On your right will be the sometimes dormant Delacorte Geyser and Roosevelt Island with its new housing developments. The bridge overhead is the stolid Queensboro or "59th Street," and right next to it, the tramway linking Roosevelt Island with Manhattan. Farther up, you'll catch a glimpse of the mayor's residence, Gracie Mansion, built in 1799 by Archibald of that name.

Then it's upstream under the Triboro Bridge (it links Manhattan to Queens and the Bronx). After several smaller spans, you'll see on the right refurbished Yankee Stadium and the nostalgic traveler may look on the Manhattan side to a cluster of red high-rises and recall the fabled Polo Grounds, scene of many dramatic sports moments, that once stood on the site.

About a mile onward, the Hall of Fame for Great Americans still looks out from a Bronx hillcrest, once part of New York University's uptown campus (the entire school is now located in Greenwich Village). Today this outdoor colonnade designed by Stanford White is on the campus of Bronx Community College. Then, rounding the northern tip of Manhattan through the Spuyten Duyvil cut, the cruise slips past Columbia University's boathouse, Inwood Hill Park, and the Henry Hudson Bridge. Once again, you're on the Hudson River flanked on the west by the towering Palisades of New Jersey. On the east you'll see The Cloisters and the heights of Fort Washington Park as you approach the George Washington Bridge, Grant's Tomb, Riverside Church, the Soldiers and Sailors Monument. The midtown towers come into view as you head back to the dock past the rebuilt luxury-liner piers between 54th and 45th streets. It's a cruise you'll long remember.

The Outer Boroughs

There are those who call Manhattan the most exciting city in the world. But just as New York City is not the United States, Manhattan is not New York City. We'll detail Manhattan's myriad offerings later, but the point for the moment is that while Manhattan is probably where you'll want to spend the bulk of your time in New York, visits to the other boroughs will help fill out your impressions of the city.

Almost everyone knows, for example, that Manhattan is at the heart of the nation's theatrical and musical activities. But the Brooklyn Academy of Music, known as BAM, has been one of the city's busiest performing arts centers since 1908. It is also the nation's oldest such complex, housing an opera house, a theater, numerous rehearsal areas, and several "performance spaces" that are used for small theatrical presentations and especially intimate concerts. Sarah Bernhardt played Camille here; Edwin Booth portrayed Hamlet, Pavlova danced *Swan Lake,* Enrico Caruso gave recitals. And all of their latter-day counterparts continue the august Academy's grand traditions.

Brooklyn may no longer have its own baseball team (the Dodgers moved to Los Angeles in 1958), but it would still rank as the fourth-largest city in the country—if it were a city unto itself. Known to some as the "Borough of Churches" because of the number of its religious institutions—many dating back to pre–Civil War days—Brooklyn's highlights also include:

• The world's largest collection of Victorian brownstones in such neighborhoods as Brooklyn Heights (where literary figures Walt Whitman, Hart Crane, Arthur Miller, and Norman Mailer have lived);

• The Brooklyn Museum, bested only by those in London and Cairo for its Egyptian art collection;

• The extensive Botanic Gardens, with its special herb garden designed for the sightless;

• The Fulton Ferry, where Robert Fulton established his steam-powered ferry route from Manhattan in 1814 (recently refurbished and brought back into service for special weekend events);

• An endless variety of ethnic enclaves, with the Middle Eastern fare along Atlantic Avenue a particular standout from a culinary point of view;

• The city's most popular beach and amusement park—Coney Island and Astroland, respectively, where more than a million and a half people are likely to congregate on a hot summer Sunday;

• The New York Aquarium (adjacent to Coney Island), where you can get acquainted with beluga whales, penguins, dolphins, and Nuka, New York's celebrity walrus-in-residence;

• And, of course, the beautiful Brooklyn Bridge, spanning the East River from lower Manhattan. The 100-plus-year-old bridge has a wonderful pedestrian lane above the roadway, popular among bicyclers, walkers, and joggers.

If Brooklyn is a borough of contrasts between industrial and shipping interests on the one hand, and 500-acre parks, miles-long beaches and well-preserved "olde New York" settlements on the other, Staten Island is the city's most rural area.

Staten Island (specifically, Tompkinsville) is where Giovanni da Verrazano landed on April 17, 1524—the first European here.

An island of low, fertile hills and valleys, the borough—alternately known as Richmond—includes a wildlife refuge as part of Gateway National Park (parts of which are also in Brooklyn, Queens, and New Jersey) and much recreational parkland. The 80-acre Snug Harbor Cultural Center constitutes the largest single restoration project going on in the U.S. Voorlezer's House—known as the original Little Red Schoolhouse and built in 1695—is the oldest elementary schoolhouse still standing in the nation. It is part of the Richmondtown Restoration, which features buildings, furnishings, and crafts of the 17th, 18th, and 19th centuries . . . and more.

Would you believe, for example, that the highest point on the Atlantic Coast between Maine and Key West is on Staten Island? That's Todt Hill, almost 410 feet above sea level. And would you believe that despite its considerable historical legacy, Staten Island is probably most famous for its ferry ride—a five-mile excursion across New York Harbor to the southern tip of Manhattan. Almost 320 million people a year make the round-trip (many of them commuting just as easily as others might by bus or subway), as beautiful a nautical experience as the Big Apple offers. The tab? Twenty-five cents—round-trip!

Queens, with 13 parks covering 6,000 acres of land, contains nearly 300,000 homes, features two of the nation's most famous tennis stadiums and two of its leading thoroughbred racetracks. It is home to the New York Mets, giving the borough its own pro baseball team. Queens also boasts New York City's two commercial airports—John F. Kennedy on the southern shore and La Guardia on the northern shore.

Although the two airports are less than ten miles apart, those shores provide 196 miles of waterfront, with fine Atlantic Ocean beaches offering a cool respite from summer heat and humidity. The Queens Museum's star attraction is the 15,000-square-foot model of New York City that was originally featured at the 1964 World's Fair. And both that museum and the Science Museum are located on the former fairgrounds site.

The Bronx is the northernmost borough of New York. It is known as the "Borough of Universities" because it has ten institutions of higher education—more than most countries in the world. Its 42 square miles (23 percent of which are parkland) include a veritable Zoo's-Who in the Bronx Zoo. World-renowned for its collection of more than 3,000 animals repre-

senting over 800 species, the Bronx Zoo is newly renovated with a monorail and a tramway, and with "cages" simulating the animals' natural habi-
tats. Nearby is the borough's other main attraction, the New York
Botanical Garden, whose 250-acre expanse includes the 40-acre wilderness
Hemlock Forest beside the Bronx River Gorge.

Because the Bronx is preeminently residential, many of its neighborhoods retain their original character. City Island, for instance, is a bit of
seafaring New England tucked away on Long Island Sound—a nautical
enclave of century-old houses and boatyards where America Cup-winning
sailboats have been built. Other Bronx features:

- Mott Haven Historic District, with townhouses dating back to the
Civil War era;
- Riverdale's fine country-style churches;
- The Van Cortlandt Mansion, dating back to before 1758, which
served as headquarters for both American and British troops during the
Revolution;
- Wave Hill, a beautiful old estate, now a city-owned arboretum and
performance center;
- And the wide avenue known as the Grand Concourse—a curving
4½-mile boulevard patterned after Paris' Champs Elysées, with the largest
collection of Art Deco residences in the world.

For recreation-seekers the Bronx offers four 18-hole golf courses, the
three-mile-long Orchard Beach, Pelham Bay Park, and an outdoor arena
whose name tells all: Yankee Stadium.

By now you get the point that the Big Apple has more to offer than
Manhattan's concrete canyons, skyscrapers, museums, theaters, nightclubs, restaurants, shopping districts, hotels, and pleasure palaces. If it is
worth going beyond Manhattan's borders to sample what the rest of the
city has to offer, there is still no denying that Manhattan is where most
of the "action" really is.

Beginning at the Beginning

New York is an easy city to explore with the aid of a city map, which
you can pick up at the New York Convention and Visitors Bureau at Columbus Circle. The bus systems and the more than 500 miles of subway
tracks will take you to almost any sight you want to see. On occasion you
may find a car more convenient for reaching widely separated attractions
on fringes of the city, but for in-town touring a car is an expensive handicap. On-the-street parking is banned altogether weekdays in midtown and
limited to very short periods in other areas. Overtime parking can result
in your car being towed away, costing $95 or more to recover. Garage
parking is often difficult to find and can cost as much as $15 for two hours
in midtown. You will find walking the most rewarding way to come to
know the city and its people, to savor its flavor, and to make little discoveries of your own. In fact, New Yorkers themselves walk, and walk a great
deal more than do the denizens of any other U.S. city. This is the key to
the vitality of the city's amazing street life—and it continues to amaze even
long-time New Yorkers. Here is what we have seen on the streets in the
past few months (a selection): mimes, jugglers, magicians, flutists and vio-
linists ("Music student needs help for tuition"), a team of "medical students" taking blood pressures, comedians, country-music groups, singers

accompanied by music taped on a cassette player, trained dog acts, cats and monkeys dressed up in Victorian outfits, a man riding a bicycle and wearing a purple silk Musketeers suit and hat with purple feathers, bagpipers, blind beggars, crippled beggars, very healthy beggars, three-card monte conmen plying their three cards on cardboard boxes—this on Fifth Avenue!—and Renaissance troubadours—all of the above soliciting our money—and street vendors selling nuts and dried fruits, fresh-squeezed orange juice, parasols, handbags and gloves, luggage, bags of lavender, "solid gold diamond" rings (for $5!), tube socks ("For Mother's Day!"), real marijuana, phony marijuana, fruit, shish kebab, Japanese dumplings and Chinese egg rolls, hot dogs (of course, with hot sauerkraut and/or onions), real New York egg creams, and giant inflatable vinyl frogs—with or without city peddler licenses. You can even sometimes play "speed chess" for a small fee at the corner of 42nd Street and Broadway, where the chessboards are set out atop garbage cans.

The Battery Park area, where the city's history began, is an excellent starting point for a day's walking tour of lower Manhattan. The bus and subway systems converge here at Bowling Green, the little "Green before the fort" where early burghers bowled on summer evenings. Within a small radius are some of the city's most historic sites.

To appreciate the strategic geographical situation of the city, which gave it a commercial advantage over all other cities, walk along the esplanade of Battery Park. It is a salt breeze-swept stroll which tycoons from Wall Street often take to help clear heads and quiet nerves when they are faced with multimillion-dollar decisions. Here you can watch a parade of luxury cruise liners and freighters steaming out to sea, tugs herding strings of barges, and ships of all flags anchored in the bay.

Look down to a point called The Narrows, where the Lower Bay funnels into the Upper Bay, and you'll see the 4,260-foot main span of the Verrazano-Narrows Bridge cinching the waist of the water between Brooklyn and Staten Island. It was at this point in 1524 that the Florentine navigator Giovanni da Verrazano, seeking a passage to Asia at the behest of King Francis I of France, discovered what he described as "this very agreeable situation located within two small prominent hills, in the midst of which flowed to the sea a very giant river."

While history does credit Verrazano with the first sighting of this magnificent harbor, the mighty river was named for Henry Hudson, an Englishman in the employ of the Dutch East India Company, who arrived eighty-five years later on another mission to "seek a new route to the Indies by way of the North."

Despite a long campaign by the Italian Historical Society of New York to make the Verrazano name better known—first by having The Narrows, and the bridge spanning it, named Verrazano—the Florentine is still not reaping the just rewards for his discovery.

The Statue of Liberty

The Statue of Liberty is probably the most symbolic structure in the United States. Its 100th anniversary celebration in 1986 was one of the most jubilant in New York history.

A visit to Liberty Island is more rewarding if one knows beforehand a bit about the forces of friendship which inspired the statue, the genius of its construction, and the long struggle to make it a reality.

The idea of the monument was first discussed at a small dinner party given by French historian Édouard de Laboulaye at his home in Versailles, shortly after the close of the American Civil War. It was to be a gift from the people of France to the people of the United States to commemorate the long friendship between the two nations—a friendship which dated from the American Revolution, when French aid to General George Washington helped to turn the tide of victory to the side of the Colonies.

The guests were prominent men in politics, letters, and the arts. One was Frédéric Auguste Bartholdi, a young Alsatian sculptor. Some of the guests had reservations about the idea. They held that it was impossible for gratitude to exist for long. They doubted that in an emergency France could count on America to remember the aid France had given and return it in kind. The idea went into hibernation for some years. When the idea was revived, it was decided that if a statue were to be constructed, it would be with the proviso that the French people would give the statue proper if the people of the United States would build the pedestal.

Bartholdi was sent to America to discuss the project with prominent philanthropists. During the ocean voyage he roughed out several concepts for the monument. But it wasn't until he sailed into New York's magnificent harbor that he conceived the idea of a "mighty woman with a torch" lighting the way to freedom in the New World. The perfect site was New York, the gateway to that world.

In France, public fêtes and lotteries were held to raise funds to build the statue. Gounod, the famous composer, wrote a song about the statue and presented it at the Paris Opera. Because the statue was to be a gift from the people of France, the government was not approached for financial aid, and it was seven years before the needed $250,000 was finally subscribed.

On this side of the ocean the proposed site for the statue stirred up old embers of hostility. Why, some states demanded to know, should they be called upon to donate money to finance the construction of a pedestal for a "New York Lighthouse"?

Piece by piece, the statue was taking form in France, while Americans continued to hassle and withhold contributions. To help kindle enthusiasm for the project, the 42-foot right arm and torch was exhibited in 1876 at the Centennial Celebration of American Independence held in Philadelphia. Public apathy could not be overcome. It looked as though construction of the pedestal never would be completed, and that the generous gift could not be accepted.

Joseph Pulitzer Saves the Statue

Philadelphia, Boston, San Francisco, and Cleveland offered to pay all the cost of a pedestal if the statue were presented to them. It was at this point that Joseph Pulitzer of the *New York World* launched a campaign to "nationalize" the project. In editorials he stormed at New Yorkers who failed to contribute according to their means; assailed the provincial thinking of citizens in other states who refused assistance because the statue was to stand in New York Harbor; called upon everyone to avert the shame of rejecting the most generous gesture one nation had ever made to another. The public's conscience was pricked and the campaign became a crusade.

Benefit balls, sporting events, and theatrical performances were held. Schoolchildren deposited their pennies and nickels in classroom containers. Contributions poured in from distant states. Completion of the pedestal was assured and the statue was packed, piece by piece, in 214 cases and shipped to New York to be assembled and mounted. The Statue of Liberty Enlightening the World was dedicated October 28, 1886, with these words by President Grover Cleveland: "We will not forget that Liberty has here made her home; nor shall her chosen altar be neglected."

The 151-foot statue is a monument to the herculean genius of its sculptor. To achieve the correct proportions of this mighty woman, Bartholdi made a four-foot study model, then cast and recast it until it was thirty-six feet high. The statue then was divided into dozens of sections and each section enlarged four times. Liberty's eyes became two feet wide, her nose four feet long, her waist an ample thirty-five feet. On the mold of each section, copper sheets 3/32-inch thick were pressed and hammered into shape. Bartholdi had chosen copper for several reasons. It was light, easily worked, strong enough to withstand shipment, and impervious to the effect of New York's salty air.

The pedestal, one of the heaviest pieces of masonry in the world, towers eighty-nine feet above its foundation, the eleven-pointed starshaped old Fort Wood. Alexandre Gustave Eiffel, the French engineer who constructed the famous Eiffel Tower in Paris, designed the framework which secures the statue to the foundation. Four huge iron posts run from the base of the statue to the top, forming a pylon which supports the weight of the whole structure. From this central tower a maze of small beams and iron straps were installed to support each section of the statue so that no piece bears the weight of the one above it. Thus, the statue is anchored to its pedestal, and the pedestal to the base in such a way that for a windstorm—and New York has severe ones—to overturn the monument, it would just about have to upend the whole island.

It is only a ten-minute ride from Battery Park to Liberty Island, and the ferry slowly skirts the monument so that you can take several closeup pictures. Once on the island, most visitors prefer to wander around on their own, and National Park Service guides are on hand to answer questions and provide you with a free souvenir pamphlet which details the history of the statue and the island.

In the base of the statue is the American Museum of Immigration. Circular in layout, the museum describes with multimedia exhibits such subjects as who settled this country, how they got here, what they brought with them (in addition to hopes and dreams), where they put down their roots, and how they fared.

Here, too, the poetic tribute written by Emma Lazarus is inscribed, its words making clear the symbolism of the Statue of Liberty:

> Not like the brazen giant of Greek fame,
> With conquering limbs astride from land to land;
> Here at our sea-washed, sunset gates shall stand
> A mighty woman with a torch, whose flame
> Is the imprisoned lightning, and her name
> Mother of Exiles. From her beacon-hand

Glows world-wide welcome; her mild eyes command
The air-bridged harbor that twin cities frame.
"Keep ancient lands, your storied pomp!" cries she
With silent lips. "Give me your tired, your poor,
Your huddled masses yearning to breathe free,
The wretched refuse of your teeming shore.
Send these, the homeless, tempest-tossed to me:
I lift my lamp beside the golden door!"

An elevator takes you up ten floors to the balcony which runs around the top of the pedestal. On each of the four sides you'll find a sketch and description of the view before you, which makes it easy to identify Staten Island, the Verrazano-Narrows Bridge, Fort Jay, Governors Island, the Brooklyn, Manhattan, and Williamsburg bridges, Ellis Island, and the skyscrapers of lower Manhattan.

For the stout of heart and strong of limb there is a staircase which spirals up twelve more stories to Liberty's crown for a stratospheric view. You are not necessarily committed to go the whole way in one uninterrupted climb. Rest platforms are located every third of the way up, where you can also cross over and climb back down if you have a change of heart about making it all the way to the crown.

The Statue of Liberty Ferry leaves Battery Park daily every hour on the hour between 9 A.M. and 4 P.M. year-round. The round-trip costs $3.25 for adults, $1.50 for children 11 and under. Donations are also accepted for maintenance. For further information: 363–3200.

Allow yourself at least two and a half hours for the ferry ride and tour of Liberty Island. It's worth the time.

Another historical site in the Upper Bay—and accessible by ferry from Battery Park (except in winter)—is Ellis Island. Its buildings were, from 1892 to 1954, the immigration processing entry point into the United States for over ten million people, primarily Europeans. **Note:** Ellis Island is scheduled to reopen to the public as a museum in April 1989.

Battery Park

On your return to Battery Park, you might find a circular stroll rewarding before continuing your tour of lower Manhattan. You'll discover statues tucked into bowers, and the handsome Marine Memorial is especially worthy of a few moments. Stand behind the memorial—an eagle on a black marble pedestal facing a corridor of huge granite slabs engraved with the names of those who gave their lives to the sea—and you will see the Statue of Liberty dramatically framed.

The Victorian-cupolaed gray building, with its gay red windowframes and bright green roof (near the park's exit), is the home of the city's fireboats. If you are lucky enough to be here on a day when a ship enters the harbor on her maiden voyage (admittedly a rare event), you'll see a fireboat or two saluting the liner with 200-foot plumes of spray.

The round brownstone building near the entrance to the park is Castle Clinton, built as a fort in 1811 to defend New York against any British attack. When the clouds of war cleared, the fort was ceded to New York City, transformed into Castle Garden in 1823, and served as a theater and public center. Here Jenny Lind, "the Swedish Nightingale," performed for $1,000 a night, an extraordinary fee in those days. From 1855 to 1890 the castle was used as the nation's principal immigrant depot, more than 7,000,000 "tempest-tossed" souls passing through its gate into a bright new world. When Ellis Island became the new depot, the castle served as the New York City Aquarium until a modern one was built on Coney Island. Today, Castle Clinton is a National Monument, and plans are underway to restore it to its original appearance.

Don't leave this area without taking a walk around the new Battery Park City complex of luxury apartments, corporate headquarters, and the striking glass-enclosed Winter Garden with its year-round palm trees. As of press time, there are weekly concerts, and a number of chic restaurants and stores are due to open within the next year. Definitely one of this city's better architectural additions.

New York is rather poor in ancient landmarks as compared to Boston and Philadelphia. Disastrous fires in the latter part of the 18th century and beginning of the 19th century took their toll of many historical homes and buildings. During the city's rapid rise as the nation's major metropolis, many fine old buildings were demolished to make way for the new. It wasn't until 1918, when Trinity Corporation decided to tear down the century-old St. John's Chapel to make way for commerce, that New York's civic pride was finally kindled. Public feeling ran high and protests were long and loud. Commerce won, however—as is usual in New York City—and the chapel came down.

It was a boom time, a period of fierce rivalry between moguls, and big buildings became an expression of this rivalry. As each tried to top the other, the old gave way to the new. In 1908 the Singer Building at 561 Broadway, between Spring and Prince streets, soared up to a record forty-seven stories (it has since been replaced). By 1913 the Woolworth Building, 233 Broadway between Barclay Street and Park Place, topped it by thirteen floors. The Equitable Life Assurance Society, 120 Broadway between Pine and Cedar streets, covered an entire city block with a 44-story straight-sided building. Its ugly functional form jarred the city fathers into action, and New York's first zoning law was enacted in 1916. Buildings, they decreed, must have setbacks, a style which became known as the "wedding cake." (By a stretch of the imagination, the progressive bottom-to-top setbacks do resemble the tiers of a wedding cake.)

In your stroll through lower Manhattan you'll find many architectural forms. Opposite Bowling Green, at the intersection of State, Whitehall, and Bridge streets, is the Custom House, an ornate Maine granite edifice studded with statuary by Daniel Chester French, which reflects the sprawling rococo period of building at the turn of the century. It seems a doughty dowager compared to the debutante across the way, the sleek new skyscraper at No. 2 Broadway, where many of New York's foremost brokerage houses have offices.

You'll find the streets down here are narrow, cut-up, and squeezed awry by the confluence of the Hudson and East rivers. If there is one place you'll need a street map to guide you, it is here. Yet, it is this crazy-quilt street pattern laid out by the first settlers which makes the scrambled spires so spectacular when viewed from a distance. Tucked into this granite-chrome-glass jungle are a few historic buildings which have managed to escape destruction or have been cleverly reconstructed.

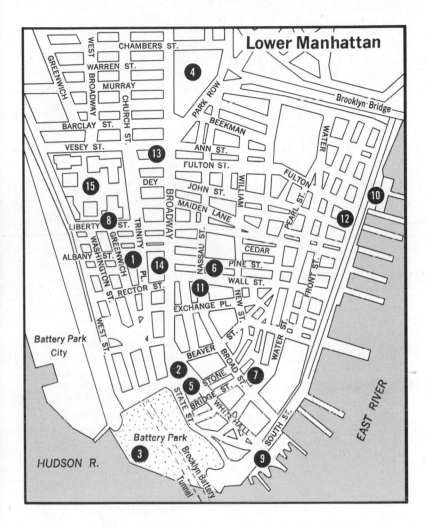

Lower Manhattan

Points of Interest

1) American Stock Exchange
2) Bowling Green
3) Castle Clinton Nat. Monument
4) City Hall
5) Customs House
6) Federal Hall Memorial
7) Fraunces Tavern
8) Federal Reserve
9) Ferry to Staten Island
10) Fulton Fish Market
11) N.Y. Stock Exchange
12) South Street Seaport
13) St. Paul's Chapel
14) Trinity Church
15) World Trade Center

Fraunces Tavern

One is Fraunces Tavern, at 54 Pearl Street (425–1778), a block east of the Custom House. Erroneously called "the oldest building in Manhattan," it is in fact an excellent reconstruction dating from 1907. Its square proportions, hipped roof edged with a light balustrade, regular window spacing, and white portico are perfect examples of the Georgian colonial style favored in the early 18th century. Built of brick—which likely saved it from going up in flames during the disastrous fires of the Revolution—and turned from a residence into a successful business building (which staved off demolition)—it has had a long, colorful history. The original building was erected in 1719 as a residence for Étienne de Lancy, a wealthy Huguenot. His grandson turned it into a store and warehouse in 1757, and in 1762 it was sold to Samuel Fraunces, a West Indian of French and Negro blood, who renovated it, making it the Queen's Head Tavern.

Taverns in those days were more than food and drink emporiums. Captains of commerce, politicians, army officers, and fraternal groups often used them as meeting halls. It was at Fraunces Tavern that the Chamber of Commerce of the State of New York was founded in 1768 to help press the fight against the Stamp Act and the tax on tea. Here, too, George Washington called his officers together in the tavern's Long Room to bid them farewell.

It was a heart-wrenching leave-taking, one officer writing in his diary: "Such a scene of sorrow and weeping I had never before witnessed, and I hope may never be called upon to witness again. It was indeed too affecting to be of long continuance—for tears of deep sensibility filled every eye—and the heart seemed so full that it was ready to burst from its wonted abode. Not a word was uttered to break the solemn silence that prevailed, or to interrupt the tenderness of the interesting scene. The simple thought that we were then about to part from the man who had conducted us through a long and bloody war, and under whose conduct the glory and independence of our country had been achieved, and that we should see his face no more in this world, seemed to me utterly insupportable . . . he walked silently on to Whitehall, where a barge was in waiting . . . as soon as he was seated, the barge put off into the river, and when out in the stream, our great and beloved General waved his hat, and bid us a silent adieu."

Fraunces Tavern is still a popular meeting place. The Sons of the Revolution in the State of New York purchased the property in 1904, faithfully re-created the original building, and today use it as their headquarters. A restaurant and bar occupy the first floor, and here, perhaps, you may see leaders of industry discussing million-dollar deals over lunch. But note: luncheon and dinner meals are served here from Monday to Friday only.

On the floors above you can view the Long Room, where Washington made his adieus, and wander through a small museum of relics from the Revolutionary period, paintings and prints depicting historical events, and such questionable Washington memorabilia as a fragment of broken tooth and lock of hair. The museum, like the bar and restaurant, is closed on weekends. Special celebrations are planned for George Washington's Inaugural Bicentennial this April.

Nearby, at 55 Water St., stands the city's newest commemorative structure. The Vietnam Veteran Memorial, dedicated in May 1985, displays 83 excerpts of letters from Vietnam servicemen and their families, which are etched on an illuminated black glass wall.

South Street Seaport

New York City gained much of its prominence and wealth as a major seaport. A nonprofit organization with a membership of more than 25,000 people established the South Street Seaport Museum, covering a four-block area around the Fulton Fish Market in lower Manhattan, in remembrance of the city's early seafaring days.

The Seaport District is a unique (for New York) combination of historical sites and lively dining/shopping complexes. Schermerhorn Row has stores and restaurants, as do other charming passages like Cannon's Walk. Don't miss the Seaport Museum on Front Street, and be sure to stop in at the Visitor's Center for complete orientation. The Fulton Market offers several floors of bustling shopping and dining, much of it casual. Early-morning visitors will find the Fulton Fish Market entertaining albeit smelly. Pier 17 across South Street on the East River is a newer center of stores, restaurants, and entertainment. The main branch of Caroline's Comedy Club is here, as are its related restaurants, The Boardwalk and The Starfish Grill. You'll find branches of Banana Republic, the Limited Express, The Sharper Image, and other familiar stores, along with inexpensive-to-moderate dining, including Chinese and Tex-Mex cuisines.

In warmer months, there's a wide variety of free entertainment on the Pier itself—everything from impromptu juggling and jazz to Skitch Henderson's New York Pops Orchestra. Note: Although parking (for a fee) is available, it's best to take public transportation to this area. During the daylight hours, The Seaport is quite safe, however it's not a good idea to wander around the adjacent neighborhoods after dark.

Not to be missed on a Seaport visit are the five late nineteenth-century and early twentieth-century square-rigged sailing ships on view: the four-masted bark *Peking,* the *Ambrose Lightship,* the three-masted *Wavertree* (still in the process of restoration), and the schooners *Lattie G. Howard* and *Pioneer;* and the multimedia show "South Street Venture" ($4.25 adults, $2.75 children; shown hourly every day).

Wall Street

Wall Street, which is only seven blocks long, has become an inclusive name. When people say "I work in Wall Street," they usually are referring to the financial district in general. Their office might be on Pine, Broad, or Cedar streets. Or they might say "I work on the street," which translates into "I work for a brokerage house."

The street, which follows what once was the walled northern boundary of the original Dutch colony, became a financial center soon after the Revolutionary War. The new Republic was $80,000,000 in debt and the first Congress, which met in a hall at the corner of Broad and Wall streets, voted to issue stock to help pay the costs of the war. Trading was a new catch-as-catch-can business carried on by auctioneers in coffeehouses and so disorganized that people were reluctant to invest. There was no assurance, they complained, that they could sell their securities when they wanted to. To give trading some semblance of order, a group of twenty-four merchants and auctioneers decided to meet each day at regular hours to buy and sell securities. They chose as their meeting place a shady spot under an old buttonwood (sycamore) tree which stood in front of the present 68 Wall Street. They were the first members of the New York Stock Exchange.

Today the Exchange has 630 member firms, with 1,366 members and 1,543 listed companies. An average 91 million shares are traded daily behind the ornate façade on Broad Street, around the corner from Wall Street. Visitors are welcome to the second-floor gallery (weekdays until 4) where you can look down on the Exchange floor and listen to a recording describing what all the frantic business is about. The self-guided tour includes audiovisual displays, a multi-image slide show, and a lecture by a guide. Guides are also present to answer your questions. The average tour takes about 30 minutes.

Around the corner from the Exchange is a handsome Greek Revival building, on the corner of Wall and Nassau streets. It is the Federal Hall National Memorial, built in 1842 on the site of New York's first City Hall. It's quite an historic corner. Here, freedom of the press and freedom of speech were won by John Peter Zenger in 1735, the first Congress convened, and on April 30, 1789, General Washington inaugurated president. It was here that the Congress adopted the Bill of Rights.

The present structure served as customs house and subtreasury building and later housed the Federal Reserve Bank of New York. In a way, the handsome building is an anomaly. If architecture is your forte, you will wonder why a circular rotunda was placed in a rectangular building (and well you should). But such were the vagaries of the period of Greek Revival. Originally the plan was to build a Roman dome over the rotunda, set squarely in the middle of this Greek temple. The dome was never built, but the handsome rotunda remains.

Administered by the National Park Service, Federal Hall Memorial Museum, 15 Pine Street (264–8711), is filled with permanent exhibits. These include displays of early historical documents (you can purchase duplicates of many of them, including the Constitution and Bill of Rights) and miniature replicas in glass cases of momentous civil liberty victories. Pick up one of the headphones, push the button, and you can even hear the proceedings of the John Peter Zenger trial.

The low marble building across the street at 23 Wall Street is the home of the powerful J. P. Morgan banking company. If you study its façade you'll find the faded scars of the bomb which, in anarchist days, was meant for his son John Pierpont Morgan, Jr., but which killed several unfortunate passersby instead.

The Federal Reserve, at 33 Liberty St., gives four tours daily. Watch millions of your dollars get the shredding treatment and take a look at all that glitters, too. One week's notice is needed for this free tour. Call 720–6130.

At the head of Wall Street, fronting on Broadway, is one of New York's richest landlords, Trinity Church. Its holdings—a land grant Queen Anne of England made to it in 1705 and bequests of large farms by early settlers—once extended along the Hudson River from about St. Paul's Chapel at Fulton Street to Christopher Street in the Greenwich Village area.

A History-Making Church

The present church building, erected in 1846, is the third one to occupy this site. The graveyard dates from even before 1697; much history is written on its headstones. If the gate is open you can wander along its tree-shaded paths to seek out the final resting places of Alexander Hamilton, Robert Fulton, and others who figured in the city's early history.

The church also contains an admission-free exhibit room. The showings cover a wide range of subjects, and there is no set schedule. It is best, therefore, to check with the church to see what exhibits are planned (602–0872). If you visit Trinity around the lunch hour, you might also stop in at the Trinity Church Coffee House directly behind the church at 74 Trinity Place.

Were it not for a favorable decision in the courts, Trinity would be just another poor parish today. After the great fire of 1776 reduced Trinity to a smoldering heap, a group of American revolutionists challenged her right to rebuild. They held that the fidelity of two of the church rectors to the loyalist cause had discredited the church; that its special status as the established Church of England in America under a royal charter was no longer valid now that the city had become part of the newly created State of New York; that the lands no longer belonged to her. Through passage of the New York State Act of 1784, however, Trinity was enabled to build chapels throughout the city with the income derived from her vast properties. It is the rentals from her large landholdings which have made Trinity one of the world's wealthiest corporations today. Leasing the land instead of selling it, Trinity was able to amass a fortune, as have other great land-holding institutions, such as Columbia University, owner of the property on which Rockefeller Center stands.

North of Trinity Church at Broadway and Fulton Street is one of the city's few remaining examples of colonial architecture, St. Paul's Chapel, one of many Trinity built throughout the city. When it was erected in 1766, it stood in a field outside the city. Townspeople complained that it was much too far to go to church; yet it is only a five-block walk from Trinity. St. Paul's Georgian-Classic revival style bears a distinct resemblance to St. Martin-in-the-Fields in London, probably for good reason, since its architect, Thomas McBean, was a pupil of Gibbs, who built St. Martin. There is much to hold you here. There is a light, cheerful air to the interior which is rare in colonial churches. Fourteen priceless Waterford crystal chandeliers glisten in the azure-tinted nave and galleries, providing an unusually elegant, if somewhat controversial, embellishment. Ever since these gleaming candlelight fixtures—they are wired for electricity now—were installed in 1802, parishioners have had some reservations about their propriety. Mumblings are still to be heard about their making the church look like a ballroom.

On either outer aisle you will find a handsome box pew. One was the special preserve of the governors who worshipped here in the comfort of upholstered chairs and draft-deflecting canopies. The pew on the left was also used by George Washington. Original William and Mary chairs in bright red satin brocade give the pew an air of elegance seldom seen in churches. Duncan Phyfe, whose cabinet shop was around the corner from the chapel, fashioned the handsome sofa you can see in the rear of the church. The altar, its railing, and a great deal of the ornamentation in the church is the work of Major Pierre L'Enfant, the designer who later planned the city of Washington, D.C.

St. Paul's congregation is probably the most scattered in the city. People who once lived in the area and were displaced when housing gave way to office buildings still return for Sunday services. They drive in from as far away as Long Island, Westchester, and New Jersey. Weekdays, the chapel serves as a quiet haven for office workers, who come to midday service or to sit on the secluded outdoor benches beside the peaceful cemetery.

Directly behind St. Paul's is the gigantic World Trade Center, operated by the Port Authority of New York and New Jersey. The Center takes up sixteen acres of lower Manhattan and stretches from Cortlandt Street on the east to West Street on the west and from Liberty Street on the south to Barclay and Vesey streets on the north.

From top (107 floors up) to bottom, the World Trade Center has become a major sightseeing attraction—and part of the lure is the food as well as the view. Its various dining rooms, cocktail lounges, private rooms upstairs, and its concourse-level dining room, bar, and café below have to be seen to be believed. And so does the view of the city from perhaps the most famous of the Big Apple restaurants, Windows on the World, and its less expensive counterpart, the Hors d'Oeuverie, a cocktail lounge and grill that is another part of the restaurant complex.

Windows on the World (we'll use the apt abbreviation WOW) has been compared to an immense spaceship, an ocean liner—you name it and pick your own superlatives—for decor, design, and view. You are seated in multi-tiered dining rooms made to seem even larger by mirrors—but it is still the skyline that is the real view, no matter what a people-watcher you may be. The main dining room is a private club Monday through Friday until 3 P.M., becoming a regular restaurant thereafter. The food doesn't match the view—but what could.

You can nibble on the hors d'oeuvres, sample the grilled entrées, or have dessert at the Hors d'Oeuverie, on the same level as WOW, or come for Sunday brunch. It is a lot less costly than WOW, a good place for snacks and drinks—and the view is equally spectacular. The phone number for these 107th floor wining and dining spots is 938–1100. (Hors d'Oeuverie is a private club at weekday lunch, though outsiders are admitted for a $7.50 surcharge. It is open to the public at other times.)

Other worthwhile (and less expensive) stops at the World Trade Center are the Observation Deck, open from 9:30 A.M. to 9:30 P.M., with sunset an especially spectacular time to be there; the Big Kitchen series of deli-style fast-food emporiums in the main concourse of Two WTC, where the crowds at lunch hour are a sight to behold; and the Skydive Café on the 44th floor of One WTC. The latter is an inexpensive-to-moderately priced luncheon cafeteria with a bar that is also open after work. The Observation Deck costs $2.95 for adults, $1.50 for children 6 to 12 years old, and $1.50 for senior citizens; telephone 466–7377.

City Hall

Return to Broadway and stroll up to City Hall. Almost any day of the week you are likely to see the welcome mat being spread out for a foreign

dignitary, a group of VIPs, a newly crowned beauty queen, a DAR delegation, or an award-winning actress. Many come to greet the mayor in legitimate roles. Others come seeking publicity. It's been the plaint of many a mayor that acting as the world's greatest greeter cuts deeply into the day's work of handling affairs for the city.

City Hall is both a museum and a municipal capital. Architecturally it is considered one of the finest public buildings in America. During the period between 1803 and 1811, when it was being built, construction costs rose to $538,000—a shocking amount in those days. The Common Council members, pinching pennies wherever they could, decided considerable money could be saved by using marble on the front and sides only. Brownstone would be used to face the back. After all, they maintained, most of the city's population lived south of the park and it would be a waste to use marble when it seldom would be seen. The city, they believed, would never grow much beyond City Hall. When the building was renovated in 1956, at a cost of $2,000,000, the outside was faced in limestone on all four sides, to afford equal respect to the citizens of each point of the compass.

The mayor's office in the west wing overlooks the triangular park where Dutch burghers once bowled and where, a century later, spunky Revolutionists raised Liberty Poles and demonstrated against British rule. Even today it is not always a peaceful view. Demonstrators often congregate here to march and shout demands for a special action by the city fathers.

A handsome, curving double staircase leads to the Governor's Room on the second floor of City Hall. The elegant quarters, "appropriated as an office to His Excellency the Governor of the State," have been the scene of many gala, historic receptions. It had been traditional, even as far back as the Dutch and English rules, to set aside an area in City Hall for the governor's convenience. Today, New York's governor is not so honored. He is housed in an archaic monstrosity upstate in Albany with not one iota of the charm of the Governor's Room, which is now a showcase of antique furnishings and priceless portraits of early American heroes. One of the most notable items in the museum is George Washington's desk. Open Monday to Friday, 10 A.M.–4 P.M. Free.

On leaving City Hall, walk around to its rear and over to the tall-towered Municipal Building. A passageway through its arch will bring you out on Park Row, near the approach to the Brooklyn Bridge, the city's oldest span. From here, it is only a five-minute walk north to Chinatown.

Chinatown, Their Chinatown

Chinatown may come as a bit of surprise or disappointment, depending on your preconceived picture of it. Many tourists are drawn to the area in hopes of glimpsing the seedy side of life they've seen in class B movies and read about in mystery-thrillers. They are due for disappointment.

Long gone are the bloody fratricidal tong wars, knifings in the night, and the stealthy slipping of dead victims into the black East River waters. Gone too are the opium dens. The tongs have turned into modern civic and fraternal organizations and the dens of iniquity have disappeared, though gangs of juvenile thugs (mostly immigrants from Hong Kong) have gained some notoriety recently.

Today, Chinatown is a colorful pocket of Oriental shops and restaurants catering to Chinese who live in other parts of the city, to local government department heads, Park Avenue matrons, Broadway stars, and out-of-town visitors (in short, to all lovers of good Chinese cuisine).

Chinatown is tiny, encompassing something like a dozen or so square blocks. Thousands of Chinese are crowded into tenements lining the narrow, crooked streets. Here, somehow, the tenements seem almost proper to their surroundings. Perhaps it's because pseudo pagodas crown their roofs, bright banners garland the streets, and temple bells and the singsong talk of venerable elders crowd out sounds of the 20th century. There is a faint aura of China's ancient civilization all around: emporiums which have modern adding machines but prefer to do their bookkeeping with the beaded abacus; apothecary and herb shops where family medicinal formulas are compounded. Stalls and shopwindows are piled high with exotic displays of condiments and herbs, snow peas, bean curd, shark fins, duck eggs, dried fungi, squid, and other ingredients used in the delectable Chinese dishes. In keeping with the Oriental theme, even the sidewalk telephone booths have been designed as tiny pagodas.

The juncture of Worth and Mott streets, across from Chatham Square, is the gateway to Chinatown. A Chinese Museum is located at 8 Mott Street, and for $1 you can view exhibits of ancient Chinese coins, costumes, deities, and dragons. There are displays of flowers, fruits, chopsticks, and incense with explanations of their history and the symbolism attached to each. Push a button at the bottom of a musical instrument display case and a Chinese combo in native costume flashes on the screen to demonstrate how they sound. Youngsters especially enjoy the educational quiz, a game of thirty-eight questions along the lines of "Which city is farthest north, Peking or New York?" and "Who invented paper and printing, the Chinese or Egyptians?" You register your choice by pressing one of two buttons and by the end of the game you have a few nuggets of knowledge to confound your friends. Open daily, 10 A.M.–midnight (964–1542). Generally, the shops in Chinatown feature jade and ivory carvings, good-luck charms, brocade dresses, tea sets, and knickknacks.

You may hear little English spoken as you wander through Bayard, Pell, and Doyers streets, though many of Chinatown's citizens can speak it if they please.

Dignity disappears when the Year of the Dragon (or Tiger, or any of the 12 in the Chinese horoscope) comes in, the whole town joining in the gay antics and colorful parades of fire-breathing monsters which mark the start of the lunar New Year at the end of January or beginning of February. Firecrackers explode everywhere. Huge dragons, unicorns, and lions prowl through the streets to scare away evil spirits. Old and young dance along behind, shouting "Gun hay fat choy!" (Happy New Year with prosperity). Merchants offer gifts to the dragon and heads of lettuce sprouting dozens of dollars to be dispensed to the poor, for the dragon is an emblem of guardianship and generosity. It is a time when Chinatown is at its liveliest, most colorful best. Not even snow flurries can dampen the high spirits of the celebrants nor those from the outside who have come to watch and participate.

To the west of Chinatown is an emerging artist's neighborhood, christened TriBeCa ("Triangle Below Canal," bounded by the West Side waterfront—Greenwich Street—and West Broadway), which offers cheaper

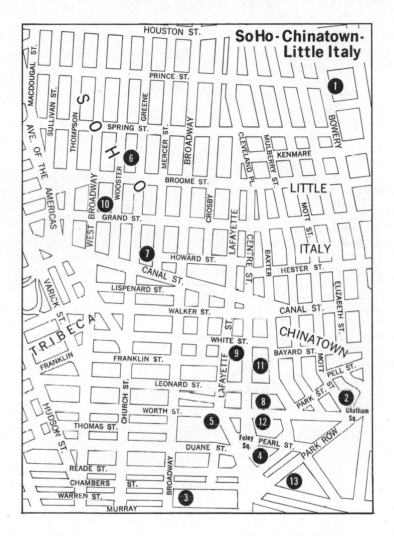

Points of Interest

1) Bowery Mission
2) Chinese Museum
3) City Hall
4) Federal Court
5) Federal Office Building
6) Museum of Colored Glass & Light
7) Museum of Holography
8) N.Y. State Office Building
9) N.Y. State Supreme Court
10) Performing Garage
11) Criminal Court
12) N.Y. County Court
13) Police Headquarters

lofts for those driven out of SoHo by rising rents. There is a growing number of trendy bars, restaurants, and night spots here.

The Bouwerie, the Bowery

Just northeast of Chinatown, in the shadow of the Williamsburg Bridge, is the Bowery. Once an Indian trail used by Peter Stuyvesant to ride to his *bouwerie,* or "farm," the thoroughfare grew into a fashionable amusement and theater center in the early 19th century, then went into a decline as people moved uptown to new neighborhoods. For almost a century the Bowery has been the "street of forgotten men."

In days gone by, the Bowery was home to most of the city's homeless. Today, the homeless are everywhere, on the streets of almost every neighborhood. They pose one of the city's most pressing social problems, one that is growing daily. One of the organizations that has been trying to help for years is the Salvation Army.

The Army began operating in the area before the turn of the century. Their lassies were not especially welcome when they invaded the Bowery in 1880 to "Go for souls—and go for the worst." Their work to reform derelicts and teach them to lead useful lives was fought by saloon and dance hall proprietors, who felt the preachings were bad for business. The Army had no church nor meeting place; so they preached and sang on street corners until a reformed Harry Hill offered them the use of his bawdy, gaudy music hall for the salvation of souls. The Army's historian recalls: "Alcoholics and prostitutes—the poor and downtrodden and discouraged—soon found new hope and comfort . . . Not only souls were saved, but minds and bodies. Roofs were put over the heads of people who had no other home on earth. Hundreds were fed and clothed by the Army's busy soup kitchens." The lassies marched on to other areas of the city and thence to other areas of public service. Despite their efforts and the efforts of many other charitable service institutions, however, derelicts still take refuge there.

The Lower East Side

Between the Bowery and the East River is probably New York's most integrated area. The entire city often has been called a "melting pot," but the mile-square east side area (bounded roughly on the south by Canal Street and on the north by Seventh Street) is, some observers feel, the most dramatic example of the blending of many races, religions, and cultures in the world.

Here, immigrants were crammed into ghettos and English was treated as a foreign language. Only those with the greatest stamina survived, and those with the greatest will succeeded in escaping from it. From here came Alfred E. Smith, a son of Irish immigrants, who became governor of New York State. Several sons of Jewish immigrants made the climb to success, too. Among them were Senator Jacob Javits, composers George and Ira Gershwin, comedian Eddie Cantor. A little Italian boy made it also— Jimmy Durante. The neighborhood also spawned its share of gangsters: a few are in jail, a few are living high.

While most shops all over the city are closed on Sunday, those on the Lower East Side bustle with activity. The Jewish Sabbath is observed on

Saturday, while Sunday is a big shopping day down here. Grand Street, often called the "Street of Brides," is lined with one shop window after another of bridal gowns. The neighborhood now has a large Hispanic community, to add to the diversity.

The stalls on Orchard Street, a street so jammed with shoppers one can hardly wiggle through, display everything from clothing to kitchen wares. Bargaining is the way most transactions are handled, and customers should be wary to inspect merchandise—sometimes these stalls or shops deal in "seconds" in order to keep their prices low. Grand Street is for fine linens, the Bowery is for lamp stores, and Allen Street is the wholesale tie district—all featuring bargain prices.

The northwestern part of the Lower East Side, around Second Avenue and St. Mark's Place (an extension of East 8th Street) is still heavily laden with Middle-European ambience. But not unmixed: St. Mark's Place, formerly the spiritual headquarters of the Hippies, is now spiritual headquarters for the Punk Rockers. The cultural juxtapositions in this area must be seen to be believed.

Little Italy

Little Italy lies east of SoHo, just north of Chinatown, and south of Greenwich Village. Centered on Grand Street and its intersection with Mulberry and Mott streets, Little Italy is the home of Ferrara's, (195 Grand Street, 226–6150), the city's foremost Italian coffee and sweet shop, as well as dozens of Italian restaurants, imported-food shops, cafés, and clam bars—including the ever-popular Umberto's and Vincent's clam bars. These clam bars feature a special hot and spicy tomato sauce with mussels, conch or squid, dishes unavailable anywhere else in the city. Best time for sampling Little Italy's fare is the early September fête of San Gennaro. During the festival the whole of Mulberry Street from Canal Street north is turned into a carnival, with food stands hawking calzone, sausage and pepper heroes, zeppole, and other standard southern Italian dishes. "Games of skill and chance" provide between-bite diversion. Chinatown seems to be crowding in on Little Italy from the south. A similar such festival honoring St. Anthony is held in Greenwich Village the first two weeks of June.

South of Houston (SoHo)

SoHo, on West Broadway (part of which was renamed La Guardia Place a few years ago), between Canal and West Houston streets, and off to the sides on Prince, Spring, and Broome streets, is an area with which many native New Yorkers aren't familiar. It is only in the last 15 or so years that (at first) artists and writers began moving into the area, bringing their imaginations to bear on buildings formerly used as warehouses and for light industry. They came because they liked what were then inexpensive rents for the lofts—often in need of plumbing and wiring but offering wide-open spaces—while gallery owners appreciated the high-ceilinged spaciousness of the old buildings, which allowed exhibit room to showcase the modern art and sculpture of today's genre. As rents rose, the area became fashionable among art patrons, jetsetters, and young professionals. So following the artists, writers, and galleries, a number of interesting and off-beat restaurants and bars came to be. Ironically, with few exceptions (the Broome Street Restaurant and Cupping Room Café on West Broadway among them), most of SoHo's more unusual spots are far too expensive for the neighborhood's natives who work at art. On weekends and most weekday evenings West Broadway is thronged with people who come to SoHo to gallery-hop and browse at the poster shops and boutiques as well as to eat and drink.

Greenwich Village

Greenwich Village is not an entity but rather a collection of little villages. Its heart is Washington Square, at the end of Fifth Avenue, and its extremities reach out farther and farther each year. Roughly, it is bounded by Houston Street (pronounced "HOUSE-ton") on the south, 13th Street on the north, Hudson Street on the west—although much of the area between Hudson (the street) and Hudson (the river) has recently been restored and taken on a "Village" look. Its eastern boundary now extends to Lafayette Street and the vague beginnings of the East Village, where most of the real latter-day Bohemians have migrated. If the Village has a "Main Street," it is 8th Street (and up onto Greenwich Avenue), centered on Village Square at Sixth Avenue.

Rents in Greenwich Village have soared out of the reach of poor poets and struggling artists. Today's Village residents are largely career people—business executives, lawyers, doctors, teachers, successful writers and artists—who have been drawn by its small-town neighborliness and convenient location to the city's business centers. Others, tired of being bound by commuter train schedules, have come down from the suburbs and live in old houses they have renovated. You'll see little clusters of these tidy row houses on such tree-shaded side streets as Charles and Perry, Bedford and St. Luke's, their tiny rear gardens bright with blooms.

The Village is also home to a large segment of New York's Italian population. Their province south and southwest of Washington Square, really an extension of Little Italy farther to the south, is a tangle of shops strung with tangy cheeses, breads, red peppers, garlic, bunches of oregano and rosemary. Housewives stream in from all parts of the Village to pinch the melons, poke through the tomatoes, and argue a bit about prices before making their selections.

In the early '20s the Village was a lively and bawdy place, a Montmartre in the midst of Manhattan. Painters and sculptors had discovered deserted lofts could be rented for a song. Poets and playwrights followed, crowding into the old buildings south of Washington Square, which became known as "Genius Row." They produced their plays in a theater converted from an old box factory, displayed their paintings in the park, scavenged for coal to heat their cold-water flats.

Since the turn of the century, it has been a center of creativity and intellectual curiosity that nurtured some of America's greatest writers and artists: Henry James, Edith Wharton, O. Henry, e. e. cummings, Maxwell Bodenheim, Rockwell Kent, and many others. Their haunts—cellar speakeasies, chile con carne joints, hole-in-the-wall restaurants, murky nightclubs with tawdry epicene shows—drew the curious uptowners who wanted a taste of *la vie Bohème.*

Many of their haunts are long gone, victims of urban renewal. Others remain as shrines to their talent and genius. This bawdy phase, however, is but one of many the Village has passed through, for its history dates back to post-Revolutionary days.

The first settlers fled to the Village during the yellow fever plagues which raged through the lower city from 1791 to 1798. Founded in haste on the site of an old tobacco plantation, the little village grew haphazardly and the streets meandered off in unplanned directions. The crazy-quilt street pattern contributes to the Village a quaint charm but drives uninitiated taxi drivers to distraction. One street changes its name in mid-block; another circles back and crosses itself; West 4th wanders across West 10th, 11th, and 12th and runs into West 13th; Little West 12th is four blocks away from its larger namesake. To explore the area, a detailed map is mandatory. Even then, it is difficult to find your way without asking directions. You'll find the Villagers friendly and willing to help you out of the maze.

Focal Point of the Village

Washington Arch, at the foot of Fifth Avenue, is the best point to start a stroll through the most colorful and historic Village areas. It is easily reached by a Fifth Avenue bus marked "8th Street," by 6th and 8th Avenue subway to West 4th Street station, or the BMT to 8th Street and Broadway.

Washington Square served as a potter's field for plague victims and public place for executions in the late 1700s. By 1823 it had been filled with 10,000 victims of the plague and the gallows. It had served its purpose and it was time for a change, the city fathers decided; so the plot was turned into a drill ground for militia. Eventually it became known as Washington Square Park, although most of its former greenery has today been changed to concrete.

Should you choose a Sunday in spring, summer, or fall for your stroll, you'll be treated to one of the town's best known free entertainments. The fountain in the square is a meeting place for jazz and bluegrass musicians, guitar-players, and pluckers of homemade instruments. Within their ranks you may run into a recording artist who has come down to play a session with a group of unknown troubadours just for the sheer fun of it. Sunday strollers are apt to include young parents with toddlers, a multitude of dog-walkers, and arms-around-each-other couples of all ages; in all manner of dress. Come Halloween on October 31 and the park is the end-point of a Mardi Gras-like costume parade that is both colorful and great fun.

The fountain is a good vantage point for viewing the red-brick, white-trimmed houses which line the north side of the square. Built around 1830, they remained a fashionable center of New York for a generation, sheltering members of old New York's aristocracy and a long-gone way of life so vividly described in Henry James's *Washington Square,* the novel which appeared on stage and in film under the title *The Heiress.*

Edith Wharton lived in the old Boorman house on the northeast corner of the square, a setting which inspired her novel *The Age of Innocence.* Down the street from her house, at No. 3, John Dos Passos wrote *Manhattan Transfer* and artist Norman Rockwell painted his own brand of "primitives." Rose Franken, author of *Claudia,* lived at No. 6 before this, while other, lovely patrician homes began to vanish.

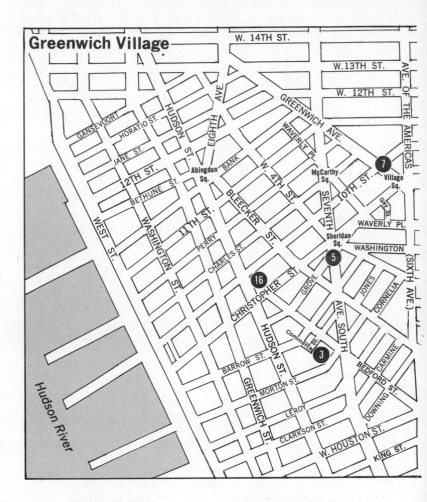

Points of Interest

1) Astor Place Theater
2) Bottom Line
3) Cherry Lane Theater
4) Circle in the Square Theater
5) Circle Repertory
6) Cooper Union
7) Jefferson Market Library
8) The New Museum/The New
   School (branch)
9) The New School for Social
   Research
10) New York University
11) Palladium
12) Players Theater
13) Provincetown Playhouse
14) Public Theater (Papp)
15) Sullivan St. Playhouse
16) Theater De Lys
17) Village Gate

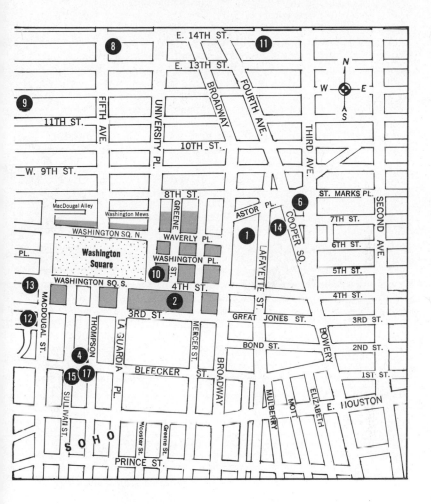

Several, including the home of William Rhinelander Stewart, which stood on the northwest corner of Fifth Avenue, have been replaced by an apartment house. Fortunately, the building has been so constructed that it blends in with the remaining old houses. Only the building's first five floors are on the square and they are aligned with the roofs of the surviving houses. The red-brick facing and white trim of the new building blends with the old homes. The granite-colored upper floors are set back and front on Fifth Avenue, making that part of the structure seem completely divorced from the square. During construction of the apartment's foundation, workers found an underground stream. It was old Minetta Brook, which was buried by fill two centuries before. The brook surfaced and now bubbles up in a glass container in the apartment's lobby. It also spouts up in a fountain at No. 33, which is now a New York University residence hall.

The university, which has been here since the 1830s, owns and leases about four-fifths of the land around the square. In its original building, which stood at 100 Washington Square East, Professor Samuel F. B. Morse developed the telegraph and Samuel Colt invented the single-shot pistol.

When its student body began bursting the seams of the campus building on and around the square, the university reluctantly gave notice to the artists and writers along Genius Row. Loud outcries were to no avail, and the row of garrets has been replaced with the Georgian-style Law School at the southwest end of the square and the modern Roman Catholic Holy Trinity Chapel. Other modern N.Y.U. additions are the Hagop Kevorkian Center for Near Eastern Studies and the Bobst Library. Up the street, the tall brick-and-glass Loeb Student Center covers the site of Madame Blanchard's boardinghouse, whose boarders included Theodore Dreiser, Eugene O'Neill, Zona Gale, Frank Norris, O. Henry, and many other literary notables.

MacDougal Street Promenade

From here it's a short walk to MacDougal Street, which is called Washington Square West at this point. A few steps up MacDougal Street brings you to MacDougal Alley, one of the most charming back streets in the Village. Most of the little homes here were former stables and carriage houses of the elegant old homes on Washington Square North. Brightly painted, with doorways lit by gas lamps, they are among the most prized studios and apartments in all New York City. At the rear of the old homes on the east side of Fifth Avenue you'll find a similar cobbled street, lined by converted carriage houses, called Washington Mews.

Returning to the west side of Washington Square, passing the Law School, and walking on into the lower part of MacDougal Street, you will see the rebuilt Provincetown Playhouse, a pioneer Off-Broadway theater made famous by the early works of Eugene O'Neill. There are boutiques where you'll find witty, trendy, and ethnic clothes and jewelry; leather goods shops and fortune-reading ateliers; a few good restaurants; coffeehouses (the latter now, alas, a Village rarity); and pizza and souvlaki eateries.

MacDougal Street leaves this mood behind as it crosses Bleecker Street, home of the Circle-in-the-Square Theater, which produced the early works of Tennessee Williams. The original theater group has now made the move uptown to Broadway and is operating at the Circle in the Square Theater. On Thompson St. between Bleecker and Houston (a Dutch term meaning "house garden") is a row of well-kept, old brick houses where well-to-do professional people live. A similar row on Sullivan Street backs onto them and the private park between is shared by householders on both sides.

Turn back to Bleecker Street, head west across Sixth Avenue—officially known as the "Avenue of the Americas"—and you'll come to Father Demo Square and the Renaissance-style Church of Our Lady of Pompeii. Spend a minute or so in the church, for its lovely stained-glass windows and religious paintings are well worth the time. You are now at the beginning of the Italian shopping mart, which stretches from Sixth over to Seventh Avenue. The pushcarts have vanished from this colorful neighborhood, as have all but a very few produce stores. But the aromatic fish stores, bakeries with their mouth-watering Neapolitan cakes and pastries, meat and cheese and grocery shops make this one of New York's unique streets, with a character and flavor all its own.

The Village's meandering streets can really defeat you at this point, but find Leroy Street and follow its bend to St. Luke's Place. Here you'll come upon a poplar-lined street of handsome Anglo-Italian houses, almost as elegant as those of Washington Square. Built in 1880, they have housed many a New York celebrity. No. 6 was once the home of New York's dashing mayor, Jimmy Walker. At an earlier time, it was the residence of the French Consul, and if you look to the left of the doorway you can still see, set in the wall, a tile bearing the arms of the French Republic.

At the end of the street, turn right on Hudson and explore the streets which twist and turn off it: Morton Street, with its attractive but seedy houses, and Bedford Street, where Edna St. Vincent Millay and John Barrymore lived (at different times) in New York's narrowest house. It is numbered 75½ and is only nine feet broad, having been built in the driveway of the old Cardoza farmhouse.

Three of the most contradictory houses in the Village are found at the corner of Grove and Bedford streets. The house on the corner, a faded historic mansion, is backed up against a little doll house which is said to have been used for slave quarters a century ago. Next door, at 100 Bedford, is a gingerbread house known as "Twin Peaks." Local legend claims it was designed as a "dream house" by a Village artist, and that the sketches of his fairytale domicile caught the eye of financier Otto Kahn, who financed the dream. To many it is a nightmare.

Follow Grove Street to the point where it bends, and you will see the gate to Grove Court, a fenced-off cluster of small brick houses circling a shady garden. Grove Court was the home of O. Henry when he became affluent and it is the setting of his story *The Last Leaf.*

While you're following these winding streets, look for Commerce Street and the Cherry Lane Theater, the famous playhouse (converted from a box factory) which has given many a struggling playwright an opportunity to display his works. Follow Grove Street to St. Luke's Chapel on Hudson Street. St. Luke's was built by Trinity Church in 1822 and still maintains many of its old traditions. The church itself burned recently, but has been rebuilt. Wings of little brick houses jut out from St. Luke's. These old row houses also date from the 1820s and one was the boyhood home of Bret Harte.

Now, follow Grove in its eastward course, and before long you'll emerge into a nine-way intersection at Sheridan Square. The area around the square is studded with restaurants, shops, theaters, and cafés.

Meandering Mood

If you still are in the mood for meandering, pick up Waverly Place, and don't be startled when you find it meeting itself after awhile. Richard Harding Davis, who lived at No. 108, often walked in circles, too. Nearby is Gay Street, a crooked little path punctuated here and there with Greek Revival houses built in the 1820s. Ruth McKenney lived in the basement apartment of No. 14 with *My Sister Eileen.* A worthwhile detour, before you reach the square, is a walk along Bleecker Street, turning left from Grove and following it to where it comes to an end, at Bank Street and Eighth Avenue. This stretch of Bleecker, like much of the Village, is a designated landmark district, and most of the buildings along it date from the early 19th century. Some of the most attractive antique and gift shops in the city are along here. The White Horse Tavern, on Hudson Street, not too far from the end of Bleecker, was the favorite Manhattan drinking place of poet Dylan Thomas. Farther west, at West Street and Bank Street, on the waterfront, is Westbeth, the former Bell Labs building converted into an artist's community. A committee screens applicants so that only working people in the arts are offered apartments.

Follow Gay to Christopher, cross that street, and then follow it westward for a few blocks' worth of good window-shopping and browsing. The entire length of Christopher Street is the center of New York's large homosexual community. This route will take you across the Sheridan Square intersection again.

Village Square

Back at the Gay-Christopher intersection, turn right into the intersection that takes in Greenwich Avenue, 8th Street, and Avenue of the Americas. This is Village Square, one of the crossroads of the Village. The open-fronted vegetable stand to the right was once Luke O'Connor's Columbian Gardens, where back in 1896 young John Masefield, the late Poet Laureate of England, hauled beer kegs and mopped floors. Across the square to the north is a block of some historic interest. Patchin Place, itself a small courtyard of great charm, off West 10th Street between the Avenue of the Americas and Greenwich Avenue, was the site of e. e. cummings' apartment for many of the later years of his life. Djuna Barnes also lived on Patchin Place. The iron-barred Women's House of Detention, across the street behind the Jefferson Market building, was demolished in late 1973. The property belongs to the city and there is doubt as to its ultimate destiny. Interested Village citizens have pushed for a semi-public park that would adjoin the neighboring Jefferson Market Courthouse, a cherished landmark since 1878. Its unusual Italian Gothic architecture is the work of Calvert de Vaux, one of the architects of Central Park, and Frederick Withers, who designed the picturesque gate of the Little Church Around the Corner. Its clock tower once served as the neighborhood fire lookout. Long unused, the Courthouse was refurbished inside and out and is now a branch of the New York Public Library.

Two major Village streets lead from this intersection in opposite directions. Eighth Street between Fifth and Sixth avenues changes personality yearly, it seems. Doorways and sidewalks are crowded and often trash-littered, especially on weekends, and shops, too, have changed radically over the years; garish snack shops and noisy record stores currently predominate. This single, busy block is still worth a visit—but a brief one. Going diagonally northwest between this intersection and Eighth Avenue is Greenwich Avenue, one of the more interesting promenades in the Village. Cafes, some good restaurants, eye-catching clothing shops (both trendy and classic), and interesting Villagers to look at make it a fun strolling route, and most of the neighborhood is out every weekend, bound on errands or the pursuit of pleasure. The farther northwest you go, the more conservative the shops and people seem. Greenwich Avenue is the Village in microcosm. The triangular vacant lot opposite St. Vincent's Hospital at Seventh Avenue and West 12th Street used to contain an apartment house inhabited by Village characters, where Edmund Wilson made his first home in the city.

The East Village

East Village, the new Bohemia, is more or less bounded by 14th Street on the north, the Bowery on the west, Houston Street on the south, and the East River. The area has inherited many of Greenwich Village's ways of the '20s. Here, every day is Freedom Day, and you'll see it celebrated in a variety of ways. This enclave of the disciples of unconventional living centers around Tompkins Square, seven blocks east of Washington Square.

Cheap rents first drew the poor painters and poets. Rooms and lofts could be rented for as little as $20 a month. Included, of course, were squalor and a lot of do-it-yourself decorating and repairs. There were other attractions, too. The new crop of artists and writers found the atmosphere lacked prejudice. Many residents live communally, sharing the work and expenses of their room and board.

The area abounds with talent, though many artists moved to SoHo or more recently to TriBeCa. Still, there is an increasingly strong "alternative gallery" presence here. Most of the area's new poets' works are published in underground magazines, mimeographed and stapled in someone's cellar, and distributed to friends and colleagues. Many an avant garde theatrical production has been given a tryout at La Mama E.T.C., 74A Fourth Street just west of Second Avenue.

St. Mark's Place is the main promenade for the East Village. It is a stretch between Third and First avenues, the extension of East 8th Street, and along it you'll see one or two emporiums that frankly proclaim themselves "head shops," a reminder that just a few years ago the East Village was one of New York's major outposts of the drug culture. Hundreds of runaway teenagers flocked here to live in anonymity and self-imposed communal poverty until sheer desperation—or the police—sent them back to their parents. Some remainder of this subculture still exists, and this is another area of the city where old-time, immigrant-family citizens and the young, free-living newcomers are learning to coexist without too much antagonism.

On St. Mark's Place, there are also several clothing shops, mostly of the wildly informal variety; boutiques with jewelry and leather goods;

record stores; and a popular movie house attracting buffs with its program of cinema classics, mostly the old musicals. Between Second and First, the architecture is considerably more attractive, and do note the charming edifice that is the First German Methodist Episcopal Church.

What was East Village before the invasion of the latter-day Bohemians? The square, named for one of New York's governors, Daniel B. Tompkins, was a nice, quiet neighborhood of mixed cultures, people of Ukrainian, Czech, German, Polish, Russian, Italian, Jewish, and, lately, Puerto Rican and Indian origins. Russian and Turkish baths, the special delicacies in delicatessen, meat, and produce stores reflect the heterogeneous ways of the neighborhood. Handsome churches of all faiths—among them, St. Nicholas Russo-Carpathian, St. Brigid's-on-the-Square, and St. Mark's Church-in-the-Bouwerie—have served generation after generation. The old-world ethnic composition of the area also makes the East Village a good neighborhood for hearty, inexpensive dining. Farther east, along avenues A and B, yet another new wave of galleries, dance clubs, and restaurants is developing.

This is the area Dutch Governor Peter Stuyvesant retired to after he surrendered Nieuw Amsterdam to the British. It became a defense post against the British in 1812, later a parade ground, then a recruiting camp for Civil War soldiers and scene of draft riots, mass meetings, and hunger strikes.

The City Moves North

Fortunately there were enough parade grounds scattered around the city to break up the forward march of square block upon square block of brownstone houses. The city was lucky, too, in having a few imaginative builders.

One was Samuel Ruggles, who had bought a large tract of land between what is now 20th and 21st streets, extending east of Park Avenue South and west of Third Avenue. It is now known as Gramercy Park, center of one of the nicer residential areas in the city. In the early 1800s, when Ruggles bought the property, the area was far north of the city. His contemporaries derided his dream of turning this woodland tract into an English-type residential square and dubbed it "Sam Ruggles' Vacant Lot." The men of little vision lived to eat their words.

Ruggles divided the tract, making a square of forty-two lots that he set aside for a park, and the bordering area, which was carved into sixty-six building lots. The elite of New York were attracted with the promise that only those who built houses around the square would have the use of the park. Two golden keys to unlock the gate of the fenced-in park were given to each homeowner. The snob appeal made the venture an instantaneous success.

Mrs. Stuyvesant Fish, leader of society's "400," became a resident and many others followed. They included Cyrus W. Field, who was responsible for the first Atlantic cable; the illustrious architect Stanford White, whose career came to a sudden end when Pittsburgh millionaire Harry K. Thaw shot him for flirting with his ladylove (showgirl Evelyn Nesbit); James W. Gerard, the pre–World War I American ambassador to Germany; and wealthy philanthropist Peter Cooper. Shakespearean star Edwin Booth's home at 16 Gramercy Park is now the headquarters of the Players' Club, and the National Arts Club is housed in the mansion at No. 15, which once had been the home of Samuel J. Tilden, the man who was almost elected president.

The social register tenants are gone and the homes have been broken up into apartments occupied by decorators, writers, business executives, and wealthy widows. You'll see the lucky keyholders sitting in the park on a sunny afternoon, reading or watching the youngsters play quiet games. It is an oasis of peace and solitude, for no dogs, bikes, or swings are permitted.

Theodore Roosevelt's birthplace (28 East 20th Street) is now a National Historic Site. It is a fine example of a typical well-to-do Victorian home. The furnishings, including the scratchy horsehair sofa which menaced a small boy in short pants, are just as they were described later by T.R. in his autobiography. The home, and the adjacent museum of the relics Roosevelt collected during his years of adventuring, are open weekdays.

Nearby, the stretch of Broadway south of 23rd Street is the center of the photographers' loft district. North, at 1 East 29th Street, is a little church with a legend, a symbol of how time has worn down prejudice. When it was built in 1849, it was named the Church of the Transfiguration, but it has been known as "the Little Church Around the Corner."

It is filled with memorials, the most famous of which is a window dedicated to Joseph Jefferson, in his role of Rip Van Winkle, leading his shroud-clad friend, George Holland, to the church. In the post–Civil War period actors were socially unacceptable. On the death of Holland, when Jefferson spoke to the pastor of the church of his choice about funeral arrangements for his friend, the pastor turned him away, suggesting that he make arrangements at the "little church around the corner, where they do that kind of thing." It is now the actors' favorite church, and many a Broadway and Hollywood star attends services here. Of course, it is a favorite with brides, too.

The church on the corner of 29th Street and Fifth Avenue is the Marble Collegiate Church, designed by Samuel A. Warner and built in 1854 during the first phase of the Romanesque Revival boom which spread throughout New York. Dr. Norman Vincent Peale, author of *The Power of Positive Thinking*, pastored the church for 52 years.

New York's Own Chelsea

The Chelsea area, on the west side across town from Gramercy Park, has let many of its historic landmarks slip through its fingers. Yet many writers find the remnants of its past gentility and the unfrenetic pace of Chelsea to their liking and the recent proliferation of cozy contemporary bars, moderately priced restaurants, and brownstone renovations has made it one of the up-and-coming neighborhoods of the city's "far west" end. Still a living symbol of the area's attractiveness to literary figures, the Chelsea Hotel, at 222 West 23rd Street, has been home to many celebrated writers. Thomas Wolfe and Dylan Thomas lived here and Brendan Behan wrote his book on New York in one of its apartments.

The hostelry, a Victorian Gothic edifice with wrought-iron balconies, turrets, and chimney stacks, has been designated by the Municipal Art Society as one of New York's architectural monuments which should be preserved at all costs. In 1978 it was named a National Historic Landmark. If you should step into the Chelsea note the teakwood fireplace in the lobby and the bas-relief mural over it. It is the work of resident Rene Shapshak and depicts the arts—painting, drama, music, dance, architecture, literature, and sculpture. Harry S Truman stopped by here many times when Mr. Shapshak was working on a bust of the former president. To the right of the registration desk is a staircase. Walk up a flight and you can see the hotel's famous web of wrought-iron railing ascending flight after flight to the skylight.

Across the street is the McBurney YMCA, the oldest "Y" in the city. Over the years its membership has included Lowell Thomas, Dale Carnegie, Arthur Godfrey, James Michener, and Brendan Behan.

Chelsea's Night Before Christmas

The most notable of all Chelsea's residents may have been Dr. Clement Clarke Moore, who penned in 1822 the poem *A Visit from St. Nicholas,* more familiarly known today as *'Twas The Night Before Christmas.* Moore grew up on his grandfather's farm here, a spread which bordered the Hudson River and ran from what is now 19th to 23rd streets. The grandfather, Captain Thomas Clarke, had come to this country from England to fight in the French and Indian War. When his tour of duty was ended in 1750, he decided to remain, buy a farm, and build a mansion, which he nostalgically named "Chelsea" after the Chelsea Royal Hospital on the Thames, a charitable institution Nell Gwynne talked King Charles II into building for old, invalid soldiers. The lovely old mansion is gone; so, too, are Dr. Moore's house and the Grand Opera House where Josie Mansfield, Lily Langtry, and Edwin Booth performed.

The oldest building in Chelsea, which dates from 1785, is a two-and-one-half-story brick house with a steeply pitched roof and dormer windows at 183 Ninth Avenue, corner of 21st Street.

If you wander through 20th, 21st, and 22nd streets between Eighth and Ninth avenues, you will see evidence of Chelsea's struggle to maintain its gentility. Many of the old brownstones have been tinted a lively pink, yellow, or blue. Their intricate wrought-iron balustrades gleam and their tiny front gardens are well tended.

The General Theological Seminary, with an entrance at 175 Ninth Avenue between 20th and 21st streets, stands on land which once was Captain Clarke's apple orchard. Dr. Clement Moore served on its staff as a professor of Hebrew. Its library, housed in a new building, is famous for its collection of rare theological books.

The rectory of St. Peter's Episcopal Church at 346 West 20th Street was built in 1831 on property donated by Dr. Moore. The adjoining Gothic Revival church was added in 1836; its parish house is a lively center of art festivals and dramatic productions. Visitors are always welcome.

This is the southern fringe of what was once "Hell's Kitchen"—20th to 50th streets, west of Eighth Avenue—an area which spawned such notorious mobsters as Mad Dog Coll and Owney Madden. It was predominantly Irish for many years, but with the coming of better times for the Irish and urban renewal, the Irish have moved elsewhere. Nightlife is picking up in the area, courtesy of two venturesome enterprises—the Ballroom, which features cabaret entertainers and revues; and Caroline's, a nightclub specializing in name and up-and-coming comedians.

The Jacob K. Javits Convention Center, which stretches from 34th Street to 40th Street, west of Tenth Avenue, is further contributing to the revitalization of the entire area.

Midtown Manhattan

Midtown Manhattan, which ranges roughly from 34th Street (the Empire State Building on Fifth Avenue marks the southern boundary) to 59th Street (Central Park begins there) and river to river, is a center of superlatives. Some of the biggest buildings, best restaurants, most art galleries, brightest lights, greatest concentration of big business, largest complex of theaters, best bargain basements, most exclusive department stores, and the most specialized services are here.

Here you can have your dog psychoanalyzed, then hire a professional dogwalker to take him for a stroll; pick up a glittery gown or mink coat at a discount at thrift shops, where Broadway and TV stars leave them to be sold on consignment; swim and sun high in the sky on a hotel roof in the morning and ice skate in the afternoon at Rockefeller Center; buy a blue wig or a sable trench coat, if you care to.

You can see more and better French Impressionist art in a day's tour of museums and galleries here than you could see in Paris in all of a week. You can make a world tour of cuisine. Name any dish and it's yours: Brazilian, Japanese, Greek, French, German, Italian, Indian, Armenian, Polynesian, Jewish, Hungarian, Chinese, Spanish, Swiss, Belgian, Irish, Mexican, regional American. You can have breakfast at 5 P.M. or 5 A.M., for New York never sleeps.

It has been said that the forest of commerce in Wall Street reflects the purpose and push of dour, determined men. If so, then uptown New York, with its elegance, culture, countless diversions, and green acres, reflects the fruits of the dour men's labors.

The midtown shopping area is without peer in America. The most elegant, extravagant, and rare fabrics, furs, jewels, and accessories are displayed in profusion. Modish copies are offered to those of modest budget. The uninitiated are hard-pressed to tell the difference between the black Dior original and genuine strand of Oriental pearls on the dowager and the "authentic" copy and simulated pearls worn by the young career woman. The world's great concentration of garment manufacturers is right at her doorstep. The "rag business," as the trade affectionately calls itself, is concentrated in the west 30s, along Seventh Avenue. Fortunes are made and lost here, depending on the consumer's whim. Those dress houses that guess wrong twice in a row go bankrupt. Often you can profit from their mistakes and buy the unpopular models (they might be exactly to your taste) for less than cost in one of the bargain basements or cut-rate specialty shops in the neighborhood. The wholesale millinery firms are here too. Many have retail salesrooms on 38th Street, where you can also buy all the trimmings for a do-it-yourself creation.

Festive Fifth Avenue

Fifth Avenue is a festival all year-round, with a continuous showing of spectaculars. Its pioneers have fought to maintain its prestige and preserve its *haute monde* image. As far back as 1907, they formed the Fifth

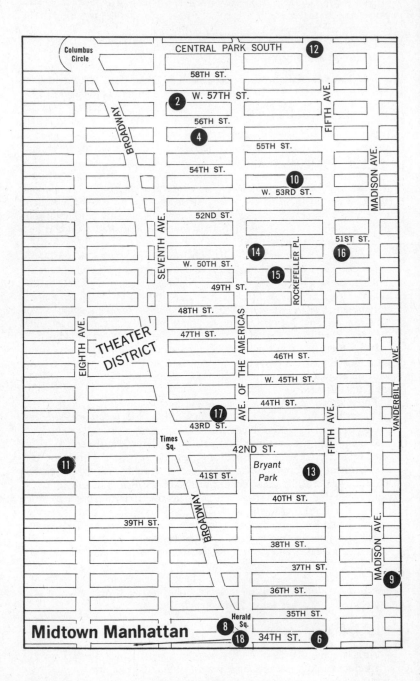

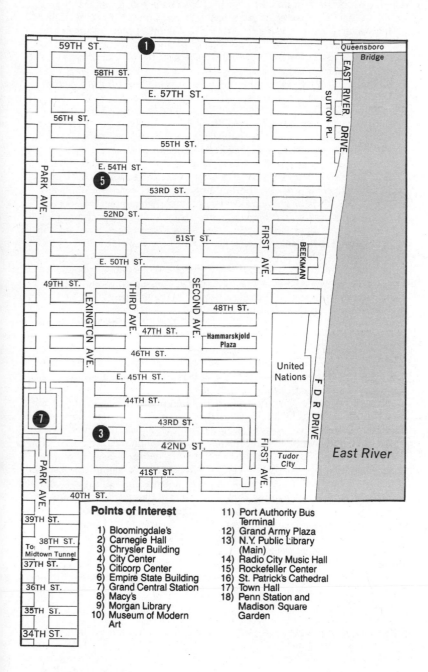

Points of Interest

1) Bloomingdale's
2) Carnegie Hall
3) Chrysler Building
4) City Center
5) Citicorp Center
6) Empire State Building
7) Grand Central Station
8) Macy's
9) Morgan Library
10) Museum of Modern Art
11) Port Authority Bus Terminal
12) Grand Army Plaza
13) N.Y. Public Library (Main)
14) Radio City Music Hall
15) Rockefeller Center
16) St. Patrick's Cathedral
17) Town Hall
18) Penn Station and Madison Square Garden

Avenue Association to do battle with any element which might threaten
its lustre. At Christmastime, the street features tinseled trees, twinkling
lights, bright garlands, and jolly St. Nicks. In springtime, awnings and
entrances bloom with artificial flowers and perfume wafts onto the street
to entice you inside. At night, windows are kept lit, offering the stroller
an incomparable window shopping tour.

No matter what the season, the Empire State Building, on Fifth Avenue
at 34th Street, remains a favorite attraction for natives and visitors alike.
Perhaps because it held the title of tallest building in the world for so long,
perhaps because it has been immortalized in so many films (not the least
of which is *King Kong*), and perhaps because it gave New York its state
title—"The Empire State"—it has retained a special place in people's
hearts despite the fact that the World Trade Center stands a full 100 feet
taller. It opened in May 1931 (it took only a year and a half to construct).
Some 15,000 people work in the building and more than a million and
a half people still visit its observatory annually for what remains a spectacular panorama of New York and its surroundings. This observatory, incidentally, is open nightly until 11:20 P.M.—two hours later than the one
at the World Trade Center. Tickets cost $3.25 for adults, $1.75 for children under 12; 736-3100.

The merchants have done battle with the city fathers about parades on
Fifth Avenue, which disrupt business. They won, up to a point. Today
most parades start at 60th Street, above the main shopping area. Despite
their efforts to keep Fifth Avenue on the highest plateau, some interlopers
have managed to open up tourist-trap linen-china-cameras-radios-
gimcracks shops.

Midtown does not readily lend itself to cut-and-dried walking tours. It
is an area to be explored according to one's whims and particular interests.
There are museums which specialize in collections of modern art, contemporary crafts, folk art, costumes of all nations, re-runs of old TV shows,
and lecture programs. There are scores of foreign tourist information centers and airline ticket offices with advice to inspire your next vacation.
There are awesome views to be seen from observatories atop midtown's
tallest buildings, a world to explore underground, a hundred little personal
discoveries to be made if you venture off the beaten track. And, of course,
there's the shopping. Virtually every one of New York's major department
stores has a character of its own—a style that is manifested in the stores'
own decor, in the merchandise they carry and in the people who shop at
them. The accent is almost always on clothing—women's more so than
men's, though Bloomingdale's gives equal if not preferential treatment to
males—with furniture and household goods almost as an afterthought,
something you might pick up "to complete the outfit" while passing
through.

Three of the city's greatest attractions are in this midtown area: Times
Square, where the Great White Way begins; Rockefeller Center; and the
United Nations.

The Great White Way starts at Times Square, a point where meandering
Broadway crosses 42nd Street and Seventh Avenue to form a tiny plaza
which is anything but square in shape.

It is a monument to the vision and the gambling spirit of three men:
Oscar Hammerstein I, an impresario who in 1894 sank a two-million-
dollar fortune, and then some, into building the first theaters here; August

Belmont, a financier who more than matched Hammerstein's gamble by extending the subway to bring the crowds uptown to the new theater district; and publisher Adolph S. Ochs, who built the Times Tower in 1904 as the new headquarters for his influential newspaper, the *New York Times,* and dedicated it with a night of revelry which has become a New Year's Eve tradition.

Theaters Move Uptown

Hammerstein's fellow impresarios knew a good thing when they saw it and moved their theaters uptown. With such a captive audience as Times Square offered, promoters of soft drinks, cigarettes, liquor, chewing gum, and two-trouser suits put up huge animated electric advertisements which outshone the sun.

Times Square became a symbol of facing life and making good. Dreams of becoming a dramatic star overnight, writing a musical hit, waxing a smash record, or marrying a millionaire swam in the heads of small-town girls and small-city boys who flocked to this street of dreams. For a special few, the dreams came true. Stars were born, fortunes were made, and millionaires wedded to their gold. Those who couldn't make the grade on Broadway took the ferry over to Fort Lee, New Jersey, and worked for the "flickers," a new form of entertainment legitimate actors deplored or ignored. The flicker performers made it big and went on to Hollywood, fame, and fortune.

The theater district has become tarnished quite a bit since the glamorous pre-Depression days when top-hatted stage-door Johnnies waited for their favorite Follies dollies, wined and dined them on the Ziegfeld Theater roof, and slipped a hundred-dollar bill under their plates for the privilege.

Broadway's Constant Lure

Times Square has taken on a midway bazaarlike look, with its soft drink and pizza stands, pinball and shooting galleries, racy lingerie and fake "fire sale" shops. Some of the old prestige theaters now feature X-rated movies and ladies of the evening roam the streets along with a hodgepodge of other derelicts and eccentrics. Within the radius of a few blocks in the 40s, however, there still remain numerous legitimate theaters, surely the greatest concentration of dramatic and musical productions you will find anywhere in the world (with the possible exception of London's West End). This tight little center of entertainment offers a rare opportunity for last-minute shopping. If you've neglected to order theater tickets in advance, make a tour of the box offices just before curtain-time and you might just be lucky enough to pick up a pair of unclaimed seats at regular prices for an otherwise sold-out hit. Or check with the Times Square Ticket Service office (the sign reads "TKTS") at 47th Street and Broadway, where theater tickets are usually available and always to be had for half the box-office price plus a minimal service fee. (Other TKTS branches are at No. 2 World Trade Center and Brooklyn's Court St. at Borough Hall. A music-and-dance half-price booth is in Bryant Park on 42nd St. at Sixth Ave.)

The Times Square TKTS booth is open daily from 3 to 8 P.M. for evening performances, 10 A.M. to 2 P.M. for Wednesday and Saturday mati-

nees, and noon to 8 P.M. for all Sunday shows. Lines for first choice of
the evening selections begin to form in late morning, much earlier for matinees. Telephone 354–5800. The WTC booth is open Monday through Saturday from 11 A.M. to 5:30 P.M. Off-Broadway tickets are sold between
11 A.M. and 1 P.M. Matinee and Sunday tickets are sold from 11 A.M. to
5:30 P.M. on the day before the performance; the lines here are generally
much shorter than those uptown, and you may well save time making the
extra trip downtown. Take the No. 2 or 3 IRT subway to the Wall Street
stop. The Brooklyn branch is open Monday through Friday 11 A.M. to
5:30 P.M., Saturday 11 A.M. to 3:30 P.M. Tickets for Off-Broadway are sold
until 1 P.M. Matinee and Sunday tickets are available on the day before
the performance (718–625–5015), while the music-and-dance booth is
open noon to 2 P.M. and 3 to 7 P.M. Monday through Saturday and Sunday
11 A.M. to 6 P.M. (382–2323).

Times Square is the object of what seems to New Yorkers like a never-
ending battle for upgrading. One major example of what appears to be
a successful move in this direction is the Manhattan Plaza apart-
ment/restaurant complex along the north side of 42nd between Ninth and
Tenth avenues. The residential units are made available to performing artists only—primarily those involved with the nearby theater—who give a
percentage of their income as rent. In response to the immediate filling
up of the apartment building, a whole slew of restaurants sprang up in
and around Manhattan Plaza, while the theaters on the south side of 42nd
have been rehabilitated as legitimate Off-Broadway houses. The latest addition to the Broadway landscape is the Marriott Marquis, a hotel-and-
theater complex at 45th Street.

For passenger ships, a series of three piers at 48th, 50th, and 52nd streets
has been turned into a climate-controlled, modern terminal for cruise ships
and the rare transatlantic liners. These piers provide not only more comfort and convenience for passengers but also excellent vantage points for
tourists to watch the whole procedure of loading, unloading, and leave-
taking.

The marble-and-glass building—formerly known as the Times Tower,
then the Allied Chemical Building—located on the north side of 42nd
Street between Broadway and Seventh Avenue, is still ushering in the New
Year with a bright ball descending the flagpole on the building, reaching
the bottom at the stroke of midnight.

The Avenue of the Americas

You might first like to stroll up Sixth Avenue, more accurately known
as the Avenue of the Americas. Note the emblems of all the nations in
North, Central, and South America hanging along the avenue. Like many
areas of mid-Manhattan, it is changing as glittering new skyscrapers take
the place of older edifices.

Bryant Park, located between 40th and 42nd streets behind the New
York City Public Library, is a green and relaxing spot to visit and rest,
if the dope-pushers and occasional crazies don't annoy you. Named in
1884 for William Cullen Bryant, poet and journalist, it is a gathering place
for impromptu public speakers and their eclectic sort of audience. A couple of booksellers have opened bookstalls there, and there is a TKTS booth
for music and dance events (382–2323). The park is also an excellent van-

tage point from which to view one of the city's more unusual skyscrapers. Located between the Avenue of the Americas and Fifth Avenue, with entrances on 42nd and 43rd streets and adjacent to the also intriguing new Graduate Center of CUNY, the Monsanto Building slopes gently upward, narrowing from its base to its towering roof, producing the rather uneasy effect of a hill carved from glass and stone. It was the city's first such structure and was designed by Gordon Bunshaft of the architectural firm of Skidmore, Owings & Merrill. A similar one curves inward from both 57th and 58th streets, also between Fifth Avenue and the Avenue of the Americas. Incidentally, this same firm also designed Lever House in 1952 at 390 Park Avenue.

Midtown is where the famous private men's clubs (many now admitting women), portrayed so often in the *New Yorker* cartoons, are thickest on the ground. Look for them as you stroll; by and large they are understated and easy to miss. A representative selection (look, but you can't enter unless you are a member): University Club, at the corner of Fifth Avenue and 54th Street; the Century Club, favored by men in the business of publishing; next to it, on 43rd Street between Fifth and Sixth avenues, is the Princeton Club, looking like an electric-power substation; down 44th Street toward Sixth Avenue is the New York Yacht Club, with interesting windows; the Metropolitan Club, at Fifth Ave. and 60th Street, in a building designed by McKim, Mead & White; the Harvard Club, 44th Street between Fifth and Sixth avenues; the Racquet & Tennis Club, at 370 Park Avenue (53rd Street); and the Yale Club, across from the PanAm Building at Vanderbilt Avenue and 44th Street.

But back to Sixth Avenue. Walk north from 42nd Street and you'll see many other recently constructed buildings. Take a short detour east on 44th toward Fifth Avenue to the Algonquin Hotel and restaurant, still operating at No. 59. Behind its rather unimposing Renaissance façade many figures have wined, dined, and discussed the hours away: Dorothy Parker, Harold Ross, and Robert Benchley, among others. East on 45th Street is a concentration of the city's best hi-fi and electronics retail outlets. East on 46th Street, still off Sixth Avenue, is an array of Brazilian shops and restaurants. At 47th Street, you just might be tempted to take another detour east for a look at the block-long area known as the city's diamond center—it's obvious why when you see the countless glittering shop windows.

For the next three blocks on the west side of the avenue you'll be passing the three newest (early seventies) skyscraper members of the Rockefeller Center community. Between 47th and 48th streets is the 45-story Celanese Building, which was completed in 1973. The next block north contains the 51-story McGraw-Hill building. Here you should plan to take an hour out to see *The New York Experience* in the building's plush Trans-Lux Experience Theater. The production is a multiple-screen entertainment that surrounds the audience with sights, sounds, and multisensory special effects utilizing thirty-seven projectors and fourteen screens and quadraphonic sound. Included as a part of the presentation is an exhibit of Little Old New York, re-creating local city life as it was in the late 19th century. On 48th Street, between Sixth and Seventh avenues, are musical instrument retail shops. The next block, on Sixth Avenue, between 49th and 50th streets, is the sleek 54-story corporate home of Exxon. This trio of buildings features open plazas and modern sculpture, where the weary sightseer can sit down with area office workers, especially at midday.

Radio City Music Hall, on the east side of the avenue at 50th Street, is a primary attraction. It is the largest indoor theater in America, with a seating capacity of 6,000. When the traditional seasonal pageant of the Nativity or the summer spectacular are presented, the four blocks bounding the Music Hall are jammed with people who will wait for hours in sleet and rain to buy tickets for the presentation. If you want to take in one of these special pageants without waiting hours in line, it would be wise to write ahead for tickets. You can order and charge tickets by phone from outside New York by calling 800–682–8080 or, in the city, 307–7171. Two major television and radio network headquarters are located several blocks beyond—CBS, between 52nd and 53rd streets and designed by Eero Saarinen, and Capital/ABC at 54th Street. Both are on the east side of the avenue. (NBC's headquarters are one block south, in Rockefeller Center.)

On 55th Street, turn left and walk almost to Seventh Avenue if you want to pick up a pair of tickets at the New York City Center, 131 West 55th Street, which usually features ballet. Now that you're this far, you might also want to continue two blocks north along Seventh Avenue, swing east around the corner of 57th Street, and check out coming concerts at Carnegie Hall. New Yorkers have been grateful ever since the last-minute decision was made not to tear down this hall in the early 1960s, when Philharmonic Hall in Lincoln Center was being built. If you're hungry, stop in at the Carnegie Delicatessen around the corner on Seventh Avenue for a real New York treat. (See *Restaurants* section below.)

Those of you with an artistic bent should backtrack to 53rd Street and turn east toward Fifth Avenue. On this block you'll find the handsome sculpture garden and avant-garde works of the Museum of Modern Art, at 11 West 53rd Street. Another art excursion—one which will require your traipsing several blocks to Columbus Circle at the southwest corner of Central Park—is to visit the statue at the corner of 59th Street and Broadway, Gaetano Russo's "Columbus," lending its name to Columbus Circle. On the park corner is architect H. Van Buren Magonigle's "Maine Memorial" with figures by sculptor Attilio Piccirilli.

Rockefeller Center

In our ramble up the Avenue of the Americas we've introduced you to several of the buildings that make up Rockefeller Center.

Rockefeller Center is a city-within-a-city; you could easily spend the whole day within its complex of twenty-one buildings. Many of its residents—it has a daytime population of 240,000—never leave its confines from their arrival in the morning until they go home. There is no need to, for the center has just about everything one could ask for. There are almost thirty restaurants, several shoe repair shops, drugstores, chiropodists, dentists, oculists, gift and clothing shops, bookstores, hairdressers, barbers, banks, a post office, movie theaters, schools, and subway transportation to all parts of the metropolis. Consulates of many foreign nations have offices in the center, as do airlines, railroad and steamship lines, and state and other travel information bureaus.

A shop-lined concourse, an underground passageway almost two miles long, ties together all its buildings and brings you almost to the doorstep of the Sheraton Centre and New York Hilton hotels. On rainy days, the concourse traffic is almost as thick as that of Times Square, but a lot drier.

It is the world's largest privately owned business and entertainment center and another monument to the courage and vision of the men who made New York City capital of the world. It was built because an opera house was not—a multimillion-dollar gamble on America's future during the height of the Depression years.

In October 1928, just before the big stock market crash, John D. Rockefeller, Jr., headed a civic drive to give New York a new opera house, arranging to lease from Columbia University the land on which part of Rockefeller Center now stands. The new Metropolitan Opera Company was to occupy the center of the plot and the remainder of the land was to be leased to private builders for commercial development. Before the grand design could get started, the opera company, plagued by legal difficulties and depressed funds, abandoned its plans for a new home and withdrew from the project. It left Mr. Rockefeller holding a long-term lease which committed him to a $3,300,000 annual rental. He was faced with a difficult decision: whether to abandon the development or go it alone? He decided to build.

The site of the center has an historic past. Until the turn of the 19th century, the area was part of Manhattan's "common lands," which stretched from 23rd Street northward. In 1801, Dr. David Horsack transformed twenty acres of these pasturelands into his famed Elgin Botanic Gardens; garden club ladies for miles around made pilgrimages to pick up ideas for their own plantings. When rising costs made the venture impractical, Dr. Horsack sold the property to New York State and a few years later the State Legislature turned over the property to Columbia College as an aid-to-education grant. At the time, the land was worth about $125 an acre. In the mid-'80s, Columbia sold the land to the Rockefeller Center Corporation.

The center gave a new life to the down-at-the-heels midtown area, changing it from a sprawling low-rent residential area to a soaring business and entertainment complex far in advance of the times. It was a pioneering approach to urban design. Skyscrapers were planned in relation to one another and fifteen percent of the land was set aside for a promenade of plantings and a breeze-swept plaza.

The Channel Gardens—six formal beds running from Fifth Avenue to the Lower Plaza—with their ever-changing seasonal plantings, draw millions of visitors. Artists, designers, and sculptors work year-round to devise new and dramatic floral patterns for the ten seasonal displays. The showings run consecutively, starting with thousands of lilies at Easter; tulips, hyacinths, daffodils, and other flowering bulbs in the spring; an all-azalea show; such perennials as foxglove, delphinium, and stock; summer lilies and snapdragons; marigolds and evergreens; tropical palms and bougainvillaea; begonias and coxcomb; chrysanthemums of every size and hue; and ending with the greatest Christmas tree of all. Even the rooftops of many buildings are landscaped, giving upper-floor tenants a soul-satisfying view of green foliage and brilliant blooms below.

The Lower Plaza, where you can ice-skate from the end of September through March and dine alfresco in the warm weather, is a kind of ceremonial town square where distinguished visitors are greeted, occasional concerts given, and special events commemorated with colorful ceremonies.

Two excellent (and expensive) restaurants are found here: American Festival Cafe and Sea Grill.

Last year, the famous Rainbow Room reopened with a grand flourish. High atop the 64th floor of 30 Rockefeller Plaza, this restored Art Deco jewel is currently the hottest dining and entertainment ticket in town. If you don't want to spring for the full (and expensive) dining and dancing tab in the Room itself, then at least have a drink in the Promenade. The Rainbow and Stars cabaret room features top singing artists. Reservations are a must; call 632–5100.

Tours of Radio City Music Hall in the RCA building are available though there is nothing to quite rival the experience of seeing a show in the Music Hall, whether a pop concert or the annual Christmas or summer shows, complete with the high-kicking Rockettes. Call 246–4600 for details.

When in doubt about what to see and where it is, visit the center's information booth in the main lobby at 30 Rockefeller Plaza, where you can also pick up tickets to television-show tapings. You might also consider an evening visit (sunset is best) to the Rainbow Room bar, which was scheduled to reopen in late 1987 following extensive refurbishing. The project has resulted in the permanent closing of the observation deck. A new entrance to the Rainbow Room will occupy the space on the 65th floor where visitors paid their admission and began their trip to the observation deck above. The view, inside and out, still promises to be spectacular. Call 757–9090 for details.

Across Fifth Avenue at 51st Street is the Gothic-styled St. Patrick's Cathedral. Based on the design of the Cologne Cathedral in Germany, work on the Roman Catholic St. Patrick's commenced in 1858, it opened as a house of worship in 1879, and was finally completed in 1906. Constructed of white marble and stone, the church's towers ascend 330 feet. Thirty-foot pillars support the cross-ribbed Gothic arches which rise 110 feet inside, where stained-glass windows from France light the nave.

The United Nations

New York City grew from a metropolis to a cosmopolis in 1952, when the United Nations moved into its elegant new home overlooking the East River between 42nd and 48th streets.

The hand of John D. Rockefeller, Jr., is imprinted on this monument to peace and brotherhood, for it was his offer of a gift of the 18-acre site that figured in the final decision to choose New York as the permanent headquarters for the UN.

Before the coming of the United Nations, the district was a crumbling conglomeration of ex-slaughterhouses, junkyards, and tenements. Today the area around the UN is studded with elegant structures and has become a showcase of new architectural design.

A bit of parkland makes the UN grounds—which are not U.S. territory—a pleasant place to stroll and watch the busy river traffic of freighters, tankers, and pleasure boats plying the East River.

The visitors' entrance to the United Nations Headquarters is at the north end of the marble and limestone General Assembly Building, at 45th

Street and First Avenue. There is a museumlike quality to the vast lobby with its free-form multiple galleries, soaring ceiling, and collection of art treasures contributed by member nations.

Visitors are welcome to attend most official meetings and admission is free. Tickets are issued in the lobby fifteen minutes before meetings are scheduled to start. Because there is no advance schedule of meetings for any given day and since they may be canceled or changed at the last minute, the majority of tickets available to individual visitors are issued on a first-come, first-served basis.

At most meetings, speeches are simultaneously interpreted in the official languages—Chinese, English, French, Russian, and Spanish—and there are earphones at each visitor's seat with a dial system which permits you to tune in the proceedings in the language of your choice.

The decor and color schemes of the meeting rooms—General Assembly Hall, the chambers of the Security Council, Trusteeship Council, Economic and Social Council—have been chosen for their soothing, subdued qualities. Sometimes they work this magic and other times they fail. At times, speeches by delegates become so impassioned that visitors may be tempted to rise and shout "bravo." Be forewarned: protocol demands that visitors remain silent throughout all the proceedings.

Taking the hour-long guided tour through the headquarters buildings is the most satisfactory way to see all the meeting rooms, to learn the aims, structure, and activities of this world body, and to appreciate fully the art works and exhibits displayed. Tours leave the main lobby approximately every 15 minutes between 9 A.M. and 4:45 P.M., seven days a week. Most are in English, although you can request and reserve for other languages on the day you plan to tour. The cost is $4.50 for adults, $2.50 for students, and $2 for children, no children under 5 permitted; phone 963-7713.

If you would like to lunch with the delegates, stop by the information desk in the main lobby and ask about making a table reservation in the Delegates' Dining Room. Tables for visitors are in short supply and are assigned on a first-come basis. The earlier you make the reservation, the better.

On the lower concourse there is a coffee shop for a quick snack and lounges to rest your weary bones. Here, too, are several shops which offer the books, art, and handicraft products of the UN's member nations. Many a returning traveler shops here for some item he forgot or could not find while on a trip to Africa, Asia, Europe, or South America.

The sliver of land you see in the middle of the East River just to the north of the UN is Roosevelt Island (formerly Welfare Island) which once served as a prison stronghold. The riptides around the island acted as prison "walls," for not even the strongest swimmer could navigate the 700-foot crossing to the mainland.

If one had money and influence there was no need for such a foolhardy escape attempt. William Tweed, for instance, came and went as he pleased, though a prisoner. Tweed was the greedy political boss of New York who fleeced the city of $150,000,000 in the four years between 1867 and 1871. When reformers caught up with him and sent him off to a cell on Welfare Island, he arranged to live a life of ease. His ill-gotten gains bought him all the creature comforts. Gourmet meals were sent in from New York's finest restaurants. A masseur came in regularly to rub away his tensions. It's said he even had the prison bars replaced by a picture window. When

Plan of the United Nations

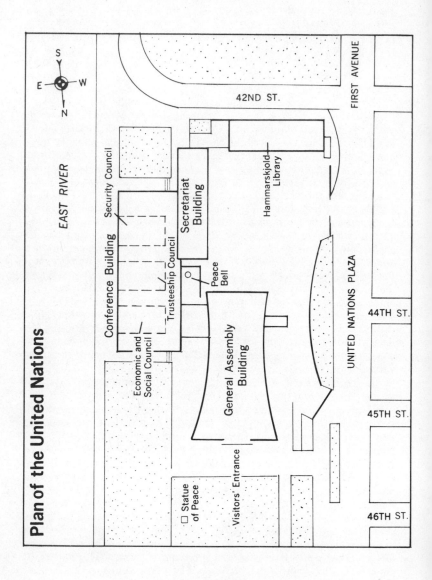

life became too boring, Tweed managed to get a night off and a launch to take him over to the mainland for a round on the town. This kindly and loving care was enjoyed by Tweed and other moneyed mobsters and racketeers until the reformers once again bestirred themselves. The prison is gone now and in its place are two modern hospitals for the aged and chronically ill—plus the Delacorte Geyser, on the southern tip, which occasionally spouts a tall plume of an estimated 4,000 gallons worth of water per minute 400 feet into the air. There are also new housing units reached from 59th Street and Second Avenue by a tramway over the East River (you may have seen it in Sylvester Stallone's movie *Nighthawks*).

Exploring Turtle Bay

As you leave the United Nations there are three general routes which you can follow, each one of which will lead you to fascinating aspects of the area extending roughly from 40th to 49th streets and from Third Avenue to the East River. It is known as Turtle Bay, whose name comes from the mid-18th century Turtle Bay Farm tract which bordered on a little cove of that name.

You can return to 42nd Street and head west. If you look up between First and Second Avenues you'll see some of the apartment buildings and hotels of Tudor City. If you've time, you might walk up the stairs along 42nd Street and enjoy this rather private little city of Tudor-style buildings around a small park. Go back down the stairs and you'll surely notice the building with the huge glassed-in garden near Second Avenue. That's the Ford Foundation Building and its offices are arranged in an L around this pleasantly leafy 130-foot-high arboretum. In the next block between Second and Third avenues is the Daily News Building, home of one of New York's three daily newspapers. Step into the lobby here if you want to scan the latest weather charts or watch the huge revolving globe. Continuing westward you'll come to the Chrysler Building at the northeast corner of 42nd Street and Lexington Avenue. When it was first built in 1930, its 1,048 feet made it the tallest building in the world. But it was soon topped by the completion of the Empire State Building in 1931. Now the twin World Trade Center towers are the highest in the city.

Westward again, between Lexington and Park avenues on 42nd Street, is the steel-and-glass Grand Hyatt Hotel, a glistening high-tech structure (built over the skeleton of the old Commodore Hotel) standing in the company of the beaux-arts classically styled Grand Central Terminal, the Art Deco Chrysler Building and other similarly spectacular delights. Grand Central was built from 1903 to 1913. If you go inside the always-busy train station, you'll be able to take escalators directly up to the lobby of the Pan Am Building, a 1963 office skyscraper addition to the terminal. At the time it was announced much protest was raised since it would—and does—effectively block the vista up and down Park Avenue.

We said you had three alternative routes through Turtle Bay from the UN. Another would be to head north along First Avenue—past the pleasant UN grounds and the posh twin 32-story apartment towers of the United Nations Plaza. Your destination on this route is Beekman Place, where the townhouses on the two blocks between First Avenue and Beekman Place on 50th Street and along Beekman Place itself between 50th and 51st streets are gracious reminders of the 1920s. The roof of the Beekman

Tower Hotel is also an excellent stop for a drink and a view of the Upper East Side.

The third jaunt is more circuitous and will serve to illustrate the dramatic juxtaposition of old townhouses and new office buildings that this city is capable of creating. Go north on First Avenue to 47th Street and turn left. Note the Holy Family Church and its pretty little courtyard on the north side of this divided street. This is where Pope Paul VI visited in 1965 in connection with a UN plea for peace. Next, a quick stop in the rock garden at Japan House (333 East 47th Street) is refreshingly tranquil. On the southeast corner of 47th Street and Second Avenue you might check out the current exhibit of alfresco, avant-garde sculpture in front of the rather conservative-looking office building. Continue on 47th Street to 747 Third Avenue, which is wonderfully imaginative with its undulating, multicolored brick walkways, circular outdoor phone booth, and benches and chairs. Look for the statue of a nude woman at the revolving doors.

Now turn right on Third Avenue and cross Third Avenue on 48th Street to peek into the "citified" courtyard of the Buchanan apartment building. On the northwest corner of Lexington Avenue and 48th Street in the Inter-Continental Hotel is the Caswell-Massey Co. Ltd., reputedly America's oldest pharmacy (1752).

A bit farther up Third Avenue is the giant Citicorp Center headquarters of the New York-based international bank. Opened in 1978, the center features a pedestrian mall. It is a refreshing change from the plain glass boxes that dominate the rest of the avenue. Indeed, Citicorp is so refreshing especially because it includes The Market, a multilevel international bazaar of restaurants and retail food shops that delight the eye as well as the palate of New Yorkers and tourists alike. The Market surrounds a skylit atrium and gives a village-square ambience. There are tables and chairs where you may just sit and people-watch or picnic by bringing your own sandwiches or buying some at one of the eateries. If you time it right, you may even enjoy free entertainment, on Saturday mornings for children and many evenings for adults, from chamber music ensembles to jazz to poetry readings. And if alfresco dining (or almost) in a stone canyon isn't what you have in mind, you can choose from a bevy of international restaurants. For sandwiches and desserts, consider the Market Coffee Shop and, for Scandinavian gourmet goodies such as herrings, salads and pâtés, consider Nyborg and Nelson. For spiritual nourishment, there is also a church—St. Peter's—in the building, and that church has staged some excellent plays of Off-Broadway caliber. All of which, together with British housegoods department store Conran's, combine to make Citicorp a nice place to visit for business or pleasure.

At Fifth Avenue and 56th Street, on the east side next to Tiffany's, is the Trump Tower. Its atrium, with swank shops, is one of New York's newest and most attractive indoor spaces. Trump Tower, with its formal doormen and extravagant prices, is a wonderful place for browsing.

Up in Central Park

Central Park, a vast oasis of rural beauty in the midst of a concrete jungle of midtown spires, runs from 59th Street to 110th Street and from Fifth Avenue to Central Park West (an extension of Eighth Avenue). Masterfully designed by Frederick Law Olmstead and Calvert de Vaux, the park was designated a National Historic Landmark in 1965.

New York can thank its good fortune that there were men of vision in 1850 who insisted that this 840-acre spread be earmarked as a park. It was none too soon, for real estate developers were gobbling up huge hunks of land just to the south and turning them into bleak stretches of look-alike brownstone residences.

A stroll through the park will reveal the woodland terrain of New York as it might have been in the days of the Dutch settlers, long before dredges and bulldozers leveled the surrounding hills and rocky outcroppings to erect a fence of luxury apartment houses.

If you take a drive down through the park from the north end at dusk, just as the lights begin to sparkle in the windows and the last rays of the sun silhouette the spires at the south end, you will be rewarded with a most strikingly beautiful sight. These roads, however, are frequently closed to traffic to allow for strollers, bicyclers, and joggers.

At this same corner of the park—a lively and interesting part of the city for people-watching—there are bookstalls open on nice days.

The park is a many-splendored mélange of fountains and ponds, statues and monuments, promenades and wooded paths. Park benches are lined with nannies gossiping away while their young Park Avenue charges swing and slide in the playgrounds. Joggers run year-round while looking over their shoulders at oncoming traffic. On warm weekdays, office workers find a favorite rock by the pond, spread out their lunches, and share them with the water birds. In the winter, they skate at Wollman Memorial Rink, recently renovated. On Sundays, families come to picnic, play soft ball, pitch horseshoes, ride the merry-go-round, fly kites, rowboats, ride bicycles on the curling, carefree drives, and absorb enough sun and fresh air to last them through another week of molelike living. The newest crazes in the park are skate-boarding and roller-skating, and on summer weekends the park mall that stretches from the Bethesda Fountain overlook at 72nd Street down to 66th Street is populated with street performers ranging from Dixieland bands to magicians to stilt walkers.

Off the 64th Street entrance on Fifth Avenue is the newly remodeled Central Park Zoo. The zoo consists of Tropic, Temperate, and Polar zones; along with birds, you can see several kinds of sea lions, penguins, and polar bears. Nearby is the Children's Zoo where kids of all ages can actually interact with friendly animals and talking birds. Don't miss feeding time! At press time, a modest admission charge was planned. Near the Conservatory Pond at 74th St. off Fifth Avenue (where model sailboats are often in the water) are the statues of Hans Christian Andersen and Alice in Wonderland.

On summer evenings you can attend outdoor performances of plays at the Delacorte Shakespeare Theater. The theater accommodates around 2,000—but get there in the early afternoon (be sure to get your place-in-the-line number as soon as you get there) to get in line for first-come, first-served tickets. Enter from Central Park West or Fifth Avenue at 81st Street. Both the Metropolitan Opera and the New York Philharmonic perform free in the park each summer as well.

The park is fringed with some of the world's great art and history centers. You could spend a week on either side of the park and never go any higher than the ground floors of these buildings.

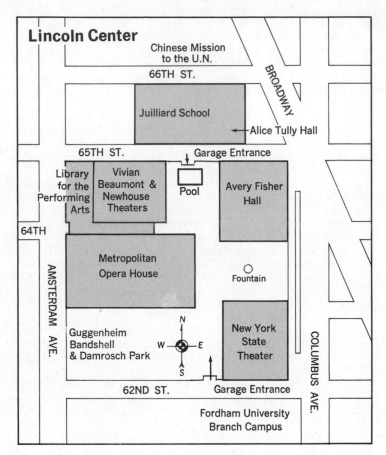

Lincoln Center

Chinese Mission
to the U.N.

66TH ST.

BROADWAY

Juilliard School

←Alice Tully Hall

65TH ST.   Garage Entrance

Library
for the
Performing
Arts

Vivian
Beaumont &
Newhouse
Theaters

Pool

Avery Fisher
Hall

64TH

AMSTERDAM AVE.

Metropolitan
Opera House

Fountain

COLUMBUS AVE.

Guggenheim
Bandshell
& Damrosch Park

N
W   E
S

New York
State
Theater

62ND ST.   Garage Entrance

Fordham University
Branch Campus

Detail of number 7 opposite

Points of Interest

1) Boat Basin
2) Columbus Circle
3) The Dakota
4) Fordham University
5) Hayden Planetarium

6) Juilliard School
7) Lincoln Center for the Performing Arts
8) Museum of Natural History
9) New York Historical Society
10) Merkin Hall
    (Goodman House)
11) Symphony Space

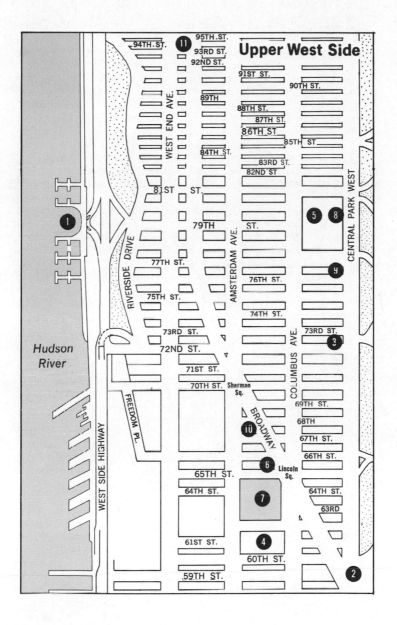

Upper West Side

Lincoln Center

Lincoln Center for the Performing Arts is an elegant four-block cultural world, located between 62nd and 66th streets west of Broadway (actually between Columbus and Amsterdam avenues). Get acquainted with the buildings by taking one of the guided tours, or wander around the open plazas and parks on your own. Tour schedules vary, so call ahead for reservations and information. The cost for adults is $6.25, Senior Citizens and students $5.25, and children $3.50. Call 877–1800. Standing on Broadway, the building you see to the left of the large central fountain plaza is the New York State Theater, home of the New York City Opera and the New York City Ballet. On the right is Avery Fisher Hall, home of the New York Philharmonic and the first of this $185 million complex to open (September 1962). Between the two is the Metropolitan Opera House, with its two colorful Marc Chagall murals depicting motifs and themes relating to music.

This is, of course, where The Metropolitan Opera company performs. It also has the Center's largest seating capacity: for over 3,700 people in its main auditorium. Tucked behind Avery Fisher Hall is the Vivian Beaumont Theater. And in back, with an additional entrance on Amsterdam Avenue, is the Library and Museum of Performing Arts, a branch of the New York Public Library. Also on these grounds is the Guggenheim Bandshell for alfresco concerts.

Across 65th Street is the Juilliard School of Music campus, which includes Alice Tully Hall, a Lincoln Center facility noted especially for its chamber music presentations.

And, at the southern end of the Lincoln Center group is the midtown campus of Fordham University.

Columbus Avenue from 67th Street to 83rd Street is the city's newest "scene," with restaurants, bars, food shops, boutiques, roller-skate rental shops, and the special New York blend of show-offs, street musicians and mimes, and with-it people.

The Historical Society

If you are interested in tracing the history and growth of New York, visit the New-York Historical Society's headquarters at 77th Street and Central Park West. Here, there are exhibits which trace the city's history from the Indian tribes which lived in the area before the white man came, through the stories of Giovanni da Verrazano, Henry Hudson, and Peter Stuyvesant. There are displays depicting the English period before the outbreak of the American Revolution; the periods of strife and struggle during the Revolutionary War; and New York when it was the capital of the new nation. There are rare collections of just about everything which shows how New York's earliest residents lived and fared.

Across 77th Street is the American Museum of Natural History, founded in 1869 "for the purpose of encouraging and developing the study of natural science, advancing the general knowledge of kindred subjects, and of furnishing popular instruction." It has been operating for over a century and houses tens of millions of zoological, geological, anthropological, and botanical specimens that are studied by scientists, students, and scholars from all over the world.

A week wouldn't be enough to see all the exhibits, which cover close to twelve acres of floor space. To make the most of your visit, pick up a guide book and check off the exhibits you want to see first. Two of the museum's greatest attractions are the 94-foot life-size model of a blue whale on the first floor and the two huge halls' worth of dinosaur fossils on the fourth floor. Other highlights include the 64-foot-long Haida Canoe, made from the trunk of a single cedar tree; the Hall of the Biology of Man, which is devoted to the evolution, structure, and function of man as an organism; reconstruction of the extinct dodo; the exhibition of the Courtship of Birds; the collection of mammals; the Northwest Coast Indian Hall; the Hall of Man in Africa; and the demonstration-participation lectures in the People Center where onlookers are invited to try on costumes or play instruments, for example, of cultures around the world.

If your time is limited, you might find it worthwhile to rent an Acoustiguide, a one-hour tape-recorded lecture tour contained in a small portable case with ear plugs. The rental sets are available at the 77th Street entrance information desk.

A connecting passageway takes you to the Hayden Planetarium, at 81st Street and Central Park West, the department of astronomy of the American Museum of Natural History. Unless you have sailed the seas or lived in the unpopulated plains and mountaintops away from the bright lights of the city, you never have seen the heavens as they are shown in the planetarium.

The first part of the program is given in the circular Guggenheim Space Center, where a mechanized model of the solar system, forty-eight feet in diameter, is suspended from the ceiling. Here you learn about the motions of the planets and their moons.

The planetarium has numerous exhibits: murals of lunar landscapes, eclipses, and the aurora borealis; collections of meteorites (some weighing up to thirty-four tons); ancient Chinese, and German astronomical instruments. But the most popular exhibits of all are the five scales which register what your weight would be in outer space. A 130-pound person would weigh 113 pounds on Venus, but on the moon he would weigh 20 pounds, on Mars 47 pounds, on Jupiter 336 pounds, and on the sun 3,550 pounds. If you want to test your weight, count on waiting, for the lines are often long. Teenagers and young adults might also be interested in Laser Rock— the star show augmented by lasers and synchronized with rock music. For information call 724–8700.

East Side Museums and Galleries

On the Fifth Avenue side of Central Park and on the side streets off Madison Avenue in the 60s and 70s is the city's greatest concentration of art galleries and museums. You might work your way up Fifth Avenue to 92nd Street, then over to Madison Avenue and down to the 60s.

A good starting point is the Frick Collection on Fifth Avenue at 70th Street, a splendid example of French classic architecture, formerly the home of Henry Clay Frick (who made millions in the steel industry). The mansion enclosing a peaceful glass-roofed courtyard and the private collection of the fine paintings, ornaments, and furnishings will give you an idea of the scale of living enjoyed by New York society before the income tax. (No small children allowed.)

Now head east to Madison Avenue and up to the 70s, where New York's art gallery district is centered. Many of the galleries which once clustered around 57th Street have moved up to these quieter surroundings; Christie's is on the East Side, over at 502 Park Avenue.

Also in this area are the Danenberg Galleries; the Graham Galleries, established in 1857 and reputedly the city's oldest; Perls Galleries, the distributor of Alexander Calder's works (he designed the cement and slate pavement in front); and the elegant Wildenstein Gallery, which presents important collections of Old Masters and French Impressionists. There are dozens of noted galleries, smaller and more intimate, besides these. In one afternoon you might be able to see more works of Renoir, Braque, Klee, Picasso, Redon, Chagall, Dufy, and Modigliani than you could in Paris.

In the midst of all this art is yet another great museum, the Whitney Museum of American Art, at Madison Avenue and 75th Street. The building itself, opened by Mrs. Flora Whitney Miller and Mrs. John F. Kennedy in September 1966, is at first startling. Given slightly less than one-third of an acre on which to build, architect Marcel Breuer was faced with the problem of creating ample exhibition and storage space for a vast collection of 20th-century American painting and sculpture which had completely outgrown the Whitney's old home on West 54th Street. (Its original home was on 8th Street in Greenwich Village.) Breuer's solution was to turn the traditional ziggurat (or "wedding cake") design upside down, with each of the second, third, and fourth floors projecting fourteen feet farther out over the street from the one below. New Yorkers' reactions were mixed, but the building has drawn students and architects from all over the world to study its design—more so, in fact, than did Frank Lloyd Wright's Guggenheim Museum.

Three blocks north and one west (on Fifth Avenue) is the Duke mansion, the former home of tobacco tycoon James Biddle Duke and his daughter Doris. Today it is the headquarters for the Institute of Fine Arts of New York University.

Across the way, facing Fifth Avenue between 80th and 84th streets, is the Metropolitan Museum of Art. The neo-Renaissance design of this imposing structure infringing on the reaches of Central Park was taken from the Columbian Exposition (Chicago World's Fair) of 1893. The museum houses one of the most comprehensive collections in the world. There are more than a million art treasures representing the work of fifty centuries. The whole of it cannot be enjoyed in one visit; so it would be best to study the floor plan and choose the galleries which hold the most interest for you. There are also Acoustiguides for rent here; the recorded tour takes approximately forty-five minutes. Its departments include Egyptian Art, Near Eastern Art, American painting, sculpture, furniture, armor, and arms. If you are interested in fashion, visit the Costume Institute, a favorite haunt of designers who come to study its period costumes. This is truly one of the world's great museums, and it is constantly expanding, so if you've only got time to visit one museum, make it the Met. They also have a wonderful gift shop with stunning antique jewelry and craft reproductions as well as posters and books.

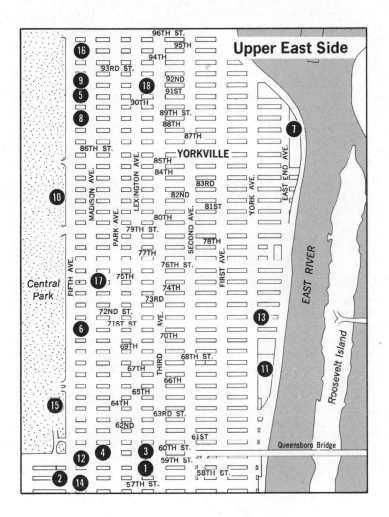

Upper East Side

YORKVILLE

Central Park

EAST RIVER

Roosevelt Island

Queensboro Bridge

Points of Interest

1) Alexander's
2) Bergdorf Goodman
3) Bloomingdale's
4) Christie's
5) Cooper-Hewitt Museum
6) Frick Collection
7) Gracie Mansion
   (Mayor's residence)
8) Guggenheim Museum
9) Jewish Museum
10) Metropolitan Museum of Art
11) Rockefeller University
12) F.A.O. Schwarz
13) Sotheby Parke Bernet
14) Tiffany
15) Central Park Zoo
16) International Center
   of Photography
17) Whitney Museum
18) YM-YWHA

Frank Lloyd Wright's Spiral

One of the most extraordinary buildings in New York is the Solomon
R. Guggenheim Museum at 88th Street. The six-story spiral structure designed by the late Frank Lloyd Wright alone is worth a visit.

Eighty-sixth Street between Third and York avenues is the center of
old Yorkville, New York's German-American community, with restaurants and shops featuring German food, records, and other items. Nearby
are lots of Czech- and Hungarian-style restaurants, too.

At 91st Street and Fifth Avenue is the former home of steel tycoon Andrew Carnegie. This handsome Georgian mansion is now occupied by the
Cooper-Hewitt Museum for design and the decorative arts. One block
north is the luxurious former home of banker Felix N. Warburg, whose
widow presented it to the Jewish Theological Seminary to be used as a
museum. The Jewish Museum has become the repository of the most extensive collection of Jewish ceremonial objects in the United States and
also is one of the three most important in the world, the other two being
in Jerusalem and Prague.

From here, even though it's a short hike north, your Fifth Avenue museum touring would not be complete without a visit to the fine Museum of
the City of New York at 103rd Street. The museum's collections are extensive and cover a wide variety of fields, reflecting both the city of today
and yesteryear. Its decorative arts collection includes outstanding examples of costumes, furniture, and silver. The print collection numbers over
half a million items of paintings, prints, and photographs of New York
City. A theater collection contains what is reputed to be the most complete
history of the New York stage ever assembled, while the toy collection
covers the whole fun world of playthings—with its dolls and dollhouses
of particular note.

Incidentally, if you have children in tow you might plan to visit on Saturday when, during the school year, special activities are planned, including puppet shows and "please touch" demonstrations.

The Upper West Side

The Upper West Side has in the 1980s become one of the trendiest
neighborhoods in the city. The development of Lincoln Center brought
musicians, singers, and other performing artists to the area in search of
convenience (the Broadway bus runs to the theater district), low rents (not
anymore), and a kind of funky ambience (rapidly disappearing). Columbus
Ave. has now taken over the heterosexual singles scene from First Ave.
Central Park West rivals Fifth Avenue as a prestigious address, particularly with its pre-1900, spacious apartment buildings. On Columbus, the restaurants and cafes are invariably overflowing with people-watchers and
people waiting to be seen. Amsterdam Ave. is up-and-coming, a handful
of trendy restaurants and boutiques sneaking onto an otherwise bleak
stretch. Broadway revolves around Zabar's, a take-out delicatessen and
housewares emporium of which Eli Zabar says, "Only God takes our customers away." West End Ave. and Riverside Drive are outstanding residential areas, teeming with spacious apartment buildings (a contradiction
in terms to latter-day urban architects) and brownstones.

One of the most scenic drives in the city is along Riverside Drive, which follows the Hudson River shoreline (inland of Riverside Park) from 72nd Street up to Inwood. The drive was another brilliant brainchild of Andrew Haswell Green, who was responsible for Central Park.

But Green, who had conservatively estimated the cost of the drive would run around $1,500,000, hadn't reckoned with Boss Tweed and his Forty Thieves. Tweed and boys liked the idea of building a park and drive; liked it so much that they made personal purchases of the land where the park was to be built and sold it to the city for a whopping profit. By the time the parkway was completed in 1885 the cost had zoomed up to $6 million.

At 79th Street, on the river, is the Boat Basin, a marina set alongside the Park promenade.

Next, at 89th Street, the Soldiers and Sailors Monument comes into view, a handsome Italian Carrara marble "silo" circled by twelve Corinthian columns. The 392-foot Gothic tower of the Riverside Church can be seen a mile to the north. Its 72-bell carillon is the largest in the United States and its range of tonal quality is superb. The largest bell, the *Bourdon,* weighs more than twenty tons, while the smallest weighs only 10 pounds.

The rocky ridge that begins in Central Park rises gradually as it travels uptown through Harlem and Morningside Heights to the precipitous lookout at Washington Heights. Here one of the big battles of the Revolutionary War was fought, and this upper end of Manhattan is rich in historic sites and lore.

Morningside Heights–Harlem–Upper Manhattan

Directly east, if you want to make a detour at this time, is the Church of St. John the Divine, on Morningside Heights (Amsterdam Avenue and 112th Street). Started in 1892, it will be the largest Gothic cathedral in the world when it is finally completed, which the church admits is probably another hundred years off!

At Broadway and 116th Street is the main entrance to Columbia University; on the other side of Broadway nearby are Barnard College and the Union Theological Seminary.

General Grant's Tomb is at 123rd Street, and at about this point Riverside Drive begins to skirt Fort Washington Park. At 155th Street you might want to make another short detour east to Broadway to visit a unique cultural center which houses four special-interest museums. Here you'll find the Museum of the American Indian–Heye Foundation, which has an outstanding collection of Indian art and relics of North and South America. The Hispanic Society of America has a museum of ancient and modern Spanish culture. At the American Numismatic Society, you can see a vast collection of coins and medals, and the country's most comprehensive library on the subject. At the American Academy of Arts and Letters, you can view the memorabilia of many famous artists, writers, and musicians.

Harlem, which begins at Central Park North (110th Street), conjures up images both romantic and repulsive. Today's truth lies somewhere in a fascinating middle replete with exciting urban renewal and, unfortunately, some of this city's worst drug dens. This legendary section is certainly worth visiting.

The Dutch first called it "Nieuw Haarlem" after their own North Holland capital city. The British later Anglicized the name. After the opening of the Harlem River Railroad in 1837, this "uptown" district became a haven for New York's monied families. During this period, the city's black population lived primarily in the West 30s, but the construction of Penn Station forced them to relocate.

In the 1920s, the now famous Harlem Renaissance cultural movement spawned a vast number of black artists, writers, and thinkers. Today, many of Harlem's developments and streets are named in their honor. During the 1960s the flowering of the civil rights movement brought tension to the area and many of Harlem's middle-class residents moved away. The result was a marked decaying of this once great section. But now there is definite improvement in the air; Striver's Row at W. 138th–139th streets is not the only "good" block in town anymore. A growing number of "Yuppies" and "Buppies" are reclaiming other stunning 19th- and 20th-century brownstones and restoring them to their original glories. One hundred twenty-fifth street, Harlem's main street, has many new storefronts and, of course, the legendary Apollo Theater is as active as ever with cable TV productions and its famous Amateur Night performances.

Other important Harlem landmarks include The Schomburg Center for Research in Black Culture at 103 W. 135th Street. This modern branch of the New York Public Library houses an outstanding collection of materials on African and Afro-American peoples. The Morris-Jumel Mansion at W. 160th and Edgecombe Ave. is the site of George Washington's 1776 headquarters and one of New York's few remaining examples of pre-Revolutionary architecture. The Graveyard of Revolutionary Heroes at 155th–153rd streets near Riverside Drive is the final resting place of many famous Americans, including John James Audubon. The Abyssinian Baptist Church at 132 W. 138th Street is where Adam Clayton Powell and Martin Luther King, Jr. preached.

Restaurants like Sylvia's and Wilson's Bakery, both near the once posh "Sugar Hill" district, have become favorites of critics and pennywise Manhattanites alike; you will often see a line of limos outside. Harlem is dusting off its favorite jazz and show places, too. Baby Grand's, Sutton's, and even Wilt Small's Paradise (currently under renovation) once again attract serious music lovers and nightlifers.

You can take the A train as Duke Ellington suggested, but the most efficient and safest way (there are still some unsavory pockets of burned-out buildings and street crime) to see Harlem's highlights is with Gray Line's group of Harlem tours, created and supervised by Harlem Renaissance Tours, or with HRT itself. This dedicated company, a member of the Uptown Chamber of Commerce, welcomes individuals and groups alike for every kind of exploration—architectural walking jaunts to champagne-filled nights of jazz and soul food, and even a visit to Sunday morning gospel services. Prices range from $30–$60 per person, depending upon the type of tour. Call 722–9534 for more information, or contact Gray Line Tours at 397–2600.

Heading north and west, pick up Fort Washington Avenue and follow it to Fort Tryon Park. This is the brow of Manhattan; from this vantage point, you have an uninterrupted view of the magnificent sweep of the

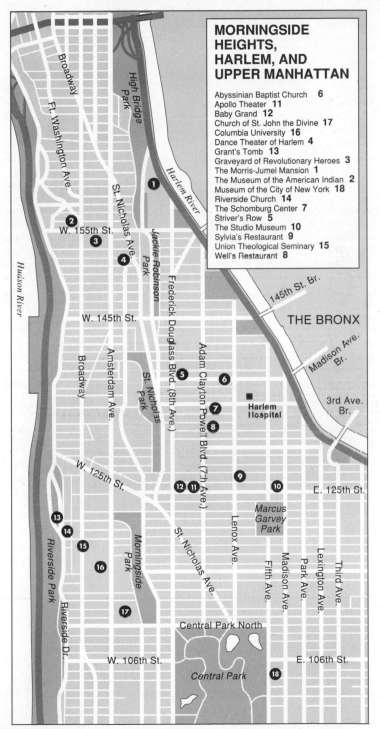

MORNINGSIDE HEIGHTS, HARLEM, AND UPPER MANHATTAN

Abyssinian Baptist Church **6**
Apollo Theater **11**
Baby Grand **12**
Church of St. John the Divine **17**
Columbia University **16**
Dance Theater of Harlem **4**
Grant's Tomb **13**
Graveyard of Revolutionary Heroes **3**
The Morris-Jumel Mansion **1**
The Museum of the American Indian **2**
Museum of the City of New York **18**
Riverside Church **14**
The Schomburg Center **7**
Striver's Row **5**
The Studio Museum **10**
Sylvia's Restaurant **9**
Union Theological Seminary **15**
Well's Restaurant **8**

Hudson River up to the Tappan Zee Bridge, the precipitous Palisades shoreline of New Jersey, the graceful arc of George Washington Bridge, and the far reaches of the Bronx beyond Spuyten Duyvil.

The Cloisters

Set in the midst of this woodland park is The Cloisters, a structure of unusual form and grace assembled from many sections of medieval European monasteries. Five different cloisters have been connected by a charming colonnaded walk and merged with a French Romanesque chapel, a chapter house of the 12th century, and a Romanesque apse which is on loan from the Spanish government.

The museum's medieval art treasures were gathered by George Grey Barnard and acquired by the Metropolitan Museum with funds provided by John D. Rockefeller, Jr. (Admission, by contribution, can be made either at the Met or at the Cloisters, and is good at both locations on the same day.) Among the museum's most notable treasures are the *Hunt of the Unicorn* tapestries, which are considered to be among the world's greatest.

At the time Mr. Rockefeller arranged for the purchase of the Barnard collection, he also bought the woodland area of Fort Tryon as the site for The Cloisters. To ensure an uncluttered vista across the Hudson on the New Jersey side Mr. Rockefeller also purchased a 13-mile strip along the Palisades and gave it to the Palisades Interstate Park Commission.

During the days of discovery, Spuyten Duyvil was a narrow, unnavigable creek which trickled between the Harlem and Hudson Rivers, separating Marble Hill from Manhattan's mainland. In 1895 a canal was cut through these flatlands, shortening the water route between the Hudson River and Long Island Sound, thus obviating the necessity of sailing way down and around the Battery to reach a berth on the Hudson River.

Within a stone's throw of Inwood Park are Columbia University's athletic fields and boathouse. On nearly any spring day you'll see oarsmen out on the Spuyten Duyvil practicing for a regatta, and in the fall, Columbia's home football games are played at Baker Field.

While you're in the neighborhood, you might want to drive down to see the Dyckman House, a museum at 204th Street and Broadway. When it was built in 1783, the wealthy Dyckman family owned most of the Inwood area. Today the little 18th-century Dutch farmhouse is squeezed between clusters of seedy apartment houses and shops, a sorry setting for such an historic gem. It has been beautifully restored by the city, is furnished with authentic pieces of the mid-18th century, and has an enchanting garden. If you ignore the surroudings, you will find it a rewarding visit.

Manhattan is a civilization on the sea and of the sea and it is from the water one fully appreciates its size, shape, and style. The Circle Line is a three-hour boat excursion around the island which reveals many of the city's characteristics one cannot observe while exploring on foot.

Outside Manhattan

As far back as 1833 there was a movement afoot to consolidate the villages around Manhattan into one Greater New York. Brooklyn, the big brother of the outlying areas, had been incorporated as a village for some time and doing very nicely on its own. In turning down the proposal to come under the wing of the bustling, brash, flourishing city of New York, its spokesman General Jeremiah Johnson echoes the sentiments of most Brooklynites with the statement that "Between New York and Brooklyn there is nothing common—unless it be the waters that flow between them. And even these waters—however frequently passed, still form and must forever continue to form an unsurmountable obstacle to the Union."

A half century later Andrew Haswell Green, having finished his big Riverside Drive project, looked around for something else to keep him occupied and hit upon reviving the Greater New York concept. The Brooklyn Bridge had been completed in 1883 and Green decreed that the waters between New York and Brooklyn no longer constituted an "unsurmountable obstacle to the Union."

In 1889 he addressed the New York State Legislature and exhorted them to move on unification. By 1894 he had managed to place a referendum on unification before the voters of Manhattan, Brooklyn, Queens, Staten Island, and lower Westchester. The vote was a toss-up. The state legislature made up the voters' minds by enacting a bill for consolidation. On January 1, 1898, Brooklyn, Bronx, Queens, and Richmond (Staten Island) joined Manhattan to become Greater New York.

The Williamsburg and Queensboro bridges, the Queens Midtown Tunnel, and miles of subway lines were built to bind the boroughs together, all save one: Staten Island, which could be reached by ferry only and remained a distant relative for fourscore years. Not until the Verrazano-Narrows Bridge was opened in 1964 was Staten Island brought fully into the fold.

The Rural Borough—Staten Island

Staten Island, the borough of Richmond, has always been the most rural area of New York City. Many of its families date back to the early 18th century, and its society is exclusive to the point of clannishness. One resident, whose family goes back to the 17th century, says that there was a time when the Vanderbilts were considered "common."

Cornelius Vanderbilt, who was born near Stapleton on Staten Island in 1794, was not to the manor born, to be sure, but he did have enterprise. At age twenty-three he started a ferry run over to the mainland and assumed the title "Commodore." Eventually he parlayed his ferry service into a railroad and hotel empire. His "rank" was given to the former Hotel Commodore on 42nd Street near Vanderbilt Avenue, which has reopened as a Hyatt hotel.

To this day Staten Island society is hard to crack, for the old families still have a tendency to stick together. Most of the old guard live up in the hills—Dongan, Emerson, Grymes Hills—in houses not exactly extravagant, but on property that has a long-time family background and a superb view of the Narrows. They are proud to point out that their Todt Hill, a 410-foot mound, is the highest point along the Atlantic coast between Main and Florida!

The island, an irregular triangle about fourteen miles long and seven miles wide, was given its name—"Staatenn Eylandt"—by Henry Hudson in 1609. It was a difficult piece of land to colonize for the original owners, the Unami Indians, were a wily lot. The Dutch started negotiating with the Unamis in 1630 and were repulsed with arrows and hatchets on three occasions before they finally were able to persuade the chieftain to sell the island. It wasn't long though before the Unamis were back to reclaim it. "They supposed that ye island by reason of ye war, by killing, burning and driving us off become theirs again," complained one colonist, Cornelius Melyn. The Dutch bought the island five times before they finally could call it their own.

When England took New Amsterdam in 1664, it appropriated Staten Island and made it a part of the province of New York. It was named Richmond County in honor of the Duke of Richmond, the son of King Charles II. Several disputes arose between the ducal proprietors from New Jersey and New York over which previous claims to the island's lush farmlands and timbered hills were still valid. It was a sticky decision to make.

The Duke of York, a man of great sporting spirit, chose a novel way of resolving the dispute. The property, he said, would be awarded to citizens who could circumnavigate the island in twenty-four hours. The first to accomplish the treacherous sail was Captain Christopher Billopp and in 1687 he was awarded the prize of 1,600 acres at the southernmost tip, which is now the village of Tottenville. The following year he built a fine mansion and it later became the scene of the famous conference Lord Howe called to determine the seriousness of American demands for independence. The Billopp Conference House at the foot of Hylan Boulevard has been restored and looks almost the same as when it first was built.

For more than a century and a half the island remained a farming area and preserve. In the 1830s fashionable bathing resorts sprang up on the north shore at Castleton, Stapleton, and New Brighton. New York socialites cruised over to spend the summer yachting, swimming, and picnicking on the beaches. Some were so taken with the bucolic atmosphere they built summer mansions and organized the Richmond Country Club, where they could meet for a stirrup cup and ride to the hounds.

For some reason Staten Island had a special appeal for Southerners, too. Many plantation owners spent their holidays here, and during the Civil War they sent their women and children to the safety of the isolated island.

The island's little scattered communities retained their rural, rustic atmosphere for almost a century more. Then came the dedication in 1964 of the Verrazano-Narrows Bridge, which opened the way from Brooklyn to Staten Island. Real-estate developers moved in, bought up many acres of farmland, and converted them into look-alike housing developments. Brooklynites have discovered that the island's beaches are a lot roomier than theirs, and now are creating weekend traffic jams.

Yet there are still miles of farm-fringed country roads, secluded parks, hilltop lookouts with superb views of Upper and Lower New York bays, historic houses, zoos, and museums, which make a whole day's excursion around Staten Island most worthwhile.

That Wonderful Ferry Ride

Bridges link the island to New Jersey and Brooklyn. The most delightful way to reach it from Manhattan is by ferry from the South Ferry terminal at the foot of Battery Park. The inexpensive ride—25 cents round-trip!—is a miniature ocean voyage past Governors Island, the Statue of Liberty, and other harbor highlights during the 15-minute run to St. George. The ferry transports passenger cars too ($1.75 plus 25¢ per passenger), and having your own car (or renting one) makes it easier for you to see all that the island has to offer. Ferries depart every half hour in each direction.

Staten Island Restorations

From St. George head for Stapleton and pick up Richmond Road. Drive through the Dongan and Todt Hills' areas of old estates and past the Richmond County Country Club on to Richmond. This is historically and geographically the center of the island and the site of a fascinating restoration called Richmondtown.

Richmondtown was called Cocclestown when it first was settled in the late 1600s, prompted probably by the quantities of oyster and clam shells left behind by the Indians. By 1730 it had grown into a compact little village with a dozen dwellings, a courthouse, jail, taverns, the Church of St. Andrew, and the center of the island's government. When the island was merged with the other boroughs into Greater New York, the abandonment of Richmondtown as the county seat left it without the incentives for change or expansion. It was a blessing in disguise.

Historically minded Staten Islanders recognized it as "a perfect setting for a life-sized model of an American town that would tell the story of the growth of such a village better than any number of pictures, exhibition cases and dioramas." You'll see the town taking shape under the auspices of the Staten Island Historical Society and the city of New York. Little 17th- and 18th-century cottages, cooperage, and basketmaker's shops, and other older buildings have been lifted off their foundations in villages around the island and brought here to form Richmondtown. The center of the settlement is the Museum of the Staten Island Historical Society, at Court and Center streets, housed in a former county building built in 1848. The museum is small and its attendants—mostly volunteer workers—outdo themselves to make you feel welcome and show you around.

On display are assorted bits of Americana which show various aspects of how people worked and lived in centuries past. The community's 19th-century country general store is also popular. Ladies in bonnets and long gingham dresses tend store, selling old-fashioned licorice whips, horehound drops, taffy, and other delectables. The shelves are lined with ornate tea canisters and spice boxes. There are cracker barrels, old apothecary jars, a cigar store Indian, an old loom, and a spinning wheel. There is an assortment of irons that housewives warmed over a wood stove: small rounded ones for pressing ruffles, heavy cumbersome ones for bedsheets and workclothes. Behind an old barber chair you'll see an unusual collection of shaving mugs, each with its owner's name fired onto the ornate designs. A doctor's bleeding instrument is mixed in with a hodgepodge of other items usually found in the old general stores which served about every need of the community.

Ask one of the attendants for the brochure which gives the location and historic backgrounds of the various buildings clustered around the museum. There is the little clapboard Voorlezer's House, built about 1696 by the Dutch congregation as a church, schoolhouse, and a home for the *voorlezer* (church clerk). It is known as America's oldest remaining schoolhouse.

Treasure House, built by a tanner in 1700, is famous for the good fortune it bestowed on a later owner. About a hundred years ago when Patrick Highland took possession he found $7,000 in gold hidden in the walls. It's thought to be the cache of an overcautious or larcenous British paymaster.

The Guyon-Lake-Tysen House is one of the outstanding restorations. It was built about 1740 by Joseph Guyon and you can see his name marked in the mud coat over the dining room door. As each new owner took possession the house grew to meet his family's particular needs. You'll notice that the mantel in the dining room is of pre-Revolutionary design, while in the parlor, which was added later, the mantel is of the post-Revolutionary type.

Another restoration project on Staten Island is the Snug Harbor Cultural Center. It consists of 26 buildings that previously served as homes for retired Staten Island seamen, on eighty wooded acres along scenic New York Harbor. In addition, seven historical landmarks dot the center's grounds. As of this writing, two exhibits have opened: the Newhouse gallery and Gallery III for the visual arts. The 260-seat Veterans Memorial Hall opened on Veterans Day, 1984. The entire complex is ultimately envisioned as a center for the performing and visual arts from around the world.

If time permits, stop by the Jacques Marchais Center of Tibetan Art near the Lighthouse (338 Lighthouse Avenue), then pick up Amboy Road for a ride through a still somewhat rural area to the Conference House at Tottenville. On your return trip to St. George you can choose either Hylan Boulevard which skirts the shoreline or the inland Richmond Parkway which ultimately leads to the Victory Boulevard route to the ferry terminal.

The Indians Sold Brooklyn

Shortly after the West India Company settled Manhattan they sailed over to the "broken lands" southeast of the Battery to negotiate with the Indians for the purchase of the whole western end of Long Island.

Their first parcel in Brooklyn (Breuckelen—broken land) was acquired in 1636 and within a few years the company had brought over a number of Walloon families to settle along the Wall-boght (Wallabout Bay), the site of the Naval Shipyard.

Under the terms of "Provisional Regulations for Colonists," the company agreed to furnish them with "necessary supplies and clothes from the company's storehouses . . . at a reasonable price," which could be paid for in installments. The colonists, in turn, were required to pledge that they would sell their farm produce and handicrafts to no one but the company's agents. They also were "bound to remain with their families for the space of six consecutive years at their destined place . . . and to faithfully fulfill their promises to the Indians and their other neighbors, whether in connection with trade or other matters."

The community grew and prospered quite separately from the earlier settlement of Nieuw Amsterdam. Brooklyn's colony burst the bounds of Wallabout Bay with the coming of Normans, French, and a group of English colonists from Massachusetts who had been excommunicated from the Puritan Church because they did not believe in the baptizing of babies.

By 1643 the colonists had cleared and cultivated the lands as far as Gravesend Bay.

On Ilpetonga (high sandy bank) where the Canarsie Indians had lived in community houses (some of which were a quarter of a mile long), wealthy merchants built elegant homes. From the heights they could watch their clipper ships round Red Hook and berth at the waterside warehouses. To prevent the warehouses from marring their river view the merchant princes planted the roofs with lawns, flowering shrubs, and trees to form ingenious backyard gardens and shortcuts to the piers below. They called the area Clover Hill. Today it is known as Brooklyn Heights. With the coming of the Brooklyn Bridge and the subways, the patrician families fled the heights. Their homes have been partitioned into studios and apartments which are handsomely restored by artists, writers, and people who enjoy the Victorian atmosphere and one of the most exciting views in the world. This view alone makes a trip to Brooklyn worthwhile.

You can reach Brooklyn Heights by driving across Brooklyn Bridge and turning south, or by IRT Seventh Avenue subway to Clark Street. A stroll through the arboreal streets—Cranberry, Pineapple, Orange, Poplar, Willow—recalls a legend of old feuds. Before the Civil War these streets were named for prominent families. Local authorities were disturbed by the personality cult which wanted their names to go down in history by way of street signs. Overnight the family names were replaced with botanical street signs by the authorities. The families replaced their names and the battle of the street signs went on for weeks. Signs seesawed back and forth between families and fruit. The fruits and trees won in some cases and the families of Hicks, Montague, Pierrepont, and Remsen won in others. Miss Middagh, a supposedly staunch supporter of the fruit and tree campaign, also has a street named for her.

You'll find remains of Old World gentility in these streets. New Orleans-type wrought-iron balconies, stately pillared entrances, delicate scrollwork embellishments, ivy-covered brownstones, hidden mews of converted carriage houses similar to those of Washington Square make the 20th-century skyline across the river seem a mirage of the future.

Along Willow Street you'll pass a few of the older homes of the Heights. At 70 Willow Street is the van Sinderen House built in the Greek Revival style in the late 1830s. The three best examples of the Federal-style row houses of the early 19th century are found at 155– 157–159.

An esplanade which extends from Remsem Street to Orange Street offers what photographic experts consider the most spectacular panoramic view of Manhattan. To the south, Wall Street's jungle of spires prick the clouds; parades of ferries, freighters, and barges ply between Buttermilk and East River Channels, often called the shipping crossroads of the world; the Statue of Liberty and the Verrazano-Narrows Bridge can be seen on the horizon. To the north, midtown's skyscrapers rise above the spidery spans of Brooklyn and Manhattan bridges.

Atlantic Avenue, nearby, is a center of Middle Eastern shops and restaurants toward its waterside end.

Fiery Sermons

Walking east from the esplanade you will come to the Plymouth Church of the Pilgrims on Orange Street, a severe, dark brick example of early

Classic Revival architecture. Inside, its severity is softened with a series of memorial windows which trace the interesting history of Puritanism. It was here that the Abolitionist movement flared into a full-scale crusade.

Soon after the church was completed in 1849 Henry Ward Beecher began a series of fiery sermons and dramatic playlets on the evils of selling human souls on the auction block. William Lloyd Garrison, John Greenleaf Whittier, and other early Abolitionists also spoke from the pulpit. It was a bold program and one which inspired citizens throughout the country to raise their voices, even in cities where public discussions of slavery were not permitted. Abraham Lincoln worshipped here on two occasions in 1860 and took his stand against slavery in his historic speech at Cooper Institute.

Brooklyn—A City of Churches

Brooklyn was long known as the city of churches, and as you drive through the borough you will see spire after spire. It also has a fair share of institutions of higher learning, including Brooklyn College, Pratt Institute, Long Island University, and St. John's University. A half dozen parks, a world renowned museum, a botanic garden, and a huge aquarium offer a variety of diversions for all ages.

Flatbush Avenue, a few blocks from Brooklyn Heights, will lead you southeastward to the monumental Grand Army Plaza with its 80-foot-high memorial arch, often open to visitors on weekends and holidays and affording an interesting view of the harbor, the Manhattan skyline, and the local neighborhoods. A little beyond the Plaza to your left, onto Eastern Parkway and behind the Public Library, you'll come to Institute Park, where the huge Brooklyn Museum and the beautiful Botanic Garden are located.

The museum's collections of primitive and prehistoric art are world renowned: North and South American Indian handicrafts; works from Oceania, Indonesia, and Africa. There is a notable collection of American painting and sculpture from colonial times to today. Its collection of Egyptian antiquities on the third floor is considered outstanding. One floor below is a fine collection of bronzes and porcelains from China, displayed in chronological order, as well as changing exhibitions from the museum's wealth of over 30,000 prints and drawings. Up on the fourth floor the costume galleries and the series of American interiors from the 17th century to the present are also of special interest.

The 50-acre Botanic Garden behind the museum, with more than 10,000 trees and plants, is especially noted for its Garden of Fragrance, one of the relatively few gardens in the world planted and maintained for the blind. The plants were selected primarily for their fragrance and shape, so that the blind might enjoy nature's beauty by the sense of smell and touch. Signs in Braille are posted at the edge of each bed to aid the blind in identifying the flowers and plants. It is noted, too, for its Japanese garden, and there are acres devoted to wild flowers, herbs, roses, tropical plants, and groves of flowering shrubs.

To the south of the Botanic Garden is Prospect Park, a 500-acre expanse of woods, meadows, footpaths, bridle trails, and tree-shaded drives. The project was designed by the same men who had collaborated on Central Park, Olmstead and de Vaux. Here you can visit the Lefferts Homestead, a Dutch colonial farmhouse which was built in 1776 and originally stood at 563 Flatbush Avenue. When the Lefferts family bequeathed it to the city, the home was moved to the park as a museum.

The Italianate villa which serves as the Brooklyn Park Headquarters (Prospect Park West between 4th and 5th streets) was once the home of railroad pioneer Edwin C. Litchfield. Built in 1857 from plans by Alexander Jackson Davis and called Ridgewood, it is said to have been one of the most elegant houses of its time and the center of Brooklyn social life.

A Day at a City Beach

Another summer day—make it a weekday when it's less crowded—can be spent in Coney Island. The island, which fronts on the Atlantic Ocean, once was a common pasture for early Dutch farmers. It became a fashionable beach resort in the mid-19th century when the enterprising Messrs. Eddy and Hart leased part of the island and built a pavilion. With the extension of the subway lines (BMT and IND), the island became accessible to all and now draws a half-billion people a year.

It was once a razzle-dazzle place with ferris wheels, carousels, roller coasters, tunnels of love, shooting galleries, penny arcades, sellers of pizza, hot dogs, saltwater taffy, and spun-sugar candy. Now Coney Island's number of amusements is diminishing, but it's still worth the excursion if only to get a taste of what the happy, gaudy, and thrilling heyday of this famous amusement park must have been like.

The New York Aquarium is here, too. Try to visit at feeding time: through portholes you can watch divers swim among the white beluga whales and feed them by hand; watch an attendant tickle an electric eel until it flashes and crackles a discharge of some 650 volts. You may see a pilot whale or seal which had gone astray and was given a home here. There are sea lions and seals, living coral, giant starfish, seahorses, octopi, and enough exhibits to keep you busy for half the day.

Another variation on the nautical theme is the fascinating Sheepshead Bay area. Take the Belt (also called Shore) Parkway east to Knapp St., head south a short way, then back west along Emmons Avenue. This mini-port for saltwater fishermen comes spectacularly alive in the predawn hours and again in late afternoon. The amazing bustle, in which you're welcome to take part, involves the all- or half-day chartering of party or private-charter fishing boats. Even if you don't want to test the Atlantic fishing in person, the returning catch—you can't get 'em any fresher—is for sale at reasonable prices. Nearby Brighton Beach is the enclave of Russian-Jewish immigrants of the 1970s. The area is filled with shops and restaurants selling Russian foods and Russian-style goods.

Back to the Shore Parkway and farther east still, straddling the Brooklyn–Queens border, and you'll be passing New York City's largest park, the Jamaica Bay Wildlife Refuge. It encompasses more than eighteen square miles (remember that Manhattan comprises only 22 square miles) of underwater island and tidal marsh terrain with 257 species of native birds. A permit is required for access to the wildlife area here; write the city's Department of Parks, Recreation and Cultural affairs. However, saltwater fishing is permitted.

Queens

Queens, covering 121 square miles, abuts Brooklyn to the south and west and Long Island to the east. The lines of demarcation are very vague. Even the native hardly knows at what point he is in Queens, Brooklyn, or Long Island. (The position of Manhattan is quite clear. It's across the East River, either over it via the Queensboro Bridge or under it via the Queens Midtown Tunnel.)

Queens is a borough of beaches, baseball parks, airports, golf courses, racetracks, yacht basins, and expressways to Long Island's beach resorts and suburban communities. The borough also has thriving manufacturing areas—especially Long Island City on the western edge—and distinct neighborhoods. Some of the large ethnic groupings are the Italians of Maspeth and Ridgewood, the Irish of Woodside, the blacks of Hollis and Jamaica, the Greeks of Astoria, the Jews of Forest Hills, and the Puerto Ricans of Corona and Elmhurst.

Until well into the 20th century Queens was a rural area. Henry Hudson had nosed the *Half Moon* into Rockaway Inlet on the south shore for a short look-see, then continued on to the Upper Bay and then to Albany in search of the Northwest Passage. Three years later Adrian Block sailed through Long Island Sound and, while navigating the roaring currents of Hell Gate on the northern extremity of Queens, didn't dare give the area a second look. He, too, was heading for Manhattan.

After the West India Company had sewed up the Brooklyn area, it approached the Reckouwacky Indians about selling a piece of their domain, in what was to become Queens, so it could continue its expansion program. Once the deal was consummated, towns sprang up all over the virgin flatlands.

By 1643 Flushing was inhabited by a small band of English Quaker refugees under the leadership of John Bowne. The same year a band of Englishmen from Hemel Hempstead had settled Hempstead, which is across the borough line in Long Island. Jamaica was chartered as a town by Governor Stuyvesant in 1656. They were followed by other English settlers and soon the area became known as Queens, in honor of Catherine Braganza, Queen of Charles II. It is not surprising, therefore, that during the Revolution, most of the people in Queens were British sympathizers.

Queens remained a loosely knit collection of small towns until the subway lines were extended to Jackson Heights, Flushing, and Jamaica. Today the borough has a population rivaling Brooklyn's, many of whom live in huge clusters of high-rise apartment houses.

There are only a few vestiges of its historic past. One is the Bowne House in Flushing (Bowne Street between 37th and 38th Avenues), which John Bowne built in 1661. For permitting Quaker meetings to be conducted in his home he was sent to Holland to be put on trial. His impassioned plea for religious tolerance won him a pardon and led to greater freedom of worship in the New World's settlements. His home is now a shrine to religious liberty.

Close by is the old Quaker Meeting House on Northern Boulevard between Main and Union Streets. It is one of the country's few remaining houses of worship dating from the 17th century. The meeting place was built in 1694 and has been in continuous use by the Society of Friends ever since, except for a time when it was occupied by the British forces during the Revolution.

Baseball, Tennis, and Racing

If horse racing, tennis, and baseball are your favorite sports, Queens is the place to head for. The National League's New York Mets (baseball) play at Shea Stadium in Flushing. The thoroughbreds run at Aqueduct in Jamaica. At the West Side Tennis Club in Forest Hills you can watch professional and amateur tennis tournaments.

For the less active pastime of strolling, sunning, and sightseeing, you might also plan on spending some time in Flushing Meadows–Corona Park in Corona. The site of both New York World's Fairs (1939–40 and 1964–65) with a few buildings of both expositions remaining, this area also contains a Hall of Science, a small zoo, a delightful aviary, a children's animal farm, and Louis Armstrong Stadium, site of the U.S. Open Tennis Championship.

The Bronx

It was a stroke of good fortune for New York City that The Bronx was slow in developing. When farsighted city officials began around 1870 to acquire lands to make Central and Prospect Parks they also turned their eyes northeastward across the Harlem River to the vast expanse of virgin forests and meadows of what was then called lower Westchester. They bought three parcels of land covering more than four thousand acres "to be held forever for the delight and well-being of the people of the city." In no other major city of the world has the country been kept this close to town (although at first glance the Bronx is hardly a "delight").

The history of the Bronx more or less parallels that of Queens. The Dutch West India Company purchased the area from the Indians in 1639 and two years later sold five hundred acres between the Harlem and Bronx rivers to a Scandinavian by the name of Jonas Bronck, later distorted to Bronx. He was joined by other colonists from New England and during the Revolution they, too, took the side of the Tories.

It wasn't until the mid-19th century that the area attracted any appreciable number of settlers. The Irish came in after the potato famine of 1840 to help build the Harlem and Hudson River Railroads. After the German Revolution of 1848 there was an influx of German farmers. They lived in small, independent settlements until 1874 when New York City enticed Kingsbridge, West Farms, and Morrisania to become wards of the city. Twenty years later they were followed into the fold by the townships of Westchester and parts of Pelham and Eastchester. Under the Greater New York Charter of 1898 these two annexations became the borough of the Bronx.

The lower Bronx is a cluster of unkempt neighborhoods and some are among the nation's most depressed areas. Its greatest claim to fame is Yankee Stadium; since its opening in 1923 it has been the home of the American League's Yankees and, from 1956 through 1972, of the football Giants.

Near the Stadium, under the Major Deegan Expressway, you can find the Bronx Terminal Market. A few years ago, it sold only to retail stores but that's changed. In one of those interesting experiments that makes living in New York a unique experience, groups of families began trying to save money by forming their own food co-ops and sending representatives to Bronx Terminal to buy wholesale lots of meat, fruit, and vegetables. Now these amateurs-turned-professionals compete with the Grand Union and A&P buyers for the best bargains.

The upper Bronx borders wealthy Westchester county and is a relatively open area with several college campuses—notably Fordham and Manhattan Universities—surburban communities, parklands, and parkways.

Those visitors to New York who say, "It's a nice place to visit but I wouldn't want to live there," probably never have crossed over the border of Manhattan into the primitive forests of Van Cortlandt Park, nor ventured up to Pelham Bay Park's breeze-swept beaches (marred somewhat in recent years by an unsightly landfill mound growing out of a garbage dump) or across the bridge to City Island and its wide views of Long Island Sound.

The parks can be reached by subway, but the pleasantest and quickest way to go is by car. The most scenic route to Van Cortlandt Park in the northwestern part of the Bronx is along Manhattan's Henry Hudson Parkway, an expressway which skirts the Hudson River just beyond Riverside Drive, crosses over Spuyten Duyvil, and leads you right into the park.

Van Cortlandt's 1,132 acres are primarily for play and relaxation. There are hiking trails through its rugged, heavily wooded terrain, playing fields, a golf course, bridle paths, tennis courts, a small lake where you can rent a rowboat in the summer and ice-skate in the winter.

Van Cortlandt House

This was George Washington country. Van Cortlandt House, at the southwest corner of the park just off Broadway, served as the General's headquarters in 1783 just before he launched his final and successful campaign to retake New York City from the British. The house was built in 1748 by Frederick Van Cortlandt, a descendant of one of the early and influential Dutch families, who managed his estate along the lines of an independent principality. Slaves tended his livestock and crops; women spun his flax, wove it into cloth, and turned the cloth into garments. A score of skilled artisans embellished his living quarters and fashioned his furniture. He was lord of all he surveyed and his word was law. It is one of the few historic houses which remained in the hands of the same family for generations. It wasn't until 1899 that Van Cortlandt's descendants sold the estate to the city, which maintains it as a museum. (The mansion is not to be confused with Van Cortlandt Manor, at Croton-on-Hudson in Westchester County, which is also a museum.)

The mansion's unpretentious square fieldstone exterior in no way prepares the first-time visitor for the elegance of its Georgian interior. The spacious rooms are furnished with handsome English, Dutch, and Colonial pieces. Its huge fireplace is framed with blue tiles. The heart of the house, the kitchen, speaks a volume on the self-sufficient way of life that was lived here: candlemakers, spinning wheel, loom, soapmakers, hand-wrought implements, and caldrons large enough to feed fifty.

Another historic house of note in the area is the Poe Cottage, a short drive southeast at Kingsbridge Road and Grand Concourse. The little farmhouse was built in 1816 by John Wheeler and was the home of poet Edgar Allan Poe and his wife, Virginia, from 1846 to 1849. Before Virginia died here, Poe wrote some of his finest works: *The Bells, Ulalume, Eureka,* and *Annabel Lee.*

Gardens and Zoos

From Van Cortlandt Park it is about 20 minutes' drive east to Southern Boulevard and 200th Street, and the New York Botanical Garden's flower displays, which spread over 230 rolling acres of the northern half of Bronx Park. In its center is a forest primeval of hemlocks. This dense stand of trees is one of the very few virgin tracts to have survived the ax in the East.

West of Hemlock Forest is a turn-of-the-century museum building which houses an herbarium, library, auditorium, and exhibition halls.

Across from the museum is a four-acre garden with hundreds of rock-loving plants. A short stroll will bring you to the Enid A. Haupt Conservatory, renovated and reopened in 1979: an elaborate complex of greenhouses where orchids, poinsettia, and other brilliant tropical plants give New Yorkers a taste of southern climes during long winter months. Behind the Conservatory, you'll come upon the vast Rose Garden, where several thousand plantings of more than 160 rose varieties are displayed in formal beds and country-style clusters.

The Bronx Zoo—the southern half of Bronx Park, at Fordham Road and Bronx River Parkway—is built with moats rather than iron bars to give the illusion of a walk through the African Veldt while elephants, deer, lions, ostriches, peacocks, and other wildlife roam around at will. The 252-acre zoo is one of America's largest, and, for the foot-weary, there's an aerial tramway that passes directly over the African Plains, the Great Apes House, and Jungle World, as well as a tractor train and monorail.

But don't forget to get off and explore the windowless World of Darkness with its nocturnal and cave-dwelling inhabitants. Another outstanding addition is the World of Birds, a series of oval aviaries connected by ramps. These contain, for example, a spectacular rain forest with a hundred species that are common to such environments in the New World. There is a forty-foot waterfall and rainstorms are simulated from time to time. There are exhibits of swamp birds, species from arid scrublands and African jungles. In The Treetops, five regional groupings are viewable only from above. Explanatory placards and drawings by artist Carlene Meeker show other facets of this World, such as the diets of various birds.

The children's zoo, the first in the country, has pigs, sheep, goats, a working beehive, and a chicken hatchery. Adults may enter only if accompanied by a child. There are pony rides, and for the more adventurous, there are even camels and llamas to ride. An outdoor restaurant and a dozen refreshment stands are spotted around the grounds.

Pelham Bay Park, a 2,000-acre jagged peninsula which juts into Long Island Sound, was part of the original 9,000-acre tract bought by English colonist Thomas Pell in 1654. Its rocky, rolling, wooded terrain is laced with bridle paths, picnic grounds, playfields, and the Pelham and Split Rock golf courses. On the sandy shores of the Sound is Orchard Beach, where you can rent bathing suits, towels, and a locker, roam the one mile crescent-shaped beach, picnic on 140 acres, visit the historic 215-acre

Hunter and Twin Island Sites, or play paddleball or handball on the extensive recreational area fields. There are fishing facilities, too. Weekends bring out hordes of city dwellers, so it would be best to plan your excursion for a weekday.

The Bartow Mansion in the park is worth a visit. The handsome Greek Revival stone house was built in 1836, and today is the headquarters of the International Garden Club as well as a museum and landscape gardening exhibit.

A causeway connects the park with City Island, a busy center of boat building, rope and sail making, and pleasure boating. Fish fresh from the sea are served at the bustling waterside restaurants where you can watch sailboats get under way, their mainsails billowing before the wind as they head out to Long Island Sound.

In the beautiful residential section of Riverdale, in the West Bronx along the Hudson, is Wave Hill, at West 249th Street, whose spacious grounds—open to the public—include formal gardens, greenhouses, a herb garden, a beautiful and historic mansion house—Mark Twain, Theodore Roosevelt, and Arturo Toscanini have lived there—and a spectacular view of the Hudson and the Palisades.

Winding Up

New York is like a giant pastry shop. It offers hundreds of delectable delights, but they cannot be consumed all at once. One must return time and again to savor a dozen or so favorite selections each visit. Nor can each one be described in a guide if it is to be of a manageable size. These have been some of New York's pièces de résistance. You'll find many more listed in the New York City *Practical Information* section, which follows.

SIGHTSEEING CHECKLIST. No matter how you come to New York City, or how many times you've been here, your state of mind will determine the best approach for exploring the Big Apple. It is a world unto itself, and an incredible world at that. Even a recent Gallup Poll of typical American travelers attested to the fact that New York is the nation's "top city," and is considered the "most interesting" city in the U.S. with the "best food" and the "best-looking women." Those quotes cover a lot of ground, territory we'll cover in the following pages with historical background and suggested walking tours. However, before we get into helpful hints about how to get around the city, and what to look for, here is New York City's "Top Attractions Checklist" as compiled by the New York Convention and Visitors Bureau. We'll go into details later on, but for starters, this is the Bureau's list of must-sees:

(1) **The Statue of Liberty,** with an observation platform 22 stories above Liberty Island, offering a superb view of New York's bustling harbor. Don't miss the fascinating Museum of Immigration in the statue's base. Nearby is Ellis Island (open for tours, spring through fall) where millions of immigrants were processed.

(2) **The Empire State Building,** 1,472 feet high, is over 50 years old, but the sleek skyscraper of steel, limestone, and aluminum is as popular as ever. Each year millions of visitors enjoy the view from observation decks on the 86th and 102nd floors.

(3) **Rockefeller Center** is a city within a city, where you can ice-skate in winter and dine outdoors in summer. This midtown Manhattan landmark offers a superb guided tour to its varied delights. Nearby is the beautifully restored Radio City Music Hall Entertainment Center, where you can take in a musical extravaganza, Rockettes and all, in the world's biggest (6,000-seat) theater, a 1930s Art Deco marvel. A separate behind-the-scenes tour is available here, too. Also nearby, in the Center's McGraw-Hill Building, is a theater showing *The New York Experience,* a multimedia, multisensory show that helps put New York City into perspective.

(4) **Lincoln Center** is a vast performing-arts complex at 65th Street and Broadway that offers opera, symphony, dance, theater, films, a library—and a guided tour of the beautiful buildings that house them. From the Chagalls at the Metropolitan Opera House and the Henry Moore statuary seemingly climbing out of the reflecting pool outside the library to the Vivian Beaumont and Mitzi Newhouse Theaters, it is nothing short of a modern-day Acropolis minus the hills.

(5) **The World Trade Center** with its twin towers—each 110 stories tall—stands like a pair of soaring sentinels guarding New York's Harbor. On the rooftop "promenade" of the South Tower, you stand on the world's highest open-air observation deck (1,377 feet). On the top of the North Tower you can drink or dine at the elegant Windows on the World, the restaurant complex that offers New York's most spectacular view (although, not, alas, the city's most spectacular food).

(6) **The United Nations** offers new sights, services, and activities for visitors taking in the imposing glass building seemingly rising out of the East River. The official meetings are open to the public, there is a one-hour guided tour (even all-day tours for small groups) and several more interesting stop-off points, including the post office, gift shops, restaurants, and gardens.

(7) **New York's neighborhoods:** Chinatown, Little Italy, Yorkville (German, Middle European), Lower Second Ave. (Middle European, Hispanic, Bohemian), Greenwich Village, SoHo (artists), the Upper East Side, the Upper West Side, Brooklyn Heights, not to mention the Russian community in Brooklyn's Brighton Beach, the Greeks in Astoria, Queens, and many more we don't have space to mention.

New York City can be understood only as a collection of neighborhoods; you can literally tour the world here. One walking tour we recommend for this purpose would start at the restored Federal-period houses at Harrison St. off the old West Side Highway in TriBeCa. Proceed through TriBeCa and over to Chinatown, then up Mulberry St. through Chinatown and across Canal St. (passing through the Kojak-type court-and-prison section before Chinatown), and into Little Italy north of Canal. At Grand St. turn west (left) and go through Broadway's discount shops and garment-manufacturing lofts to West Broadway. Then up West Broadway through the heart of the SoHo art district and across Houston Street into Greenwich Village.

The Village itself is many neighborhoods, as you will see if you start from the west end of Christopher Street and stroll east, weaving north and south of the 8th St.–St. Mark's Pl. axis, ending at the Romanian delicatessens at lower Second and First aves. But for seeing all the most interesting neighborhoods, the first commandment is: Walk.

(8) The Great Museums: The Metropolitan Museum of Art and the Museum of Modern Art, the Frick Collection, the American Museum of Natural History, the Museum of the American Indian, the Museum of the City of New York, the New-York Historical Society, the Cooper-Hewitt, the Guggenheim, the Whitney, and the hundreds of galleries that make New York City the world's undisputed art center.

(9) Sports: The full gamut of sporting events can be observed at Madison Square Garden, Shea and Yankee Stadiums, the Flushing Meadows and Forest Hills tennis complexes, and the Belmont, Aqueduct, Roosevelt, and Yonkers racetracks. Baseball, boxing, hockey, soccer, basketball, tennis, track and field, horseracing—you name your game, New York City plays it.

(10) Times Square is the glittering "Great White Way" with its theaters, movie houses, skyscrapers, and shops. If you can see only one play or one musical your visit will be greatly enhanced.

(11) Houses of Worship offering food for the soul and impressive works of art and architecture include such landmarks as St. Patrick's Cathedral, the Cathedral of St. John the Divine (the world's largest Gothic cathedral), Temple Emanu-El, Riverside Church, Trinity Church and St. Paul's Chapel, and more than 2,500 other religious edifices.

(12) New York and American Stock Exchanges offer free tours during trading hours in the nation's marketplaces—the money capitals of the world. But beware of bulls and bears.

(13) South Street Seaport, an indoor-outdoor "museum" consisting of several blocks and three piers stretching along the East River waterfront at Fulton Street, near the site of the famous fishmarket. The entire area is being restored to its original appearance, as it was when South Street was one of the world's great ports for sailing ships. Among the attractions: a collection of historic ships, an old printing shop, a model-ships museum, the Fulton Market, the Titanic Memorial Lighthouse, and some of the best seafood restaurants in town.

That's a baker's dozen sightseeing attractions to give you something to think about while you're deciding where to eat, shop, stay, or be entertained. One way—perhaps the easiest and most relaxing way—to get your bearings is to take a sightseeing bus tour or a Circle Line three-hour sightseeing cruise around the island of Manhattan. Or maybe even a sightseeing helicopter trip. How to find these places, sights and sites? When in doubt, write or stop by the New York Convention and Visitors' Bureau, 2 Columbus Circle (58th St. and Eighth Ave.), New York, NY 10019. Or call 397–8222. They will even supply you with free folders on all the city's boroughs. And, of course, read on.

Outside the City

Fire Island. From Memorial Day to late September, especially on weekends, the Fire Island beaches and beach communities are home for a good portion of New York City's business and creative people and journalists. Many of the summer rentals are taken by groups of singles or young married people. The ferry ride over and back—there is no other way to reach Fire Island proper than by water—is part of the experience.

The Hamptons. Farther out than Fire Island, the Hamptons have become widely popular only in recent years, drawing off some of what used to be the summer Fire Island regulars. Beaches in the Hamptons tend to be less accessible than on Fire Island, where all the oceanside beaches are open to everyone, but the Hamptons seem to have a higher social cachet—or so the Hamptons regulars believe.

Sleepy Hollow, below Tarrytown in the Hudson Valley, was the estate of Washington Irving.

Hyde Park, near Poughkeepsie in the Hudson Valley, was the home of Franklin Delano Roosevelt and is now a National Shrine. The house and library are open to the public.

West Point, on the west bank of the Hudson River, is open to the public, who can enjoy its museums, battle monuments, and other sights—including frequent parades.

Woodstock, New York, is the center of an art colony in the Catskill Mountains.

Western Connecticut and the Berkshire Mountains provide a taste of New England scenery and town life close to New York City. The best time to go is in October, when the foliage turns.

Princeton University, an hour by bus, train, or car from the city, is a peaceful gothic-style oasis compared with hectic Manhattan. Try to see the Graduate School and the Institute for Advanced Studies there.

The Jersey Shore is prime for fishing and the summer beach life.

Atlantic City, where you'll find the only legalized gambling on the East Coast and the attendant entertainment, is an interesting side trip from New York City, one that can be combined with sunning on the beach in season.

Other Suggestions

Check with your travel agent (no fee to you in most cases) for information on other ways to see the city and extend your trip's potential. For example, there are special weekend packages at most of the better Manhattan hotels that, for relatively low rates, offer free drinks, meals, and maybe entertainment (plays or concerts or nightclubs) as part of the rate. For another example: Visit the city tied in with—to take one possibility—a one-day cruise out of Manhattan with the Holland-American Line, or a long-weekend cruise to the Bahamas, possibly even taking along your car. The possibilities are seemingly endless, and a travel agent will be up on the latest offers.

PRACTICAL INFORMATION
FOR
NEW YORK CITY

HOW TO GET THERE. By air: Virtually every major (and most minor) airline serves New York City. The three largest airports serving the city are *John F. Kennedy,* in southeastern Queens; *La Guardia,* in northern Queens; and *Newark,* in nearby New Jersey. A few private flights come in at *Teterboro,* in northeastern New Jersey. This choice of where your flight lands may be relevant, depending on where you are planning to stay in the metropolitan area. (For airport transportation, see *Getting Around,* below.)

By bus: The newly modernized Port Authority Building (8th Ave. at 41st St., 564–8484, Manhattan) is a fantastically busy place, with over 200 platforms where commuter and transcontinental buses alike load and unload. A few of the individual carriers who serve the region around New York City are: *Asbury Park-New York Transit; Hudson Transit; Red and Tan Lines; Surburban Transit; Community Transit; DeCamp, and New Jersey Transit.* These all run from New Jersey.

From the Hudson Valley, try *Pine Hill, Leprechaun,* or *Rockland Coaches.* The Berkshire area is connected to New York City by *Bonanza Bus Lines,* the Poconos by *Martz Trailways.* Of course, the busing giants, *Greyhound* and *Trailways,* have service to and from New York City from and to every region of the United States. Their passenger platforms are below street level in the terminal; those of the smaller lines are on the upper stories.

By car: The *Lincoln Tunnel* from New Jersey, and the *Midtown Tunnel* and *Queensboro Bridge* from Long Island, are the most direct arteries to mid-Manhattan. The *Holland Tunnel* from New Jersey, and the *Brooklyn-Battery Tunnel* from Brooklyn, reach lower Manhattan. The *George Washington Bridge,* from New Jersey, and the *Triborough Bridge,* from Queens and the Bronx, give access to upper Manhattan.

The *Brooklyn-Queens Expressway,* from Queens and Long Island, and the *Verrazano-Narrows Bridge,* from Staten Island, will get you to Brooklyn. The expressway, of course, continues on through western Queens, which may also be reached from the north via the *Triborough Bridge.*

From upstate New York and New England, the city is accessible via many highways, both free and toll. The *New England Thruway* leads to the Bruckner Traffic Circle in the east Bronx, from which you may go to Queens *(Bronx, Whitestone,* or *Throgs Neck bridges),* Manhattan *(Bruckner Expressway* and *Triborough Bridge)* or the west Bronx and Manhattan *(Cross-Bronx Expressway).* The *New York (Dewey) Thruway* extends via the *Major Deegan Expressway* (both I–87) to the south Bronx and Triborough Bridge. The bridge gives access to both Queens *(Grand Central Parkway)* and Manhattan *(Franklin D. Roosevelt Drive).*

By train: Long-distance *Amtrak* routes reach New York from Chicago and the West, Washington, Florida and the South, plus Boston, Montreal, and Toronto, and all terminate in the city at either Grand Central Terminal (42nd to 44th Sts. on Park Ave.) or Penn Station (31st to 33rd Sts., 7th to 8th Aves., 212–736–4545). Suburban lines stretch about 75 to 100 miles north (Metro-North's Hudson, Harlem and New Haven Lines, 212–532–4900) and east (Long Island Railroad 718–454–5477). Both stations are quite good at giving out information; both have uncomfortable waiting areas. *PATH Train Lines,* 212–466–7649, service Jersey City, Newark, and Hoboken into Manhattan, terminating at the World Trade Center or Penn Station. All the commuter lines are notorious for their erratic service, lack of punctuality, and frequent equipment failure.

TELEPHONES. The area code for Manhattan and the Bronx is 212; 718 for Brooklyn, Queens, and Staten Island. To get directory assistance, dial the proper area code (if other than the one from which you are calling) plus 555–1212. When dialing a number in another area code, the full number must be preceded by a 1. Pay telephones cost 25 cents for the first three minutes of a local call—though calling within the five boroughs is not always local; if this is the case you will be asked for an additional deposit.

HOTELS AND MOTELS. Manhattan is an island literally filled with hotels, or so it seems when a visitor is trying to make up his or her mind where to stay. From the chic super-deluxe establishments to the modest, more reasonably priced ones, there is an incredibly wide range of accommodations available.

Those accustomed to the hotel situation in almost all other parts of the United States may be taken aback by (1) the paucity of motels in the city and (2) the lack of or limited parking areas at those that do exist. Motels by design were intended for motorists, and most everywhere but New York you can park in front of your motel room or in an open lot nearby. That is rarely the case in Manhattan, where space is at such a premium that monthly parking spots in some neighborhoods cost in excess of $300—the equivalent of rent for a studio or one-bedroom apartment in some other parts of the country.

Nor will you find the simple, inexpensive roadside stopover motels that are otherwise the norm in the U.S.—the $19.95 to $29.95 double rooms complete with color TV, outdoor pool, etc. In other cities, or on the road, you can usually pull into one of these places in late afternoon and get a room for the night. As in so many other things, Manhattan is the exception. As for room rates, the $19.95 to $29.95 range is about what you'd pay for a single at the YMCA or YWCA; and no matter how much or how little you anticipate paying, it is always best to have a reservation ahead. That way you're assured of a room awaiting you upon arrival and that the rate will be confirmed. While you might be lucky once hitting town with no reservation and finding a suitable room, you might just as easily arrive simultaneously with five or six mammoth conventions—with not a room to be had.

Another important suggestion in selecting a hotel or motel to suit your needs: If you have the luxury of planning ahead, consult a travel agent or, if you can get a copy ahead of time, the Sunday *New York Times* Travel section. We've listed many hotels for you to choose from, including the range of rates for a *double* room—i.e., for two persons. Many of these hotels, however, offer special packages for visitors—particularly for non-expense-account sightseers. Most of these deals are built around weekend stays at reduced rates (when there are fewer businesspeople in town) and often include tickets to top Broadway shows, a bus tour, a bottle of wine or champagne on arrival, Sunday brunch (and the *Times*—a tradition among New Yorkers themselves) or other similar amenities.

Even if you have to pay a higher rate during the week, these weekend packages are definitely worth your consideration. In comparing them, however, be aware that in order to bring the numbers down to eye-catching appeal, some advertise the rate per person, based on double occupancy. Others give you the full weekend rate, all inclusive. Some are also available for one night, while others require longer stays. In other words, read the fine print carefully.

Because of the unique nature and diversity of New York City hotels and motels, we have tried to add a little extra detail to our general categories, and advise you to give consideration to geographic location as well as price and appointments. Getting around the city is time-consuming and expensive; thus a few extra dollars per night to be in the area in which you plan to spend most of your time (the theater district, lower Manhattan, the upper East Side, etc.) are probably well spent.

We've categorized our selection (it is only a selection) of New York's hotels based on price. Exact prices are generally misleading; most major properties change their room rates every eight to 12 months. What we've done is to group some of the city's best lodgings into five price categories: *Super Deluxe* (over $250 per night), *Deluxe* ($200 – $250), *First Class* ($150 – $200), *Exceptional Value* (hotels priced between *First Class* and *Budget* that offer above-average accommodations and amenities for the money), and *Budget* (under $150). In each case, the price range applies to a **quality double room** for two people. It is important to remember that there is an occupancy tax ($2 per room) and, as of this writing, a 13¼% city and state sales tax. For the convenience of visitors in transit, we've also included a short section on airport hotels.

Since high prices are not always perfect indicators of impeccable service, designer decor, or delicious cuisine, our brief write-ups indicate shortcomings as well as outstanding features. Common sense can also help you to figure out where your expectations would be best fulfilled. For example, it would be unwise to anticipate the same level of service from a top-flight convention hotel like The Marriott Marquis and a smaller luxury property like The Mayfair Regent, even though both appear in the *Deluxe* section of this chapter. On the other hand, if bright lights, lots of lobby activity and a central location is your idea of a perfect New York hotel experience, then you might well be disappointed with the city's more residential-style lodgings, no matter how elegant.

Speaking of residential, those popular suite-style hotels, many of which contain full kitchen units, are finally catching on. We've included both new and already established properties in our *Exceptional Value* section. As for those on rock-bottom budgets, we strongly suggest telephoning the YMCA, YWCA, and various youth-hostel organizations (preferably before your arrival), or contacting local colleges and universities, many of which have available dormitory space during the summer months. As with hotels, the further in advance you can make your reservation, the more likely you'll get the best available accommodation.

As we've already said, what follows is only a selection. There are, to be sure, many more hotels to be found around this vast city, especially in the *Budget* category. However, we've only listed lodgings that are in safe parts of town. If we wouldn't feel comfortable leaving or returning after dark, then you won't find it within these pages.

Super Deluxe

The Carlyle. 35 E. 76th St.; 744–1600. Located in one of New York's poshest residential areas, it is also handy to two of the city's best museums—the Metropolitan and the Whitney. All rooms are air-conditioned, suites have a pantry with refrigerator and some suites have private terraces and/or wood-burning fireplaces. *Café Carlyle* offers elegant dining, and the *Bemelman's Bar* is decorated with murals by that whimsical artist himself. Bobby Short's piano often echoes in the Vertès-decorated Café Carlyle. There are 175 available rooms (the best are for full-time residents). Garage facilities.

Grand Bay Hotel at Equitable Center. 152 W. 51st St.; 765–1900. The old Taft Hotel has recently been transformed into one of New York's most exciting luxury cooperative apartment and hotel complexes. The Grand Bay's guest rooms are among the most beautifully appointed in the city (all the baths feature deep tubs, TVs, and bidets). The hotel features *Bellini,* Harry Cipriani's chic Italian restaurant. This is the only luxury hotel in the city that's within easy walking distance of the theater district. Guests can use Equitable's corporate health club, too. 178 rooms.

Maxim's. 700 Fifth Ave. at 55th St.; 247–2200. The city's newest luxury hotel with a delightfully French accent has finally opened on the site of the former Gotham. Rooms and public areas are filled with striking touches of art nouveau and rich fabrications. Bathrooms are outstanding (many have bidets) and the cuisine at the *Adrienne Restaurant* is winning compliments. The rooftop health and swim club was scheduled to open by mid-1988. 250 rooms and suites.

Park Lane. 36 Central Park South; 371–4000. A relatively new addition to the list of classic hotels on the southern boundary of Central Park, and one that quickly established itself as ranking right alongside them for dignity and service. There are views of the park, the skyline and, if you're high enough, the Hudson and East Rivers; a rooftop dining room; and a staff conversant in several languages. A favorite especially among knowledgeable foreign visitors. 640 rooms.

Parker-Meridien New York. 118 W. 57th St.; 245–5000. New and big (700 rooms), the Meridien is operated by Air France's hotel subsidiary. Unique features include a health club, rooftop pool, squash courts, jogging track, and that it is in walking distance from Carnegie Hall and the Russian Tea Room. The in-house restaurant *Maurice* is one of the city's most elegant French dining rooms, serving outstanding nouvelle cuisine. Very formal and very expensive.

Pierre. 61st St. & Fifth Ave., opposite Central Park; 838–8000. This fine hotel, which opened in 1930, is primarily a residential hotel (cooperative apartments) and more than half of its 633 rooms are permanently occupied. Those which are not are available to transients, and these guests often occupy the highest echelons of society and celebrity. The *Cafe Pierre* has garnered critical acclaim for its stylish cuisine; tea in the *Rotunda* is a romantic treat.

Hôtel Plaza Athénée. 37 E. 64th St., near Madison Ave.; 838–3110. This "sister" hotel to the Paris original, also run by Trust House Forte, is definitely elegant, but not as polished or comfortable as it should be for the money. Rooms are small, though opulent, and the service can be lax. However, lunch or dinner in the *Le Regence* dining room can be a transporting experience. Special weekend rates available. 160 rooms.

Stanhope. Fifth Ave. at 81st St.; 288–5800. Its atmosphere is particularly gracious, and above all it features classic service. Free Rolls-Royce shuttle service to 50th St. in the morning. Fine cuisine, elegant atmosphere in the main dining room and lobby tea lounge. And on a summer Sunday, having brunch outside at *The Terrace* as you watch the crowds amble to the Met is an experience you'll long remember. 275 rooms. (Note: At press time, the hotel was involved in a possible change of ownership, which may affect services.)

Vista International. 3 World Trade Center; 938–9100. Vista International's first property in the Continental U.S. is a flagship hotel in every sense. Located within walking distance of Wall Street and the entire southern tip of Manhattan's financial district, Vista is a sparklingly alive edifice with beautiful public areas, including the *Tall Ships* bar, the outstanding and friendly-but-formal *American Harvest* restaurant, and the less imposing but equally satisfying *Greenhouse.* A fitness center and pool, racquetball court, full range of business services, free transportation to the theater district every evening, and a variety of special weekend packages are some of the ways this unusual hotel goes about making its out-of-the-way location an asset. The only serious drawback is that rooms and hallways show more wear and tear than they should at these prices. 825 rooms.

Deluxe

Algonquin Hotel. 59 W. 44th St.; 840–6800. Long a favorite for its warm hospitality and literary history (its bar—and drinks are also served in the comfortable lobby lounge—and restaurant continue to be the watering hole and outpost of the *New Yorker* magazine staff), the Algonquin prides itself on the traditions of Europe's finest family-owned hotels. The modern comforts are here, the location absolutely perfect whatever your purpose in town, and the rates surprisingly reasonable. *The Oak Room* is still one of the city's most popular supper clubs, attracting top cabaret names like Julie Wilson and Michael Feinstein. 165 rooms.

Drake Swissôtel. 440 Park Ave.; 421–0900. The Drake underwent a major modernization and restoration program in 1987, and the rejuvenation has been effective and tasteful. In addition to having pleasant surroundings the hotel is well located, with telephone and loudspeaker in each of the new bathrooms. There is also a lobby lounge, full concierge service and the *Lafayette Restaurant.* 640 rooms. 1,347 rooms.

The Essex House. 160 Central Park South; 247–0300. Park Avenue has the reputation but Central Park South has the view, and is probably as attractive a location as can be found in the city. With 700 available rooms, the Essex House is one of the largest along this mini-hotel row, but it still manages to provide personal service. For an unusual dining experience, try the new *Ben Kay* restaurant featuring Japanese dishes and imported seafood, flown over regularly for this Nikko-owned property.

Grand Hyatt New York. Park Ave. & 42nd St.; 883–1234. On the site of the old Commodore Hotel right next to Grand Central Station. This renovated masterpiece, done with lavish amounts of brass, glass, chrome and marble, features *nouvelle cuisine* at *Trumpet's* and a spectacular lounge overhanging 42nd St. Summer and weekend rates are available.

Helmsley Palace. 455 Madison Ave. at 50th St.; 888–7000. Constructed above and around the landmark Florentine Renaissance-styled Villard Mansions, originally built in 1855, the Helmsley is extravagantly rich-looking and in a location central to just about everything. 875 rooms. Summer rates available.

Inter-Continental New York. 111 E. 48th St.; 755–5900. (Formerly the Barclay.) Located half a block off Park Ave., one of this hotel's prime advantages is a degree of withdrawal from the bustle of the city while still being at the heart of the goings-on. This is an older, gracious hotel with pleasant, spacious atmosphere. Live birds frolic in the aviary in the lobby, restored to its original 1920s grandeur as part of a recent renovation. 686 rooms, garage facilities, and health club.

The Lowell. 28 E. 63rd St., between Madison and Park Ave.; 838–1400. This chic tiny hotel is located in one of New York's best neighborhoods. Rooms and suites are at once homey and luxurious. The staff makes you feel as though you're the only guest on the premises. Breakfast and lunch are served in the romantic *Pembroke Room.* Steak lovers will enjoy the connecting *Post House* restaurant for dinner. 60 rooms.

Marriott Marquis. 1535 Broadway, at 45th St.; 398–1900. Almost 2,000 rooms in the heart of Broadway, with a revolving restaurant and a bar with spectacular views. Mostly a convention hotel—and there are usually several going on simultaneously. Very modern, very high tech, right down to the glass elevators. Convention and weekend rates are lower.

Mayfair Regent. 610 Park Ave., at 65th St.; 288–0800. Fine, dignified hotel on one of the most elegant stretches of Manhattan Island. 200 rooms means superior personalized service. This delightful residence is home to one of the city's most elegant tea lounges and to the much-touted celebrity restaurant, *Le Cirque.*

Morgans. 237 Madison Ave.; 686–0300. One of New York's most innovative hotels. Rooms are on the small side, but stunning high-tech furnishings (baths have aluminum sinks and checkered tile walls), and extras like VCRs and tape players make this yuppie heaven. On weekends, rooms take a dramatic tumble in price and come with free passes to the Palladium disco. Not for Aunt Martha, but your favorite out-of-town trendsetter will love running into Cher or Billy Crystal in the elevator. 110 rooms.

New York Helmsley. 212 E. 42nd St.; 490–8900. Another new Helmsley hotel, close to the United Nations but catering to the executive. The New York Helmsley is sleekly modern with such unusual touches as phone extensions in the bathrooms. 790 rooms.

New York Hilton. 1335 Ave. of the Americas; 586–7000. The Hilton name is becoming synonymous with large, fancy, modern (and impersonal) hotels; this one is no exception. One of the biggest and most popular among conventioneers and tourists alike, the Hilton can offer such conveniences as extra-long beds and heated bathroom floors. Central to everything in midtown. There is also entertainment in the way of jazz combos at *Pursuit of Happiness.* 2,130 rooms.

Omni Berkshire Place. 21 E. 52nd St.; 753–5800. Since it was refurbished in 1979, the Berkshire Place has become a most popular haunt, largely because of the *Rendezvous,* an attractive bar and restaurant where the food is seriously lacking in distinction and highly overpriced, and the bright gardenlike atrium in the foyer. The rooms are simple and modern, the ambience young-and-on-the-go but with good attention to detail in the service. 420 rooms.

The Plaza. Fifth Ave. & 59th St.; 759–3000. The grandest hotel in the city (now owned by Donald Trump) has been on a major campaign to regain all its former glory, remodeling and touching up its public areas and redecorating rooms floor by floor. And even as the renovations have gone on, The Plaza has remained the most imposing and beautiful place to stay in New York. With Central Park on one side, and a small plaza complete with graceful fountain in front, this is New York's enclave of tradition and elegance in the European manner. None of the original 1907 flavor of this hotel has been lost. The 837 rooms are richly decorated, mostly in the French Provincial manner. Service is superb, the staff trained to the point of remembering guests' names—and using them. The Plaza's restaurants are famous in their own right, and include the staid *Oak Room*, the popular *Oyster Bar* (great for lunches and snacks), the *Palm Court* (where strolling musicians entertain during tea daily), and the elegant *Edwardian Room*, where you dine by candlelight and dance to live music.

Regency. Park Ave. at 61st St.; 759–4100. French tapestries, Italian marble floors, gilt mirrors, guests such as Audrey Hepburn (though the Beatles tried, they never got in), and a garage ideally suited for 140 Rolls-Royces—that's the level of elegance to be expected at the Regency. There are 400 rooms and suites, most decorated in traditional Louis XVI style. White-marble baths feature scales, deep tubs, and in some cases, TVs. Suites have small kitchenettes. The stunning *540 Park* and adjacent *Regency Lounge* now have cuisine that can match any number of New York's finer dining spots. And to work off the calories, guests can use the on-premises health club. All of this luxury can be had for less than at many other hotels in this category if you aren't tempted to spring for Prince Albert of Monaco's digs.

St. Moritz. 50 Central Park South; 755–5800. Another fine hotel on Central Park South, and although it is a little bit less expensive than the others, it doesn't sacrifice too much in the way of service or furnishings. Rooms are small but tastefully done, and the hotel is another favorite of foreign visitors. During the summer, the hotel sets up the *Café de la Paix* along the sidewalk. It may not be Paris, but the effect is still refreshing. 680 available units.

Sheraton Park Avenue. 45 Park Ave., at 37th St.; 685–7676. Located on Murray Hill and a little removed from the heart of the city, the hotel offers a calm dignity that contrasts well with the trials of city life. The hotel is used mainly by businesspeople, but its generous rooms, some with fireplaces, should appeal to other visitors. 170 rooms, parking facilities.

Sherry-Netherland. 781 Fifth Ave.; 355–2800. Though somewhat less well-known than its neighbors, the Plaza and the Pierre, the Sherry-Netherland is a distinguished hotel with an aura of grandeur all its own. The accent is unquestionably Continental. The rooms are lovely and the location chic. 375 rooms.

Tuscany. 120 E. 39th St.; 686–1600. This is a smaller luxury hotel just south of Grand Central. All of its rooms are studios, complete with service pantries and other extras, such as bathroom telephones and color televisions. The charming *Time & Again* restaurant features turn-of-the-century atmosphere and traditional cuisine with a lighter touch. 120 rooms.

Waldorf-Astoria. 301 Park Ave. at 50th St.; 355–3000. Some hotels seem to improve with age, and the Waldorf is in some ways a prime example. It is certainly the most renowned of American hotels, and the very mention of its name conjures up images of luxury. The Hilton Corporation has really spruced up the majority of its 1,900 guest rooms and baths, especially in the middle and upper price ranges. Public areas, including the Art Deco Park Avenue entrance and the famous *Peacock Alley* bar and restaurant, look equally fresh. For a real splurge, try one of the 88 exclusive Tower accommodations *(Super Deluxe)*.

Westbury. 15 E. 69th St.; 535–2000. In many ways this is one of the better hotels in the city. The neighborhood surroundings are unimpeachable (especially for high-fashion shoppers, museum buffs, and gallery browsers), and the dignified tone of the hotel is intended to complement them. The furnishings reflect a grand style and the rooms are tastefully comfortable. Farther uptown than most, this hotel's personal attention and ambience more than make up for any inconvenience. 235 rooms.

First Class

Beverly. 125 E. 50th St.; 753–2700. Transient guests are usually business types, though tourists have found it increasingly well-suited to their needs. Some of the suites have pantries and terraces. Comfortable though not distinguished. *Kenny's Steak Pub* downstairs. Excellent multilingual concierge who knows the city well. 300 rooms.

Doral Court. 130 E. 39th St.; 685–1100. Just East of the Doral Tuscany is this new Doral renovation of its former *Tower* residence. Double rooms are set up as junior suites with spacious separate sitting areas. Color schemes run to rich burgundy and bright florals. Baths are new but dull. There is a restaurant-bar complex with outdoor dining in season. 199 rooms, some with kitchenettes.

Doral Inn. 541 Lexington Ave.; 755–1200. (Formerly the Belmont Plaza.) One of several commercial hotels along Lexington in the upper 40s. There is nothing impressive about it, but it is comfortable and centrally located. Frequented by airline personnel and often the site of labor negotiations. 700 rooms.

Dorset. 30 W. 54th St.; 247–7300. One of the lesser known of NYC's top stopping places, the Dorset is a very quiet, traditional hotel adjacent to the Museum of Modern Art and the corporate headquarters for such communications conglomerates as CBS, ABC, Capitol-EMI, and MGM. 190 available rooms.

Golden Tulip Barbizon. 140 E. 63rd St.; 838–5700. Formerly a hotel for women only, the fashionably located Barbizon (right near Bloomingdale's) has reopened as a regular hotel, completely renovated and redecorated. Its 348 rooms are charming, but some might find them too cramped for comfort. Formal restaurant specializes in Dover sole.

Gramercy Park. 2 Lexington Ave.; 475–4320. Among the greatest beauties of London are its scattered parks and squares, forming oases in the city pattern. The namesake of this hotel is one of the few locations in the city that meets the London standard. The area is dignified and quiet. The hotel faces out on a small private park and is unpretentiously inviting. Yet many well-known rock groups stay here. Very comfortable bar. 500 rooms.

Halloran House. Lexington Ave. and 49th St.; 755–4000. Good central midtown location with modest accommodations—but costing considerably less than its high-powered neighbors. 650 rooms.

Lexington. 511 Lexington Ave.; 755–4400. This is a good hotel which was recently renovated. The rooms are more than adequate even if the decor is routine. There is a branch of the famous British "grazing" restaurant, *Menage a Trois,* along with a pricey Chinese eatery and a coffee shop. 800 rooms.

Kitano. 66 Park Ave. at 38th St.; 685–0022. New York's only Japanese owned and operated hotel, with half of its 80 rooms featuring Japanese decor. Good location, and a peaceful retreat, though rooms, both Oriental and traditional, are somewhat dark and a bit down-at-the-heels. Excellent and beautifully done Japanese restaurant off the lobby on the second floor.

Loew's Summit. Lexington Ave. & 51st St.; 752–7000. The Summit has been completely redone in recent years. Ultra-modern guest rooms; lobby cocktail lounge; *Maude's* turn-of-the-century restaurant; tower suites; color televisions; refrigerators; phone in bathroom. ESP (Extra Special People) floor for those who want super-deluxe special services. 770 rooms, garage.

Mayflower. 15 Central Park West, at 61st St.; 265–0060. Unpretentious but most accommodating, this is the type of hotel New Yorkers wish they knew about to recommend for visiting friends. The views of Central Park are as good as from the south, and the feeling is simple friendliness. Close to Lincoln Center and Carnegie Hall but convenient via the Columbus Circle bus and train stations to just about everything. 240 available rooms.

Milford Plaza. 270 W. 45th St.; 869–3600. In the heart of the theater district; package deals often run half the official rate. Very popular with tourist groups.

New York Penta. 401 Seventh Ave., at 33rd St.; 736–5000. This is a huge (1,700 rooms), busy hotel directly across from Penn Station and Madison Square Garden and practically in the heart of the garment center. Very popular among businesspeople trying to get in and out of the city quickly, and among those coming into town for concerts, sporting events, or trade shows being held at the Garden. The rooms are unspectacular but comfortable.

Novotel. 226 W 52nd St.; 315–0100. At the northern boundary of the Great White Way, and perfect if you're dividing your time between Broadway and Carnegie Hall. Also central for midtown Fifth Avenue shopping. The real highlight, though, is a wine bar overlooking the neon nights of Broadway. Weekend and "getaway" packages trim even the usual rates, which are relatively low for the area and level of accommodation. 470 rooms.

Omni Park Central. Seventh Ave. & 56th St.; 247–8000. Standing in the lobby here is something akin to trying to meet somebody at the information booth in Penn Station. Tours are constantly arriving and leaving, the people who work at the hotel are rarely cognizant of which are which or who's who. Upstairs is as quiet as being in midtown ever gets and the rooms are attractive—some even luxurious. If you can get by without much in the way of service you'll be fine. 1,600 rooms.

Sheraton Centre. 811 Seventh Ave. between 52nd & 53rd Sts.; 581–1000. Formerly the Americana. The new owners have done more than refurbish—they've essentially redesigned the lower public floors and meeting rooms in order to make them more attractive and more practical. With 50 floors, the Sheraton Centre lacks warmth and the rooms tend to be small, but many opt for it simply because it is situated so close to the theater district. There are five restaurants, including a disco.

Sheraton City Squire. 790 Seventh Ave.; 581–3300. In recent years a number of motels have been built in the city, mainly on the West Side. They are uniformly modern and attractive. The City Squire is one of the better ones, and closer to the city's activities than most. An indoor swimming pool is also open to the public for a fee. 700 rooms.

Southgate Towers. 371 Seventh Ave.; 563–1800. Opposite Penn Station on 31st St., this large hotel is somewhat removed from the main attractions and tends to attract people doing business in the garment center directly to the south. Accommodations are suitable to most ordinary demands. 1,200 rooms, garage facilities.

Warwick. 65 W. 54th St.; 247–2700. The harried pace and uninspired lobby are misleading here. Once upstairs the rooms bespeak a simple, straightforward elegance. The hotel attracts people in the communications, advertising, recording, and fashion industries, but it has all that is necessary to appeal to the average appreciative visitor. The rooms are large and generally handsome. *Sir Walter's Restaurant* has long been a favorite of show people. 500 rooms.

Exceptional Value for the Money

Beekman Tower. 3 Mitchell Pl. (First Ave. at 49th St.); 355–7300. The Beekman is a small gem of a hotel. Subdued elegance. All rooms—whether studios or one- or two-bedroom suites—include kitchens and dining areas. Across from the United Nations and backing onto one of the loveliest little streets full of private houses in the city, the rates are surprisingly reasonable weekdays, with half-price packages often available for weekends (which can include Sunday nights, unlike most such offers). No room service, but the rooftop bar is romantic, and the new *Coq d'Or* restaurant has already received two stars from the *New York Times* for its superb cuisine and well-priced (as well as well-chosen) wine list. 157 rooms.

Dumont Plaza. 150 E. 34th St.; 481–7600. This new all-suite hotel looks more like a deluxe apartment house. Its 250 suites come with a complete kitchen area (some with dishwashers), although there is a Chinese restaurant on the premises. Furnishings are generally nicer than those found in more expensive "convention" hotels. This is one of the few high-quality, reasonably priced options on a direct bus route to the Javits Convention Center. Full-time concierge and health club. Near to Fifth Ave. shopping.

Élysée. 60 E. 54th St.; 753–1066. This small hotel is elegantly tucked away between Madison and Park Avenues on 54th St. Its size permits the management to extend more than token service. Some individuality is maintained by assigning you a room having a name as well as a number, and the decor of each room varies. Among the suprising amenities (for the price) are VCRs. We've seen far less gracious living at far higher prices. A new formal restaurant should be open by early 1989. 110 units.

The Helmsley Windsor. 100 W. 58th St.; 265–2100. We think that rooms at this reasonably priced, full-service hotel are at least as attractive as the less-expensive ones at some *Deluxe* or even *Super Deluxe* establishments. Traditional decor, more than adequate baths (with amenities), and a great location for exploring both the East and West sides of town make The Windsor a great value. No restaurant, but otherwise everything you would expect of a top-of-the-line first-class lodging. Close to the Coliseum, Carnegie Hall, and Fifth Ave. 300 rooms.

The Roger Smith Winthrop. 501 Lexington Ave.; 755–1400. Don't let the humble entrance fool you. The rooms and suites are generous in size, tasteful in decor (even a few canopy beds), and extremely fair in price. As of this writing, the lobby should be redecorated too. A better buy than many of its neighbors, the hotel rate includes Continental breakfast. 200 rooms.

San Carlos. 150 E. 50th St.; 755–1800. A small, friendly hotel with pleasant, modern rooms that are at least as good as some of its grander neighbors. Women on business will appreciate the extra security measures taken by the caring staff. Most rooms and suites contain kitchenettes. No room service, but a full breakfast can be ordered in the morning. Good Japanese restaurant on premises. 143 rooms.

Budget

Bedford. 118 E. 40th St.; 697–4800. A small, almost inconspicuous hotel two blocks south of Grand Central, the Bedford offers pleasant rooms, all with serving pantries. It attracts mostly businesspeople. 145 rooms.

Best Western Skyline Motor Inn. 725 Tenth Ave. at 50th St.; 586–3400. One of the first real "motels" built in New York. Quite far west but comfortable and within walking distance to most theaters. That walk late at night, however, is not suggested. Indoor pool, free parking.

Blackstone. 50 E. 58th St.; 355–4200. A good midtown address, convenient to the best of the city's shops, theaters, and movies. 200 rooms.

Century Paramount. 235 W. 46th St.; 764–5500. This economical old-timer is about to get a smartening up from the same people who own Morgans. Until it does, you can count on basic but clean rooms and baths, a well-lit lively lobby, and a reliable coffee shop and bar. The entire hotel should soon become a sleek born-again Broadway baby. Ask for the Palladium disco package for even lower prices on all days. 600 rooms.

Chelsea. 222 W. 23rd St.; 243–3700. The Chelsea probably deserves a category unto itself—a study in contradictions, and totally unique among New York hotels. It was the first hotel in the city designated a historic and architectural landmark. It has a long history of sheltering creative talent—including the likes of Mark Twain, Thomas Wolfe, Dylan Thomas, Brendan Behan, Arthur Miller, Virgil Thomson, Ben Shahn, and Larry Rivers, to name a few. Some of the Chelsea's history is described in our *Walking Tours* section, and it is worth a brief visit even if you stay elsewhere. Today it is, shall we say, funky, attracting many rock stars who use it as home base when in New York. It is not for everyone. 400 rooms.

Days Inn. 440 W. 57th St., between Ninth and Tenth aves.; 581–8100. A bit off the beaten track, but the location avoids a lot of traffic for those arriving via the Jersey approaches to the city. Decor and room appointments conform to the standards of the chain. Rooftop pool and kennel. 600 rooms.

Hotel Edison. 46–47th sts., west of Broadway; 840–5000. This hotel is popular with tour groups and budget-minded theater lovers. Recently refurbished restaurants and rooms are nothing special, but perfectly respectable. Some lovely original Art Deco embellishments in the lobby. Part of *The Godfather* was shot here. 1,000 rooms.

Empire. 44 W. 63rd St. at Broadway; 265–7400. Located opposite Lincoln Center, you'd expect this once-flourishing hotel to be ritzy to the hilt. It is not. It is simple and modestly comfortable, popular for organized tours and among visiting musicians and performers. Weekly rates available. 600 rooms.

Excelsior. 45 W. 81st St.; 362–9200. Out of the way but convenient to bus and subway transportation. Far from fancy, but offers basic accommodations. 300 rooms.

Howard Johnson's Motor Lodge. Eighth Ave. between 51st and 52nd sts.; 581–4100. Right in the heart of the theater district and a few blocks from "Restaurant Row." Color televisions, radio, in-room movies. Free guest parking. Cocktail lounge and restaurant. 300 rooms.

Mansfield. 12 W. 44th St.; 944–6050. The location is good, just off Fifth Ave., and not far from Times Square. The Harvard and Princeton clubs are virtually next door. There are no pretensions and the quarters are not for the fussy. The staff is particularly good for a hotel in this price range. 200 rooms.

Murray Hill. 42 W. 35th St.; 947–0200. A small hotel offering quiet in a busy neighborhood. Pleasant, large rooms. Near *Altman's* and *Lord & Taylor,* but not in the Murray Hill district itself. 140 rooms.

Ramada Inn–Midtown. 790 Eighth Ave., between 48th & 49th Sts.; 581–7000. Center of the theater district. Color televisions, radio, in-room movies. Free guest parking. Cocktail lounge and rooftop restaurant. Rooftop pool (seasonal). 370 rooms.

Shoreham. 33 W. 55th St.; 247–6700. A small hotel just off Fifth Ave., the Shoreham presents a dignified appearance and is splendidly located for shopping activities, the Museum of Modern Art, and Broadway. The rooms are modest but clean and each has its own pantry. 150 rooms.

Travel Inn Motor Hotel. 515 W. 42nd St.; 695–7171. Almost beside the Manhattan-side Lincoln Tunnel exit, the location is particularly convenient for those entering the city from the west. Off the mainstream but convenient to the 42nd St. crosstown bus. Pool. Parking. 250 rooms.

Tudor. 304 E. 42nd St.; 986–8800. On the East Side of the city and a part of the Tudor City apartment complex, this hotel is near the UN and not far from Grand Central. The area is pleasant, quiet, and refined, and so are the accommodations, which have been recently refurbished. 475 rooms.

Wales. 1295 Madison Ave.; 876–6000. The location on E. 92nd St. places guests in the heart of one of NYC's best neighborhoods, and close to the Metropolitan Museum of Art—though it is a mite uptown from the heart of the city. 100 clean and functional rooms, some with views of Central Park.

Wellington. 871 Seventh Ave.; 247–3900. Convenient to Carnegie Hall, the Coliseum, Broadway, and the Stage Deli. The rooms are contemporary but the hotel rundown. Provides most of the services of more expensive establishments to compensate. Used often by airline personnel. 700 rooms.

Hotel Wentworth. 59 W. 46th St.; 719–2300. Located on a street that could be known as "Little Brazil," this small but perfectly adequate hotel is indeed frequented by many middle-class South American visitors. No restaurant, but who needs one with dozens just outside the door? A good money-saver for visitors interested in theater and shopping since it's within easy walking distance to Broadway and Fifth Ave. 200 rooms.

Wyndham. 42 W. 58th St.; 753–3500. This residential-style hotel has some of the coziest suites and doubles for the price in town. Large beds, bright floral fabrics, and attractive window treatments make this a pleasant place to come home to, whether you're a single, couple, or family of four. No room service, but the friendly desk staff will be happy to help you find anything you need in the Carnegie Hall vicinity. A favorite among theatrical and musical folk. 225 rooms.

Airport Hotels

Most of the hotels and motels near New York City's three major airports (JFK, La Guardia, and Newark) fall into the *First Class* or *Budget* category. Obviously, these hotels were designed primarily for convenience, so don't expect superlative accommodations or service. Still, they are useful for overnight stopovers, and those near JFK are in close proximity to Aqueduct and Belmont racetracks. Most offer courtesy buses and limousines to the airports.

Airway Motor Inn at La Guardia, 718–565–5100; **Hilton Inn at JFK,** 718–322–8700; **Holiday Inn at La Guardia,** 718–898–1225; **JFK Airport Marriott,** 718–659–6000; **La Guardia Marriott,** 718–565–8900; **Sheraton Inn, Newark,** 201–527–1600; **Viscount International Hotel at JFK,** 718–995–9000.

HOW TO GET AROUND. For those using public transportation, a handy number to keep in mind is the *New York City Transit Information* phone, 718–330–1234. Open 24 hours a day, they'll give you the best route from wherever you are to wherever you're going. If calling from a phone booth, however, have a few extra nickels ready—the wait "on hold" can be a while.

By subway: The city's extraordinary subway system is your best bet for speed-thrift-convenience—usually. Late at night, when waits between trains are much longer, safety is a problem. When traveling at night, stay at or near the center of the train. Police patrol is spotty, so the volunteer Guardian Angels group (look for them in their white T-shirts and red berets) do their civic best to deter foul play on the trains. The weekday rush hours, usually cruelly overcrowded, are particularly oppressive on very hot summer days.

Of course, you'll want to know what stop is closest to your destination. A pocket atlas—obtainable at book stores and in the magazine kiosk on the Times Square island (between 7th Ave. and Broadway, just north of 42nd St.)—superimposes subway routes onto the street maps. Once you've targeted the proper stop, check a map of the subway system—you can get one at any token booth or at the New York Convention and Visitors Bureau (at Columbus Circle). Subway maps also appear in the Yellow Pages for each borough. The map's main fault is that it is not drawn to scale. Rather, it enlarges areas such as downtown Brooklyn, mid-Manhattan and Jackson Heights, Queens, where many routes converge and mass changes from train to train occur at busy times. But it does help.

With the map you can utilize every stretch of track in the vast network. But remember to study it before you embark on a subway adventure. *Don't* grab a map as you rush to catch a train and expect to unfold and read it on a crowded platform en route. Use it patiently. You'll see, for example, that you can get from major terminals (Times Square; Roosevelt Ave.–Jackson Heights, Queens; Atlantic Ave.–downtown Brooklyn) to all but a few stops with no more than one change of train. And if you still have questions—about routes, schedules, rates—ask at a change booth or a conductor. Or call the Metropolitan Transit Authority, 718–330–1234.

A subway token costs $1 at press time. Reduced fares are offered Senior Citizens and the disabled during certain hours. Note: You can use subway tokens on city buses, and get a free transfer, too. You cannot use a transfer from bus to the subway, however.

Be cautious about using the subways after 7 P.M. If you must, stay on the platform in view of the entrance; on the train, travel in a middle car, near the conductor.

Staten Island has a surface train from the ferry at St. George to Tottenville.

Remember: Some trains have more than one route, depending on the time of day. It's all clearly explained on the map.

By car: While we urge all visitors not to attempt touring Manhattan by automobile, some people may wish to have a car at their disposal for trips to the outlying boroughs or for travel to other areas. It is worth noting that car-rental rates are considerably cheaper when you pick up a car at one of the airports than they are when renting from midtown locations operated by the same companies. Similarly, parking cars at centrally located midtown hotels is far more expensive than leaving them at lots and garages on the far west side of the island. Just make sure of the hours these garages are open so that you'll be able to retrieve your car when you want to. For short stays in the theater district, the Municipal Garage, which can be entered from 53rd and 54th Sts. between Broadway and Eighth Ave., is relatively inexpensive. In other garages, don't be surprised having to pay $8 to $15 for two hours' parking. Many restaurants (including Windows on the World at the World Trade Center) will "validate" your parking stub, entitling you to a discount or free parking at *designated* garages. The city itself attempts to discourage city drivers with a 14 percent parking tax added onto every bill.

Trying to drive around in Manhattan can be an educational, if searing, experience. The main drawbacks: heavy traffic, scarcity of legal parking spots, and very expensive garages—and unbelievable, car-wracking potholes. The police in Manhattan *will* quickly remove an illegally parked car from a zone marked "tow away," and it will cost $100 for the towing plus whatever the fine is for the parking violation. No excuse or plea sways the officers who man the West Side pier where cars are stored (these may be argued later in court), so prepare to pay. Better yet, don't drive or park illegally, or, best of all, forget about driving, except on weekends and holidays.

If you insist on driving, let's take the parkways first. *Manhattan's West Side Highway* is undergoing repairs south of 72nd St. and is closed south of 57th St., with West St. running south to the Battery. North of 57th St. the highway is known as the *Henry Hudson Parkway.* It parallels the Hudson and meets I–95 where the George Washington Bridge (to New Jersey) becomes the *Cross-Bronx Expressway* (to the Bronx and New England or to Long Island via the Triborough Bridge). The Henry Hudson Parkway continues north, crossing the Harlem River into the West Bronx. It leaves the city above Van Cortlandt Park and goes through Yonkers into Westchester.

On the east side of Manhattan, with access to the Brooklyn Bridge, the *Franklin D. Roosevelt Drive* (also called *East River Drive*) runs from the Battery to 125th St. and to the bridges to Queens (Triborough) and the Bronx (Willis Avenue). The road still continues beyond 125th St., however, along the east side of Manhattan, under the name *Harlem River Drive*. On it, you can get to upper Manhattan (Washington Heights and Inwood sections) or cut off to I–95 (George Washington Bridge west, Cross-Bronx Expressway east). The F.D.R. Drive, being rehabilitated one portion at a time, is old, twisting, subject to dense traffic and, in a heavy rain, flooding.

The *Bronx* has three big, relatively new roads. The *Cross-Bronx Expressway* (I–95) passes through the Bronx at about 174th St. and has exits onto almost every major north-south avenue. From west to east, it also gives access to the *Major Deegan Expressway* (I–87, the southern extension of the Thruway).

The *Bronx River Parkway* (to White Plains and central Westchester) terminates at the new Bruckner Traffic Circle. At that gigantic interchange, you can go to New England via I–95 or eastern Queens via the Whitestone or Throgs Neck bridges.

The Bruckner Circle also leads to another major highway in the borough, the *Bruckner Expressway,* which runs southwest to the Triborough Bridge. Use the bridge to reach Manhattan or Queens. If you don't take the Triborough, the same road also loops around the southern tip of the Bronx and heads up the west shore of that borough as the Major Deegan Expressway (I–87). It has exits for Yankee Stadium and for the Cross-Bronx Expressway, and moves out of the Bronx as the New York State Thruway, later passing by Yonkers Raceway.

The *Henry Hudson Parkway* runs up the west side of the Bronx, from Manhattan's West Side Highway, and leads to the *Saw Mill River Parkway,* among others.

Queens is accessible from the west by two highways. From the Triborough Bridge, the *Grand Central Parkway* runs through the northwestern communities of Astoria and Jackson Heights, passing La Guardia Airport and Shea Stadium. After an interchange with the *Long Island Expressway* (I–495), it dips south, touching Forest Hills and Kew Gardens, then bolts away to the northeast again, past Springfield Gardens and Queens Village. The Long Island Expressway runs fairly straight west to east from the Queens Midtown Tunnel (E. 36th St., Manhattan) as far as Rego Park (you'll see Lefrak City and other high-rise developments crowding in on both sides). Then it jogs northeast, connects via the *Grand Central Parkway* to Kennedy Airport and continues on to Nassau and Suffolk Counties. These two roads are the principal automotive corridors for commuters, shoppers and theatergoers from Long Island, and traffic is invariably formidable.

KEY TO MANHATTAN STREET NUMBERS

Here is a handy guide to finding most addresses in Manhattan. To get the cross street nearest to a building number, just cancel the last figure of the building's number. Divide remainder by two and add the key number below. Result is approximately the nearest cross street.

*Exceptions: Cancel last figure of house number and add or deduct.

Example: 350 Park Ave. Cancel last figure (0), divide by 2, and add key number (35). **Answer: 52nd Street.**

Aves. A, B, C, D	3	8th Ave.	10
1st Ave.	3	9th Ave.	13
2nd Ave.	3	10th Ave.	14
3rd Ave.	10	11th Ave.	15
4th Ave.	8	Amsterdam Ave.	60
5th Ave.		Columbus Ave.	60
1 to 200............................	13	Lexington Ave.	22
201 to 400............................	16	Madison Ave.	26
401 to 600............................	18	Park Ave.	60
601 to 775............................	20	West End Ave.	60
776 to 1286................ *deduct	18	Central Park West	*divide by
			10 and add 60
Ave. of the Americas.. deduct	12	Riverside Drive	*divide by 10
7th Ave.		Broadway	and add 72
1 to 1800............................	12	1 to 754..............	below 8th St.
above 1800...........................	20	743 to 858....................	deduct 29
		858 to 958....................	deduct 31
		above 1000...................	deduct 31

To find street numbers on cross streets commence as follows:

East Side	West Side
1 at 5th Ave.	1 at 5th Ave.
101 at Park Ave., Park Ave. S, or 4th Ave.	101 at 6th Ave. (Ave. of the Americas)
201 at 3rd Ave.	201 at 7th Ave.
301 at 2nd Ave.	301 at 8th Ave.
401 at 1st Ave.	401 at 9th Ave.
501 at York Ave. or Ave. A	501 at 10th Ave.
601 at Ave. B	601 at 11th Ave.

The main north-south highways in Queens are the *Brooklyn-Queens Expressway, Van Wyck Expressway,* and *Cross Island Parkway.* The first begins just east of the Triborough Bridge ("Brooklyn" exit from the Grand Central Parkway) and has interchanges with most major Queens thoroughfares as it passes over the mainly industrial western edge of that borough. The last exit in Queens is to the Long Island Expressway (L.I.E.).

The Van Wyck, important as the road to Kennedy Airport, connects with the *Southern State Parkway* for Nassau County. It intersects the

Grand Central Parkway (which you must take to get onto the L.I.E.) and then becomes the Whitestone Expressway (I–678) through Whitestone and Bayside, Queens, on its way to the Bronx Whitestone Bridge. The Van Wyck is almost invariably—except, maybe, at 3:30 A.M.—snarled with traffic; leave early if you plan to use it.

The Cross Island starts in the north at the Whitestone Bridge and roughly parallels the north shore of Queens until it crosses Union Turnpike (a city street). Then it angles south past the Belmont Racetrack and traces the borough's eastern border until it is swallowed up by the Southern Parkway just east of Kennedy Airport. (Note: as your map will confirm, Southern and Southern *State* Parkways are not quite the same.)

Let's continue into *Brooklyn* with the Southern Parkway. Known as the Belt Parkway or Shore Road in Brooklyn, it girdles the entire borough along the southeast boundary around to the L.I.E. at the northwest. Major exits include Cross Bay Blvd. (to Rockaway), Flatbush Ave. (to Rockaway's northern tip, Breezy Point, Gateway National Park, and eastern Flatbush), Ocean Parkway (to Sheepshead Bay) and Cropsey Ave. (to Coney Island and Bensonhurst). Along the way, you'll see signs for the Verrazano-Narrows Bridge to Staten Island. The Belt Parkway, after passing under that huge span, continues up the west shore past Bay Ridge (exit at 65th St.) and Borough Park (exit at Prospect Expressway). Finally, it reaches downtown Brooklyn and the three main routes to Manhattan (Battery Tunnel and the Brooklyn and Manhattan Bridges). Having now changed its name to the Brooklyn-Queens Expressway, the highway passes over Williamsburg and Greenpoint. If you're heading in the opposite direction—*from* Queens—you'll have a chance to cut over the Williamsburg Bridge onto Delancey Street in Manhattan.

City Streets

Manhattan has probably the most regular and gridlike pattern, except that the *Lower East Side* and *Greenwich Village,* two of its most interesting and vital neighborhoods, lie outside the grid. (Another confusing area for out-of-town drivers: downtown—the *Wall Street* area.) Almost all the east-west streets and most of the north-south avenues are one-way. The two-way streets are spaced rather evenly from south to north: Canal, Houston, 14th, 23rd, 34th, 42nd, 57th, 72nd, 79th, 86th, 96th, 106th, 116th, 125th, 135th, and 145th. North of that, the island is considerably narrower and the last really wide one is 207th, just about a mile from the upper end of the borough.

All the north-south avenues are parallel except Broadway, whose traffic winds from northwest (the 225th Street Bridge to the Bronx) to southeast *(South Ferry)*. Traffic on Broadway is one-way southbound below 59th Street, two-way above there. An attractive parallel to the West Side Highway is Riverside Drive from 72nd Street to the George Washington Bridge.

Central Park offers a lovely interior roadway. It is beautiful, especially at night, when thousands of distant skyscraper lights are framed by trees. This road is closed to motorists on weekends and evenings for the benefit of the city's many bike-riders.

The table on the previous page will help you find your way around town.

Brooklyn is accessible from lower Manhattan via three bridges. The most northerly is the *Williamsburg,* from Delancey St., followed by the

Manhattan (Canal St.) and the *Brooklyn* (Chambers St.). Broadway will take you to Canal St. or Chambers St., and for Delancey, take Bowery, which is just a continuation of 3rd Ave. below 9th St.

Brooklyn is often said to be impossible to navigate (perhaps Thomas Wolfe had this in mind when he wrote his famous short story, "Only the Dead Know Brooklyn"). But this reputation is undeserved. Most neighborhoods there are also grids; problems arise only because they meet one another at odd angles (note the half-left turns in the routes outlined below). Brooklyn's most famous street, Flatbush Ave., runs diagonally from northwest (at the Manhattan Bridge) to southeast *(Marine Park, Floyd Bennett Airfield* and the Belt Parkway). Along the way it passes through *Prospect Park* and very near the *Brooklyn Museum.* From the opposite direction, southwest, corner of Prospect Park, three wide and well-maintained roads run almost due south toward the Atlantic: Ocean Parkway, Ocean Ave. and Coney Island Ave. About two miles farther east, Utica and Ralph Avenues trace parallel paths through *Crown Heights, Brownsville,* and *Flatlands.*

Routes across the breadth of Brooklyn are more complicated. The only continuous one is Atlantic Ave., from the East River to the Queens border, on the north edge of the borough. In the center, take 39th St. (eastbound exit from the Belt Parkway) across *Borough Park* to McDonald Ave. Turn right, then quickly left on Ave. F, which you follow to Coney Island Ave. Turn right and at Ave. J, turn left. This avenue runs block after block through the lovely and peaceful residential area of *Flatbush.* When you cross Utica Ave., start watching for Flatlands Ave., where you take a half-left. Flatlands keeps you on the crosstown route, becoming Fairfield in the *East New York* region. Follow on to Fountain, the border between Brooklyn and Queens. Take a left to Linden Blvd., then a right. In about a mile, Linden meets the Southern Parkway, west of *Kennedy Airport.* If you continue on Linden, you'll soon reach the *Aqueduct Racetrack.*

The southern tier of the borough contains the comparatively conservative communities of *Bay Ridge, Fort Hamilton, Bensonhurst, Sheepshead Bay,* and *Canarsie.* The route through here is, from the west, 86th St. to Stillwell Ave., where you take a half left onto Ave. U and follow it east to Flatbush Ave. near *Marine Park.*

It might be helpful to know about a few main streets in *Queens.* One route across the borough, west to east, begins with Metropolitan Ave. (exit from the southbound Brooklyn-Queens Expressway). It passes through a mostly industrial area at first, but soon becomes the main street in the *Ridgewood-Glendale* neighborhood you've probably seen in the opening of *All in the Family.* This is Archie Bunker "country." In *Forest Hills,* a block beyond 75th Ave., go left onto Union Turnpike, which angles northeast through *Kew Gardens, Flushing,* and *Bellerose.* It passes two of Queen's largest parks, *Cunningham* and *Alley,* before crossing into Nassau County.

The lower level of the Queensboro (59th St.) Bridge out of Manhattan lets the driver choose between the borough's two busiest roads, Queens Blvd. and Northern Blvd. The first runs east, connecting with Woodhaven Blvd. (to *Rockaway*), and the L.I.E., then curves south connecting with the Van Wyck Expressway (JFK Airport or the Bronx Whitestone Bridge) and leads onto Hillside Ave. (eastern Queens communities, *Hillside, Hollis,* and *Queens Village*).

Northern Boulevard runs northeast past *La Guardia Airport,* the Grand Central Parkway–Van Wyck Expressway interchange, Shea Stadium and the *Flushing, Auburndale,* and *Bayside* areas. It is State Rte. 25A and continues into Nassau at *Great Neck.*

North-south through streets are scarce in Queens. In western Queens, use the Brooklyn-Queens Expressway; in east Queens, the Cross Island Parkway. In between, Woodhaven Blvd. runs from Queens Blvd. (at about 97th St.) south to *Rockaway,* becoming Cross Bay Blvd. en route. The Whitestone/Van Wyck Expressway combination goes from the Whitestone Bridge to Kennedy Airport at about 136th St. and thus serves *Whitestone, Murray Hill, Corona, Kew Gardens, Jamaica,* and *South Ozone Park.*

The Bronx is probably the most confusing of the four most populous boroughs. In the west Bronx, the main north-south roads are Jerome Ave. and Grand Concourse, the latter much broader and more attractive, but ending about 205th St. (The Grand Concourse serves as the east-west divider for the Bronx.) Jerome Ave. runs from *Yankee Stadium* all the way to Westchester, with driving made somewhat more "challenging" by the pillars of the IRT elevated subway line. In the center of the borough, the Bronx River Parkway begins at the Bruckner Expressway, goes into Westchester at *Bronxville;* White Plains Road is parallel, about ½ mile to the east; it too has an "el" structure.

There are only a few east-west roads. Tremont Ave. begins just south of the 179th St. exit from the northbound Major Deegan Expressway (I–87) and runs through many different neighborhoods, rich and poor, eventually leading to the Throgs Neck Bridge. Fordham Rd., beginning at the bridge from 207th St., Manhattan, runs cross-borough at about 190th St., passing *Fordham University* and the *Bronx Zoo.* As US 1, it continues east under the name Pelham Parkway and ends with interchanges for the Hutchinson River Parkway and New England Thruway (both lead to Westchester).

The Staten Island Expressway crosses that borough's northern tier, directly off the Verrazano-Narrows Bridge from Brooklyn to the Goethals Bridge for New Jersey. Other limited access roads are planned around the perimeter, but, for now, Hyland Blvd. is the most reliable route to the more rural sections, like *Tottenville.* It connects to the interchange with the recently completed West Shore Expressway which crosses south to the Outerbridge Bridge.

By bus: Of course, buses are slower than subways (during rush hour, they crawl along). But the routes are varied and, since there are almost always stops every two blocks, you can often get closer to your destination than on the subway. Midtown bookstores will sell you a large-print map and explanatory guide; it should make the subway look easy by comparison. In *Manhattan,* there are routes on all north-south avenues and major crosstown streets, as well as several trips that zigzag along a wandering path through (and sometimes out of) the borough. Look on the front of an approaching bus for a sign hinting at its destination. But to know *how* it gets there, you'll need to ask the driver or consult the map. Free maps are also available on some buses, but your best bet for a free map is the Convention and Visitors' Bureau, the MTA booths at Grand Central or Penn stations, or the Yellow Pages.

Buses also cost $1 (to ride you need *exact* change, a token, or a transfer; dollar bills not accepted); Add-a-Ride tickets, which are free, allow you to transfer from one route to a connecting line. Ask for the transfer as you board.

By ferry: The famous nickel ride from the Battery to *Staten Island* now costs 25¢ (round-trip). It is most glorious at night when city lights create a spectacular show. The trip takes about half an hour each way, the boat moves swiftly, has a snack bar and room for cars, and passes close to the Statue of Liberty.

From the airports: Some hotels serve the airport terminals with their own limousines, so check when you make reservations. There are usually plenty of taxis available. The fare to Rockefeller Center, for example, will be about $12 from La Guardia, $25 (tip included) from Kennedy if traffic moves steadily. *JFK Express:* Subway-bus service, connecting points in Manhattan and Brooklyn with Kennedy International Airport, is available for $5.50, one way plus $1 for subway entry. Travelers can board a specially marked subway train (look for a white airplane on a blue background) at its starting point at 57th St. and Sixth Ave., or at seven other express stops: 47th–50th sts. and Rockefeller Center; 42nd St. and 6th Ave.; 34th St. and Herald Square at 6th Ave.; W. Fourth St. at 6th Ave.; Chambers St. and World Trade Center; Broad and Nassau Sts.; Jay St. and Borough Hall in Brooklyn. The subway will terminate at the Howard Beach–JFK Airport station and passengers will be picked up by buses that will transport them to any of the airline terminals. Passengers leaving the airport can take the service into Manhattan for the same fare. The JFK Express operates at 20-minute intervals, seven days a week, from 6 A.M. to 11 P.M., from both terminals, and takes about one hour. *Helicopter* service into Manhattan is available, weather permitting, from all three major area airports. Heliports are located on the East River at Pier 6 in the Wall Street area, at 34th St., and at 60th St. Metropolitan (883–0999) serves the Wall St. Heliport; Island (718–895–1626) goes to all three East River landing strips. All are also available for sightseeing, with Metropolitan offering special camera mounts on its choppers. The fares vary from $35 to $75, one way. The Carey Bus Co. will bring you into Manhattan for $6 from La Guardia or $8 from JFK. Buses leave from and return to the Grand Central Terminal (42nd St. and Park Ave., near the Grand Hyatt Hotel). There is a free airport-bus shuttle van to Grand Central from the Port Authority.

The most convenient and probably least expensive way to and from Newark Airport is via New Jersey Transit bus. Buses run between the Port Authority Terminal in New York and Newark every 15 to 30 minutes between 5 A.M. and midnight. Another line, Olympic, goes to the World Trade Center, East Side Airlines Terminal and Grand Central; cost is $4. Unless you get stuck in especially heavy traffic, the ride is less than half an hour. A cab from New York to Newark will run the meter about $38, with the meter reading in effect until the end of the tunnel and doubling from there to the airport. From Newark there is a flat rate depending on your destination that runs about $20–$25. Helicopter is $55 each way, and Abbey's minibuses (718–786–0073) run between midtown hotels and Newark for about $13.50. Share-and-save taxis are $11–$14.

By taxi: If you carry an atlas, you can discuss the route of a long or complicated trip before you set out. The driver, by law, may not refuse to take any "orderly" passenger anywhere in the five boroughs, Nassau, Westchester, or to Newark Airport (the last three destinations entitle him to twice the fare shown on the meter). Neither may he charge each passenger separately when there is more than one passenger. These rules, along with the phone number of the city's Taxi and Limousine Commission, (212–869–4237), are posted inside each cab. On the back of the roof-light, you'll find the vehicle's medallion (identification) number. Sharing of taxis is permitted between New York's airports and certain midtown Manhattan hotels. Inquire at the airport or at your hotel.

The fare is $1.15 for the first ⅛ mile, 15¢ for each additional ⅛ mile. (That comes to about $2.20 for a one-mile trip, before tip.) You also pay for waiting time (including red lights and traffic jams). The driver expects, because he usually gets, about a 15 to 20% tip. A larger tip is appropriate if your destination is an area far from where he can reasonably expect to find a return-trip passenger. The rider pays bridge, tunnel and/or highway tolls. Certain cabs are also entitled to a 50¢ surcharge per ride between 8 P.M. and 6 A.M. Those drivers permitted to charge the extra fee will have a sign indicating so posted in the passenger compartment.

Whenever you're traveling within the city limits— *including all five boroughs* —be sure the meter is running. Don't let cabbies try to offer you a "bargain" off-the-meter rate. Those bargains just don't exist. Officially, a driver cannot refuse to take you anywhere within the five boroughs, though in practice this isn't always the case—particularly if you wish to go to the far reaches of Brooklyn or Queens or into crime-infested areas such as the South Bronx. If you know you're headed far, it may well be best to phone ahead for a cab (regular meter rates apply except for "car services"); check the Yellow Pages of the telephone directory for companies and phone numbers. Hailing a cab on the street is simple: available cabs have the number on their roofs lit. A wave of the hand should flag them down. Take their advice with a grain of salt, though. As stated, some are genuinely proud of the city and feel as if they are ambassadors of good will. Alas, many also prey on those who don't know their way around.

More and more fleets and independent drivers are using two-way radio equipment to handle telephone orders. There may be an extra charge for this service if reserved in advance; ask the dispatcher on the phone rather than waiting until the cab arrives and trying to work it out with the driver. Some of the better-known radio fleets are: *Minute Men,* 718–899–5600; *XYZ,* 718–768–9251; *Last Taxi,* 718–706–7300; and *UTOG,* 212–741–2000.

By limousine: If you really want to do it up right, there's only one way to go—chauffer-driven car. *Carey Cadillacs,* 986–5566, have a fixed price of $40 per hour or $1.45 per mile, whichever is greater. A special airport fee system runs along these lines: from midtown to JFK is $65, all fees mentioned plus tips and tolls.

On foot: Several famous sections of Manhattan are easily seen on foot. They include, but are not limited to, Greenwich Village, Midtown, Wall Street, Lincoln Center, and the UN-Turtle Bay area.

TOURIST AND GENERAL INFORMATION SERVICES. The *New York Convention and Visitors Bureau* at Columbus Circle has multilingual aides to assist you in making your sightseeing plans. At their headquarters, you can also obtain subway and bus maps, and information about hotels, motels, and restaurants, as well as seasonal listings of the city's special entertainment attractions. The Bureau is open Monday to Friday, 9 A.M. to 6 P.M., weekends and holidays, 10 A.M. to 6 P.M. call 397–8222.

The Times Square Ticket Center (TKTS) at Broadway and 47th Street and at No. 2 World Trade Center (354–5800) sell Broadway and Off-Broadway tickets at half-price on the day of performance. Ditto the music-and-dance booth, Bryant Park, 42 St. between Fifth and Sixth Aves. (382–2323).

New York magazine, published weekly and incorporating the listings sections from the old *Cue* magazine, does an excellent job of keeping a finger on the pulse of New York City. Weekly features include comprehensive information on cultural events, shopping, sports, street fairs, walking tours, museums and galleries, activities for children, and all manner of special events. *New York* also maintains a free ticket service information phone—880–0755, Monday to Friday, 12:30 to 6:30 P.M.—which will advise you regarding ticket availability for theater, dance, and concerts.

New Yorker magazine, most famous for its literary efforts, also has excellent theater, music, dance and movie reviews, and listings (with brief, pithy commentary) of what's happening at art galleries, museums, nightclubs, opera, and ballet.

The city's daily papers—the *New York Times, New York Post, New York Newsday,* and *Daily News*—list current attractions, with the Friday weekend sections always geared to the most promising upcoming events. On Fridays, too, both the *Times* and the *News* list theater ticket availability through that Sunday. The huge Sunday *Times* is perhaps the best buy in town, though, with its "Arts and Leisure" and "Guide" sections overflowing with useful entertainment information and ads.

Of the city's varied weekly newspapers, the *Village Voice* is the one to consult for the latest on pop music, jazz, modern dance, and off- and off-off-Broadway theater.

Weather forecasts, time, traffic conditions, sports information, a jazz hotline, your daily horoscope, jokes . . . all can be obtained over the phone. For these and other numbers consult the white pages of the telephone directory.

RECOMMENDED READING. A selection of books for visitors with specialized interests:

The American Institute of Architects' *AIA Guide to New York City,* by Norval White and Elliot Willensky (Collier), is a comprehensive guide to city architecture and history. The Landmarks Preservation Committee of the City of New York published a booklet, *A Guide to New York City Landmarks,* that is sold at most city bookstores and cultural institutions, such as museums and libraries, usually for one dollar.

The Street Book, by Henry Moscow (Hagstrom), is, as its subtitle suggests, "an encyclopedia of Manhattan's street names and their origins" and a good source of city lore.

Manhattan Menus (Manhattan Menus Inc.), revised annually, is a compilation of approximately 175 menus from a representative cross-section of New York eateries, complete with prices and specialties of the house. For serious *gourmands,* there is Seymour Britchky's *The Restaurants of New York* (Random House) for an almost bite-by-bite account of meals at an equally wide variety of establishments and Mimi Sheraton's *The New York Times Restaurant Guide.*

The Lower East Side Shopping Guide, by Alan Teller and Sharon Greene (Shopping Experience, Inc.), is an oversize pamphlet-type publication that gives a store-by-store account of the wholesale/retail shops along Orchard, Grand, and their surrounding streets. Other similar guides will lead to you warehouse and discount outlets throughout the metropolitan area.

The New York Walk Book (Doubleday) is the joint project of the New York–New Jersey Trail Conference and the American Geographical Society. It gives detailed information and maps for trails in all parts of the state, with a special section devoted to the five boroughs.

Walking Tour Tapes for use in a Walkman, etc., are available for Greenwich Village, Fifth Ave. mansions, etc., at Gotham Book Mart (see *Shopping*).

SEASONAL EVENTS. If New York City is normally overflowing with more exhibits, shows, and galleries than even its natives can take in, it is also home to numerous annual special events that range from car shows to ethnic food festivals, from the Ringling Bros., Barnum & Bailey Circus to the St. Patrick's Day Parade. As a general rule (of course there are exceptions), you can expect outdoor happenings to be free, although the temptation to purchase food or merchandise at most street fairs and carnivals will be high. Indoor events at the Javits Convention Center (11th Ave. and 38th St.), Madison Square Garden (32nd St. and Seventh Ave.), the Seventh Regiment Armory (66th St. and Park Ave.), and Lincoln Center (64th St. and Broadway) usually require the purchase of tickets. Phone numbers cited below are all in the 212 area code.

January. *The National Boat Show,* open to both the trade and the general public, is held at the Jacob Javits Convention Center. With the latest models being displayed, crowds can be almost overwhelming, particularly on weekends. Call 216–2000. . . . The *Winter Antiques Show* is resident at the Seventh Regiment Armory late in the month, featuring some of the nation's finest dealers and their latest acquisitions. Call 665–5250. . . . The spectacular *Ice Capades* glide and spin at Madison Square Garden for a two-week stint. Call 563–8300. . . . Rounding out the month is the explosive *Chinese New Year,* which arrives at the first full moon after January 21 (Tet, in the lunar calendar). Fireworks, food, and fun mark this 10-day celebration. Call 397–8222.

February. The two-day *Westminster Dog Show* finds hundreds of competitors strutting their stuff at Madison Square Garden. Call 563–8300. . . . *Black History Week* is marked at the American Museum of Natural History, Central Park West at 77th St., by way of films, exhibits and discussions. Call 769–5000. . . . *White Sales*—offering huge savings on towels, linens, and other merchandise—fill the major department stores with bargain-seekers on Washington's and Lincoln's Birthday weekends.

March. The Javits Center hosts two popular events: The *Sport, Camping, Travel and Vacation Show,* where you can buy direct from the exhibitors; and for stay-at-homers, the *Antiques and Garden Show.* Call 216–2000. . . . You don't have to be Irish to tag along in the *St. Patrick's Day Parade* on the 17th. Just follow the green stripe down the middle of Fifth Avenue and join the politicians and tens of thousands of marchers all decked out in green. . . . If that's not enough of a three-ring circus for you, get your tickets for the *Ringling Bros., Barnum & Bailey Circus* at Madison Square Garden. The good seats at the kiddie matinees sell out first for performances through the end of April or early May. Call 563–8300.

April. The *Easter Parade* (admittedly, sometimes in March) starts at St. Patrick's Cathedral, Fifth Ave. at 49th St., immediately following the morning services. Put on your Sunday best and stroll uptown with the rest of the crowd. . . . For children, in the past there's been an *Easter Egg Rolling Contest* in Central Park, but the event has grown so popular, and the crush so bad, that its future is in question. Check the newspapers to be sure. . . . When the New York Knicks are contenders, the *pro basketball playoffs* can be seen at Madison Square Garden. Tickets are very difficult to get so try to reserve early. The same is true for the Garden's resident hockey team, the *Rangers.*

May. Parades abound: *Armed Forces Day, Brooklyn Bridge Day, Martin Luther King, Jr., Memorial Day* and *Norwegian Independence Day.* For dates and route information call 397–8222. . . . The street festival season gets underway in earnest with the *Ninth Avenue International Festival,* a multi-ethnic feast (plus much free entertainment) that stretches along Ninth Ave. from 37th to 59th Sts. Call 581–7029. . . . *The Park Avenue Antiques Show* is a week-long, nationally recognized display of American and European collectibles at the Seventh Regiment Armory. . . . The *Washington Square Outdoor Art Exhibit* sprawls out covering lower Fifth Ave. at Washington Square Park, Broadway, University, and La Guardia Place for three weekends beginning the last weekend in May. There's *some* good art to be found here, but most is pedestrian and uninspired. . . . *Memorial Day Weekend* is marked by parachute and acrobatic flying shows at Brooklyn's Coney Island. . . . Little Italy comes alive for the *Feast of St. Anthony* on Mott St. from Canal to Grand for the last weekend of the month. You'll be overcome by the luscious smells of sizzling calzone (oversize cheese-filled dumplings, deep-fat fried), grilled sausages, and fresh shellfish. Rides, raffles, and games of chance and skill are also featured. Call 226–2978.

June. The *Feast of St. Anthony of Padua* continues the Italian festivities a wee bit north on Sullivan St. between Houston and Spring Sts. Call 777–2755. . . . It's *Basically Bach* (with a few other well-tempered selections) at Lincoln Center's Avery Fisher Hall for six days—call 874–6770—while the free *Goldman Band Concerts* commence across the Lincoln Center Plaza in Damrosch Park. The latter run through August Wednesdays through Fridays, and Sundays, from 8 to 10 P.M. Call 594–5151. . . . George Wein's annual *JVC Jazz Festival* brings a large congregation of jazz musicians and fans together for 10 days of concerts all around the city—in concert halls, on the Staten Island ferry, and in the parks. After the first week of May, call 787–2020 for performance and ticket information . . . *Shakespeare in the Park,* under the auspices of Joseph Papp's New York Shakespeare Festival Public Theater, brings the Bard free to the minions at the Delacorte Theater in Central Park (enter the park at 81st Street from either Central Park West or Fifth Ave.). The line for tickets, which are distributed on the day of performance beginning at 6 P.M., forms early in the afternoon. After June 15 call 861–7277. . . . The *Metropolitan Opera* also brings free concert performances of complete operas to various city parks during the month. No tickets necessary, but you might want to stake out your space early, and bring a blanket and a picnic dinner. Call 362–6000. . . . *Museum Mile* finds Fifth Ave. turned into a pedestrian mall as the ten museums between 82nd and 105th Sts. open their doors for a special midweek evening. . . . The *Great Irish Fair* carries the spirit of St. Patrick into the summer with a two-day festival along the Brooklyn waterfront. . . . Parades mark *Puerto Rican Day* and a *Salute to Israel.* Call 397–8222.

July. The *Fourth of July* is America's Independence Day and the fireworks literally begin at 9:15 P.M., sponsored by Macy's Department Store and most recently emanating from barges on the waters around the Statue of Liberty. Check newspapers for best vantage points and for details regarding the *Great July 4th Festival.* . . . It's *Mostly Mozart* at Avery Fisher Hall for the next six weeks, while Lincoln Center Plaza is given over to the *American Crafts Festival* for the first two weekends of the month. More than 300 craftsmakers sell their leather, furniture, glass, jewelry, and other wares with children's activities including mime, singing, magic, and clowns. Call 677–4627. . . . Joe DiMaggio usually shows up for *Old Timers' Day* at Yankee Stadium. Call 293–6000. . . . More Italian-flavored street festivities are part of the nightly (for ten days) *Lady of Pompeii Feast* on Carmine St. south of Bleecker St. in Greenwich Village. Call 989–6805.

August. The *New York Philharmonic* takes a portable stage to Central, Clove Lakes, Prospect, and other city parks for a series of alfresco performances. Blankets and picnics in order once again. Call 580–8700. . . . *Lincoln Center Out-of-Doors,* at that cultural center's Plaza, is a three-week marathon of free shows drawn from all the performing arts. Call 877–2011. . . . It's the Mets' turn for *Old Timers' Day* at Shea Stadium. Call 718–507–8499. . . . The annual *Bluegrass Club of New York Amateur Band Contest* is held at various locales. Check the papers. The *U.S. Open* at the National Tennis Center in Queens' Flushing Meadow Park features top international pros competing for top national honors. Call 718–271–5100.

September. Labor Day is the scene of the West Indian carnival parade along Eastern Parkway in Brooklyn. In addition to the bands, floats, and spectacularly costumed marchers representing various Caribbean islands, food sellers along the parade route sell delicacies like jerk chicken, souse, johnnycake, and *maubi* to wash them down with. The *San Gennaro Festival* on Mulberry and Grand Streets is yet another chance to fill up on Little Italy's best goodies—for 11 nights running! Call 226–9546. . . . German-Americans celebrate *Steuben Day*—honoring one of the Europeans who aided the Colonists during the Revolutionary War—with a parade ending on East 86th St. Call 397–8222. . . . *New York Is Book Country* is the theme on Fifth Ave. from 47th to 57th Sts. for one Sunday this month, with major publishers setting up kiosks in order to tout their authors' latest literary efforts. Some authors are in attendance, there are some publishing demonstrations, and street performers line the route. . . . The *New York Film Festival* previews art films as well as the latest soon-to-be-released Hollywood blockbusters for three weeks at Alice Tully Hall, Lincoln Center. Tickets are available—and often sold out—in advance. Call 362–1911. . . . The *TAMA Country Fair* and *Festival of the Americas* street fairs, with about 800 booths each, get one Sunday apiece on Third and Sixth Avenues, respectively. For TAMA information, call 684–4077; for Festival of the Americas, call 921–8122. . . . Brooklyn's Atlantic Avenue is turned into an *Atlantic Antic* for a celebration of Middle Eastern foods and crafts. Call 718–875–8993.

October. For walkers, parades: *Columbus Day, Pulaski Day, Hispanic Day,* and *Veterans Day* (for dates and routes call 397–8222). . . . The fall foliage season is the perfect time for a hike through any of the city's parks, with the Cloisters up at the northern tip of Manhattan island perhaps the most spectacular of all. . . . It's *United Nations Day* on the 24th, though there are no regular, official ceremonies. . . . *Old Home Day* at the Richmond Restoration, 411 Clarke Ave., Staten Island, finds the doors open to period houses throughout the area. Call 718–351–1611. On Halloween there is a colorful and somewhat bizarre *Halloween Parade* in Greenwich Village between Bank St. and Washington Sq., starting at about 5:30 P.M.

November. For runners, the 26-mile *New York City Marathon* begins on the Staten Island side of the Verrazano-Narrows Bridge and ends at Tavern-on-the-Green in Central Park. Hopefully, everyone starts and finishes on the first Sunday of the month. Call 860–4455. . . . *Macy's Thanksgiving Day Parade* is a thrill to see live as it wends its way down Central Park West (beginning about 8:30 from 77th St.), Broadway, and Seventh Ave. Everyone's wide-eyed as Snoopy, Bullwinkle, and other favorite cartoon characters march by as building-high balloons. Even Santa makes his first seasonal appearance! Call 397–8222. . . . As of Thanksgiving weekend, the windows at *Lord & Taylor, Altman's,* and *F.A.O. Schwarz* are done up with spectacular, moving Christmas displays. Go at night, if possible, for the lines during the day at Lord & Taylor especially can be long and deep. . . . The *National Horse Show* trots around Madison Square Garden for six days. Call 563–8300. . . .

December. The annual Christmas tree lighting ceremony at *Rockefeller Center,* 47th Street between Fifth and Sixth Ave., is always an event. . . . Tchaikovsky's *Nutcracker Suite* ballet is the seasonal offering by the New York City Ballet at Lincoln Center's State Theater. The regular company is augmented by children from the School of American Ballet, and there are daily performances—which invariably sell out—for about three weeks. Call 870–5570. . . . For crafty holiday shopping try the *American Crafts Holiday Festival* at NYU Loeb Student Center, La Guardia Place and Washington Square South. Plenty of jewelry, clothing, furniture, glass, leather, and other goods. Call 677–4627. . . . And if you're lucky enough to be ringing out the old and ringing in the new in New York City, you can join the *New Year's Eve* revelry in Times Square as thousands watch an illuminated apple descend from the top of the Allied Chemical building at the stroke of midnight, a ceremony whose continued practice is dubious. Alternately, there are midnight celebrations (complete with fireworks and live music) in *Central* and *Prospect* parks.

FREE EVENTS. Summer is especially full of outstanding free cultural offerings throughout New York City. Both the Metropolitan Opera (in late June and early July) and the New York Philharmonic (in late July and early August) travel the various city parks giving free performances—the Philharmonic concerts in Central and Prospect Parks usually augmented by fireworks accompanying the *1812 Overture* or some similarly suitable work. The Goldman Band concerts are held all summer long at the bandshell in Damrosch Park, in the southwest corner of Lincoln Center. Lincoln Center Plaza is also the scene of numerous free events, from the American Crafts Fair, held for two weekends beginning July 4th, to three weeks of daily performing-arts shows in August. A handful of Jazz Festival concerts around the end of June are also free. At the Delacorte Theater in Central Park there are free Shakespeare productions, while the city's various other parks have extensive schedules of free dramatic, pop, jazz, classical, dance, and other offerings. (Call the individual parks or borough presidents' offices for full listings.)

The Mall in Central Park south of the 72nd St. transverse and the area north around Bethesda Fountain are always overflowing with street entertainers—musicians, mimes, jugglers, magicians, and the like—who perform summer weekends and holidays from about noon to dusk. Most, though, do pass the hat.

On the Fourth of July, Macy's sponsors a spectacular half-hour-long fireworks display from different parts of New York Harbor. And on New Year's Eve, rain or snow or bone-chillingly cold, Central and Prospect Parks shine from the glimmer of overhead lightshows.

Beginning with the Ninth Ave. International Fair in mid-May, city streets are given over to carnivals, street fairs, and festivals right through to the end of September. Strolling and entertainment are always free at these extravaganzas (the Ninth Ave. fair attracts half a million people annually; other smaller ones a few thousand on a single block) although there's always food, rides, and merchandise to be bought. Call the Visitor Information Center, 397–8222.

Many of the attractions in the *Museums, Historic Sites,* and *Walking Tours* sections of this book are free—with some additional museums asking only a voluntary contribution. Others that usually have fees, such as the Guggenheim and the Whitney, are free Tuesday evenings. Tickets for television shows—live or taped—are always free, and available at the Convention and Visitors Bureau, or frequently from station personnel stationed outside the NBC and CBS buildings. All of the city's parks, zoos, and gardens are free, with the exception that there is a charge at the Bronx Zoo Fridays and weekends.

Floral displays begin with those at Rockefeller Center's Channel Gardens on Fifth Ave., but include Easter and Christmas displays in the Pan Am Building and a Spring Flower Show at One World Trade Center. At the Citicorp Center, there are daily (including weekend) popular and classical music programs in the Atrium, 153 E. 53rd St. Lincoln Center's Library of the Performing Arts, Amsterdam at 66th St., has free concerts on weekdays at 4, Saturdays at 2:30. Each Sunday at 5, there are jazz vespers at St. Peter's Church, 54th St. at Lexington Ave. Other new office buildings and culturally minded religious institutions also feature free performances, with increasing regularity; check the weekly entertainment pages of the Sunday *Times, Village Voice, New York,* and *New Yorker* for specifics.

Free outdoor art exhibits are common from spring to fall. Among the more famous are the Washington Square Outdoor Art Show, late May–early June and early September. Greenwich Village; and the Brooklyn Heights Promenade Fine Arts Show, in May. The Canal Street Flea Market, 335 Canal St. (near Chinatown), is open Saturday and Sunday. Also in lower Manhattan is a self-guided Heritage Trail, which you can pick up anywhere, though Trinity Church at the head of Wall Street is as good a place as any to begin. The Manhattan Art & Antiques Center,

1050 Second Ave. (55th St.) has free admission to its complex of 72 shops, open every day. There are free guided Central Park tours Sun.; call 397–3091. Finally, you can tour a winery (the only one functioning in Manhattan) by calling at Schapiro's, 126 Rivington St., Sundays 11 to 4, every hour on hour. (Phone 674–4404 for weekday appointment.)

For other free tours, refer to the *Tours and Special-Interest Sightseeing* section, which follows.

TOURS AND SPECIAL-INTEREST SIGHTSEEING. Before you begin walking or busing around town, we urge you to take in *The New York Experience,* a multisensory film which will introduce you to the city and help you get your bearings. (Lower plaza, McGraw-Hill Building, 1221 Sixth Ave., between 48th and 49th sts., 869–0345.) Adults, $4.75; $2.90 for children under 12. Shows Monday through Thursday are every hour on the hour from 11 A.M. to 7 P.M.; Friday and Saturdays, 11 A.M. to 8 P.M.; Sundays, noon to 8 P.M. A similar multimedia show available at the Translux Seaport Theatre is *The Seaport Experience* (608–7888). Adults, $4.25; $2.75 for children. Shows are every hour on the hour from 11 A.M. to 4 P.M. (Mondays–Thursdays); Fridays, Saturdays and Sundays, 11 A.M. to 6 P.M.

General-interest bus tours are still available from midtown. *Gray Line of New York,* 900 Eighth Ave., 397–2600, offers 15 different tours covering uptown, downtown, and Atlantic City. Reservations necessary. *Crossroads Sightseeing,* 701 Seventh Ave., 581–2828, covers many well-known Manhattan spots. *ShortLine Tours,* 166 W. 46th St., 354-5122, also has good touring choices.

There are a number of specialized services offering guided tours of the theater district, architecturally important areas, historic districts, and other notable areas of the city. Harlem Your Way! (690–1687), for example, will show you what this famous uptown neighborhood looks like. Ask for the *Big Apple Specialized Services* flier at the Visitors' Center at Columbus Circle.

If you want to skim the waters of the Big Apple, *Circle Line* cruises leave Pier 83 at the foot of W. 43rd St. and 12th Ave., 563–3200, approximately every 45 minutes beginning midmorning. Details of the sights en route are included in the introduction to the *Walking Tours* section, but it's a leisurely 2½- to 3-hour ride around the entire island. Adults $12, children $6, April–November. More intimate and adventurous are the daily sailings of the triple-masted schooner *Pioneer* and *Andrew Fletcher* from the South Street Seaport Museum Pier. $14 and $19 for adults for 2- and 3-hour trips respectively, $11 for children; advance reservations (669–9416) are necessary for the *Pioneer;* tickets to the *Fletcher* can be purchased at the dock. Riders are invited to help raise the sails and steer— to relax, picnic, and enjoy the view. Or you can take to the air via *Island Helicopter,* heliport at the foot of E. 34th St. on the East River, 683–4575. Flights day or night, from $35 per person. *Manhattan Helicoptor Tours* (247–8687) leave from the heliport at W. 30th St. and 12th Ave. *The Petrel* is a sailing-yacht cruise of New York Harbor—great close-up views of the Statue of Liberty, Ellis Island, more—leaving from Battery Park 4 or 5 times daily, starting at 12 noon. Cruises are from 45 minutes to 2 hours, and cost $8–$20. There are moonlight cruises leaving at 9:30 P.M. on weekdays and 8 P.M. weekends. 825-1976.

Still another unique perspective of Manhattan can be had by taking a hansom cab—horse-drawn carriage—through Central Park, down Fifth Ave., or wherever the spirit guides you. Carriages are always lined up at 59th St. and Fifth Ave., just outside the Plaza Hotel. The usual routes are a brief ramble through the park, or down Fifth Ave. for eight or ten blocks and back up Sixth Ave., but drivers will tailor a trip to your desires. It is not an inexpensive mode of travel, though, given the leisurely pace and the possibility of hitting traffic. Official rates are $17 for the first half hour, and $5 for each additional 15 minutes, although a rate hike is in the works. It is best that you confirm the rate with the driver you choose before setting out.

Tours of some individual attractions in the city are also popular. These are described fully as part of the *Walking Tours* section but a brief reminder that they are available is in order. Among them: the *New York Stock Exchange,* Visitors Center, 20 Broad St., 656–5167. Self-guided via automated narration and participant-activated exhibits. Mon.–Fri., 9:20 A.M.–4 P.M. Free; *United Nations,* First Ave. at 45th St., 963–7713. Hour-long tours are run daily every 10 minutes 9 A.M.–4:45 P.M. Adults $4.50, students $2.50, children $2.; *Radio City Music Hall,* 50th St. at Sixth Ave., 757–3100, $5; *Lincoln Center,* Broadway at 64th St., 877–1800—Avery Fisher Hall is the starting point but times vary, so call before you go for the current schedule. Adults $6.25, students and Senior Citizens $5.25, children $3.50.

For offbeat tours, contact *Adventure On A Shoestring, Inc.,* 300 W. 53rd St., 265–2663, and meet new people in unusual surroundings at budget-minded but imaginative events. *Discover New York* is a series of six Sunday-afternoon walking tours, sponsored by the *Municipal Art Society Tours,* 457 Madison Ave., 935–3960. Brooklyn Heights, Upper West Side, Upper Fifth Avenue are some of the areas on the itinerary; $8 for members, $12 for non-members. Other walking tours are listed regularly in the *Cue* section of *New York* magazine.

In addition to all of the above, and the museums, historic sites, and places to be seen on walking tours, all of which are described under those entries in this book, there are other fascinating places which don't fit into such convenient categories, yet deserve mention. Here are a select few:

Guinness World Records Exhibit Hall, Empire State Bldg., 34th St. and Fifth Ave., 947–2335. Over 200 exhibits, including moving light displays, replicas, etc., all from that wonderful book. Open seven days 9:30 A.M.–5:30 P.M.

Supreme Court of New York County and the *Criminal Court* are located at 60 and 100 Centre St., respectively. If a publicized trial interests you, or if you simply want to see the routine business of a court, they—and smaller courts—are open to the public.

The *Mormon Visitors Center,* Columbus Ave. & 65th St., 595–1825, features archeological exhibits in replica of artifacts from both Eastern and Western cultures. A diorama with talking mannequins relates the story of a contemporary Mormon family, a 19th-century pioneer family, and a *Book of Mormon* family of 2,000 years ago. Open seven days, 10 A.M.–8 P.M. Free.

If you're interested in—or puzzled by—our nation's fiscal and monetary policies, visit the New York *Federal Reserve Bank,* 33 Liberty St., 720–6130. You must call a week in advance to set up a tour, but they will then explain the Federal Reserve System and central banking, show you check processing and the gold vault.

Gallery Passports, 1170 Broadway, 686–2244, organizes tours to artists' studios and lofts in the city and to other art attractions outside New York that can be seen in a day (Baltimore, Md., and Williamstown, Mass., for instance). Sept.–May.

The largest theatrical community in America is in mid-Manhattan and you can glimpse its workings close up through *Backstage on Broadway,* 228 W. 47th St. (575–8065). The tour guides are professionals from all branches of the industry and the program draws praise from educators around the country.

Con Edison, New York's public utility for electricity, has installations all over the metropolitan area and several of these are visited by bus provided by the company. Con Ed's *Energy Museum,* 145 E. 14th St., 460–6244, displays the past, present, and future of electricity. Open Tues.–Sat., 10 A.M.–4 P.M.

If you've never been in a transoceanic port before, the busy piers and luxury liners may prove fascinating indeed. The newspaper shipping pages list departure schedules, and if you call the line for its visiting policy (on ocean liners visitors are generally allowed about two hours before sailing), you'll be ready to stroll the decks while passengers board.

PARKS. These cover nearly a sixth of the city's land and provide welcome contrasts to its concrete canyons and crowded sidewalks. Vandalism and inadequate maintenance have taken their toll, but a spirit of preservation and renewal is increasingly in evidence.

The parks may disappoint those seeking pure pastoral beauty and restful solitude. They *are* beautiful—there's something very special about looking at the skyscrapers of Manhattan from a snow-covered Central Park, where cross-country skiers wend their way across the Sheep Meadow; or getting a feel of New England during the fall foliage season in the Bronx's Van Cortlandt Park. But New York's parks have gradually evolved into recreational and cultural areas, especially in summer.

If there's a promenade for strollers you can rest assured that there'll be street entertainers—musicians, magicians, jugglers, and even comedians—all along the route. More formally, both the Metropolitan Opera and the New York Philharmonic offer series of free park concerts during the summer, travelling from one borough to the next. And it is not unusual for these concerts to draw several hundred thousand fans a night. (Take a blanket, a picnic dinner, and arrive late afternoon for an 8:30 performance if you want to plant yourself within view of the stage.)

There are marathons, walk-a-thons, and races for men, women, children and handicapped in the different parks. There are weekend festivals sponsored by various ethnic, civic, and commercial organizations. The *Parks Department* sponsors drama, film, poetry readings, music and dance throughout the boroughs, with schedules available in local newspapers and magazines (see *Tourist Information* section). And of course there are miles and miles of trails for leisurely walking (not recommended for night), lakes for boating, bicycle lanes for two-wheel enthusiasts . . . and more.

Unique among Metropolitan New York parks is Gateway National Recreation Area, a federally administered park that stretches through parts of Brooklyn (Floyd Bennett Field, a former navy airstrip, is where

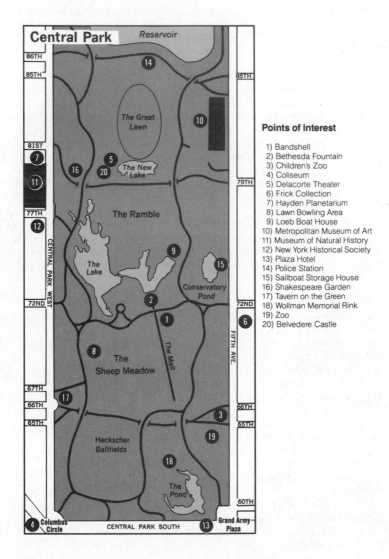

Central Park

Reservoir

86TH
85TH
81ST
77TH
72ND
67TH
66TH
65TH

85TH
79TH
72ND
66TH
65TH
60TH

The Great Lawn

The New Lake

The Ramble

The Lake

Conservatory Pond

The Mall

The Sheep Meadow

Heckscher Ballfields

The Pond

CENTRAL PARK WEST

FIFTH AVE.

Columbus Circle

CENTRAL PARK SOUTH

Grand Army Plaza

Points of Interest

1) Bandshell
2) Bethesda Fountain
3) Children's Zoo
4) Coliseum
5) Delacorte Theater
6) Frick Collection
7) Hayden Planetarium
8) Lawn Bowling Area
9) Loeb Boat House
10) Metropolitan Museum of Art
11) Museum of Natural History
12) New York Historical Society
13) Plaza Hotel
14) Police Station
15) Sailboat Storage House
16) Shakespeare Garden
17) Tavern on the Green
18) Wollman Memorial Rink
19) Zoo
20) Belvedere Castle

numerous special events are staged), Queens (the Jamaica Bay Wildlife Refuge on Cross Bay Blvd. is a lure to birdwatchers from all over, while Jacob Riis Park is one of the city's most popular—and cleanest—beaches), Staten Island, and New Jersey. Ranger-guided tours, hikes, and educational programs are offered regularly all year round.

We must also reluctantly note that with the exception of nights when there are special planned events, most of New York's parks are not very safe strolling areas after dark.

Manhattan

Central Park has 840 acres which include lakes for rowing (you may rent a boat, at the Loeb Boat House), stable and trails for horseback riding, dozens of baseball diamonds and playfields, a bocci green, a zoo, and a skating rink.

The New York Shakespeare Festival makes use of the Delacorte Theater near the 81st St. entrances (from either Central Park West or Fifth Ave.) for free performances of the classics. (Tickets are given out on a first-come, first-served basis beginning at 6 P.M. the night of the performance only; the line for tickets starts forming in early afternoon.)

The Goldman Band Shell is in the Mall midway between East and West 72nd Street, and has frequent free concerts. The Mall itself is where most of the park's regular street performers congregate (best times for a stroll are Saturday or Sunday afternoons from May to October, from noon to dusk). North of 72nd St. is the Bethesda Fountain, another popular meeting place right by the edge of a lake. On nearby Conservatory Pond, you may see people maneuvering their battery-operated remote-controlled model sailboats in good weather; the boats are stored in a building to the east of the pond. A jogger's track and bridle trail circle the Reservoir in the 80s. The Metropolitan Museum of Art borders the park at Fifth Ave. and 82nd St.

Strawberry Fields, a memorial to the late John Lennon, is due north of the 72nd St.–Central Park West entrance.

Cars are banned from all park roads except the east-west transverses almost all but rush hours from May to mid-October.

Riverside Park runs along the Hudson River beginning at 72nd St. and north through Harlem. Invariably less crowded than Central Park, Riverside is a neighborhood outpost, full of families and sunbathers. A favorite stroll is along the promenade by the 79th Street Boat Basin, where a number of yachts serve as full-time city residences.

Fort Tryon Park at the northern tip of Manhattan, high over the Hudson, runs south of the Cloisters. Besides the view of the Palisades across the river there is an attractive but somewhat wild garden area.

Battery and *Washington Square Parks* in lower Manhattan are small and don't even pretend to bring the country to the city. The latter, in fact, is mostly concrete. However, Battery Park gives a good harbor view and cooling breezes off the water in summer, while Washington Square is an active mingling ground for Greenwich Villagers. Some sing, play guitars, and smoke dope; some argue social issues, some play chess, and some romp with their children and pets. Washington Square is also the scene of a very New Orleans-like carnival every Halloween night (late in October).

Brooklyn

Prospect Park's northeast corner is right at Brooklyn's Grand Army Plaza, near the Brooklyn Public Library, Brooklyn Museum and Botanic Gardens. The park itself is more than 500 acres, with lakes, boathouse, riding stables, a Quaker cemetery, the historic Lefferts Homestead and Litchfield Mansion (both open to the public) and a bandshell at 3rd St. and Prospect Park South that is used for small jazz, pop, and classical concerts during the summer.

Also of interest: *Marine Park,* with its 18-hole public golf course.

Queens

Flushing Meadows/Corona Park is partially on the site of the 1964 World's Fair grounds, near La Guardia Airport and Shea Stadium. Housed in what was formerly the New York State Pavilion are the Queens and Science Museums, and a few rides and mildly "glamorous" playgrounds also survive. Top of the Park is a restaurant overlooking the park and its immediate surroundings.

Cunningham and *Kissena Parks* are, as is Flushing Meadows, in the central part of the borough.

Jacob Riis Park, best noted for its beach but full of picnic and play areas, is now incorporated into the Gateway National Recreation Area.

Staten Island

Clove Lake is the most popular of Staten Island's parks, with boating, fishing, horseback riding, and wooded paths. A short ride from the Staten Island Ferry terminal on a Victory Blvd. bus makes the park easily accessible to the visitor.

Although not actually a park, *Fort Wadsworth* is one of the quieter spaces in New York City. It is situated under the Staten Island end of the Verrazano Narrows Bridge and commands an impressive view of New York harbor. To get there, take the Bay Street bus from the ferry terminal. On the grounds is the Fort Wadsworth Military Museum (closed Tues. and Wed.) which traces the history of the fort, which is still an active military post.

Other area parks include *Silver Lake, Latourette,* and *Willow Brook.*

Bronx

The woods-and-flowers highlight of the Bronx is easily the *Botanical Garden,* with its 250 acres and thousands of trees, shrubs, and plants. Depending on the season, you'd want to look out for the rose, rhododendron, magnolia, or azalea gardens. (For further details see the *Gardens* section below.)

Pelham Bay Park is almost entirely surrounded by water and is the largest of the Bronx's public parks. Also especially scenic is *Van Cortlandt Park,* which includes the Van Cortlandt Mansion Museum—an 18th-century colonial manor, furnished today just as it was when built in 1748.

ZOOS. New York has several zoological centers, but the *Bronx Zoo* (Fordham Road & Southern Blvd., Bronx; 220–5100) is something special. Over 250 acres, with more than 3500 animals, it is one of the largest in the world. It has recently been modernized and wherever possible the animals are not caged, which makes sections such as the African Plains most fascinating. A tractor train will allow for a quick survey, the Bengali Express monorail covers the Wild Asia area May through October, and a Skyfari cable car affords an overview of the entire zoo.

The Bronx Zoo is open 10 A.M. to 5 P.M. Admission is free Tuesdays, Wednesdays, and Thursdays; $3.75 for adults, $1.50 for children; Senior Citizens and children under 2 free at all times. There are $1 additional fees for the various rides. There is also a children's zoo opposite the elephant house where admission is 75 cents for kids and $1 for adults. The Bronx Zoo can be reached via the IRT No. 2 or 5 trains to the East Tremont Ave. stop or by car at the intersection of the Pelham and Bronx River Parkways.

New York's other zoos can hardly rival the Bronx Zoo for size, in maintenance, or for educational value. The *Central Park Zoo* is in the process of being rehabilitated, but the *Children's Zoo* is still open 10 A.M. to 4:30 P.M. (E. 64 St. & Fifth Ave.; 408–0271). The *Prospect Park Zoo* (Empire Blvd. & Flatbush Ave., Brooklyn; 718–965–6560) is open 11 A.M. to 4 P.M. Also of possible interest is Staten Island's *Barrett Park Zoo* (614 Broadway; 718–442–3100).

The *New York Aquarium* (Surf Ave. & W. 8th St., at Brooklyn's Coney Island; 718–266–8500) is filled with mammals, fish, and birds from the world's water environments. They are displayed and publicly fed to the delight of adults and children alike.

GARDENS. A youngster who grows up in New York City is sometimes called "a child of cement." As you have seen from our discussion of parks, it need not be so. And giving surprise to the visitor who expects to see no green in New York at all are the New York and Brooklyn *Botanical Gardens*, each ranking among the world's most beautiful public gardens. They have horticultural displays all year round, are open daily, and admission is free.

New York Botanical Garden, directly north of the famed Bronx Zoo, has brought pleasure to New Yorkers since 1891. Its 250 rolling acres contain some 12,000 different species of plants, some of which bloom on such specialized sites as Rhododendron Slope, Daffodil Hill, Azalea Glen, and Magnolia Dell.

There is also a spectacular 40-acre Hemlock Forest, virgin land unchanged since the days the Indians camped out there. Ancient hemlock, maples, giant oak, poplar, beech, hickory, ash, and tulip trees shade the forest floor. The Bronx River slices through this forest primeval, cascading over a falls not far from *Snuff Mill.* There you will find a post-primeval restaurant, the *Lorillard Snuff Mill,* with dining terrace overlooking the river. There is a picnic area nearby.

The garden's 11 greenhouses feature a world of flowers: lush jungle blooms from Asia, desert plants from Africa, pineapple, oranges, and pomegranates from the tropics. There's also a plant sales area. Almost worth a trip to New York itself is the glass conservatory (inspired by London's Kew Gardens Conservatory). Admission to the Conservatory, where special exhibitions are held, is $2.50.

The *Museum* (Italian Renaissance style) has displays explaining the evolution of plants and their use to man. The paleo-botanic exhibit has some 30,000 plant fossils, some of which date from the year 500 million B.C.

There are five acres of wild flowers, meadows, and rock gardens, and there is an herbarium with some 3,000,000 species. There are flower-bordered pools, three miles of roads, 15 miles of paths. There is an *Easter Show* in March, a *Rose Day* in June, and a *Christmas Show* in December. Call 220–8777 for general information.

To get there: Take New York Central Harlem Division to Botanical Garden Station; or, 6th Ave. Concourse-205th St. (D) subway train to Bedford Pk. Blvd. Walk east eight blocks. By car, Pelham Pkwy. west from New England Thruway and Hutchison River Parkway; Bronx River Parkway to Mosholu Pkwy. Use Mosholu Pkwy. from Henry Hudson Pkwy.

The 50-acre **Brooklyn Botanic Garden,** directly behind the Brooklyn Museum, features two of the most beautiful *Japanese gardens* in this hemisphere. The pond-and-hill garden, built in 1913 by Takeo Shiota, is a landscape of symbols. The pond takes the shape of the Japanese character for the word "heart." There is a tori, or gate, in the pond; a shrine on top of the hill. And there are caves which echo the delicate sound of five tiny waterfalls.

The second Japanese garden, which was opened in 1963, is an exact replica of the 15th-century Ryoanji (Buddhist) Temple of Kyoto, one of the most famous abstract gardens of contemplation in the Far East. There is a replica of the viewing wing of the ancient Ryoanji Temple. The tennis-court-size garden area is filled with swirling patterns of gravel, and fifteen stones (imported from Japan) arranged in five groups. The original purpose of the starkly simple design: to draw the minds of monks into meditation.

Another unique feature of the Brooklyn Botanic Garden is its *Fragrance Garden for the Blind.* The plants, raised in beds, are specially selected for identification by taste, touch, or smell. The plaques describing the flowers are in Braille.

There is also a *Shakespeare Garden* (with the various plants and flowers mentioned in the Bard's works), a wild flower garden, a rose garden, a range of greenhouses, and an abundance of cherry trees which burst into sudden bloom in late April, retain their pink glory through early May.

Hours vary according to season; open seven days a week. Call 718–622–4433 for information.

To get there: From the East Side, take Lexington Ave. IRT subway downtown express marked Utica Ave. or Atlantic Ave. to Nevins St. Change to B'way 7th Ave. train. Ride to Eastern Parkway, also called Brooklyn Museum Station. From the West Side, take B'way 7th Ave. IRT, downtown express marked New Lots Ave. or Flatbush Ave. Get off at Eastern Parkway. (Trip takes about 25 minutes from Times Square.)

Japan House, at 333 E. 47th St., has both indoor and outdoor gardens. The gardens are a favorite relaxation spot for office workers on their lunch hour. There is also a library, art gallery, and auditorium here.

If you delight in strolling through quiet *formal gardens,* you'll be glad to learn that Gallery Passport, 1170 Broadway, 686–2244, often includes them in tours to spots in the city and the supporting areas, like *Boscobel* in Westchester. Bus transportation to the various attractions is included in the service.

Manhattan's own **Conservatory Gardens,** in Central Park near Fifth Ave. at 105th St., is just what the name suggests: a greenhouse featuring blooming plants, displays changing seasonally. It's about a 15-minute stroll uptown from the Guggenheim Museum.

The **Ford Foundation** at 320 E. 43rd St. has an indoor garden with a 130-foot ceiling. The garden is in the lobby on this impressive building and has all kinds of flowers, shrubs and vines. Open weekdays.

The **Queens Botanical Gardens,** 43–50 Main Street, Flushing, is a recent addition to the city's attractions. Noted for its summer rose garden and fall chrysanthemum show, the garden also offers a shop (reasonable prices) and popular horticultural programs. Environmentalists will be pleased to learn that this 30-acre Gardens is "planted" on a former garbage dump! *To get there:* IRT subway Flushing Line uptown to Main St. (the last stop); then take the Q44 bus, south on Main St., ask for the Botanical Gardens stop.

Also worth a visit is the **Wave Hill Center for Environmental Studies** in Riverdale, Bronx (West 249th St. and Independence Ave.). It offers an outdoor sculpture garden, greenhouses, and gardens (formal, "wild," aquatic, herb, rose), as well as concerts, lectures, etc. The view of the Hudson River and Palisades is spectacular. *To get there:* We recommend a cab or your car. The trip by subway-bus-foot is a trip itself (IRT Seventh Ave. subway, No. 1 train to 231st St. station; No. 10 or No. 100 City Line Bus from NW corner of 231st St. and Broadway to 252nd St.; cross Parkway Bridge, on foot; walk on 252nd St. to Independence Ave. The entrance to Wave Hill is a few blocks down the road—at 249th St.).

BEACHES. By far the most famous of New York City beaches is **Coney Island** a 3½ mile stretch of Brooklyn facing out on the Atlantic Ocean. Upwards of a million and a half people will descend upon Coney Island's breezy shores on a hot summer day. Yet for all its continued popularity, this is a sadly rundown area, of which author Mario Puzo has written, "There was a time when every child in New York loved Coney Island, and so it breaks your heart to see what a slothful, bedraggled harridan it has become, endangered by the violence of its poor and hopeless people, as well as by the city planners who would improve it out of existence. If I were a wizard with one last magic trick in my bag, I would bring back the old Coney Island."

Coney Island is not quite that bleak; it retains a certain tacky charm, with the idle parachute jump at nearby *Astroland Amusement Park* towering above the beach and boardwalk—and with what invariably seem like the best frankfurters, French fries, and cotton candy in the world. Coney Island remains an experience, safe certainly by day, if only by dint of the massive crowds that include representatives of every racial group and ethnic community in the city.

In addition to Astroland, the *New York Aquarium* is also nearby, and the side streets are dotted with some of the best Italian restaurants in New York (*Gargiulo's* on W. 15th St. is a garish, 500-seat remnant of Coney Island's bygone glory days; it also consistently garners raves for outstanding food and service).

The B, D, F, M, N, and QB trains all converge at Stillwell Ave., Coney Island; it is also accessible by car via the Belt Parkway, heading east from lower Manhattan by way of the Brooklyn Battery Tunnel. Take the Ocean Parkway exit south about ½ mile until you reach the waterfront. The main beach area and other attractions will be to your right. There are also express buses that go to the Coney Island area, which you can pick up at designated stops between Wall St. and E. 50th St. in Manhattan.

Almost as famous and easily as popular is **Jones Beach,** just beyond the city limits on Long Island. Jones Beach is more parklike than Coney Island, without Coney's array of distractions—with the noteworthy exception of the nearby *Jones Beach Marine Theater,* an outdoor arena where the stage floats in the water. (Pop, jazz, and country-and-western concerts in the evenings.) The beach itself is usually very clean, despite the millions who come to bathe and swim there daily during the June to August season.

To get to Jones Beach by car, take either the Long Island Expressway or the Southern State Parkway to the Meadowbrook Parkway and follow the signs to the parking lots. Despite their size, these lots fill up quickly, and the area is then closed to further traffic. So if you're planning to make the one-hour trip (unmercifully longer on a hot Sunday), leave early in the morning.

Alternatively, leave from the Port Authority Bus Terminal (41st St. and 8th Ave. in Manhattan). In the past, buses ran to and from Jones Beach on a regular basis, but fares and schedules for the upcoming summer had not been published at press time. Call 564–8484 for information.

Jacob Riis Park in Queens, named for the turn-of-the-century photographer and philanthropist, and recently incorporated into *Gateway National Park,* is another popular seaside resort. The beach and its waters are generally rated among the cleanest of any in the city and within the park's borders are an 18-hole pitch-and-putt golf course; numerous playgrounds for children of all ages; free tennis, shuffleboard, handball, and squash courts; boardwalk; and some grassy, shaded picnic areas. It should be noted that the far eastern end of the beach has in recent years evolved into an unofficial and illegal nude sunbathing area popular especially among New York's homosexual community.

Riis Park has parking facilities for 10,000 cars, and is easily reached in about an hour via the Belt Parkway going east from Lower Manhattan. Take the Flatbush Ave. South exit and continue over the Marine Parkway Bridge onto the Rockaway Peninsula. Using public transportation, take the No. 2 or 3 IRT line to Flatbush Ave. in Brooklyn; at the Flatbush/Nostrand junction upstairs, take a bus marked Riis Park or Beach 116 St. (it's best to ask for the bus stop, as there are different lines running from every corner).

New York's beach lovers do run the risk of oil spills or shark alerts periodically closing their favorite haunts, but with the above, as well as *Orchard Beach* near City Island in the Bronx, and *Wolfe's Pond Park* in Staten Island, they're never at a loss for alternative sun-'n'-fun spots.

BABYSITTING SERVICES. For parents who may be hesitant to bring their children to the Big Apple, there should be comfort in the fact that there are a number of reliable sources for babysitters here. Perhaps the best known is *The Babysitters Guild,* 60 E. 42nd St., 682–0227. Their prices will be steep by the usual babysitting standards, but their reputation is impeccable. Rates start at $7.50 an hour, and escalate depending on the number and age of children, and where the sitter is to work; for example, the fee for two children aged 8 and 10 staying at the Plaza would be $8.50 an hour. In all cases there is a four-hour minimum and an additional fee for carfare: $4 round-trip during the day and until midnight, $7 after midnight. Rates for infants up to six months are higher because the Guild uses only people trained as baby nurses for children that young. Other possibilities: *Barnard College Babysitting Service,* 606 W. 120th St., 280–2035; Gilbert Child Care, 115 W. 57th St., 757–7900; and *Stern College For Women,* 245 Lexington Ave., 340–7715.

CHILDREN'S ACTIVITIES. There are very few places or activities in New York City that do not hold some fascination for youngsters or that can't be adapted to children's interests. Nonetheless, there are numerous things to see and to do that seem to have younger visitors especially in mind.

Museums

Most of the major museums have special programs designed for children of different ages, but none seem to garner wide-eyed enthusiasm more consistently than the *American Museum of Natural History* (Central Park West at 79th St.; 769–5100) and its sister *Hayden Planetarium* (can be entered from the Museum or separately at CPW and 81th St.; 769–5920)—the former with its life-size dinosaur skeletons and moon rocks, the latter with its changing sky shows and laser-lit rock shows to prerecorded music.

The laser shows, produced by an outside organization in cooperation with the Planetarium, make use of the Planetarium's star projectors but add laser lights and music (sometimes rock, sometimes classical) for a multimedia assault that can be quite impressive. On Wednesdays, when the Museum and Planetarium are open until 8 P.M., you can time your visit to include *Laser Rock,* though that is quite a full day; remember, the Museum and Planetarium span two square city blocks, each with several floors—so be sure everyone is wearing comfortable shoes. Museum open daily 10 A.M. to 5:45 P.M., and until 9 P.M. Wednesday, Friday, and Saturday evenings. Admission is on a pay-as-you-wish basis with suggested contribution: adults $3, children $1.50, except on Friday and Saturday evenings when admission is free. Planetarium open essentially the same hours, though it's best to check the precise times of the sky shows. Admission is $3.75 for adults, $2 for children under 12. Check for *Laser Rock* times and ticket prices. There are also half-hour shows throughout the day in the Nature Max Theatre; $3.50 for adults, $1.75 for children.

Also very popular among younger travelers are the *Museum of Broadcasting* (1 East 53rd St.; 752–7684), where the entire family can select old TV shows to watch together and explore the history of broadcast media; and the *Museum of Holography* (11 Mercer St.; 925–0526), with its unusual displays of three-dimensional light projections known as holograms.

The *South Street Seaport Museum* and its surroundings provide an outstanding afternoon's tour for children. An excellent introduction to the revitalized neighborhood is "Seaport Experience," a multimedia show at the Trans-Lux Seaport Theater (608–6696). Shows are daily every hour on the hour from 11 A.M. to 5 P.M.; Saturdays and Sundays, 11 A.M. to

7 P.M.; admission is $4.50 for adults, $3.75 for Senior Citizens, $3 for children.

Not to be missed on a Seaport visit are the late nineteenth century and early twentieth century square-rigged sailing ships on view. These are open to the public for a fee ($4 for adults, $2 for children, $3 for senior citizens). During the summer there are free concerts and other activities at the foot of the pier—a spectacular setting with the Brooklyn Bridge to the north, the East River to the east and the lower Manhattan skyline to the west. The indoor Museum and Gallery are full of New York nautical history and there are literally dozens of places to eat, from an international array of fast foods to full sit-down restaurants. General information: 669-9424.

Fun and Games

The Manhattan Children's Museum, 314 W. 54th St. (765–5904), *Brooklyn Children's Museum,* 145 Brooklyn Ave. (718–735–4400), and *Staten Island Children's Museum,* 1000 Richmond Terr. (718–273–2060), always have some special performances for children, in addition to their permanent and temporary exhibits. The New York Public Library has an ongoing program of youth-oriented entertainment at its branches throughout the city.

Long-running efforts include *The Party Center* at 1 P.M. every Saturday and Sunday at the West Side YMCA, 5 W. 63rd St. (874–3297). Story hour is held regularly at *Eeyore's,* a children's bookstore, at 11 A.M. every Sunday, 2212 Broadway (between 78th and 79th Sts., 362–0634). Free admission.

Mostly Magic, 53 Carmine St., 924–1472, combines magic and comedy with audience participation, Saturdays at 2 P.M., and for adults at 9 and 11 P.M.

Original plays, fairy tales, and musicals are given at the following theaters: *Courtyard Playhouse,* 39 Grove St., 765–9540, Saturday and Sunday, Labor Day to June, 1:30 and 3 P.M.; *Thirteenth Street Theater,* 50 W. 13th St., 675–6677, Saturday and Sunday, 1 and 3 P.M. Also check the Friday editions of the *New York Times* and the *Post* for extensive listings for that weekend.

Zoos

Bronx Zoo, Fordham Road and Southern Blvd., 220–5100. There is a brand-new children's zoo opposite the elephant house where the admission is 75 cents for kids and $1 for adults! As for the main zoo—also recently renovated—rides include the Bengali Express monorail through the spectacular Wild Asia exhibit (where the animals roam free), a tractor train, and a Skyfari cable car. Open 10 A.M. to 4 P.M. Admission is free Tuesdays, Wednesdays, and Thursday; parking is $3; admission $1.50 for adults, 75¢ for children. Senior Citizens free. There are $1 additional fees for the various rides.

Central Park Zoo, Central Park, E. 64th St. and Fifth Ave., 408–0271. Newly renovated and reopened to the public. The nearby *Children's Zoo* remains open from 10 A.M. to 4:30 P.M.

New York Aquarium, Surf Ave. & W. 8th St., Coney Island, Brooklyn, 718–265–3474. Over 3,000 varieties of marine life are shown in outdoor and indoor exhibits. The whale and dolphin show is very popular with children. Open every day, 10 A.M.–4:45 P.M.; $3.75 adults, $1.50 children.

Other good animal facilities include: *Jamaica Bay Wildlife Refuge,* Cross Bay Blvd., between Howard Beach and Broad Channel, Queens, 718–474–0613, open every day, 8 A.M.–5 P.M., free; *Prospect Park Zoo,* Empire Blvd. and Flatbush Ave., Brooklyn, 718–965–6560, 11 A.M.–4 P.M., free; *Staten Island Zoological Park,* 614 Broadway, Staten Island, 718–442–3100, open every day, 10 A.M.–4:45 P.M., $1; children under 3 and senior citizens free; free to all Wednesday.

Sightseeing

There is also, of course, the *Statue of Liberty,* which is reached by ferry from the South Ferry subway stop of both the IRT 7th Avenue and IRT Lexington Avenue lines. Children love to climb up the narrow, circular ramp to the statue's crown. An elevator can take you up to the first 10 stories, the last 12 stories are on foot.

The 102-story *Empire State Building* on Fifth Ave. between 33rd and 34th sts. is always popular. From the terraces of the 86th floor one can rent binoculars and look out across the whole city—and simply being in one of the world's tallest buildings is an unforgettable experience for a child. And don't forget the *World Trade Center* and the *RCA Building* at Rockefeller Center. A ride on the *Roosevelt Island* tramway at 59th St. and Second Ave. also provides still a different type of bird's-eye view of the Upper East Side.

Between Memorial Day and Labor Day, the city opens many outdoor pools for *swimming.* Van Cortlandt Park has one in the Bronx, Greenwich Village (Clarkson St. and 7th Ave.) in Manhattan, Flushing Meadows in Queens and Bedford-Stuyvesant (Kosciusko St. and March Ave.) in Brooklyn—but the area is rough. An indoor pool open all year is at 342 E. 54th St., Manhattan.

Several plots in the city have been protected from development and preserved as *nature areas.* Most notable are Wave Hill's 28 acres in the Bronx (675 W. 252nd St.) and the larger High Rock Conservation Center on Staten Island (Nevada Ave.). Central Park's *Ramble* is a favorite for birdwatchers; hilly and wooded, it lies just north of the 72nd St. lake and can be reached on foot in 10 minutes from the Museum of Natural History.

Toys and hobbies galore can be seen—or bought—at F.A.O. Schwarz (59th St. and 5th Ave.; 644–9400) and Polk's Hobby Shop (32nd St. and 5th Ave.; 279–9034.), and Central Park has plenty of space, on weekdays, to fly kites or model airplanes.

Many of the sites covered in the essay "New York City: A Congregation of Neighborhoods," as well as those listed under *Historic Sites* and *Museums* will likely also prove exciting and memorable for children. And you might want to check the daily papers for the regularly touring circus, ice, Disney and Sesame Street shows that play Madison Square Garden.

Other Suggestions

Radio City Music Hall's various spectacles are always designed as family entertainment, and the occasional concerts held there are usually also by big-name entertainers who appeal to all ages. Backstage tours here, as well as through the NBC television and radio studios across the street, or at ABC around Lincoln Center, give everyone a behind-the-scenes look at the technical side of New York theater. Also check Broadway and Off-Broadway listings.

Periodically throughout the year, the *Big Apple Circus* sets up its one-ring tent in parks around the city. Though small in scale, the company is wonderfully reminiscent of traditional European-style circuses. Phone: 391–0767.

The *Ringling Bros., Barnum & Bailey Circus* comes to Madison Square Garden for the months of April and May every year. With a company of dancers to complement the high-wire acts, human rocket ship, and trained animals, it is a show that in recent years has regained much of the glamour and excitement that had been lost. Various other traveling ice, cartoon character, and fantasy shows can also be seen at the Garden throughout the year, though these are hardly unique to New York. Check the daily papers for current attractions.

At Christmas time, be sure to stop at the Fifth Avenue department stores to see the windows. Of special note are *Lord & Taylor*, at 39th St., *Altman's* at 34th St., and *F.A.O. Schwarz* at 59th St. If the children are old enough to go at night, that's your best bet—the lines are shorter and the atmosphere better, and you can linger to your heart's content. Moving indoors, the fifth floor at *Macy's* (34th St. at Seventh Ave.) is spectacular with Santa Claus in residence and toys galore. Also during the holiday season catch the Christmas tree at *Rockefeller Center*. Come April, the Easter Parade along Fifth Avenue and the egg hunt in Central Park are noteworthy. And Macy's Thanksgiving Day Parade, broadcast live around the world, can be watched in person all along the 2-½-mile marching route—from 77th Street at Central Park West, down around Columbus Circle, and southward on Broadway until it reaches the department store itself.

During the summer, the major city parks have bicycle and rowboat rentals, with roads generally closed to car traffic during non-rush hour times and on weekends for cyclers, strollers, and runners. Also, Coney Island's *Astroland Amusement Park* and Rockaway Park's *Playland* offer rides, "games of skill and chance," and miles of white sand beaches for sunbathing and swimming, plus occasional fireworks displays. July 4th is the time for Macy's spectacular fireworks show, set off from various points in New York Harbor and best viewed from Battery park on the west side of the island. Between Memorial Day and Labor Day, various city-run pools are open all over the city; check in the Parks Dept. listing at the back of the white pages under "New York City Government Offices." An indoor pool is open year-round at 342 E. 54th St. in Manhattan.

Always a special treat is a real old-fashioned ice cream soda—best had at *Rumpelmayer's* (50 Central Park South), *Serendipity* (225 E. 60th St.), or the *Agora* (87th St. and Third Ave.). Further details on these and other possibilities are in the *Desserts* section, below.

PARTICIPANT SPORTS. The sports most participated in by New Yorkers are probably **jogging** and **bicycling.** Statistics bear this out, as do two major events created by interest in these two sports—the annual New York City Marathon (run through all five boroughs and a great way to sightsee on foot if you're up to covering 26 miles, 385 yards) and the five-borough Bicycle Tour in May sponsored by the New York City Parks Department (360–8165).

The reasons for the popularity of jogging and bicycling are fairly obvious: They are relatively inexpensive, require no in-place equipment (just some park space), and their exercise and health value are intensified in the city environment, where the air is never better than "kind of pure" and so many people work inside sitting down. The reasons for the popularity of the New York City Marathon are not so obvious—but it must have something going for it because the cut-off number for participants is 16,000—and the waiting list to get into the run is usually over 20,000! In any event, the Marathon is always held in late October/early November when the weather is usually fall crisp, cool, and clear. And the guiding spirit behind the race is the New York Road Runners Club, headquartered at the International Running Center, 9 East 89th St., New York, NY 10028, 860–4455.

Indeed, the Road Runners Club is a treasure trove of Big Apple running information for joggers of every speed. They can tell you about races scheduled while you are in town, or of the city's best running routes. These routes range from the obvious—such as the reservoir loop in Central Park or the scenic strip along the East River Drive leading to Randall's Island—to the not so obvious, such as the "Museum Mile" from 82nd to 104th Sts. passing ten museums along Manhattan's Fifth Avenue, or another lake loop in Flushing Meadows Park. The club even has a book filled with mapped running routes all around the city, yours for a nominal fee. For further information about running around the Big Apple, and for Marathon entry forms, write the Road Runners Club, Box 1388, GPO, New York, NY 10116. And if you are interested in running the Marathon, make sure to write early and to follow the instructions regarding earliest acceptable postmark.

Central Park in Manhattan and Prospect Park in Brooklyn have automobile roadways that are closed to cars and reserved for walkers, runners, and pedalers during daylight hours on weekends and often during non-rush hours weekdays. You can find plenty of places to rent a bike on the nearby side streets and avenues—check the Yellow Pages—or you can rent in Central Park at the Loeb Boathouse near the 72nd Street lake. You must bring some identification and at least $10–$25 or a major credit card as a security deposit. The bikes cost about $2.50 per hour, with special rates for the day, and a couple of brisk circuits of the park are certainly worth it for the activity and the view of the city and its citizens at leisure. Central Park is especially interesting for the various ad hoc music parties that fill the air in summertime, while Prospect Park is more of a family and community park.

There are plenty of informal participatory sports such as **softball, volleyball, soccer, rugby, frisbee,** or **pushball** in all the city's parks, and even the more formal league teams often look for "pick-up" players to substitute for their own absentees. In winter, cross-country **skiing** and **tobogganing** are popular in Central Park, while spring brings the **roller-skaters** out en masse. In good weather, there are a number of vans set up along Columbus Ave. in the 70s for renting skates, and on good days there is a shop near the corner of Columbus and 75th St. that rents skates also. In Central Park, most of the team games are played in the 60s and 70s, although there are many playing fields farther uptown as well. If you are brave enough to play rugby with total strangers, bring your own ambulance!

For special events information call 360–8165.

For a variety of inexpensive sports choices, from **handball** and **paddleball** to **swimming** and **jogging/exercise classes,** consider the "Y" 's way, where a daily guest membership runs in the $10–$12 range, offered by various YM-YWCAs and YM-YWHAs around town. Call the Y general information number (564–1300) for the address of the Y nearest you so you can check what they have to offer. Two handy Ys to keep in mind because of their location and facilities are the West Side Y at 5 West 63rd St. (787–4400) and the Vanderbilt (a k a Grand Central) Y, 224 East 47th St. (755–2410). The former has an indoor track, one of the best-organized running clubs in town, locker and shower facilities and pool, and is almost directly across the street from Lincoln Center and from Central Park. The Vanderbilt offers paddleball, handball, volleyball, sauna, swimming, and a convenient Grand Central Station area location close to the East River and the United Nations.

Increasingly, you'll come across Y-like health clubs and spas throughout the city, some with tennis and racquetball courts, pools, and extensive exercise rooms. Access to these is almost always by membership only, although you may be able to purchase a day-pass if you have a friend who belongs to one or another of the clubs. If on business, you might also be able to gain admittance through a company membership. Some hotels, including Vista International at the World Trade Center, the Marriot Marquis in Times Square, and the United Nations Plaza Hotel, also have health club facilities that can be used by guests.

Chess and backgammon, and sometimes Go, are not exactly participant sports, but this is what is available at the Chess Shop, 230 Thompson St. near 3rd St., in the Village.

There are plenty of **bowling alleys:** in lower Manhattan, Bowlmor (110 University Pl.) is for regular bowling most of the time, but adds a disco beat after midnight several times a week; in midtown, New Mid-City Lanes (625 8th Ave.); check the Yellow Pages for other lanes.

Billiard Academies—or, if you prefer, pool halls—are similarly numerous, though not all for innocent visitors. You can cue up, in Inwood, near the Cloisters, at Guys and Gals (500 W. 207th St; 567–9279) and the venerable, but not necessarily respectable, Julian's, 138 E. 14th St. (475–9338). Venture carefully, though.

The city's numerous public **golf courses** are playable for a weekday green fee of $10, $12 on weekends; senior citizens, $5. Phone ahead to get a "best guess" on how long a wait you'll have before teeing off. In Brooklyn, play at Dyker Beach (86th St. and 7th Ave.; 718–836–9722). In Queens, there's the Clearview in Bayside (202–12 Willets Point Blvd.; 718–229–2570), Douglaston Park in Douglaston (Commonwealth Blvd. & Marathon Parkway; 718–224–6566), Forest Park in Ridgewood (Interboro Parkway and Main Drive; 718–296–2442), and Kissena Park in Flushing (N. Hempstead Turnpike and Fresh Meadows Rd.; 718–939–4594). Staten Island's courses are Silver Lake (Victory Blvd. and Park Rd.; 718–447–5686), South Shore (Huguenot Ave.; 718–984–0108), and LaTourette (Forest Hill Rd.; 718–351–1889). The Bronx offers Van Cortlandt (Broadway near 242nd St.; 543–4595), and Pelham–Split Rock (City Island and Pelham Bay Park W.; 885–1258). There are two courses at the latter, and Split Rock may be the toughest challenge within the five boroughs. There are also large driving ranges and miniature golf layouts near the City Island Causeway in the Bronx and across from Floyd Bennett Field (near Gateway National Park and the Rockaways) in Brooklyn.

Ice-skating is popular, even fashionable, at the famous Rockefeller Center rink and the Wollman Memorial Rink near 59th St. in Central Park, as well as at the Lasker Rink (397–3142) at the north end of Central Park. Other city locations are Sky Rink (450 W. 33rd St. in Manhattan, where the New York Rangers work out), Riverdale and another Wollman Memorial, this one in Brooklyn's Prospect Park. A brand new facility is Rivergate Terrace Rink, 401 E. 34th St. (689–0035).

Roller-skaters gather in Central Park on a mall at about 70th St. due east of Central Park West—follow the skaters or the sound of blaring radios and tape players to find them. Beginners flock to Greenwich Village's Village Skating (15 Waverly Pl.; 677–9690), while only the most experienced venture out to Brooklyn for the standard-bearing roller rink of them all, the Empire (200 Empire Blvd.; 718–462–1570). Check the Yellow Pages for additional neighborhood locales.

Fishermen can rent or charter boats to try their luck in the waters surrounding New York. Favorite launching points are City Island in the Bronx (Jack's Bait and Tackle) and the Sheepshead Bay area of Brooklyn (Bay End Dock Co. or Canarsie-Jamaica Marine at the Canarsie Recreation Pier, east of Sheepshead Bay). There are numerous other fishing excursions at both these locations.

Tennis courts maintained by the Parks Department are used by city residents, who purchase a season permit, valid from early April to the end of October, for $35; but visitors may buy individual $4 passes at the Central Park Courts (93rd and Central Park). These passes entitle the player to one hour of tennis on any of the city-run courts, a list of which may be obtained from the Parks Department. The Central Park courts are very popular, and players often have to wait an hour or two after signing in for a court, but at other locations, though they are sometimes tricky to find and not as well maintained, one can often sign in and walk right on to the court. For privately owned courts, rates vary considerably from summer to winter, often running as much as $25 an hour higher in the winter. The rates also vary according to the time-slot required: the hours before work, 7–9; lunch hours, 12–2; and the evening hours from 6–10, being generally most in demand and therefore most expensive. Prices per hour range from a low of $16 to a top of $25 for inexpensive courts, to a low of $27 to a high of $58 for the most expensive. (And many courts will be raising their prices soon.)

Courts in *Manhattan,* starting south and working uptown: *Wall Street Racquet Club,* foot of Wall St. at East River (952–0760); free parking; 9 new indoor Har-tru courts; low weekday rates. *Village Tennis Courts,* 110 University Place (989–2300); Acrycushion 6 surface courts; ball-machine practice courts; moderate. *Midtown Tennis Club,* 341 Eighth Ave., corner 27th St. (989–8572); eight Har-tru tournament courts; indoor and outdoor courts; limited back line space; moderate. *Tennis Club, Grand Central Terminal,* 15 Vanderbilt Ave. (687–3841); two Elastraturf courts; very expensive but luxurious. *Manhattan Plaza Racquet Club,* 450 W. 43rd St. (594–0554); new Elastraturf courts; excellent tennis pros; expensive. *Sutton East Tennis Club,* 488 E. 60th St. at York Ave. (751–3452); eight clay courts; cramped space; moderate to expensive; open Oct. to Apr. *Tower Tennis Courts*, 1725 York Ave. between 88th and 89th Sts. (860–2464); Deco-turf indoor courts, limited side lines; expensive.

In the boroughs outside Manhattan the price range is considerably lower, being as low as $4 for open-air courts in the summer, and in the winter ranging from a low of $8 to a high of $23.

Brooklyn: Brooklyn Racquet Club, 2781 Shell Rd. (718–769–5167); 14 indoor and outdoor clay courts; free parking and babysitting; inexpensive. *The Bronx:* Stadium Tennis, 11 E. 162nd St. (293–2386); only open to transients in the winter, in the summer it reverts to a city court; eight unevenly laid, rubberized cork surface courts; moderate to inexpensive. There are also courts in Van Cortlandt Park. *Queens:* Sterling Tennis, 40–15 126th St, Corona. (718–446–5619); Har-tru courts; open-air in summer; inexpensive. Boulevard Gardens, 51–26 Broadway, Woodside (718–545–7774); indoor and outdoor clay courts; moderate to inexpensive. U.S.T.A. National Tennis Center, Flushing Meadows Park, Flushing (718–592–8000); this is the tennis complex where the U.S. Open Championships are played—there are nine indoor and 24 outdoor courts, all in excellent condition; surfaces are Deco II; moderate to inexpensive.

Squash courts are available at the following Manhattan locations: Fifth Avenue Racquet Club (2 W. 37th St., 594–3120), Park Avenue Squash and Racquet Club (3 Park Ave.; 686–1085), Uptown Racquet (151 E. 86th St.; 860–8630). Manhattan's only platform tennis courts are at the Apple Platform Tennis Club (215 E. 24th St.; 684–0970); these courts are closed during the summer. Because racquetball courts come and go as quickly as the ball flies off the wall at you, the Yellow Pages are your best source of information. Fees are generally somewhat lower than for tennis.

Some of the larger city parks maintain bridle paths for **horseback riding.** Near Forest Park, along the Brooklyn–Queens border, the nearest riding stable is Lynne's in Forest Hills (88–03 70th Rd.; 718–261–7679); in Staten Island, riding horses and horse-drawn hayrides are available at West Shore Stables, 52 Hughes Ave., 718–494–9816; in Manhattan, the Claremont Stable (175 W. 89th St.; 724–5100) is right near Central Park; in Brooklyn, there are Prospect Park Riding Stables (51 Caton Place, off Prospect Park West; 718–438–8849) and Jamaica Bay Riding Academy (7000 Shore Parkway; 718–531–8949). All the stables listed also offer instruction. You can expect to pay $15–$22 per hour, without instruction, but usually including a trail guide.

Some other sports opportunities in New York center around schools. Consult, according to your special interests.

SPECTATOR SPORTS. Baseball season, April through October, features the Yankees and Mets, and each schedules about 75 home dates, of which nearly half are night games. The Mets' ballpark is Shea Stadium, in Flushing, Queens (718–507–8499), while the Yankees play at their famous stadium in the Bronx, "the house that Ruth built" (293–6000). Tickets are available at many Ticketron outlets throughout the metropolitan area and a fairly good seat is usually not too hard to find unless the team is involved in crucial, late-season action. Caution: Shea Stadium can be uncomfortably chilly on spring and autumn nights. And the Yankee Stadium area isn't the safest place in the world, so don't linger too long after the game.

Pro football is a furious business, and New York's two pro teams, Giants and Jets, put their fury on display at Giants Stadium in the Meadowlands Sports Complex in New Jersey, a few miles and about 15 minutes from midtown Manhattan via the Lincoln Tunnel by car or, more wisely, by bus. Season ticket holders claim most of the seats for home games, although a few general admission seats—particularly for Jets' games—may be available on a day-of-the-game basis. Jets reserved seat tickets cost $15 and if you think it can get cold nights during baseball season, wait until the winter winds come howling in across the Meadowlands. Bring blankets, antifreeze, hats, gloves—you name it, because, Baby, it gets cold outside when you root, root, root for the home team Jets. For ticket and game information call the stadium at 201–935–3900.

The pro Giants left Yankee Stadium for the greener pastures of the nearby New Jersey Meadowlands sports complex in East Rutherford, New Jersey. Tickets for games at Giants Stadium are $14 and $17; phone 201–935–3900. The season runs from September through January.

Yankee Stadium is most readily accessible via the IRT No. 4, and the IND D and C subway lines to the 161 St. stop. Shea Stadium can be reached by way of the No. 7 Flushing line to the Willets Point–Shea Stadium station. The Shea parking lot (follow the signs from the Van Wyck Expressway or Grand Central Parkway) accommodates thousands of automobiles, though the traffic on both of these highways is always great. To get to the Meadowlands, inquire at the Port Authority Bus Terminal, Eighth Ave. at 42nd St.; 564–8484.

Basketball and **hockey** are the major attractions at Madison Square Garden, which stands above Penn Station at 32 St. and Seventh Ave. Known simply as "The Garden" to generations of athletes and sports fans, this 20,000-seat arena hasn't grown a real winner in recent seasons in either the Knicks—New York's pro basketball entry in the National Basketball Association—or the Rangers, the Big Apple's National Hockey League representative from Manhattan. Again, the result is that tickets are readily available on any given night, at prices ranging from $8–$20 for Knicks games and $8–$25 for Rangers games.

Both teams play a regular season that runs from early October to early April, excluding post-season playoffs that may go another six weeks. The regular season involves about 40 home dates. To find out who's battling either of these home teams call 563–8300. Parking near the Garden is difficult and expensive, so try using the IRT 1, 2, or 3 train, or the IND A, C, or E line to Penn Station.

Diehard sports fans can catch more pro basketball action by venturing out of Manhattan to the Meadowlands to see the scrappy New Jersey Nets play their version of NBA ball (201–935–8888). Hockey fans wanting to get their fill can venture to the Meadowlands to see the New Jersey Devils, or the Nassau Coliseum on nearby Long Island to see the New York Islanders (516–587–9222).

The Garden used to be famous for its **boxing** matches but has fallen on hard times of late for a variety of reasons. The *Daily News* still sponsors the exciting Golden Gloves programs each spring; the very lack of polish and ring experience guarantees action galore. And Madison Square Garden is still home for the final rounds of its post-season collegiate National Invitational Basketball Tournament, offering a Holiday Festival over the Christmas semester break that brings in excellent college teams and is occasional home court for such exciting local college squads as St. John's, Fordham, Manhattan, and Seton Hall. The Garden also hosts some prizefights, indoor pro tennis, prestigious track and field events such as the Millrose Games and entertainment events such as ice shows, the circus, rodeos, wrestling, horse shows, and even rock 'n' roll headliners who play the main arena (563–8300) as well as the smaller Felt Forum (563–8300).

Flat and harness tracks draw millions of **horse racing** enthusiasts each year. Thoroughbred racing takes place at Aqueduct Racetrack in Ozone Park, Queens, and Belmont Racetrack in Elmont, on nearby Long Island, with the season running from October through April at Aqueduct and from May through October at Belmont, except for the month of August when racing shifts upstate to Saratoga. Belmont is where the third and final leg of the "Triple Crown," the Belmont Stakes, is run to determine the nation's best three-year-old racehorse. Since post times vary seasonally it's best to check first with the New York Racing Association (718–641–4700) before heading out to the tracks. Working folks benefit from the night-time programs of standardbred harness races at Yonkers in Westchester County (914–968–4200; just over the New York City border at the edge of the Bronx), and the Meadowlands (from January through August), new home of the Hambletonian, in East Rutherford, New Jersey (201–935–8500). The Meadowlands also runs thoroughbred horses *at night* from September through December. To get there, inquire at the Port Authority Bus Terminal, Eighth Ave. at 42nd St. (564–8484).

The New York City Off-Track Betting Corporation (OTB) is the nation's first government-run off-track betting operation. OTB offers betting programs from some of the best thoroughbred and harness tracks in America. It is a source of entertainment and sport for thousands of New Yorkers and visitors who want to get a bet down or just study the Damon Runyan characters who frequent OTB. There are over 150 branch offices throughout the city's five boroughs, many open seven days a week. Free admission. For further information, the New York City OTB phone number is 704–5100.

Tennis reaches its peak here in early September when the U.S. Open Tennis Championships are played at the USTA National Tennis Center, Flushing Meadows, Queens (718–592–8000). This is one of four titles which enjoys supreme status worldwide, and although tickets for the finals are scarce, you can catch most of the big names as they work their way through the early rounds. The prestigious tournament was recently moved from the West Side Tennis in Forest Hills (718–268–2300) which is still synonymous with the best tennis in the world. Forest Hills stages its own major pro tennis event in the early fall.

Golf tournaments are proliferating so fast that almost any area is a candidate for the next one, although the annual Westchester Classic in early June at the Westchester Country Club in Rye (914–967–6000) is one of the major steps on the Pro Golfers Association Tour.

College football, basketball, and **baseball** can provide some exciting moments on a highly skilled amateur level—as well as the opportunity to see some of the Big Apple's most beautiful campuses. Columbia University, for example, plays football against Ivy League rivals such as Harvard, Yale, and Princeton at the new Wein Stadium at Baker Field. Broadway at 218th St. in the colorful Inwood section of upper Manhattan. St. John's in Brooklyn, Manhattan in the Riverdale section of the Bronx, and Fordham in the Little Italy section off Fordham Road in the Bronx, play a very competitive brand of club- and small-college-division-level football, as does Wagner on rural Staten Island, Iona in Westchester, and Seton Hall in nearby New Jersey, where Rutgers plays the closest thing to a big-time football schedule in the metropolitan area.

All of the above-named colleges and universities have top basketball, baseball, and track and field programs and compete actively in such relatively minor sports as soccer, lacrosse, crew, and swimming. Indeed, Columbia is a perennial Ivy League soccer powerhouse. Most field women's teams in major sports as well. In fact, Fordham has become a national power in women's basketball.

LOTTERIES. At any given time, New York State will have several lotteries going, all benefiting local school districts across the state. Bets range from 50 cents up, with prizes ranging up to multimillion dollar amounts. There are three daily games, the three-digit *Daily* number, *Win-4*, and *Keno*. On Mondays there is the *Cash-40 Lotto*, with lump-sum payments to winners. Wednesdays and Saturdays drawings are held for the *54-number Lotto*, where the million-dollar (usually much more) first prizes are paid out in annual installments over 20 years. The "games" for each vary, ranging from scratch-and-match-the-pictures to genuine lotteries whereby individuals choose a series of digits and compare their numbers to ones drawn at random. Tickets can be purchased at thousands of newsstands and candy stores, but winners for each game are drawn on a different basis. For the daily contests, winning numbers are drawn at 7:40 P.M. on Channel 11 TV (WPIX), with a Keno summary at 10:15. Also on Channel 11, Cash-40 numbers are drawn Mondays at 11:15 P.M., Wednesday Lotto at 11:15 P.M., and Saturday Lotto at 10:55 P.M. For a recording with the current winning numbers, call 488–7796, or check the newspapers the following day. Instant Winners tells you immediately after purchase what you have won in the preliminary rounds, with winners eligible for a grand prize drawing. Each day's or week's numbers are reported in the daily papers as well. Even if you don't win anything, you'll have an interesting souvenir—and you'll have helped the state's school system.

HISTORIC SITES. Wall Street Area and the Harbor: If you are conducting your own walking tour of historical sites and sights, you might do well to start out where the city did—at the harbor. Henry Hudson, an Englishman employed by the Dutch East India Company, sailed his ship, the *Half Moon,* into the harbor in 1609 and the area's inclusion in what Europeans called the "New World" dates from then.

Battery Park. Time your explorations to arrive Tuesday at noon (from the end of June to early September) and your explorations can be accompanied by the brassy beat of a Battery Park Band Concert. A few of the historic sites of note (walking clockwise):

Shrine of Saint Elizabeth Ann Seton, 7 State St. Canonized in 1975, the first American-born saint, she once lived at 8 State St.

Jewish Immigrant Memorial. In front of the Staten Island Ferry Terminal, it commemorates the 23 Jewish men and women who arrived in Nieuw Amsterdam (then chiefly inhabited by Mana-hatta Indians) in 1654, and stayed to found several of America's most distinguished families.

Verrazano Statue. Honors the Florentine navigator who pre-dated Henry Hudson, entering the harbor in 1524. Despite the fact that he boldly took possession of "this island-bay, river, and all countries, rivers, lakes and streams contiguous and adjacent thereunto," his employer, Francis I of France, did nothing further about it, and the island, therefore, never was colonized by France.

Castle Clinton National Monument. Originally built as a harbor fort in 1811, it has been substantially restored as such. It has also served as the Castle Garden amusement center, where P. T. Barnum staged the musical "event of the century" by presenting Jenny Lind. Those who could not obtain tickets formed rowboat parties and listened to the Swedish Nightingale from the river. From 1855 to 1890 the ex-fort played host to some 7,000,000 "new Americans" as the country's chief immigrant entrance station. After that it served as a station for fishes—the city's aquarium—until 1941.

Bowling Green. This is the site, many believe, where Peter Minuit bought the island Manhattan from the native Algonquins. A century later, it was indeed a lawn where sportsmen played bowls. The original 1771 fence around the green is intact today.

U.S. Custom House. It was built by Cass Gilbert in 1907, when America was newly conscious of its central position on the world stage. This may account for the themes of the white marble sculpture: the great continents and commercial cities of the globe.

Fraunces Tavern (corner of Broad and Pearl Sts.). One of the few remaining restored Colonial buildings in the city. Built in 1719 as a handsome private house for Etienne de Lancey, it was bought in 1762 by a Frenchman, Samuel Fraunces, otherwise known as "Black Sam." He ran it as the Queen Charlotte, or Queen's Head Tavern, and it was there, in the second-floor dining room, that General Washington gave the farewell dinner to his officers. Souvenirs of the occasion can be seen in the third floor *Museum of the Revolution.* The ground-floor restaurant open for lunch and dinner weekdays, Washington's birthday. The Tavern once offered "first-class regular dinner for 25 cents, for gentlemen only." The prices are now somewhat more elevated. The entire Tavern is closed weekends. The Museum is open Monday–Friday, 10 A.M.–4 P.M. Free.

To reach Battery Park, take East or West Side IRT (local) to South Ferry.

While at Battery Park you will no doubt want to visit the *Statue of Liberty.* The 151-foot-high lady, the world's best-known symbolic monument, may be visited via the special ferry which leaves from Battery Park every hour on the hour from 10 A.M. to 4 P.M. Wednesday through Sunday, with additional sailings Saturdays, Sundays, and holidays, April through October round-trip fares for adults, $3.25; children (11 and under) $1.50. For ferry information call 269–5755; for Statue information, 363–3200. The boat trip takes 20 minutes; allow two hours for round-trip plus inspection of the Statue. Refreshments and souvenirs available on boats. The Statue has been raising her torch over New York Harbor since 1886.

There is also a ferry from Battery Park to *Ellis Island,* the former immigrant-processing center, through which the ancestors of many, many Americans reached the New World.

Lower Manhattan

A few old streets: Stone Street was the first cobbled under the orders of Nieuw Amsterdam's governor, irascible peg-legged Peter Stuyvesant, who also built a wall along the north edge of the settlement in 1658 as protection against the Indians.

Wall Street follows the course of that original wall. Several years later the first road was built (1668), linking the first colony to a suburban village called Nieuw Haarlem. The road was called Broadway. At 45 Broadway there is a tablet at the site of the first house built on Manhattan in 1613. Nearby is the historic *Trinity Church* (602–0872), reputed to be the wealthiest single church in the world. In 1705, Queen Anne gave Trinity Parish a grant of land covering a substantial chunk of lower Manhattan; the church still owns much of it. Alexander Hamilton and Robert Fulton are buried in the graveyard. The church (built in 1845, the third on the site) and graveyard are open daily from 7 A.M. to 6 P.M. The Trinity Museum is open Monday–Friday 1 P.M.–3:45, P.M., Saturday and Sunday 10 A.M.–3:45. P.M. Admission to all is free.

Nearby is the *Federal Hall National Memorial,* on the site of the country's first capital, where our first President took his first oath of office. A statue of Washington stands on the spot today. The museum includes the Zenger Room, with documents relating to John Peter Zenger's fight for freedom of the press. Also, call for schedule of free weekly concerts, 264–8711.

In the busy City Hall-financial district stands *St. Paul's Chapel,* where Washington worshipped. You can see his pew in the north aisle. The church was also the site of a special service after Washington's inauguration. This handsome church was built in 1761–66, and is the oldest public building in Manhattan. It fills the block between Broadway, Vesey, Church, and Fulton Streets.

Some other Historic Sites in Lower Manhattan: St. Mark's-in-the-Bouwerie, at 10th St. at intersection of Stuyvesant St. and Second Ave., was consecrated in 1799. It stands on the site of a chapel originally built on the edge of Peter Stuyvesant's 300-acre farm (or—in Dutch—Stuyvesant's *bouwerie*). You can see Stuyvesant's grave, and a statue of him, in nearby Stuyvesant Park. Nearby Stuyvesant Town, a "city" within a city—35,000 call this middle-income development "home"—covers part of his riverfront farm.

At the east end of Fulton Street is the *South Street Seaport,* an area that has undergone restoration. Pier 16 has several tall ships, some of which the public may board and view; a museum with displays and folklore about the history of the Port of New York; and many shops and restaurants in restored 18th- and 19th-century buildings often with goods and services in the manner of the era.

Have lunch at nearby *Sweets* (Schermerhorn Row, Fulton St. near Front), one of the world's finest seafood restaurants, little changed in style or excellence since it was founded in 1845. To reach Sweets and/or the Fulton Fish Market, take IRT or BMT line, or Broadway bus to Fulton St. and walk east.

Civic Center

City Hall. The present structure was opened in 1812, restored in 1956. In 1824, Lafayette, the great French ally of the colonists during the Revolutionary War, was officially entertained here. You may sometimes see ceremonies on the steps in honor of a person or group that has performed a good deed. Also of interest is *The Governor's Room,* where period furniture and portraits of George Washington, Alexander Hamilton, and John Jay, among others, are on view. Open to the public, Monday–Friday, 10 A.M.–3 P.M. Free.

Nathan Hale Statue. West of City Hall, but still within the surrounding park, a statue commemorates the patriot whom the British hanged as a spy in 1776. As he prepared to ascend the gallows, he uttered his historic farewell, "I regret that I have but one life to give for my country."

Greenwich Village

The Village was the city's first residential suburb, started in the late 1730s when people fled "north" to escape the plague. *Washington Square* was originally used as a potter's field and public execution ground. By 1826, when it became a drill ground for militia, some 10,000 bodies, victims of the plague or the gallows, had been buried there. Around this time the Square's red brick, white-trimmed houses were built. The old *Boorman House* on the northeast corner was the home of Edith Wharton, William Dean Howells and Henry James.

Washington Arch, at the foot of Fifth Ave., was first built in 1889 when the city celebrated the centenary of Washington's inaugural. The present version was designed by the famous Stanford White, and built in 1895.

Two blocks over from the Square, at the corner of 6th and Greenwich Ave., is the *Jefferson Market Courthouse,* built in 1877 and more recently saved from the wrecker's ball and turned into a branch of the N.Y. Public Library.

There are many other historic houses in the Village—for example, *The narrowest house in the city* at 75½ Bedford St., whose tenants included Edna St. Vincent Millay and John Barrymore. But the only house in the district which you can visit is *The Old Merchant's House,* 29 E. 4th St., 777–1089. The house was built in 1830, was lived in by the same family, the Tredwells, from 1835 to 1933 when the last of the Tredwell sisters died, in her nineties. The house was bought by a grandnephew and presented to the city. Sundays, 1–4 P.M., group tours by appointment. Adults, $2; students and Senior Citizens, $1. *To get there:* take Third Ave. bus to 4th St.; or IRT Lexington local to Astor Place.

Another noteworthy old house not far from the Village is the *Theodore Roosevelt Mansion,* 28 E. 20th St. 260–1616. The Rough Rider was born and grew up in this typical upper-middle-class brownstone which is well kept up, and open to visitors. Daily 9 A.M.–5 P.M., except Monday–Tuesday. Adults, $1; children and Senior Citizens, free.

Midtown and Uptown

The Abigail Adams Smith Museum at 421 E. 61st St. 838–6878. One of Manhattan's last 18th-century buildings. Originally the carriage house for the home the then Vice-President John Adams had built for his daughter Abigail. A gem kept in perfect condition by the Colonial Dames of America. Guide on duty. Monday–Friday, 10 A.M.–4 P.M. Adults, $2; Senior Citzens, $1.

Far Uptown: *Morris-Jumel Mansion,* W. 160th St. and Edgecombe Ave. This Georgian colonial hilltop house was built in 1765. A year later, George Washington slept here for a night. His camp bed may still be seen. Here too Aaron Burr married the wealthy Mme. Jumel, then in her sixties, and soon divorced her. *To get there:* Madison Ave. uptown bus 2 or 3 to 162nd St.; or IND Eighth Ave. subway to 163rd St. (B or K local). Tuesday–Sunday, 10 A.M. to 4 P.M. Adults, $2; students and Senior Citizens, 50 cents. Phone 923–8008.

The Dyckman House, 204th St. and Broadway, was built in 1783, and was the farm residence of the wealthy Dyckman family, which once owned most of northern Manhattan. The only remaining Dutch farmhouse in New York City. *To get there:* IND (Eighth Ave.) subway (A) to 204th St. Tuesday–Sunday, 11 A.M.–4 P.M. Free.

General Grant National Memorial, Riverside Dr. and 122nd St., 666–1640. The Civil War general and two-term president is buried in the crypt, with photo and other exhibits also housed in the tomb. Open daily, 9 A.M.–4:30 P.M.; closed Monday and Tuesday. Free admission.

The Other Boroughs

Brooklyn: *Brooklyn Heights,* a picturesque neighborhood of brownstone, brick, and old wooden houses high on a bluff overlooking New York Harbor, was designated New York's first "historic district." The New York Landmarks Commission calls the Heights "by far the finest remaining microcosm of our city as it was more than 100 years ago." Once a year the Brooklyn Historical Society conducts walking tours of some of the private homes, but even at other times you may wish to wander through the streets and trace the evolution of the New York townhouse: wooden and brick Federal style, Greek Revival, Gothic Revival (which came into style in the 1840s), Romanesque Revival, and Renaissance Revival. The Heights' *Lady of Lebanon Church* is the first Romanesque Revival building in the U.S. An esplanade reached by way of Montague Street, the residential area's primary shopping block, affords a spectacular view of the lower Manhattan Skyline and the New York Harbor.

Lefferts Homestead, Prospect Park, 718–965–6505. A homestead built in Dutch Colonial days. Call for schedule. Free.

Bronx: *Van Cortlandt Mansion Museum* 543–3344. Built in 1748, this house, now run by the Colonial Dames, has furnishings and household goods which reflect both its Dutch and British owners. The house was being renovated at press time; plans were to reopen it in September 1988. Tentative hours: 10 A.M. 4:30 P.M. Wednesday–Saturday, 12–4:30 P.M. Sunday. Small admission prices were not set at press time. *To get there:* IRT Broadway subway to Van Cortlandt Park (end of line).

Poe Cottage, Poe Park, Kingsbridge Road at the Grand Concourse, 881–8900. Edgar Allan Poe wrote many of his works (including *Annabelle Lee*) in this small cottage, which has barely been preserved as it was in the poet's day. Adults $1, children free. Open 9 A.M.–5 P.M. Wednesday–Friday; 10 A.M.–4 P.M. Saturday; 1 P.M.–5 P.M. Sunday.

Queens: *Bowne House,* 37–01 Bowne St., Flushing, 718–359–0528. The Society of Friends assembled in this old house. Built in 1661, it is today a shrine commemorating the struggle for religious freedom. Tuesday, Saturday, Sunday, 2:30–4:30 P.M. Adults, $1; children 25 cents.

LIBRARIES. The New York Public Library System is divided into research and branch libraries. The branch libraries are the lending libraries, but the research libraries don't allow their materials to be taken out, though they can be used in-house. The system includes a number of outstanding individual branches, some of which will be detailed below. The library operates an excellent telephone reference service: 340–0849.

The crown jewel of the system, on Fifth Avenue from 40th to 42nd streets, is, ironically, a private library open to the public—funded originally by the Samuel J. Tilden Trust and the Astor and Lenox libraries of the 1890s. The city contributed to its founding by donating the site and constructing the $9 million building that was to house the collections.

This, the *Central Research Library,* is a familiar city landmark. It has a two-block-long Beaux-Arts façade, with twin lions perched alongside the steps leading to the entrance. With a public card catalog containing 10 million entries, and more than half an acre of reading rooms, it includes resources for virtually every field of endeavor. Only the Library of Congress and Harvard's Widener Library are larger. No books are lent out at the Main Library, but anyone, resident or not, may use the Main Library's volumes within the confines of the building.

The 42nd St. library, however, is something of a museum as well as a research center. Sixteen years under construction, it opened in 1911, christened at the time by President Taft. The expansive marble foyer bespeaks extravagance in a way that is rarely seen in New York. In addition there are several galleries throughout the building, and such specialty reference rooms as the Economic and Public Affairs Room and the Science and Technology Room. Most of these are open to the public; for some, including the Manuscript Room, a special pass is needed. There are always two or three special exhibitions at the library in the lobby and along the second- and third-floor corridors—prints, books, or manuscripts—as well as the Berg Collection, which has large exhibits that change twice a year. The Berg specializes in literature, and, except for the exhibit area, is open to qualified scholars and researchers only. The Gottesman Exhibition Hall, right off the first-floor lobby is the site of large special exhibits. The Edna Barnes Salomon Room, located on the third floor, opened in May 1986, is the headquarters for the library's special collections and the showplace for new acquisitions. It also serves as the library's main picture gallery. One of the most elegant rooms in the library is the newly restored, sky-lit domed Celeste Bartos Forum, which houses the library's Public Education Program. Also available for party rentals, it has a capacity of 400 people.

Several midtown Manhattan branches are of particular interest, and worth noting here. These include the *Mid-Manhattan Library,* the main circulating library in the system, at 40th St. and Fifth Ave. Whereas the 42nd St. Main Library is purely a reference and research facility, the Mid-Manhattan Library is a lending library whose collection emphasizes science, education, business, history, and sociology. The *Library and Museum of Performing Arts* at Lincoln Center (111 Amsterdam Ave.; there are

New York Public Library at 42nd Street

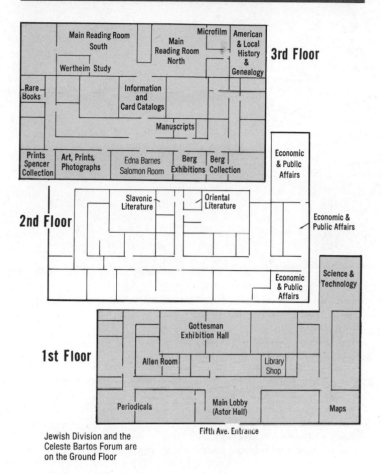

3rd Floor

Main Reading Room South
Wertheim Study
Main Reading Room North
Microfilm
American & Local History & Genealogy
Rare Books
Information and Card Catalogs
Manuscripts

2nd Floor

Prints Spencer Collection
Art, Prints, Photographs
Edna Barnes Salomon Room
Berg Exhibitions
Berg Collection
Economic & Public Affairs
Slavonic Literature
Oriental Literature
Economic & Public Affairs
Economic & Public Affairs
Science & Technology

1st Floor

Gottesman Exhibition Hall
Allen Room
Library Shop
Periodicals
Main Lobby (Astor Hall)
Maps
Fifth Ave. Entrance

Jewish Division and the
Celeste Bartos Forum are
on the Ground Floor

really two libraries here: one, open to the public, for records, printed music, dance, film and drama books, and the other, open to qualified researchers by permission. This library also has regular exhibits of performing arts materials such as set models, designers' sketches, music manuscripts, etc.). The *Donnell Library* (20 W. 53rd St., also strong on performing and fine arts and popular books in foreign languages). The *Library for the Blind and Physically Handicapped* (166 Avenue of the Americas).

There are 82 branch libraries in Manhattan, the Bronx, and Staten Island. Hours vary, so it is best to check with individual branches when planning a visit.

Special-Interest Libraries

New York has numerous specialized libraries on almost all subjects. Some, listed below alphabetically by subject area, are open to the public. Others may be found by consulting the *Special Libraries Directory of Greater New York,* available at the Mid-Manhattan Library, 8 E. 40th St. If the library you are interested in is not open to the public, you may know someone in a professional association who is allowed in. In all cases, we suggest you call before going.

Advertising and marketing. *Batten, Barton, Durstine & Osborne Information Resource Center,* 1285 Ave. of the Americas, 415–5000, ext. 101.

Architecture, crafts, and design. *Fashion Institute of Technology Library,* 227 W. 27th St., 760–7590, and *American Craft Council,* 45 W. 45th St., 869–9422. An appointment is necessary for nonmembers, and hours are erratic; call ahead.

Banking. *New York Stock Exchange,* 20 Broad St., 656–3000.

Behaviorial sciences. *American Society for Psychical Research,* 5 W. 73rd St., 799–5050 (open to members only), and *Kristine Mann Library,* 28 E. 39th St., 697–7877, the latter specializing in the work of C.G. Jung.

Biblical studies. *American Bible Society,* 1865 Broadway, near Lincoln Center; 581–7400, where Bibles can be found in more than 1,700 languages.

Black studies. *Schomburg Center for Research in Black Culture,* 515 Lenox Ave. at 135th St., 862–4000. A research division of the New York Public Library.

Broadcasting. *Museum of Broadcasting,* 1 E. 53rd St., 752–7684. Includes a large videotape collection of historic TV broadcasts.

Business subjects. *American Institute of CPA Library,* 1211 Ave. of the Americas, 800–522–5434, and the *Brooklyn Public Library,* Grand Army Plaza, Brooklyn; 718–780–7700.

Chemistry. *Chemists' Club Library,* 52 E. 41st St., 679–6383.

Civil liberties. *ACLU,* 132 W. 43rd St., 944–9800.

Economics and commerce. *Dun and Bradstreet,* 99 Church St., 312–6500, asks that you call ahead for an appointment. Another source is the *U.S. Department of Commerce,* 26 Federal Plaza, 264–0630.

Education. *Borough of Manhattan Community Colleges,* 199 Chambers St., 618–1000, has an extensive collection of Third World materials. *Children's Book Council,* 67 Irving Pl., 254–2666, is self-explanatory.

Flowers and plants. *Horticultural Society of New York,* 128 W. 58th St., 757–0915.

Geography. *Explorers Club,* 46 E. 70th St., 628–8383. An appointment is needed.

History and Genealogy. *New York Genealogical and Biographical Society,* 122 E. 58th St., 755–8532.

Industry and labor. *American Arbitration Association,* 140 W. 51st St., 484–4000. Data, laws, and court decisions in this field can be found at the *Worker's Compensation Board,* 180 Livingston St., Brooklyn, 718–802–6600.

Insurance. *College of Insurance,* 101 Murray St., 962–4111.

Medicine. *New York Academy of Medicine,* 2 E. 103rd St., 876–8200.

Music. In addition to the previously mentioned Lincoln Center and Donnell Branches of the Public Library, the *Wallace Library,* 799–5000, at Juilliard's Lincoln Center building requires advance arrangements. Also see the *Metropolitan Opera Association Archives* at Lincoln Center, 799–3100; appointment required.

Public administration. *John Jay College of Criminal Justice,* 444 W. 56th St., 489–5183, has special collections on police work.

Publishing. *Oxford University Press Library,* 200 Madison Ave., 679–7300.

MUSEUMS.

Examples of all manner of artistry from throughout the ages are on view in New York, much of it housed in buildings which are of great architectural interest themselves.

The fine arts lead, and such museums as the Metropolitan and the Museum of Modern Art are among the best in the world, but if the Old (or New) Masters don't move you, stimulation can be found in other museums. There are studies of nature and the stars, of man's history on earth, and more particularly, of his life in New York City. Smaller museums, or portions of larger ones, are devoted to coins, musical instruments, rare books, crafts and folk art, ships, interior decoration, clothing, textiles, medicine, historical figures—the list is endless. Once a year, usually in mid-June, the stretch of upper Fifth Ave. known as "Museum Mile" becomes a pedestrian mall between 6 and 9 P.M. From 82nd to 105th sts., strollers are free to come and go at ten of the city's best-known museums, including the Metropolitan, the Museum of the City of New York, the Jewish Museum, and the Cooper-Hewitt. Admission to all is free that night, with street musicians, mimes, and clown troupes entertaining the walkers outside. Check with any of the above museums for exact date and additional details.

Lastly there often are exhibitions sponsored by banks, oil companies, and large industrial corporations, usually in the lobbies of their office buildings; or you may find a display of anything literally from soup to nuts squirreled away in some corner of a school, church, YMCA, or firehouse—you name it.

The following New York City museums are all in Manhattan unless otherwise noted.

American Craft Museum, 40 W. 53rd St.; 965–6047. Exhibitions spotlighting contemporary craftspersons working in clay, glass, fiber, wood, metal, and paper. Open Tuesday 10 A.M.–8 P.M., Wednesday–Saturday 10 A.M.–5 P.M. Admission is $3.50 for adults, $1.50 for children under 16, students and senior citizens. Children under 12 admitted free when accompanied by adult.

American Museum of Natural History. Central Park West at 79th St.; 769–5100. Billed as the world's largest natural history museum, where everything involving animal, vegetable, and mineral is dramatically highlighted, the American Museum of Natural History has an incredible array of marvels too numerous to be taken in on a single visit. (The museum's collections comprise some 36 million artifacts and specimens!) A few notables are the exquisite 563–carat (golf-ball-size) Star of India star sapphire; one of only two dinosaur mummies known to exist in the world (part of the largest and most complete dinosaur collection anywhere); an enormous crosscut of a Giant Sequoia tree over 90 feet in circumference and

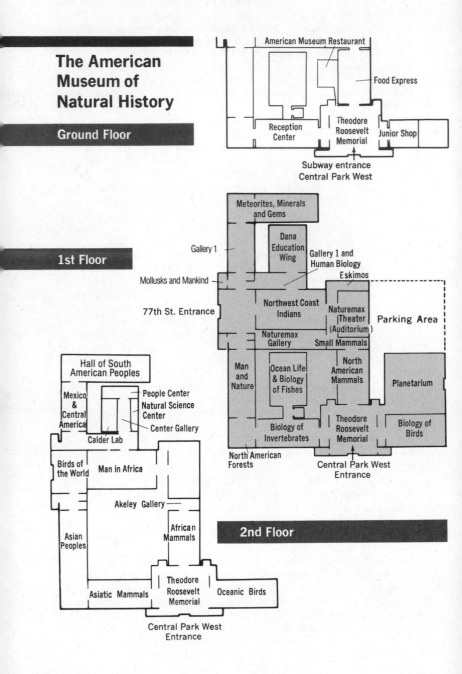

The American Museum of Natural History

Ground Floor

American Museum Restaurant

Food Express

Reception Center

Theodore Roosevelt Memorial

Junior Shop

Subway entrance
Central Park West

1st Floor

Meteorites, Minerals and Gems

Gallery 1

Dana Education Wing

Gallery 1 and Human Biology

Eskimos

Mollusks and Mankind

77th St. Entrance

Northwest Coast Indians

Naturemax Theater (Auditorium)

Parking Area

Naturemax Gallery

Small Mammals

Man and Nature

Ocean Life & Biology of Fishes

North American Mammals

Planetarium

Biology of Invertebrates

Theodore Roosevelt Memorial

Biology of Birds

North American Forests

Central Park West Entrance

Hall of South American Peoples

Mexico & Central America

People Center
Natural Science Center
Center Gallery

Calder Lab

Birds of the World

Man in Africa

Akeley Gallery

African Mammals

2nd Floor

Asian Peoples

Asiatic Mammals

Theodore Roosevelt Memorial

Oceanic Birds

Central Park West Entrance

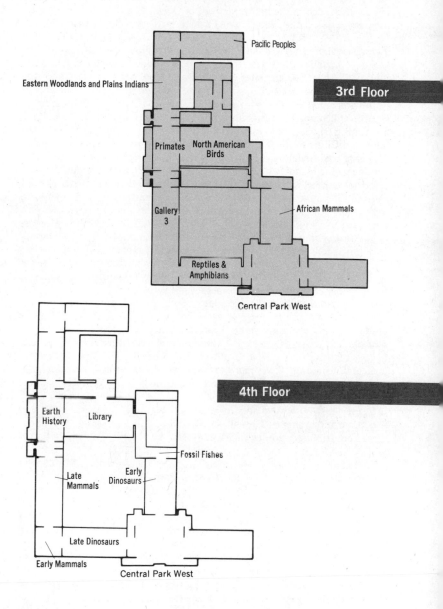

3rd Floor

Pacific Peoples

Eastern Woodlands and Plains Indians

Primates

North American Birds

African Mammals

Gallery 3

Reptiles & Amphibians

Central Park West

4th Floor

Earth History

Library

Fossil Fishes

Late Mammals

Early Dinosaurs

Late Dinosaurs

Early Mammals

Central Park West

dating back to A.D. 550; and, of course, the 94-foot Blue whale, which hangs suspended in the first floor Hall of Ocean Life. The newest permanent attraction is the Naturemax Theater, with New York City's largest indoor screen (40 feet by 66 feet) and a special projection system that creates an incredibly realistic and spectacular film experience. The film schedule includes films guaranteed to leave audiences gasping in their seats. Call 769–5650 for times and admission fees. Another treasure is the Gardner D. Stout Hall of Asian Peoples, focusing on the rich cultures of Asia with 3,000 artifacts and artworks from the dawn of civilization to the present, many of which have never been shown to the public. It's a fascinating trip back into time, from 600,000 years ago when Peking Man inhabited China to the late 19th century when Western technology began changing traditional ways of life. Explore the Arab world, the Indian Subcontinent, the Himalayan Mountains, the Mongolian steppes; and be dazzled by the peerless Chinese jades, rare Tibetan religious tapestries, and exquisite Japanese ivory carvings. You can also journey from the Amazon to the Andes in the museum's newest permanent exhibit, the Hall of South American Peoples, opened in Oct. 1988. The Arthur Ross Hall of Meteorites showcases a wide variety of meteorites, rock samples from the moon, an audiovisual program showing the impact of meteorites, and a series of exhibits examining the origin and significance of meteorites. The Margaret Mead Hall of Pacific Peoples is on the third floor. In other parts of the museum are exhibitions of minerals and gems, birds, dinosaurs, fishes, invertebrates, reptiles and amphibians, shells, forests, ecology, mammals, and man. There are frequent lectures and movies, special exhibitions, a graduate-study program, three theaters, library (400,000 volumes represent one of the largest and most valuable research collections on natural history on this continent), laboratories, the Whale's Lair Cafe, and a cafeteria and restaurant. Two major exhibits scheduled at press time for 1989 are: Madagascar, Mar.–July; and Crossroads of Continents, Dec. 1989–May 1990.

Open daily, 10 A.M.–5:45 P.M., and to 9 P.M. on Wednesday, Friday, and Saturday evenings. Closed Thanksgiving and Christmas days. Suggested contribution: adults, $3.50; children, $1.50; free Fri. and Sat. evenings after 5 P.M.

Hayden Planetarium, a separate division of the American Museum of Natural History, at 81st St. and Central Park West, 769–5920, presents its ever-popular Sky Show. A huge, star-filled dome brings the heavens to life via a Zeiss Star Projector and other dazzling special-effects techniques. The Guggenheim Space Theater, a circular area with 22 screens for projecting a wraparound slide presentation serves as an introduction to the Sky Show. Adults, $3.75; students and senior citizens, with ID, $2.75; children under 13 years, $2. Also, Cosmic Laser Light Concert, Fri.–Sat. evenings, $6. Call 769–5921 for all schedules.

American Numismatic Society. Broadway at 155th St.; 234–3130. The society advances numismatic knowledge as it applies to history, art, archeology, and economics. A major exhibit, The World of Coins, surveys the history of coinage and money. Lectures on numismatic research are open to the public. Library. Open Tuesday–Saturday, 9 A.M.–4:30 P.M., Sunday, 1–4 P.M. Free.

Asia Society. 725 Park Ave. at 70th St.; 288–6400. A $16.6-million, eight-story, red-granite building, designed by Edward Larrabee Barnes, is the new headquarters for this nonprofit educational group that concentrates on Asian affairs. Although not exactly a museum, the facility offers exhibits accenting Far Eastern art. The permanent collection features three sections: an installation of South Asian stone and bronze sculptures, including art from India, Nepal, Pakistan, and Afghanistan; the Chinese section, displaying ritual bronze vessels, ceramics, sculptures, and paintings, along with a small group of Korean ceramics; and the Japan section, which houses ceramics, paintings, and wood sculptures. Three galleries are used for large special exhibitions in the fall. During the rest of the year the *C.V. Starr Gallery* holds temporary exhibits, the *Arthur Ross Gallery* is the location for informal exhibits primarily from local collections, and the *Mr. and Mrs. John D. Rockefeller 3rd Gallery* contains an exhibition from the Rockefeller collection.

The following exhibits are tentatively scheduled for 1989: Aboriginal Art, Oct. 6, 1988–Jan. 8, 1989; Emperor's Classic/H. Shum, Jan. 15–Apr.; Imperial Enamels: Chinese Cloisonné from the collection of Pierre Uldry, Feb.–Apr.; The Spiritual Art of Bhutan, June–Aug.; Major Landmarks of Indian Architecture (photography), Oct. 1989–Apr. 1990.

Open Tuesday–Saturday, 11 A.M.–6 P.M., Sunday, noon to 5 P.M. Admission: $2; senior citizens and students, $1.

The Brooklyn Museum. Eastern Parkway and Washington Ave., Brooklyn; 718–638–5000. Flanked by the Brooklyn Botanic Gardens, this museum is a real find for museum lovers who enjoy viewing the sights but not battling the crowds. Though the museum is the seventh largest in the nation and houses a truly outstanding collection of artistry dating from ancient history to contemporary times, visitors are able to relax and enjoy the collection in an atmosphere of quiet peacefulness far removed from the hustle-bustle so often associated with many major museums. Perhaps most highly acclaimed for its world-renowned collection of ancient Egyptian art, the museum also has extensive collections of the primitive arts of Africa, Japan, and Indonesia, as well as American Indian primitive art. Also on view are the arts of India and the Orient, American painting and sculpture, prints, drawings, costume collections, pewter, silver, ceramics, china (Wedgwood buffs will be pleased with the Emily Winthrop Miles gallery, which contains a vast collection of the fine china), glass, and 28 completely furnished American period rooms—from colonial days through the 20th century. Another standout not to be overlooked is the museum's outdoor sculpture garden; amidst the ivy, you'll find a vast array of ornamentation taken from Manhattan buildings, including one very lifelike dragon who looks as though he could have flown directly from Tolkein's Middle Earth.

The tentative schedule of 1989 exhibits is as follows: Cleopatra's Egypt: Age of the Ptolemies, Oct. 7, 1988–Jan. 2, 1989; Courbet Reconsidered, Nov. 4, 1988–Jan. 16, 1989; 19th Century French Watercolors and Drawings from the Brooklyn Museum Collection, Dec. 2, 1988–Jan. 23, 1989; Four Americans: Aspects of Current Sculpture, Feb. 10–May 15; The Stubborn Genius of W. Eugene Smith 1918–1978, June–Aug.; Pearlstein: Sphinx Prints, June–Aug.; Hispanic Art in the United States, June 10–Sept. 4; Andrew Wyeth: The Helga Pictures, June 16–Sept. 18; 25th National Print Exhibition, Oct. 1989–Jan. 1990; Fin de Siecle Couture: Worth, Pingat and Doucet 1885–1905, Nov. 1989–Feb. 1990.

Points of Interest

1) Sculpture Garden
2) Museum Shop
3) Lobby Gallery
4) Grand Lobby
5) Robert E. Blum Special Exhibition
   Gallery
6) African Art
7) The Americas
8) Oceanic
9) Community Gallery
10) Cafeteria
11) Himalayas/Southeast Asia
12) Japanese Art
13) Korean Art
14) Library
15) Chinese Art
16) Indian Art
17) Islamic Art
18) Print Gallery
19) Art School
20) Greek Art
21) Roman and Coptic Art
22) Lecture
23) Court
24) Coptic Art
25) Wilbur Library of Egyptology
26) Middle Kingdom and Dynasty XVIII
27) Monor Arts
28) Ancient Near Eastern Art
29) Old and Middle Kingdoms

30) Predynastic Period
31) Old Kingdom
32) Funerary Arts
33) Egyptian Deities
34) Ramesside and Late Periods
35) 19th-Century American Period Rooms
    and Decorative Arts
36) Wedgwood Gallery
37) Neo-Classical Period Rooms and
    Gallery
38) Ceramics
39) Glassware
40) American Folk Art
41) 18-Century Period Rooms:
    New England
42) Danbury Alcove
43) Metalwares
44) 18th-Century Period Rooms: the South
45) Special Exhibition Gallery
46) 20th-Century Decorative Arts
47) Jan Martense Schenck House
48) 17th- and 18-Century Decorative Arts
49) Costumes and Textiles Gallery/Costume
    Theatre
50) American Painting III
51) American Painting II
52) American Painting I
53) American Painting IV
54) European Painting
55) Rotunda
56) Modern Painting

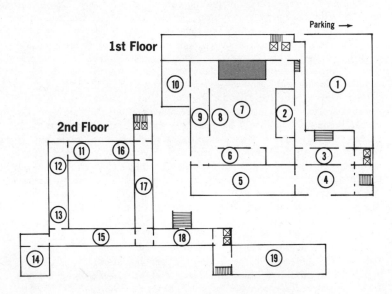

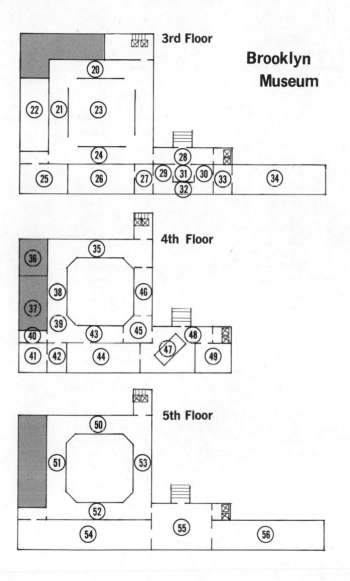

3rd Floor

Brooklyn Museum

4th Floor

5th Floor

The museum has concerts, films, and lectures (write or call for a schedule), and there is a cafeteria in the building. The Gallery Shop sells folk art and handicrafts from over 65 countries. Open daily, 10 A.M.–5 P.M. Closed Tuesdays, Thanksgiving, Christmas, and New Year's Day. Suggested contribution, $3 adults, $1.50 students with valid ID, $1 senior citizens. Free to members, and children under 12 with an adult.

China House Gallery. 125 E. 65th St.; 744–8181. Changing exhibitions of classical Chinese art is exhibited at this facility operated by the China Institute in America, Inc. Open Monday–Friday, 10 A.M.–5 P.M.; Saturday and Sunday, 11 A.M.–5 P.M. Suggested contribution, $1.

The Cloisters. Fort Tryon Park; 923–3700. A branch of the Metropolitan Museum of Art, this medieval art complex is perched on a hill overlooking the George Washington Bridge and the Hudson River. Constructed from the ruins of five French cloisters, some of the highlights include: 12th- and 13th-century Spanish frescoes; the extraordinary Unicorn tapestries; a Romanesque apse; a complete 12th-century architectural ensemble from a ruined abbey of Gascony; Romanesque wooden figure of the Enthroned Virgin and Child; the Bury Saint Edmunds Cross; stained-glass lancets from the Carmelite Church of Boppardam-Rhein; early Christian chalice of Antioch; an arcade from a Benedictine priory of Froville in eastern France; and scores of other priceless objects. It's well worth the trip uptown to this very peaceful retreat. Can be reached on the M4 bus, which goes up Madison Ave. in midtown. Open Tuesday–Sunday, 9:30 A.M.–5:15 P.M.; closed Mondays. Suggested contribution: adults, $5; senior citizens and students, $2.50; children under 12, free.

Cooper-Hewitt Museum, the Smithsonian Institution's National Museum of Design. 2 E. 91st St.; 860–6868. Founded in 1897 by Eleanor, Amy, and Sarah Hewitt as an adjunct to the Cooper Union (established by their grandfather, Peter Cooper), the museum collections were later entrusted to the Smithsonian Institution in 1967. In 1976, the Cooper-Hewitt opened in the historic mansion of American industrialist and philanthropist, Andrew Carnegie. The collection's accent is on decorative arts of all periods and countries, highlighting architecture and ornament drawings, prints, textiles, jewelry, ceramics, wallpapers, metalworks, woodworks, and specialized materials. (The permanent collection is never shown in its entirety; pieces are usually shown in changing exhibitions related to design.) Gallery space is predominantly made up of small, intimate rooms and hallways, many with magnificently carved Scotch oak or teak ceilings and walls.

The museum boasts the largest drawing and print collection in the U.S., and its textile department is one of the nation's most comprehensive. These materials are available as a research resource to the general public, and are of especial interest to designers, architects, and scholars, all on an appointment basis. An extensive reference and picture-research library is also open to the public by appointment. A lovely garden, true to Carnegie's day, provides a perfect escape from the city's hectic pace, while extensive book and catalog publications are available by subscription from the museum shop.

At press time the only exhibit scheduled for a Mar. 1989 opening is *L'Art de Vivre:* Decorative Arts and Design in France 1789–1989. The exhibit, a special celebration of French design commemmorating the bicentennial of the French Revolution, is to span four floors of galleries. Open

Plan of the Cloisters

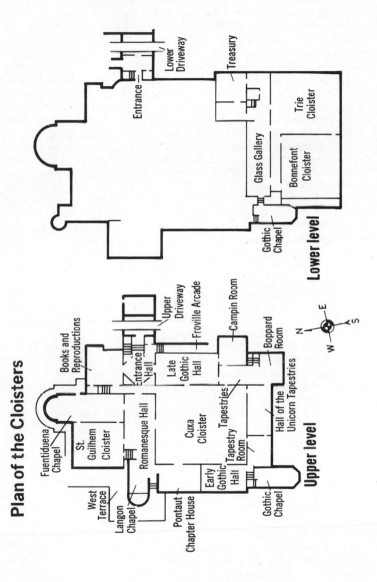

Upper level

Books and Reproductions

Fuentiduena Chapel

West Terrace

Langon Chapel

St. Guilhem Cloister

Romanesque Hall

Entrance Hall

Upper Driveway

Froville Arcade

Late Gothic Hall

Campin Room

Boppard Room

Pontaut Chapter House

Cuxa Cloister

Early Gothic Hall

Tapestries

Tapestry Room

Hall of the Unicorn Tapestries

Gothic Chapel

N E S W

Lower level

Entrance

Lower Driveway

Treasury

Glass Gallery

Bonnefont Cloister

Trie Cloister

Gothic Chapel

Tuesdays–Saturdays 10 A.M.–5 P.M., Sunday noon–5 P.M., Tuesday evenings til 9 P.M. Admission is $3 for adults, $1.50 for students, senior citizens, and children under 12, free on Tuesday evenings.

The Frick Collection. 1 E. 70th St.; 288–0700. In a word, The Frick Collection is magnificent. While most museums are simply a display area for works of art, the Frick has an elegant aura of an art lover's private home. Room after room is filled with masterpieces that make one's head spin. Even the most casual art-watcher will appreciate these works by the grand masters of art, including Renoir's *Mother and Children,* Vermeer's *Mistress and Maid,* Rembrandt's *Self Portrait,* Corot's *The Boatman of Mortefontaine,* and others by Fragonard, Bellini, Titian, El Greco, Turner, Whistler, Van Dyck—and the list goes on. Paintings, sculpture, exquisite furniture, decorative arts, stunning enamels, huge Oriental rugs—The Frick Collection has them all. Some highlights: South Hall—Vermeer's *Officer and Laughing Girl* and *Girl Interrupted at Her Music;* Boucher Room—Eight panels showing the *Arts and Sciences* painted by Boucher for Madame de Pompadour; Dining Room—18th-century British paintings including Hogarth's *Miss Mary Edwards,* Gainsborough's *Mall in St. James's Park;* Fragonard Room—Fragonard's *The Progress of Love,* 18th-century French furniture, including pieces by Riesener, Lacroix, Gouthière, Dupré, and Carlin, and Sèvres porcelains; Living Hall—Titian's *A Man in a Red Cap* and *Pietro Aretino,* El Greco's *Saint Jerome;* Library—British portraits and landscapes by Gainsborough, Reynolds, Lawrence, Romney, and Turner.

To add icing to the cake, the building in which they are housed provides the sumptuous background necessary for such a collection. Overlooking Central Park (which can be glimpsed through the floor-to-ceiling French doors lining many of the rooms), the museum was the residence of Henry Clay Frick, the Pittsburgh coke and steel industrialist. A gorgeous indoor court, complete with fountain and tiered-glass ceiling, is the perfect resting place to sit and catch one's breath after seeing so many treasures. Be sure not to miss the Enamel Room with its 16th-century painted enamel dishes and triptychs, or the West Gallery, a huge room with a truly impressive display of art, among them Constable's *The White Horse,* and Bronzino's lovely *Portrait of Lodovico Capponi.*

A museum shop sells prints, cards, books, and detailed catalogs of the collection. Open Tuesday–Saturday, 10 A.M.–6 P.M.; Sunday, 1–6 P.M.; closed Monday and major holidays. Adults, $3; students and senior citizens, $1.50. Sunday, $3. Children under 10 not admitted; those under 16 must be accompanied by an adult.

The Solomon R. Guggenheim Museum. 1071 Fifth Ave. at 88th St.; 360–3500. The ultramodern façade and interior created by Frank Lloyd Wright is the centerpiece for the modern works on display. The *Justin K. Thannhauser Collection* consists mainly of French works from the Impressionist and Post-Impressionist eras, including Pissarro, Manet, Renoir, Cézanne, van Gogh, Gauguin, Toulouse-Lautrec, and Degas, and heavily emphasizes works by Picasso and Braque. *Masters of Modern Art,* another permanent collection gallery, contains a selection of 90 of the finest and most famous paintings of Kandinsky, Klee, Léger, Chagall, and many others. Artists represented in the *Peggy Guggenheim Collection* (in Venice) include Klee, Ernst, de Kooning, Gorky, Kandinsky and Pollock, among others. The main, spiral gallery is used exclusively for the temporary ex-

The Frick Collection

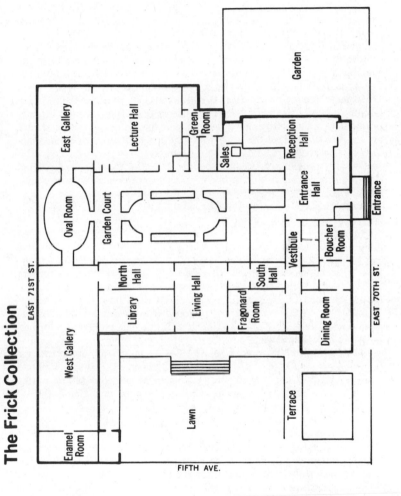

hibits for which the Guggenheim is famous; check the newspapers or *New York* and *New Yorker* magazines.

Taped or guided tours are available by appointment; 360–3558. The Guggenheim also offers an extensive bookstore and a café. The museum is open Tuesday, 11 A.M.–7:45 P.M. Wednesday–Sunday and holidays, 11 A.M.–4:45 P.M., closed Mondays. Admission: $4; students and adults over 62, $2; children under seven, free; Tuesday evenings, 5–7:45 P.M., free.

Harbor Defense Museum. 101st St. at Fort Hamilton Pkwy., Brooklyn; 718–630–4349. Situated at Fort Hamilton at the Brooklyn end of the Verrazano-Narrows Bridge, this museum is for military buffs. Its collection includes artillery equipment dating back to the 18th century, small arms, uniforms, and a wide array of military miniatures. Museum and souvenir shop open Monday, Wednesday, and Friday 1–4 P.M.; Saturday, 10 A.M.–5 P.M.; and Sunday, 1–5 P.M. Free. Group tours can be arranged.

Hispanic Society of America. Broadway and 155th St.; 690–0743. The famous Spanish masters El Greco, Velasquez, and Goya are elegantly displayed here, along with collections of metalwork, sculpture, pottery, tiles, and textiles that reflect the history and culture of Hispanic people. Open Tuesday–Saturday, 10 A.M.–4:30 P.M., Sunday, 1–4 P.M. Closed Monday and holidays; the library reading room is closed for the month of August. Free, but contributions are appreciated. Group reservations recommended; call 926–2234.

International Center of Photography. 1130 Fifth Ave. at 94th St.; 860–1777. The only museum in New York City devoted exclusively to photography. Opened in 1974 and housed in a neo-Georgian landmark building that was once headquarters for the prestigious Audubon Society, the galleries display continuous, changing exhibits of works by such as Henri Cartier-Bresson, Alfred Eisenstaedt, Berenice Abbott, and others.

The museum shop sells books, postcards, posters, and limited-edition prints. Also offered are lectures, courses, and workshops. Open Tuesday, noon–8 P.M., Wednesday–Friday, noon–5 P.M., Saturday–Sunday, 11 A.M.–6 P.M., closed Monday. Admission, $2.50; students and senior citizens, $1. Free Tuesday, 5–8 P.M.

I.C.P./Midtown. 77 W. 45th St., 536–6443. This branch of the International Center of Photography, opened in October 1985, displays photographic exhibits. The museum bookstore, in addition to selling books, prints, posters, and cards, also has bookstore exhibitions. Call 860–1485 for details and group tours. Open Monday–Friday, 11 A.M.–6 P.M., Saturday, noon–5 P.M., Free.

Japan Society. 333 E. 47th St.; 832–1155. Organized in 1907 to bring the peoples of Japan and the United States closer together through the examination and appreciation of their respective cultures, this gallery features a wonderfully serene setting for exhibits from well-known Japanese and American museums and private collections of Japanese art. Other Japan Society programs include movies, lectures, classes, audiovisual presentations, concerts, and drama. Call 752–3015 for reservations. Open daily 11 A.M.–5 P.M. Suggested contribution, $2.50.

Jewish Museum. 1109 Fifth Ave. at 92nd St.; 860–1888. Established in 1904, the Jewish Museum is dedicated to collecting and displaying art and artifacts that represent Jewish tradition spanning nearly 4,000 years. Elegantly housed in the former residence of the Warburgs (donated in 1944), the collection, one of the largest of its kind in the world, includes ceremonial objects, antiquities, paintings, sculpture, photographs, textiles, decorative arts, and more—all created by Jewish artists or dealing with Jewish subjects. A new permanent exhibition, Israel in Antiquity: from David to Herod, opened in 1982, and a second addition, the National Jewish Archive of Broadcasting, opened late March 1984. A major work, *The Holocaust,* by George Segal, was permanently installed in Jan. 1986. Exhibits tentatively scheduled for 1989 include shows on the Jews of Italy and the Golem in art. Events accenting Jewish themes include concerts, lectures, films, and workshops. The museum shop has an impressive range of items. Open Sunday, 11 A.M.–6 P.M., Monday–Thursday, noon–5 P.M. Closed Friday, Saturday, major Jewish holidays, and some legal holidays. Adults, $4; children 6–16, students with ID, and Senior Citizens, $2. Free guided tours; group tours by advance arrangement.

Library and Museum of the Performing Arts. 111 Amsterdam Ave. (Lincoln Center); 870–1630. A division of the New York Public Library, this library/museum touches on just about every imaginable aspect of the performing arts. While the collection's subject matter is concentrated solely on the performing arts, the media involved can be expressed in anything from Katherine Cornell's makeup kit to holographic manuscripts of Bach, Mozart, and Stravinsky. Set designs, costumes, letters, records (the library has a circulating collection of over 30,000 records touching just about every Broadway show ever to hit the stage), paintings, models, posters, and lithographs are just part of the vast (and vastly entertaining) holdings. The Bruno Walter Auditorium has frequent performances, many of which are free to the public. Small fry can also get in on the fun with the world's largest children's library, which houses the Heckscher Oval Theater, an exotic puppet exhibit (shown at child height), and lots of interesting memorabilia including a slipper hand-embroidered by Mark Twain for turn-of-the-century child actress Elsie Leslie.

Metropolitan Museum of Art. Fifth Ave. and 82nd St.; 535–7710. At the top of the grand staircase on the second floor of this venerable institution is a stunning eighteen-foot mural by the 18th-century Italian painter Tiepolo, whose masterpiece heralds the *European Paintings Gallery,* devoted exclusively to European paintings from the 15th century to the first half of the 19th century. All the great masters in the museum's general collection are housed in this one section. Some representative works include El Greco's *The Miracle of Christ Healing the Blind,* Vermeer's *Portrait of a Young Woman,* Rubens's *Self-Portrait with Helena Fourment,* Rembrandt's *Aristotle with a Bust of Homer.* (See the accompanying *Plan of the Museum* for a more detailed breakdown of this gallery.)

The *Robert Lehman Wing* contains a special collection, primarily European old master paintings and drawings from the 15th to the 18th centuries, but some 19th and 20th. The *André Meyer Galleries* house the Museum's later 19th- and early 20th-century European paintings: from Goya and Delacroix through the Impressionists—and that is where these galleries are at their best—to the Post-Impressionists.

The *American Wing* is arguably the most impressively mounted of the Museum's permanent exhibits. It has room settings from the 17th to 20th centuries (among which is a living room designed by Frank Lloyd Wright), as well as paintings, sculptures, and all sorts of decorative arts, including a lovely collection of turn-of-the-century stained glass from Tiffany Studios. It is a bit hard to find your way around the wing; basically, there is an inner structure (it faces the Engelhard Court) surrounded by an outer structure.

The most recent addition to the museum is the new $26-million *Lila Acheson Wallace Wing.* Opened on Feb. 3, 1987, spanning three floors, this wing contains 10 galleries all devoted to the museum's large and very impressive collection of relatively unknown 20th-century art. The *Sharp Gallery* houses paintings ranging from Picasso's *The Blind Man's Meal* to Balthus's *The Mountain.* The *Helen and Milton A. Kimmelman Gallery* contains special exhibitions that change twice yearly. *The Gioconda and Joseph King Gallery* holds changing exhibitions of drawings, prints, and photographs. Other highlights include a survey of American painting between 1905 and 1940; selections from the personal collection of Alfred Stieglitz, donated by his wife, Georgia O'Keeffe; a gallery housing collections of design and architecture; selections of modern sculpture displayed in a dazzling 30-foot-high, 136-foot-long mezzanine-level court along with paintings by Al Held, Matta, and Andy Warhol; a chronological display of modern American painting from 1943 to 1980; and a gallery that contains recent paintings by younger artists.

Located on top of the Lila Acheson Wallace Wing, *The Iris and B. Gerald Cantor Roof Garden,* opened on August 1, 1987, is devoted to the display of the museum's 20th-century sculpture collection. Offering spectacular views of Central Park, the roof garden will be open from May 1 through Nov. 1, weather permitting. *The Astor Garden Court* and *Ming Furniture Room* and the *Douglas Dillon Galleries for Chinese Painting,* mark the first phase in the permanent reinstallation of the museum's collections of Far Eastern art. The Astor Garden Court alone is worth a visit to the museum; it is a reconstruction of an actual 19th-century Chinese scholar's garden. It is on the second floor but can be reached only from below on the first floor.

The north wing houses the *Egyptian Galleries,* including the Temple of Dendur, a gift of the government of Egypt to the Met, brought over disassembled and then reassembled on the present site, and the splendid Lila Acheson Wallace Galleries, displaying 18,000 of the Met's Egyptian treasures.

The mammoth *Michael C. Rockefeller Collection of the Art of Oceania, Africa, and the Americas* is devoted entirely to primitive art spanning 3,000 years, three continents, and an array of islands in the Pacific. The collection's 1,500 objects represent a rich diversity of cultural tradition, and include sculpture of wood stone, terra cotta, precious and semiprecious stone, gold, and silver.

Other galleries and collections are: *Islamic Art; Ancient Near Eastern Art; Greek and Roman Art; Prints and Drawings; Asian Art*—especially ceramics and sculpture; *Musical Instruments of the Past and of Non-European Cultures; European Sculpture and Decorative Arts; the Costume Institute; French and English Period Rooms; Medieval Art* (in impressive churchlike settings); *Arms and Armor;* and, of course, usually, two or three featured temporary exhibitions.

Visiting the Met can be frustrating. There are *always* galleries closed for reworking, and when you visit they will probably be the ones you wanted to see.

Be sure to inquire at the desk for audio cassette tours of selected galleries. And for the kids' enjoyment, pick up a few of the gallery hunt booklets, which contain the Met's version of an Easter-egg hunt.

A ground floor complex, *The Ruth and Harold D. Uris Center for Education,* includes classrooms, a gallery, and auditorium, and a visitor-information center. Children's exhibits and activities are stressed. The *Thomas J. Watson Library,* for research, has more than 155,000 art books and 1,000 periodical items. In the southern wing of the museum, on the main floor, there is an indoor restaurant (serving so-so food). The museum also provides free lectures and films from time to time, plus subscription concerts and lecture courses on art.

In a way, the museum is also a sort of art supermarket, with these shops: A reproductions shop, for pendants, other jewelry, sculpture, and so forth, up to and including solid-silver reproductions of Early American silverware; a Christmas card shop; a children's shop; a regular—and very extensive—bookshop; and a poster shop.

Call or write for the museum's monthly calendar of events. Floor plans, friendly staff members, and special services are available. Note: Highlight tours are conducted weekends.

Open Tuesday, 9:30 A.M. to 8:45 P.M., Wednesday–Sunday and holidays, 9:30 A.M.–5:15 P.M., closed Mondays, including Monday holidays. Suggested admission: $5. for adults, $2.50 for students and senior citizens. Members and children under 12 with an adult are free.

(In good weather and especially on weekends, there is almost always some sort of street theater going on for the tired museumgoers sitting on the steps outside the main entrance, usually mimes or magicians, plus, say, a brass quintet playing Gabrieli, and lots of hot-dog vendors.)

Pierpont Morgan Library. 29 E. 36th St.; 685–0008. The Library's collection is contained in a neo-Renaissance palazzo built in 1906 to house the already burgeoning collection of medieval and Renaissance manuscripts, old-master drawings, and rare books amassed by financier J. Pierpont Morgan. Since that time, the Library, located in midtown Manhattan, has become one of the city's classic landmarks. A treasure house of literary, historical, and artistic collectibles, the Library contains manuscripts dating back to the Middle Ages and on through the Renaissance, a comprehensive collection of bookbindings, many intricately wrought in precious metals and jewels, plus a good number of rare books dating from their original printings. The collection also includes such items as the Stavelot Triptych (reputedly containing fragments of the True Cross), and, on an historical note, Lord Cornwallis's letter to George Washington asking for surrender terms, which eventually led to the colonies' victory over England. Prominently displayed is the Library's newly acquired first printing, first state of the Declaration of Independence, the finest of 21 copies.

The walls of the West Room, formerly Pierpont Morgan's study, are clad in a vivid red-silk damask that provides a dramatic backdrop for the paintings, sculpture, stained-glass windows, furniture and intricately carved ceiling that adorn the room just as they did in Mr. Morgan's day. The East Room houses three tiers of bookcases extending from floor to ceiling. A scholar's reading room is open for study and research—accreditation is necessary, and the library asks visitors to abide by its very strict rules when using materials.

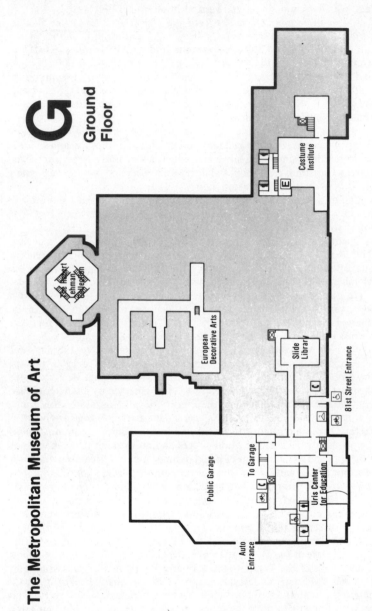

The Metropolitan Museum of Art

G
Ground
Floor

Robert Lehman Collection

European Decorative Arts

Costume Institute

Slide Library

81st Street Entrance

Public Garage

To Garage

Uris Center for Education

Auto Entrance

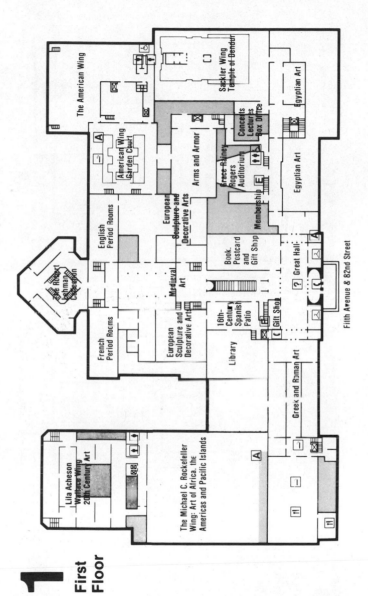

First
Floor

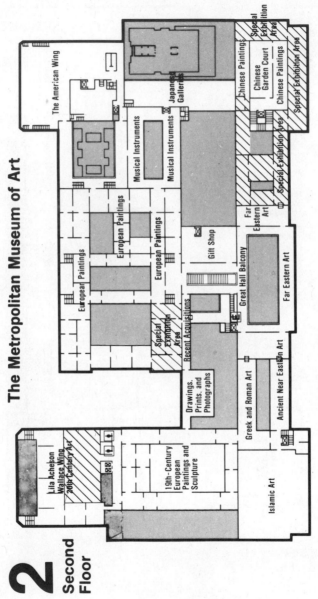

The Metropolitan Museum of Art

2 Second Floor

The Metropolitan Museum of Art
European Paintings Galleries

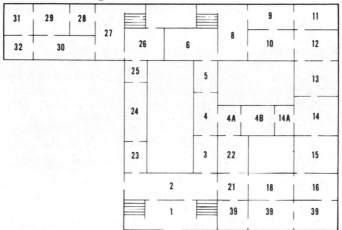

(This area is No. 37 at the top of the main staircase on the 2nd floor.)

1) Tiepolo
2) Reynolds, Gainsborough, Pannini
3) Giotto, di Paolo, Sassetta
4) Italian secular painting
4A) Pinturicchio
4B) Botticelli, Mantegna
5) Bellini, Mantegna, Tura
6) Botticelli, Lippi, di Cosimo
8) Titian, Tintoretto, Veronese
9) Moretto, Moroni, Correggio
10) Claude, Poussin
11) La Tour
12) Vermeer, De Hooch, Steen
13) Ruisdael, Cuyp, Van Goyen, Hobbema
14) Rembrandt, Hals, Vermeer
14A) Memling, Dürer

15) Rembrandt, Hals
16) Lawrence, Raeburn
18) Greuze, Chardin, Robert
21) Watteau, Boucher, Fragonard
22) Guardi, Hogarth, D. Tiepolo
23) Van Eyck, Van der Weyden
24) G. David, Bosch
25) Holbein, Cranach, Clouet
26) Bruegel, Cranach, Patinir
27) Rubens, Van Dyck, Jordaens
28) Van Dyck, Jordaens
29) El Greco
30) Caravaggio, Carracci, Reni, Rosa
31) Velazquez
32) Murillo, Zurbaran
39) Special Exhibitions

The following exhibits were scheduled for 1989 at press time: Drawings and Watercolors by Maurice Sendak: Wilhelm Grimm's *Dear Mili,* Nov. 3, 1988–Feb. 12, 1989; The Romantic Spirit: German Drawings 1780–1850 from the German Democratic Republic, Nov. 17, 1988–Jan. 29, 1989; Charles Dickens: *A Christmas Carol,* Nov. 25, 1988–Jan. 15, 1989; From Michelangelo to Rembrandt: Master Drawings from the Teyler Museum, Feb. 10–Apr. 30; Hebrew Manuscripts and Books from the Valmadonna Trust, Feb. 15–May 7; and Words of Blood, Images of Fire: The French Revolution, May 12–Aug. 20.

Hours: Tuesday–Saturday, 10:30 A.M.–5 P.M., Sunday, 1–5 P.M. Closed Monday, holidays, and the last two weeks in August. Group tours available upon advance request. Contribution $3 for adults, and $1 for students and senior citizens.

Museum of American Folk Art. Until its new building on W. 53rd St. between Fifth and Sixth aves. is completed in 1990, the museum is presenting exhibitions at various buildings throughout the city on a 3-month basis. Exhibits are listed in *New York* magazine and art publications; call 481–3080 for information. The museum has a collection of over 1,000 objects representing the nation's folk art heritage. The museum shop, now located at 62 W. 50th St., offers handmade items crafted in the folk tradition, postcards, and books on folk art. The shop is open Monday–Saturday 10:30 A.M.–5:30 P.M.; 247–5611. The museum is planning to open a branch at 2 Lincoln Square (Columbus Ave. and 65th St.), in mid-1989. In addition to serving as the museum's headquarters until the 53rd St. building is ready, this space will house four exhibits, both rotating and permanent. Call for details. Free.

Museum of the American Indian—Heye Foundation. Broadway at 155th St.; 283–2420. Indians from North, South, and Central America are represented here with artifacts of hides and feathers, masks, totem poles, pottery, stone, jade and turquoise, and painted wooden sculptures. Open Tuesday–Saturday, 10 A.M.–5 P.M., Sunday, 1–5 P.M., closed Monday and holidays. Adults, $3; students and senior citizens, $2; Native Americans and members, free.

Museum of the City of New York. Fifth Ave. at 103rd St.; 534–1672. This museum houses many fascinating exhibits highlighting the history and culture of New York City—from a small Dutch town into the "Big Apple." Formidable portraits of New York's founding fathers look down on dioramas of historic scenes; a small-scale model shows the island of Manhattan when the "town" was walled off from the "country." The Dutch galleries contain a life-size reconstructed portion of Fort Amsterdam. A Toy Gallery, the Dolls' House Gallery, and the John D. Rockefeller Sr. Rooms are now on permanent view. The museum also mounts changing exhibits from its theater collection, the most complete record of the New York stage. In the spring and fall, the museum's popular Sunday walking tours give visitors a chance to explore New York neighborhoods; $6 for members, $10 for nonmembers. Children's events include puppet shows, after-school programs, and family workshops. Open Tuesday–Saturday, 10 A.M.–5 P.M., Sunday and holidays, 1–5 P.M., closed Monday, Thanksgiving, Christmas, and New Years Day. Suggested contribution $3; children, $1.

Museum of Modern Art. 11 W. 53rd St.; 708–9500. In 1989 the museum will celebrate it 60th anniversary. In May 1984 after a four-year expansion project, the museum (usually referred to by its nickname, MOMA) re-opened with twice the gallery space it previously held. Perhaps the most dramatic addition is the glass Garden Hall, a four-story, steel-and-glass structure overlooking the refurbished Abby Aldrich Rockefeller Sculpture Garden, with balconies looking down on the garden and escalators moving between floors. Other improvements included a 200-seat theater (the museum's second), a public restaurant, and an enlarged museum shop.

The expanded museum now has three public floors with permanent exhibitions and two for temporary installations. The Painting and Sculpture Collection is on the second and third floors, its works in chronological order. Special galleries have been created for the museum's Matisse and Picasso collections, as well as a special room for Monet's *Water Lilies* and one for Matisse's large work *The Swimming Pool.*

The Photograph Gallery is on the second floor; separate galleries for Prints and Illustrated Books and Drawings Collections on the third. Architecture and Design occupy several galleries on the fourth floor of the new West Wing. Museum has two state-of-the-art theaters. Call 708–9490 for schedules.

The Museum was founded in 1929 for the purpose of introducing to the public works of modern art—an area not then being covered at all by the Met. In acquiring works for the Museum, Alfred H. Barr, Jr., the first director, acted on the belief that art was not limited to painting and sculpture, drawings and prints, and extended the scope of the collections to include films, photographs, architecture, and design.

The museum's collections now include masterpieces of modern art from about 1880 to the present. The great movements of the late 19th and 20th centuries are all represented with outstanding, first-rate examples: Post-Impressionism, Cubism, Dada, Surrealism, Expressionism, Futurism, Constructivism, Abstract Expressionism, and more. Some of the most famous paintings on exhibit are van Gogh's *The Starry Night,* Matisse's *Red Studio,* Picasso's *Les Demoiselles d'Avignon,* Henri Rousseau's *The Sleeping Gypsy,* Jasper John's *Flag,* and Jackson Pollock's *One (Number 31, 1950).* The architecture, design, and photography collections are now probably the best in the world, including architectural models from Le Corbusier's studio, Edward Steichen photographs, Tiffany glass, posters, and so much more. Classic films have usually been shown at least once a day at the museum.

The exhibits scheduled at press time are: Anselm Kiefer, Oct. 17, 1988–Jan. 3, 1989; Richard Diebenkorn, Dec. 15, 1988–Feb. 21, 1989; Emilio Ambasz and Steven Holl, Dec. 17, 1988–Mar. 7, 1989; Andy Warhol, Feb. 5–May 2; Liubov Popova, Mar. 15–May 30; Minor White, Mar. 23–June 6; Helen Frankenthaler, May 24–Aug. 8; The Prints and Illustrated Books of Antoni Tapies, June 15–Aug. 22; California Photography, June 22–Aug. 22; and The Unique Collaboration: Picasso and Braque 1907–1914, Sept. 24, 1989–Jan. 16, 1990. Call 708–9480 for recorded information on current shows. Museum shops selling cards, books, posters, and reproductions are located in the lobby and at 37 West 53rd St. Information on Gallery talks is available from the museum desk. Open daily, 11 A.M.–6 P.M., Thursday, 11 A.M.–9 P.M. Closed Wednesday and Christmas day. Adults, $5; full-time students with I.D., $3.50; senior citizens, $2; children under 16 with adult, free. Thursdays 5–9 P.M. pay what you wish.

The Museum of Modern Art

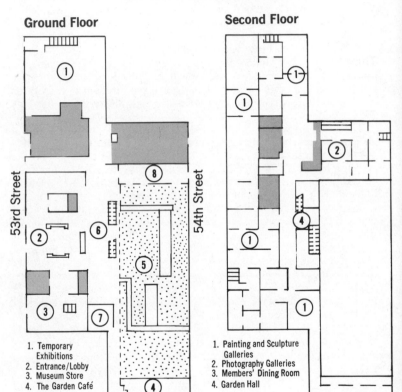

Ground Floor

53rd Street

54th Street

1. Temporary Exhibitions
2. Entrance/Lobby
3. Museum Store
4. The Garden Café (Public)
5. Sculpture Garden
6. Garden Hall
7. Video Gallery
8. Education Center

Lower Level and Theater Level not shown

Second Floor

1. Painting and Sculpture Galleries
2. Photography Galleries
3. Members' Dining Room
4. Garden Hall

Shaded areas closed to public

The Museum of Modern Art

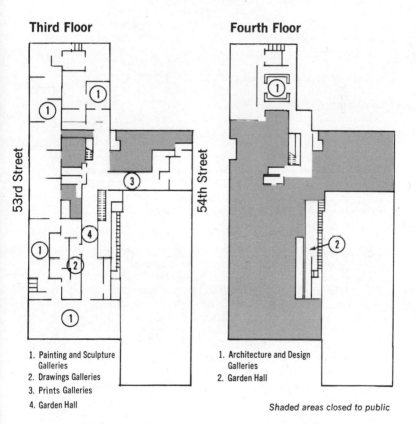

Third Floor

Fourth Floor

53rd Street

54th Street

1. Painting and Sculpture
   Galleries
2. Drawings Galleries
3. Prints Galleries
4. Garden Hall

1. Architecture and Design
   Galleries
2. Garden Hall

Shaded areas closed to public

National Academy of Design. 1083 Fifth Ave. at 89th St.; 360–6794. Founded in 1825, the Academy's collection comprises works solely by American artists—Winslow Homer, Rembrandt Peale, Samuel Morse, Thomas Eakins, Reginald Marsh, George Grosz, Edwin Dickinson, and others—and ranges from the early periods of American art up to the present day. The permanent collection represents only those artists who have been invited to membership, and since the requirements specify that the applicant submit a self-portrait plus a representative work of art, the Academy now boasts a vast holding of more American portraits than any other institution. Art genres represented are painting, sculpture, drawing, architectural drawing, engraving, prints, and photography. Exhibitions of the Academy's collection serve to document the considerable artistic activity in the United States throughout the 19th and 20th centuries.

Open Tuesdays, noon–8 P.M.; Wednesday–Sunday, noon–5 P.M. Admission is $2.50 for adults; $2 for students and senior citizens; members, free. Tuesday evenings 5–8 P.M. are free. Group reservations necessary; call 369–4880.

New-York Historical Society. 170 Central Park W. at 77th St.; 873–3400. Founded in 1804, and still using the hyphen between New and York that was standard spelling back then, the New-York Historical Society showcases American history and art, with an emphasis on the city's and state's contributions. The exhibits include fine American paintings, furniture, sculpture, and decorative arts such as original Audubon watercolors, Gilbert Stuart portraits, early American toys, Tiffany lamps, and Hudson River school landscapes. It also has one of our nation's finest reference libraries of American history, housing over 500,000 volumes and many more manuscripts and prints. Open Tuesday–Saturday 10 A.M.–5 P.M., Sunday 1–5 P.M., closed Mondays. Adults, $2; children, $1.Tuesdays, contribution.

New York Public Library. Fifth Ave. and 42nd St.; 869–8089. Stored in what is certainly one of New York's finest architectural works are treasures far beyond what one normally thinks of in relation to a library. But the New York Public Library is no ordinary library. A Gutenberg Bible, early Shakespeare folios, the manuscript of Washington's Farewell Address (in his own hand), the Lenox Globe (one of the earliest global reproductions, dating from around 1510), and other rare books, prints, and manuscripts are all part of the Library's collection of things other than "just books." Frequently changed exhibits display selected portions of the Library's constantly growing holdings.

Some artworks to note are the four huge murals by Edward Laning on the second floor depicting the story of the written word from Moses and the tablets to the first printing press; *Kindred Spirits,* which hangs in one of the main hallways; and the gigantic *Blind Milton Dictating Paradise Lost to His Daughter,* located on the main stairway. Also of interest is the lion motif found throughout the library, even extending as far as the rather amusing lion water-fountains which dot the hallways. The Library's main exhibition room has been magnificently restored and renamed the Gottesman Exhibition Hall. Tentative Gottesman exhibits for 1989 include A Sign and a Witness: 2000 Years of Hebrew Books and Illuminated Manuscripts, late-1988–Jan. 14, 1989; Revolution in Print: France 1789, Feb. 18–May 13; Botanical Illustrations from Kew Gardens England and the New York Public Library, June 3–Sept. 2; and The Memory of Mankind:

Treasures from the Bibliotheque Nationale France, Oct. 7, 1989–Jan. 3, 1990.

Special Collections are housed on the third floor: the Edna Barnes Salomon Room, opened in May 1986, which houses special exhibits and new acquisitions; the Berg Collection, containing important editions, manuscripts, and autograph letters in the field of English and American literature; the Manuscripts and Archives Room; the Rare Book Room; and others. To use the materials in the Special Collections, a card of admission is required which can be obtained from the Office of Special Collections, Room 226.

Guided tours available Monday–Saturday, 11 A.M. and 2 P.M. The museum is open Mondays and Wednesdays 10 A.M.–9 P.M. Tuesdays, Fridays, and Saturdays 10 A.M. to 6 P.M. Free. (See the plan of the Library in the *Libraries* section, above.)

South Street Seaport Museum. 207 Water St., 669–9424. New York's historic waterfront has undergone dramatic restoration, and the museum, with its collection of historic ships and 19th-century buildings, is the centerpiece of activity. You can tour several old ships that are moored at the South Street pier, including the 378-foot, four-masted, square-rigged, *Peking*. Recent additions include a new children's center, opened in June 1986, and several new shops and restaurants. The museum shops (in the Museum Block) sell stationery, boat kits, and souvenirs. Concerts are held on the pier throughout the summer. Call for hours. Admission to Museum programs, Seaport Galley and vessels: adults, $4; senior citizens and students, $3; children, $2; children under 4, free. This fee also includes admission to three tours of the area and two film presentations.

From May to September sailing trips are available on the schooner *Pioneer*. Prices range from $11 to $21. Call for details and reservations.

Studio Museum in Harlem. 144 W. 125th St.; 864–4500. Making its home in the renovated Kenwood Building (with three times the exhibition space as the old location), the Studio Museum is hailed as the principal center for the study of Black art in America. The museum exhibits works by local and international Black artists, in addition to African artifacts; some jewelry and crafts on sale at gift shop. Special events include children's workshops, films, lectures, and poetry readings; call the museum for schedules. Located one-half block from the Lenox Ave. subay station (the West Side IRT 2 and 3 trains). At press time plans had just been approved for the museum to build a sculpture garden in the vacant lot adjacent to the building. Plans were also approved for the expansion of the gift shop to begin in 1989. Open Wednesday–Friday, 10 A.M.–5 P.M., Saturday and Sunday, 1–6 P.M., closed Monday and Tuesday. Admission: $1.50 for adults, 50¢ for students with ID and senior citizens; on Wednesdays free for senior citizens.

Whitney Museum of American Art. 945 Madison Ave. at 75th St.; 570–3600. This museum contains the world's most comprehensive collection of 20th century American art, with special emphasis on the work of living artists. Marcel Breuer's massive granite structure contains a sunken sculpture garden, lobby floor, three cantilevered gallery floors, and office space. There's a restaurant, and the museum shop sells catalogs, posters, and postcards on American art. Daily gallery talks are popular.

Open Tuesday, 1 P.M.–8 P.M., Wednesday–Saturday, 11 A.M.–5 P.M., Sunday, noon–6 P.M., closed Monday and all major national holidays.

Adults, $4; seniors over 62, $2; children under 12 with adult, and college students with current I.D., free. Free Tuesday, 6–8 P.M.

A Selection of Other Museums

(All are located in Manhattan)

Abigail Adams Smith Museum. 421 E. 61st St.; 838–6878. Built in 1799 as a coachhouse and stable on a 23-acre estate, the structure has gone through many phases, functioning at various times as a country inn, a private home, and an office building housing Con Edison. Abigail Adams, daughter of President John Adams, owned the estate with her husband, William Stephens Smith, an aide to George Washington. As a museum its Greek Revival interior includes parlors, bedrooms, library, music room, dining room, and kitchen, with authentic appointments from the early 1800s. Special programs, lectures, music performances, and seminars take place year-round; call for schedules. Open Monday–Friday, 10 A.M.–4 P.M. Closed holidays and August. Children under 12, free; adults, $2; senior citizens, $1.

Afro Arts Cultural Centre, Inc. 2191 Adam Clayton Powell, Jr., Blvd., between 129th and 130th Sts.; 996–3333. Artifacts from East, West, North, and Central Africa. Daily, 9 A.M.–5 P.M. Contributions: Adults, $2.50; children, $1.75.

Alternative Museum. 17 White St., below Canal St.; 966–4444. Mixed-media works by known and unknown artists, mostly of avant-garde nature. Tuesday–Saturday, 11 A.M.–6 P.M., closed in July and Aug. and all major holidays. Contribution requested.

American Academy and Institute of Arts and Letters. Audubon Terrace, Broadway between 155th and 156th sts. 368–5900. Works by and about members, which include paintings, music, sculpture, and graphics. Research facilities open to accredited scholars, by appointment. Three annual exhibits open to the public; call for dates. Open Tuesday–Sunday, 1–4 P.M. Closed Mondays and holidays. Free.

American Institute of Graphic Arts. 1059 Third Ave. at 63rd St.; 752–0813. Competitive graphic design exhibits, on display Oct.–May. Monday–Friday, 9:30 A.M.–5 P.M. Free.

American Museum of Immigration. Statue of Liberty Monument, Liberty Island; 363–3200. Part of the National Park Service, the permanent exhibit contains photographs, artifacts, and films depicting the history of American immigration. The new Statue of Liberty exhibit, which opened on July 5, 1986, shows artifacts, artwork, and video presentations on the history of the statue, and features a full-size copper replica of the statue's face and left foot. Museum shop; handicap facilities. Open daily from 9:30 A.M.–5 P.M. Extended hours July-Labor Day are Sunday, 9 A.M.–7 P.M., Monday–Saturday, 9:30 A.M.–6 P.M. Suggested donation is $1 plus the fee for the boat ride over to the island, $3.25 for adults, $1.50 for children under 12.

Americas Society. 680 Park Ave. at 68th St.; 249–8950. This organization has exhibits concerned with the Western Hemisphere, from pre-Columbian to contemporary times. Tuesday–Sunday, noon–6 P.M. Suggested contribution $2.

Aunt Len's Doll and Toy Museum. 6 Hamilton Terrace at 141st St.; 281–4143. Almost 5,000 dolls and accessories, plus wind-up, mechanical, and tin toys. Open every day by appointment only. Adults, $2, children, $1.

Bible House. 1865 Broadway at 61st St.; 581–7400. Among 40,000 volumes two leaves from the Gutenberg Bible, fragments from the Dead Sea Scrolls, an 18-volume Braille Bible originally belonging to Helen Keller, and a replica of the original Guttenberg Press. Monday–Friday, 9:30 A.M.–4:30 P.M. Free.

Children's Museum of Manhattan. 314 W. 54th St.; 765–5904. Founded in 1973 as an innovative classroom program the Children's Museum of Manhattan has grown into a unique cultural center designed especially for kids. The catchword here is participation; all the exhibits encourage children to touch and explore the science and art experiences. In addition to several permanent exhibits, the museum has extensive education programs, after-school services, puppet and theatrical shows, and much more. A perfect place to take the kids for a full day of fun. Open Tuesday–Friday, 1–5 P.M., Saturday and Sunday, 11 A.M.–5 P.M. Admission is $2 for children and $1 for adults on weekdays; $3 children, $2 adults on weekends. In 1989 the museum will be moving to its new building at 212 W. 83rd Street so check before you go.

Drawing Center. 35 Wooster St., 219–2166. From September to March the center features four group exhibits by promising unknown artists. From April to July, each year the Center features a historical exhibit. In 1989 it is Architectural Drawings by Inigo Jones. Open Tuesday–Saturday, 11 A.M.–6 P.M., Wednesday til 8:00 P.M., closed in Aug. Suggested donation, $2.

Fashion Institute of Technology Gallery. 27th St. and 7th Ave.; 760–7760. Historic and contemporary displays of European and American fashions, textiles, furnishings, fashion illustrations, and photographs. Tuesday, 10 A.M.–9 P.M., Wednesday–Saturday, 10 A.M.–5 P.M. Closed major holidays. Free.

Federal Hall National Memorial. 26 Wall St.; 264–8711. This Greek Revival building occupies the site of George Washington's inauguration and the first capitol of the U.S. Exhibits include Washington memorabilia and models of the original building. In the Bill of Rights Room a diorama depicts the debate over that famous document. Open Monday–Friday, 9 A.M.–5 P.M. Closed most major holidays. Free.

Goethe House New York—German Cultural Center. 1014 Fifth Ave. at 82nd St.; 744–8310. Exhibitions, films, video, lectures, readings, recitals offered on premises or at American partner institutes. Library with books, periodicals, and records. Gallery hours: Tues. and Thurs., 9 A.M.–7 P.M.; Wed. and Fri., 9 A.M.–5 P.M.; Saturday, noon–5 P.M. Library hours: Tues. and Thurs., noon–7 P.M.; Wed., Fri., and Sat., noon–5 P.M. Both the library and gallery are closed Sunday and Monday. Free. Write for the calendar of events.

Grey Art Gallery. 33 Washington Pl.; 998–6780. The New York University Fine Arts Museum is regularly given over to shows of mostly 20th-century fine arts; also, the Abby Weed Grey Foundation Collection of Contemporary Asian and Middle Eastern Art. Call for hours and exhibition schedule. Suggested contribution, $1.50.

Grolier Club of N.Y. 47 E. 60th St.; 838–6690. Rare books, manuscripts, and prints, occasional special exhibits. Monday–Saturday, 10

A.M.–5 P.M. with breaks between exhibits for remodeling; call for information. Free.

Interchurch Center. 475 Riverside Dr. at 120th St.; 870–2931. Displays pertaining to interfaith concerns including the final manuscript copy of the Revised Standard Version of the Bible. Visiting arts and crafts exhibits. Monday–Friday 9 A.M.–4 P.M. Free.

Intrepid Sea-Air-Space Museum. Pier 86 on the Hudson River at W. 46th St.; 245–2533. Unusually housed in a refurbished U.S. naval aircraft carrier, this fascinating museum features exhibitions revolving around 20th-century history and technology in sea, air, and space science. Exhibits are divided into five main theme halls spanning two full decks and several island bridges; these exhibits succeed admirably in taking the visitor back to the early days of technology and then far forward into the next century for a prediction of what the years ahead may hold. The *Intrepid* also houses the Congressional Medal of Honor Society's Hall of Honor Museum, which contains the single largest collection of actual medals received by U.S. heroes along with artifacts donated by their survivors. Open Wednesday–Sunday, 10 A.M.–5 P.M. (ticket office closes at 4 P.M.). Adults $4.75; senior citizens, $4; children, $2.50. Call for group rates.

The Kitchen. 512 W. 19th St.; 255–5793. A center for mixed media and alternative arts, with exhibits by day and "performance arts" events at night. A mecca for experimentation with video, film, music, dance, unstructured (or nonlinear) drama, and other avant garde forms. Tuesday–Saturday, 1–6 P.M. September–May only. Free. Evening performance prices vary; call for schedules.

J. M. Mossman Collection of Locks. 20 W. 44th St.; 840–1840. Historic survey of security instruments. Monday–Thursday, 10 A.M.–4 P.M. Groups must call in advance. Free.

El Museo Del Barrio. 1230 Fifth Ave. at 105th St.; 831–7272. Puerto Rican and Latin American fine arts. Wednesday–Sunday, 11 A.M.–5 P.M. Suggested contribution $2.

Museum of Broadcasting. 1 E. 53rd St.; 752–7684. Enormously popular for its ever-growing library of classic and contemporary radio and television programs, all available for individual screening. Tuesday, noon–8 P.M., Wednesday–Saturday, noon–5 P.M. Suggested contribution: adults, $4; students, $3, children under 13 and Senior Citizens, $2.

Museum of Holography. 11 Mercer St. in SoHo; 925–0581. This museum, which was founded in 1976, is the first of its kind anywhere in the world. Holograms, are three-dimensional pictures created with laser light. A permanent exhibit focuses on the history of the medium and its current state. A film called *An Introduction to Holography* is shown continuously in the 35-seat theater. Special exhibits change three times a year. Open Tuesday–Sunday, 11 A.M.–6 P.M., Adults, $3; children and senior citizens, $1.75. Group rates available.

New Museum. 583 Broadway, between Houston and Prince Sts; 219–1222. This young museum, founded in 1977, shows the work of contemporary artists who have had little exposure elsewhere. Open Wednesday–Sunday, noon–6 P.M., Friday and Saturday til 8 P.M. Donation, $2.50; students, senior citizens, and artists, $1.50; members, free.

New York City Fire Museum. 278 Spring St.; 691–1303. One of the richest and most comprehensive collections of authentic firefighting equipment used during the 18th, 19th, and early 20th centuries. Hand-pulled and horse-drawn apparatus, engines, sliding poles, uniforms, and fireboat equipment are scattered throughout the museum. Children will love touring this renovated firehouse. Open Tuesday–Saturday, 10 A.M.–4 P.M.; call for Sunday and holiday hours as they vary. Suggested donation, $3 adults; 50 cents children.

Pen and Brush. 16 E. 10th St.; 475–3669. Painting, sculpture, and graphic arts exhibits sponsored by the oldest professional women's creative arts organization in New York. Open daily except Monday, 1–4 P.M. September–June. Closed July and August. Free.

Society of Illustrators Museum of American Illustration. 128 E. 63rd St.; 838–2560. Contemporary; historical, solo, group, and theme shows drawn from the Society of Illustrators' 1,000-piece collection. Monday–Friday, 10 A.M.–5 P.M. Tuesday until 8 P.M. Closed in August. Free

Theodore Roosevelt Birthplace. 28 E. 20th St.; 260–1616. Here is where our 26th President was born and lived during his formative years. The reconstructed Victorian brownstone row house contains memorabilia and historical items highlighting the Rough Rider's life. Such items include personal diaries, eyeglasses, relics of the Spanish-American War, campaign buttons. Open Wednesday–Sunday, 9 A.M.–5 P.M., closed Mondays and Tuesdays. Adults, $1, senior citizens and children under 12, free.

Urban Center. 457 Madison Ave. at 51st St.; 935–3960. Architectural and urban-issue exhibits and programs are housed in the North wing of the historic Villard Houses, at the foot of the Helmsley Palace Hotel. The bookstore specializes in architecture, urban design, and historic preservation. Open Monday–Thursday, 10 A.M.–8 P.M.; Friday and Saturday, 10 A.M.–6 P.M.; Sunday, noon–5 P.M. Free.

Other Boroughs

Bronx. *Bartow-Pell Mansion Museum and Garden,* Shore Rd. North in Pelham Bay Park; 885–1461. The mansion, built in 1842, is a Greek revival restoration with sunken gardens, period furnishings, paintings, and a 200-volume library, closed to public, containing books on architecture, gardening, and herbs. Open Wednesday, Saturday, and Sunday, noon–4. Admission $1, children under 12 with adult, free.

Bronx Museum of the Arts, 1040 Grand Concourse; 681–6000. This museum, founded in 1971, displays contemporary and modern art. Open Monday–Thursday, 10 A.M.–4:30 P.M. Saturday and Sunday, 11 A.M.–4:30 P.M. Suggested contribution, adults, $1.50; senior citizens and students, $1.

Hall of Fame for Great Americans, W. 181st St. and University Ave.; 220–6920. Original bronzes of 102 prominent Americans are on display in the turn-of-the-century Stanford White edifice located on an important Revolutionary War site. This site is now on the campus of the Bronx Community College. Groups should call in advance. Open daily, 10 A.M.–5 P.M. Free.

Valentine-Varian House Museum of Bronx History 3266 Bainbridge Ave.; 881–8900. Isaac L. Varian, mayor of New York City from 1839–1841, was born in this house, which was built in 1758 and was later the site of several Revolutionary War skirmishes. Indian and military artifacts, natural history displays, paintings, and prints and photographs tracing the history of the Bronx. Open Saturday, 10 A.M.–4 P.M., Sunday, 1–5

P.M. Weekday tours available by appointment only, 9 A.M.–5 P.M. Admission, $1.

Queens. *Bowne House Historical Society,* 37–01 Bowne St.; 718–359–0528. Known for the *Flushing Remonstrance.* John Bowne, advocate of religious freedom when New York was still Nieuw Amsterdam, lived in this house built in 1661. It contains 17th-century furnishings, a pewter collection, and Bowne family memorabilia. Open Tuesday, Saturday, and Sunday 2:30–4:30 P.M. School and adult groups by appointment. Admission, adults $1; children, 25 cents.

Hall of Science of the City of New York, 4701 111th St., Flushing Meadow Park; 718–699–0675. Children almost always enjoy the museum of science and technology; this one has "hands-on" exhibits, a cafeteria, and scientific toys for sale. The museum features several exhibits including some on color and illusion, the atom, self-sensory machines, and the biological sciences. Open Wednesday–Sunday, 10 A.M.–5 P.M., Adults, $2.50; senior citizens and students, $1.25. Wednesdays and Thursdays 2–5 P.M. free admission. Groups of 10 or more require reservations; call 718–699–0301.

Queens Museum, NYC Bldg., Flushing Meadow, Corona Park, 718–592–5555, on site of 1964 World's Fair. This is the home of the Panorama, an 18,000-square-foot architectural model of New York City's five boroughs. Also exhibits major public and private collections, as well as the works of younger artists. Open Tuesday–Friday, 10 A.M.–5 P.M., Saturday and Sunday, noon–5:30 P.M., closed Monday. Suggested contribution: Adults, $2; senior citizens, $1; children, free.

The Store Front Museum. At press time the museum was looking for a new building in which to relocate. Founded in 1971, this black art and history museum has a collection of paintings, drawings, and sculpture by black artists in the United States and abroad, including tribal art from Africa as well as special exhibits. Call 718–465–6455 for details on location and schedules. Free.

Brooklyn. *Brooklyn Children's Museum.* 145 Brooklyn Ave. at St. Mark's Ave.; 718–735–4400. A natural history museum designed especially for children with exhibits showing American Indian and other prehistoric cultures, fossils, mounted mammals, tame live animals. Open Monday, Wednesday–Friday 2–5 P.M.; Saturday, Sunday, most holidays, and public school vacations, 10 A.M.–5 P.M.; closed Tuesdays. Admission, $2; children, $1.

Brooklyn Historical Society. 128 Pierrepont St.; 718–624–0890. If your ancestors come from any of the four counties that make up Long Island (Kings, Queens, Nassau, or Suffolk), you might be interested in spending time in the reading room of this research library/museum, which has 125,000 volumes pertaining to local history and genealogy. The museum also has a collection of paintings, graphics, and costumes. A new display gallery opened in October 1983. Open Tuesday–Saturday, noon–5 P.M. Free. Library open Tuesday–Saturday, 10 A.M.-5 P.M. Admission, $2.

Staten Island. *Staten Island Museum* (Staten Island Institute of Arts and Sciences), 75 Stuyvesant Pl.; 718–727–1135. Permanent science exhibits provide an introduction to the Natural History of Staten Island. The museum's changing fine arts exhibits contain paintings, graphics, and decorative arts which illustrate the history of Western Art. Open Tuesday–Saturday, 9 A.M.–5 P.M., Sunday, 1–5 P.M. Open Mondays for groups by appointment only. Suggested donation: adults, $2; children and senior citizens, $1.

Conference House Association, Conference House Park (7455 Hylan Blvd.); 718–984–2086. The only peace conference during the Revolution was held September 11, 1776, in a stone house constructed in 1675 known as the Conference House, or Billopp House, which now may be seen by guided tour. Open daily, 1–4 P.M., closed Monday and Tuesday. Admission $1, children 50 cents.

Jacques Marchais Center of Tibetan Arts. 338 Lighthouse Ave.; 718–987–3478. Here you may view examples of Tibetan and Buddhist art, study Eastern religions and philosophy in the 20,000-volume library, and meditate in one of the gardens. The galleries are closed in Dec. through March; research can be done by appointment only. Open Friday–Sunday 1–5 P.M. in Apr., Oct., and Nov. From May to Sept., open Wednesday–Sunday, 1–5 P.M. Sunday afternoons at 2 P.M. are slated for special presentations. Admission $2.50; senior citizens, $2; children, $1. Group tours available by appointment only.

Richmondtown Restoration/Staten Island Historical Society Museum, 441 Clarke Ave.; 718–351–1611. This is New York City's only settlement restoration, representing three centuries of regional history and culture. The village, constructed upon 96 acres, consists of 25 historic structures including private residences, craftsmen's shops, a general store, a 1696 Dutch schoolhouse, and several municipal buildings. Thirteen buildings are open to the public and manned by authentically costumed interpreters who recreate the daily work activities and trades of an earlier way of American life. Open Wednesday–Friday, 10 A.M.–5 P.M., Saturday and Sunday, 1–5 P.M. General admission (Village Tour and Museum) $3; senior citizens, children, and students, $1.50.

MOVIES. Since 1963, the Film Society of Lincoln Center has produced what many regard as the most important film event in the country, the New York Film Festival, where many of the most innovative and critically acclaimed American and foreign films receive their first New York showing. It is the Big Apple's answer to Cannes, usually runs around two weeks from late September to mid-October at Lincoln Center and includes a "New Directors/New Films" annual series co-sponsored with the Museum of Modern Art. Tickets range from $5 to $7, opening and closing night are at Avery Fisher Hall, all other performances at Alice Tully Hall.

But New York is a year-around film festival. You'll hear many New Yorkers referring to movies as *films, flicks,* or *cinema,* and this art form is taken very seriously by fans, aspiring filmmakers, and professional critics. If two weeks pass and you haven't read about a W. C. Fields, Humphrey Bogart, or Marx Brothers Festival, better check to see if you're really in New York.

Movies are advertised daily in all the papers, but for a complete listing look to *New Yorker* and *New York* magazine's *Cue* listings, or to the Friday and Sunday *New York Times.*

There are at least five common formats for the presentation of movies here. First come the expensive ($6 or more) and prestigious East Side houses like the *Coronet* (993 3rd Ave. at 59th St.) or the *Beekman* (Second Ave. at 66th St.).

Multiscreen neighborhood houses like *Loew's 84th Street* (at Broadway) show features that have gained enough critical acclaim and made enough money in their first-run engagements to justify wide dissemination. They also host premieres of action-packed, star-studded "flicks."

Ten years ago, art film houses were known for foreign movies. Since film has come to be regarded as a kind of literature that can be experienced more than once, the situation has changed. Venerable theaters like *80 St. Marks* (8th St. and 2nd Ave.) and the *Bleecker St. Cinema* (Bleecker and La Guardia) have done well with old foreign and American classics and more recent works whose true values have surfaced since they first (sometimes unsuccessfully) came out. Some houses also have special midnight showings, on the weekend, of strange and often offensive cult films; read the listings carefully for these as they are frequently not advertised.

A fourth category includes museums, libraries, and churches that show films, often seldom-seen ones, in the course of retrospective examinations of great careers in the industry. Admissions are usually modest and the setting interesting beyond the film itself (such as the *Museum of Modern Art,* 53rd St. between 5th and 6th Aves., or the *Whitney Museum* on Madison Ave. at 75th St).

Finally, filmmakers not yet established in the big time want their work seen and occasionally have showings in out-of-the-way lofts or college buildings. They sometimes exhibit individually, sometimes band together in "collectives." Since they have little money for publicity, the best way to learn about a showing is to keep your eyes open for handbills and posters in Greenwich Village and near campuses around the city. Read the *Village Voice* for news of offbeat films.

Although ambitious plans for the facelifting of the Times Square area of Broadway are underway, some of its theaters are currently given over to X-rated films (this is true of W. 42nd St. and 8th Ave. as well). Those which are not show primarily first-run action features—sure moneymakers. But colorful though the area may be, beware of the low lifes that infest some of the movie houses on this neon-lit strip.

There are some movie houses, however, that are as interesting as the movies they show because of their locale. The *Paris,* for example, at 4 W. 58th St., shows first-run foreign and art films right across the street from the venerable Plaza Hotel and Central Park. The *Little Theatre,* in Joe Papp's Public Theatre complex at 425 Lafayette St., opens late in the afternoon to show old art films, giving one the opportunity to catch an off-Broadway play in the same building that evening. There are a number of other locations with unusual film offerings, including *Theatre 80* at 80 St. Marks Pl. in the East Village; the *Film Forum* at 57 Watts St., and *Thalia Soho* at 15 Vandam St., both on the Lower West Side; and *Cinema Village* at 22 E. 12th St. in Greenwich Village. Farther uptown is the *Biograph Cinema* at 225 W. 57th St. On the fashionable East Side from the 50s into the 80s, is a veritable Hollywood movie belt of first-run films in "piggy back" theaters, with as many as five different films playing in different showcases in the same complex.

MUSIC. Manhattan is beyond serious dispute the most active musical city in the world, and the one with the largest population of professional musicians. (Most of them live and/or perform on the Upper West Side near Lincoln Center, where you will see many people carrying violins, cel-

MUSIC 191

los, and the like to and from lessons, rehearsals, and performances, and
where it is not uncommon to hear tenors practicing scales as they do their
grocery shopping.) Your only real problem is which performance to
choose. In their daily entertainment sections, the *New York Times* and
other daily papers list all the day's musical events—and Friday's papers
include the entire weekend's goings-on, including church performances.
The Sunday *Times* has the week's list. There is a "Music & Dance" booth
for half-price tickets, open from noon, in Bryant Park at 42nd St. and Ave.
of the Americas; 382–2323.

Lincoln Center, Broadway at 64th St. (877–2011) is the musical heart
of New York City, with *Carnegie Hall* (247–7800) its soul. Within the 20-
year-old Lincoln Center complex are *Avery Fisher Hall* (home of the New
York Philharmonic, American Philharmonic Orchestra, the Mostly Mozart festival, and many visiting orchestra performances—874–2424); the
New York State Theater (home of the New York City Opera and New
York City Ballet as well as for many visiting ballet troupes—870–5570);
Alice Tully Hall (probably the most acoustically perfect of the halls, and
site of numerous chamber music recitals—362–1911); the *Juilliard School
of Music* (799–5000)—one of the world's most respected institutions; and
the *Guggenheim Bandshell* in the outdoor *Damrosch Park* (877–1800).
Also part of the complex are the *Library and Museum of Performing Arts*
(where some concerts and recitals are also held, especially for children—
870–1630); and the *Vivian Beaumont* and *Mitzi Newhouse theaters*
(362–7600). The plaza at Lincoln Center is also the base for dozens of free
concerts daily throughout the summer.

The various buildings opened one at a time, beginning with Avery Fisher Hall in 1964—then called Philharmonic Hall, but renamed after a
donor contributed $5 million to have the acoustics adjusted. Interestingly,
attractive as all the buildings at Lincoln Center are—the Met with its Chagall murals lighting up the plaza, the Calder sculpture that adorns Damrosch Park—designed by such recognized architects as Max Abramovitz
(Avery Fisher) and Philip Johnson (State Theater, and later overseer of
the reconstruction of Avery Fisher), they have almost all been beset by
acoustical and structural problems. Avery Fisher and the Beau-
mont/Newhouse theaters have all undergone serious reconstructions, and
the New York State Theater had its interior rebuilt for acoustics in the
summer of 1982. Indeed, in Avery Fisher Hall, only the outside façade
and general shape of the auditorium remain as originally constructed.

Thus New Yorkers, and musicians and fans around the world, were especially appreciative of the efforts to save Carnegie Hall (154 W. 57th St.)
from destruction following the completion of Lincoln Center. It took great
musicians like Isaac Stern to spearhead the campaign to save Carnegie
when it was threatened with demolition in order to make way for yet another midtown office building. Opened in 1891 with a concert conducted
by Tchaikovsky, it remains an acoustical marvel and leaves New York's
musical heart and soul intact.

They say New York's longest running musical hit is the New York Philharmonic. The oldest symphony orchestra in the U.S., it is nearly 150
years old yet incredibly vital under music director and conductor Zubin
Mehta, who gets the best out of the 105-plus extraordinarily gifted musicians in the orchestra. The Philharmonic season runs September through
May at Avery Fisher Hall. Tickets cost from $7.50 to $35. The orchestra,

of course, attracts outstanding guest soloists and conductors. And Avery Fisher Hall is the home of the Mostly Mozart Summer Music Festival, New York City's version of Tanglewood, with more than 40 low-cost concerts (about $9 to $12 for a reserved seat) from mid-July through late August. Basically Bach, another low-cost music festival, spills over from Carnegie Hall to Avery Fisher Hall and various churches in early June.

The Metropolitan Opera is now into its second century. The season runs from September to mid-April.

Throughout the season opera's greatest names can be heard, and the house, with its Chagall murals and cut-crystal chandeliers, is a spectacular setting for any event. Tickets range from $7 to $75, with standing-room and partial-view seats available.

Across Lincoln Center Plaza, in the New York State Theater, the New York City Opera operates under an unusual schedule—July through November performances. General Director Beverly Sills, the company's most famous star a few years ago, feels that a connected season will shore up the sometimes tenuous financial base of the City Opera. Tickets there range from $2.40 to $35, and Miss Sills tries to draw a younger, less elitist audience.

Both companies emphasize American singers, with the City Opera almost totally American and generally younger. The growing popularity of opera generally and the full houses in New York come in large part from the televised operas of both companies and the more than 40 years of Texaco-sponsored live Saturday matinee Metropolitan Opera broadcasts.

Alice Tully Hall in Lincoln Center's Juilliard Building is small, intimate, and perhaps the best acoustical building in the complex—a suitable home for the Chamber Music Society of Lincoln Center, which has commissioned over 30 compositions and has given many New York or American premieres since its inception in 1969. Also attracts outstanding performers, from pianists to vocal groups, as well as stages (usually free) performances by Juilliard students.

Many guest artists, composers, and visiting orchestras perform at various times at each of these Lincoln Center auditoriums and theaters. For information on performances and prices write for the Lincoln Center Calendar, Lincoln Center, 1865 Broadway, New York 10023. Tickets are also available by mail, but they should be ordered a month in advance, or through most Ticketron outlets. There are also occasional free outdoor performances at Lincoln Center, either on the plaza or at the Guggenheim Bandshell, in the summer.

For sheer musical variety and artistry, Carnegie Hall is hard to beat with instrumental recitals by the likes of Rudolf Serkin, Nathan Milstein, and Mstislav Rostropovich, visits by orchestras such as the mighty Chicago under Solti, the Cleveland under Maazel, the Philadelphia under Muti, the Boston under Ozawa, and an atlas of other famed orchestras as well as vocal recitals by world greats. Performances go on virtually year-round. Tickets vary, from around $5 to $25.

The Off-Broadway equivalent in the Big Apple music world may well be the 92nd St. YM-YWHA, 1395 Lexington Ave., which offers major chamber music and orchestral series as well as performances by individual artists of international stature and a fun series featuring Broadway tunesmiths performing and speaking about their work. Colleges such as Hunter and the College of the City of New York (CCNY) also offer programs featuring major musicians, as does Merkin Concert Hall at Abraham Goodman House, 129 W. 67th St., sort of the Off-Off-Broadway of the music world. Town Hall, the famous old concert facility on W. 43rd St. near Sixth Ave., is newly restored and offering light classics, ethnic concerts, and jazz. *Symphony Space* at Broadway and 95th St. (864–1414) offers an eclectic schedule of music, dance, and other performing arts at reasonable prices.

Here are some other possibilities:

Amato Opera Theatre, Inc., 319 Bowery 228–8200. Two generations of Amatos have produced this showcase company for student and young professional singers.

The *Light Opera Company of Manhattan* (affectionately known as "LOOM") presents excellent Gilbert and Sullivan operettas throughout the year at its small theater at Playhouse 91, 316 E. 91st St.; 831–2000.

The Manhattan and other borough parks have an extensive free concert series June through August. The New York Philharmonic performs twice each summer in the Sheep Meadow at Central Park and at least once in a park in every borough. So does the Met.

Free concerts are also offered at the *Greenwich House Music School* (IRT 7th Ave. subway to Christopher St. stop; ask for directions to 46 Barrow St.; 242–4770); *The Museum of the City of New York* (5th Ave. bet. 103rd and 104th St.; Sunday, October–May; 534–1672) and *The New-York Historical Society* (107 Central Park West, near 77th St., Sunday, November–April; 873–3400).

Check the listings in the music section of the *New York Times* Sundays for news of frequent concerts at the Metropolitan Museum of Art, the Guggenheim, the Nicholas Roerich Museum, the Brooklyn Museum, the Frick Collection, the concerts of live or recorded music on certain Sundays in the medieval splendors of The Cloisters (which are part of the Metropolitan Museum of Art but located uptown in Fort Tryon Park), and, usually, many other places every day.

The sound of music—usually free—fills some of the city's great churches. Some suggestions: The beautiful Riverside Church, Riverside Drive at 122nd St., presents carillon concerts at noon Saturdays and 2 P.M. Sundays. St. Peter's Lutheran Church, in the Citicorp Center at 54th St. and Lexington Ave., has Jazz Vespers Sundays at 5 P.M. as well as interesting theater performances. And Trinity Church, at Broadway and Wall St., presents organ recitals on three varying weekdays.

The Library and Museum of the Performing Arts at Lincoln Center also showcases outstanding young concert artists, as do other branches of the New York Public Library. Check the Events Calendar of the New York Public Library, free at all branches. And don't overlook the Brooklyn Academy of Music (BAM), 30 Lafayette St., Brooklyn (718–636–4100), the nation's oldest performing arts center, with its various chamber and orchestral series as well as performances by internationally acclaimed guest artists in its four theaters (where dance, theater, films, and children's programs are also staged). Most renowned in recent years: the Next Wave Festival of avant garde and performance arts. The BAM season usually runs from October through June. Tickets range from around $9–$30.

Popular Music

Pop and rock concerts are presented all over town all year long. The Millertime Concerts series runs from June to August, usually at Pier 84. The *Ritz,* a former ballroom, on E. 11th St., draws young people from the suburbs as well as the neighborhood and Manhattan. The biggest attractions, such as Bruce Springsteen or The Grateful Dead, can fill *Madison Square Garden, Radio City Music Hall,* or the *Bottom Line,* 15 W. Fourth St., for several nights. Other halls that play big-name pop, rock, or jazz headliners are Carnegie Hall, Avery Fisher Hall (Lincoln Center), and sometimes even Alice Tully Hall, also at Lincoln Center.

The *South Street Seaport,* Pier 16 at Fulton St. on the East River, presents pop, jazz, bluegrass, and folk dance concerts throughout the summer, many for free or a nominal admission charge, and Save-Our-Ships concerts, on the waterfront from June through August in one of New York's more unusual but pleasant settings.

George Wein's *JVC Jazz Festival,* from the last week in June through the first week in July, percolates in Carnegie Hall, Avery Fisher Hall, and other places around town.

For events, dates, and times while you are in town, check the daily papers, *New York* magazine, the *Village Voice* or the *New Yorker.*

For information on other nonclassical music, that performed in club settings where drinks or meals are served, refer to the *Nightlife* section later in the book. But serious nonclassical music thrives in New York in less formal places, such as "performance lofts" in SoHo and TriBeCa; read the *Voice* carefully for the minute notices, or scan the handbills posted on poles and walls.

DANCE. New York is now the dance capital of the world, and the Metropolitan Opera House is perhaps the largest and most important impresario of ballet, with the entire Lincoln Center complex the vital nerve center that keeps the Big Apple on its toes. (You will see students of the ballet around Carnegie Hall on 57th St. and Broadway in the '60s, '70s, and '80s, going to and from the many ballet schools there.) Three Russians have helped New York maintain its dance excellence: the late George Balanchine, Rudolf Nureyev, and Mikhail Baryshnikov.

It is Balanchine, of course, who built the *New York City Ballet* (NYCB) into one of the great ballet companies in the world, his dancers whirling through abstract geometrical patterns choreographed by Balanchine in plotless ballets whose very simplicity reflects the lines in the NYCB's home, the New York State Theater in Lincoln Center. With 110 dancers, the NYCB is the largest dance organization in the Western world. And it was Balanchine who brought the proud traditions of Russian Imperial ballet to the New World and put them to work in creating the sleek, neoclassical, and decidedly American NYCB. Balanchine and the NYCB's other principal choreographer, Jerome Robbins, have created more than 160 ballets. These ballets are now regarded as *the* classic repertoire of the 20th century. The fall dates are November through February. December is reserved for Balanchine's Christmas classic, *The Nutcracker.* Tickets from $4 to $20.

Across the Lincoln Center Plaza, at the Metropolitan Opera House, the *American Ballet Theatre* (ABT) usually stages its fall season from October through November and its summer season from mid-April through June. ABT has made its reputation by becoming America's prime repertory company. They perform the great 19th-century classics as well as important works of the early 20th century and a regular crop of story and contemporary ballets.

While NYCB prides itself on being a "starless" company where dance is the true star under the first of America's great balletic émigrés from Russia, the legendary Balanchine, the ABT is nonetheless the Big Apple's—and America's—"star" ballet. The ABT is now under the leadership of its talented superstar, Mikhail (Misha) Baryshnikov, the latest of the dance defectors from Russia's brilliant Kirov Ballet, noted for its soft, lyrical style and its brilliant interpretations of story ballets. The dashing Misha and one of his leading ladies, Natalia Makarova, another defector from the Kirov, have managed to inject the Russian spirit into the American dance tradition that makes the ABT so special. Misha choreographs, too, a budding Balanchine. ABT tickets vary, from around $5 to $35 and climbing.

It was, of course, Nureyev, the first of the great Russian dancers to defect from the Kirov, who, with his superstar quality slowly dimming over the years, gave ballet its mass appeal in America. And it was the box office power of Nureyev's name that helped fill the Met when Rudi danced as visiting guest star with some of the world's best troupes—troupes first imported to America by another Russian great, the late impresario Sol Hurok. Hurok's death left a void. And the Met stepped into that void, acting as its own impresario to keep its house full during the summer months. But it is names like Balanchine, Nureyev, and Baryshnikov that bring the crowds in.

It is their popularity that helps keep both the State and Met filled with visiting dance companies when the NYCB and ABT aren't performing, and when the respective house opera companies aren't doing their thing. So it is possible for a dance aficionado to look forward to seeing, say, the athleticism of Russia's *Bolshoi,* the lyricism and story ballets of Germany's *Stuttgart,* the statelines of the *National Ballet of Canada,* the pageantry of Britain's *Royal Ballet,* and the avant-garde leanings of the *Netherlands Dance Theater*—to name just a few of the great troupes that have come to the Big Apple in recent seasons.

But the troupers go beyond the classical greats. The Moorish-style City Center Theater at 131 W. 55th St., for example, which has been extensively renovated, is, along with several Broadway theaters, home for such world-class companies as the *Alvin Ailey* (with its haunting blend of spiritual, modern jazz and story ballet rising out of the Black experience), the up-and-coming *Harlem Dance Theater,* and the mod, hip, with-it *Joffrey Ballet* that dances classics as well as rock-inspired pieces. (The Joffrey is now partly based in Los Angeles.) *Paul Taylor* and his company fuse the classics with modern dance, humor and a marvelous athleticism; so do *Twyla Tharp, Murray Louis,* and *Alwin Nikolais* (who uses more lights than the hippest disco). New to the city is the Joyce Theater at 18th St. on Eighth Ave., where the *Eliot Feld* company is in residence. The theater hopes to become the base for many contemporary and avant-garde companies.

The Brooklyn Academy of Music draws all kinds of dance companies, too. Indeed, its *Ballet America* series is a national celebration of dance paced from October to June. Companies from Los Angeles, San Francisco, Pennsylvania, Cleveland, and Utah are among the visitors. In addition, *Martha Graham* (usually in early spring) and *José Limon* bring their respective companies here regularly, as do many international companies.

The entertainment pages of the Sunday *Times* and the *Village Voice* are always full of dance events, ranging from those mentioned above to smaller presentations given in lofts, on college campuses, at churches and elsewhere, and ranging from avant-gardists such as *Merce Cunningham* to folk troupes from Senegal and the Ukraine. In fact, a directory of Big Apple dance troupes lists over 140 companies in all!

Some things to keep in mind when buying tickets for performances at some of the more expensive houses: Dance has become very, very popular in recent years. The major companies sell out regularly, and in advance. If you can, write for your tickets ahead, or call and charge them to a major credit card to ensure seats for the performance you want. If you're planning to be here during Christmas season and want to take the kids to see *The Nutcracker* at the State Theater, write as far ahead of time as possible. Despite a month of daily performances, *The Nutcracker* is invariably a hot ticket.

The best seats for dance at the State Theater are in the first ring, where you can look down and see the dancers' feet. Because there are no aisles down the center of the sprawling auditorium, you may get tired of climbing over people and vice versa if you sit in the center, so consider aisle seats at the ends of the row, or seats as near the aisle as possible. They cost less, too.

Because the acoustics are so bad at the Uris, dance home of many a visiting troupe, you may want to sit further back, in a lesser priced seat that still affords a good view of the dancers. And because the glitterati sit up front at the Met doesn't mean you have to; dance and music critics have found the viewing and hearing is actually better farther back in the orchestra rows. The Dress Circle seats offer an excellent vantage point at considerable savings over an orchestra seat—an important consideration in these days when ballet tickets at the major houses are edging into the $40 and up category. Substantial savings can be made by purchasing an obstructed-view seat at the Met or State theaters.

Lastly, don't overlook the fact that discount ballet (as well as theater, symphony and opera) tickets go on sale the same day as the performance at the music-and-dance TKTS booth, Bryant Park (42nd St. between Fifth and Sixth aves.), daily from noon to 2 P.M. and 3 P.M. to 7 P.M. Sunday noon to 6 P.M. Call 382–2323.

STAGE. This year, at New York's legitimate theaters, more than 8 million people will attend Broadway shows. And with an estimated 40 percent of the ticket buyers from outside the New York metropolitan area (nine percent foreigners), all those numbers add up to Broadway being New York City's number one tourist attraction. And that's not even counting the tickets sold at the nearly 15 Off-Broadway theaters in the Greenwich Village area and the more than 230 Off-Off-Broadway showcases found everywhere from SoHo to the Upper West Side, from Chelsea to the Bowery. As Ethel Merman used to sing it, there's no business like show business—and theatrical show business is obviously big business here.

At least part of Broadway's renaissance can be attributed to a combination of promotion and marketing campaigns undertaken by the League of Theater Owners and Producers, the city and the state. Most prominent among these is the effort to simplify ticket buying and, indeed, it is easier to buy Broadway tickets today than it ever has been. You can phone for reservations for a particular show from virtually anywhere in the world, charge the tickets to a major credit card, and have them waiting for you at the box office the night of the show. In the metropolitan area (and sometimes throughout the Northeast) you can purchase theater tickets and seats for other performing arts events at computerized Ticketron outlets (call 399–4444 for the location nearest you) up until the day before a performance. On the day of the performance, you can pick up last-minute seats to many plays, musicals, and other attractions for half price (plus a small service charge) at one of three TKTS booths—the first at Broadway and 47th St., the second at No. 2 World Trade Center, and a third near Borough Hall in Brooklyn. And, of course, you can always go directly to the box office of the show you want to see and get tickets there.

Some facts and hints: The Times Square TKTS booth is open from 3 to 8 P.M. daily for evening performances, from noon to 2 P.M. for Wednesday and Saturday matinees, and from noon to 8 P.M. for both matinees and evening performances on Sunday. At the World Trade Center the hours are 11 A.M. to 5:30 P.M. Monday through Saturday; matinee and Sunday tickets are sold 11 A.M. to 5:30 P.M. the day before the performance; Off-Broadway tickets are sold 11 A.M. to 1 P.M. for evening performances only. In Brooklyn, the booth operates Monday through Friday 11 A.M.–5:30 P.M., Saturday 11 A.M. to 3:30 P.M. for evening performances only. Matinee and Sunday tickets are available on the day before the performance; Off-Broadway tickets are sold till 1 P M Lines at the Times Square booth can be very, very long. If you have very specific preferences you'd probably want to be on line by 10:30 or 11 in the morning for matinee tickets, by 2:30 or so for evening performances. It is often worth a little extra subway time to travel to the Trade Center or Brooklyn. The lines and wait (except at lunchtime) are shorter, and the selection just as good as uptown. The TKTS booth, however, accepts traveler's checks or cash only—no credit cards, no checks.

You should also look into "twofers"—tickets that entitle you to buy two tickets for the price of one when presented at the box office for specified performances—and, if you're in town for an extended stay, the Theater Development Fund. Twofers are usually available at hotel desks, at restaurant cashier booths, and at offices of the New York Visitors and Convention Bureau, 2 Columbus Circle. Sometimes they are even distributed while you're waiting on line at the TKTS booth.

The emphasis here on half-price tickets is simple: Broadway prices have skyrocketed in recent years, and although tickets for equivalent presentations elsewhere—in Las Vegas or Tokyo or London—are often even more expensive than full price in New York, the $45–$50 top-price seat for a Broadway musical is increasingly the norm, while one show imported from England during a recent season had a $100 top-ticket (the "cheap" seats were to be $70) for a two-part, eight-hour show. Thus it is easy to understand why more than 20 percent of all theater tickets in New York are sold through the TKTS booths.

The best advice for getting to see the biggest hits on Friday and Saturday nights is to write well in advance to the box office, or to phone a reservation via credit card. If you're writing, send a certified check or money order for the exact amount, give several alternate dates and enclose a stamped, self-addressed envelope. Tickets for these same hits are usually easier to get for weekday evenings and matinees, though the sooner you make your decision as to what you want to see and when you want to see it, the better chance you have of getting your first choice. For sold-out shows, you might try waiting at the box office around 6 P.M. the night *before* you want to see that show. That's when unused "house seats" (a handful of the best seats held by the management for VIPs) are put on sale. This is admittedly a risky bet. Many shows also sell standing room—usually on the day of the performance, at prices ranging from about $5 to $10. And if there's only "must see" sold-out show for you, try a ticket broker. Brokers charge full price plus a commission, the latter *legally* limited to $2.50 per ticket, and all too often the hottest tickets go only to favored customers. Check the major hotels, most of which cater to out-of-town clientele.

Picking a new show is as easy as ABC. Study the classified listings on the theater pages of the daily newspapers or in the *New Yorker* or *New York* magazine (the latter includes concise capsule reviews of all offerings), where you'll find casts, telephone numbers, prices, curtain times, and theater addresses. The *New York Times,* especially on Sunday, has similar information. Ticket-availability boxes appear in the amusement pages of the *New York Times* and *Daily News* on Fridays. Hint to reading between the lines: When the availability chart says "all sections, all performances" or even "most sections," chances are you can get tickets to that show at the TKTS booth. For quick suggestions, scan the ads for major Tony Award winners—Broadway's equivalent of Hollywood's Oscars. Among recent winners that should be playing through the 1988–89 season: *Cats, 42nd Street, Les Miserables, Me and My Girl, Phantom of the Opera, Serafina,* and *A Chorus Line.*

A recent trend on Broadway has been toward quality revivals of both musical and straight-play classics of the American stage. Witness such recent and popular offerings as *Anything Goes, The Music Man, Cabaret,* and *A Streetcar Named Desire.*

Another recent trend on Broadway has been toward short-run one-man or one-woman shows featuring young talents such as Lily Tomlin in her Tony award-winning performance in *In Search of Intelligent Life in the Universe,* Liza Minelli, Neil Diamond, Bette Midler, Gilda Radner, and Peter Allen, and older standbys such as Lena Horne, Tony Bennett, Jackie Mason, and Andy Williams.

Many of the city's theaters themselves are handsome, steeped in theatrical history and designated city landmarks. Indeed, no visitor should bypass *Shubert Alley,* a narrow private walkway (open to the public) between 44th and 45th Sts. west of Broadway. It is named for the three famous producing and theater-owning brothers of the early part of the century, Sam, Lee and J.J. Shubert. Both the *Shubert Theater* and the *Booth* are on the alley (along with an "I Love New York" souvenir shop, restaurant, and ticket agency). At the foot of Shubert Alley on 44th St. is also *Sardi's,* famous theatrical hangout and site of numerous opening-night parties. Its walls are lined with caricatures of the famous Broadway personalities who have wined and dined there—though neither the food nor the service seems as pleasing to nonregulars as to those who are instantly recognized.

Broadway means different things to different people. To most, it means the New York City theater district situated around the bright lights of Broadway. But to theater people, it means a geographic entity of 36 square blocks bounded by Sixth and Eighth Aves. and 41st and 53rd Sts. In the theaters on those blocks are tried-and-true dramas and musicals and British imports on the main featuring the best talent money can buy. Since it can cost $3–$5 million to stage a musical and up to $1½ million for a straight play, Broadway doesn't take chances and leaves the risk-taking on new and unproven plays to Off-Broadway (OB) and Off-Off-Broadway (OOB).

There are many differences between Broadway, OB, and OOB. For openers, Broadway performers work under an Equity (actors' union) contract for a basic minimum pay. The OB minimum is a lot less because the theaters are a lot smaller, the cost of mounting a play a lot less because of relaxed union regulations. And the OOB performers may be working for the experience, exposure, and contributions in everything from SoHo lofts to church basements to showcases in Queens short on scenery but long on desire.

OOB is, to the Alliance of Resident Theaters/New York (ART), "alternative theatre—a place for testing potential, for experimentation and the discovery of new talent . . . the research and development division of the American Theatre. Pulitzer Prize winners *A Chorus Line, No Place to Be Somebody, Talley's Folly,* and *Buried Child* are among the many works introduced in this arena for emerging artists." For information about OOB performances, read the *Village Voice.* Keep your eyes open as you walk around, too. There are lots of theater endeavors not advertised on a regular basis, but you'll see posters or signs. Churches frequently host such theater.

OB was born in much the same way when it started in the 1930s in Greenwich Village around the time when the *Provincetown Playhouse* on MacDougal St. began showcasing playwright Eugene O'Neill there. Bette Davis and Henry Fonda worked OB, so did Geraldine Page, Jason Robards, George C. Scott, and Colleen Dewhurst, and so did—and do— Meryl Streep, Dustin Hoffman, and Al Pacino. Edward Albee and Lanford Wilson got their playwriting start there, Jose Quintero became an OB legend for his direction of O'Neill works there, and Brecht, Weill, Ionesco and Beckett got some of their first important U.S. exposure there. Indeed, Joe Papp's Public Theater complex there is a veritable supermarket of lively theater choices.

In brief, some of the best theater in America was—and is—presented OB in Greenwich Village theaters such as the *Cherry Lane, Circle-In-the-Square* (downtown), *Theatre de Lys, Roundabout, Public, The Negro Ensemble,* and *Circle Repertory* at less than half of Broadway prices. America's longest running show, *The Fantasticks,* has been playing since May 3, 1960 at the *Sullivan St. Playhouse.* Some OB companies—most notably, *Circle Repertory,* in TriBeCa and the *Manhattan Theater Club* on the Upper East Side—get their big hits to Broadway. Newest members of this OB community—right on the fringe of Broadway itself—are the 14 theaters of *42nd Street Theater Row,* between Ninth and Tenth Aves., across from Manhattan Plaza. Sadly, despite their relatively consistent quality and quest for innovation, just about all of these theaters and companies are in constant financial trouble, struggling from one production to the next, forever hoping to hit upon that one huge Broadway possibility—as *Chorus Line* and *Pirates of Penzance* were for Joseph Papp's *New York Shakespeare Festival Public Theater*—whose proceeds will finance other endeavors. Tickets for OB shows are usually about half the price of Broadway seats, and often less. They are even cheaper OOB.

Papp's theater complex on Lafayette St., near Astor Place, generates some of the most exciting theatrical events in the city. The various theaters play host to young playwrights honing their craft in workshop situations, to experienced actors and directors needing the feedback of a small intimately housed audience, to short-lived experimental works, jazz concerts, dance series, film retrospectives and anything related to the performing arts. Other reliable sources of interesting theater are the internationally famed *LaMama Experimental Theater Club* (74A E. 4th St.; 475–7710), *Playwrights Horizons* (406 W. 42nd St.; 279–4200), the *American Place Theater* (111 W. 46th St.; 246–3730), *CSC Repertory* (136 E. 13th St.; 677–4210), *Jean Cocteau Repertory* (330 Bowery; 677–0060), and *New Federal Theater Group* (466 Grand St.; 598–0400). OB may also mean a trek even farther uptown—to the *Riverside Church,* (122nd St. at Riverside Drive; 222–5900). Experimental outposts of the theater—such as the *Wooster Group, Re-Cher-Chez Studio,* and *Theatre for the New City,*—are usually found in the Village, or in SoHo.

Central Park's *Delacorte Theater* continues to be home to summertime Shakespeare productions co-sponsored by the city and Joseph Papp's Public Theater. Tickets to these generally first-rate outdoor productions are free, distributed beginning at 6 P.M. on the night of performance. The line for tickets, however, begins forming in the afternoon, so take a blanket, a book, and maybe a picnic for before the show. (Get a place number immediately.) There are usually two productions each summer, running about a month each. The theater is set beside a rock-bounded lagoon near W. 81st St., and is accessible via the 81st St. entrances to the park from Central Park West or Fifth Ave.

Sitting in the Delacorte listening to Shakespeare's words will make you feel far removed from the pass-the-hat informality of OOB, from the OB of Greenwich Village, or the bright lights of the Great White Way. But it's all there for the taking, and all part of New York's great theatrical life. After all, the theater in Manhattan has to strain to outdo the everyday theater of the streets.

SHOPPING. Whether or not you came to New York for the shopping, you probably won't be able to resist it while you're here. The city offers such a variety of stores, goods and services that, even if you don't buy, a shopping expedition can be exciting and fascinating.

First, though, you should know where to look for what you do want. The telephone book Yellow Pages are valuable guides (there is one volume for Consumers, another for Businesses). Or check the local newspapers and magazines for ads or articles on current sales. If you're not looking for something too esoteric, the major department stores (Macy's, B. Altman, Bloomingdale's) may surprise you with the completeness of their stock. Although a specialty store might have a collection that more exactly matches your tastes, the department stores have at least a little bit of almost everything, and after seeing some particular sections—both Macy's and Bloomingdale's for example, have lavish cookware departments—you may feel no need to look further. Many department stores now open their doors for Sunday shopping. The hours are usually noon to 5 or 6. Also, you need not have a store's own card to charge; many stores, including Bloomingdale's, Saks Fifth Avenue, and Macy's, now accept American Express and even Diners Club. So far, only B. Altman accepts MasterCard or Visa.

Nonetheless, it's fun to explore. Most of New York's serious shopping is done in the midtown area, between 34th St. and 60th or so. This corresponds to the "downtown" of other American cities. But other areas have valuable resources too. On the residential Upper West Side, from 72nd to 86th Sts. for instance, there's a concentration of quieter, neighborhood-type stores along Broadway, and the southern parts of Amsterdam and Columbus Aves. are now arcades of new, trendy shops and restaurants. This part of town has traditionally been the middle-class area of Manhattan, and though it's rapidly becoming fancier and more expensive, you'll still find some very civilized browsing there in the way of books, foodstuffs, antiques, and so on. The more fashionable Upper East Side, from the 60s through the 90s, is terrain for the serious collector of antiques and art (the auction houses are here, and the galleries of Madison Ave.) and for lovers of handsome boutiques. For bargains you really go downtown. For apparel, for example, a long stretch of Orchard Street from Houston Street south is the nearest the city comes to an old-fashioned marketplace. Don't go on Saturday, when many businesses shut for the Sabbath—though they do open Sunday—and don't be deterred by the countless small, poky stores—there are good buys here for those with the patience to look. *A. Altman,* for example, at 182 Orchard, is renowned for women's fashion.

But if shopping is at all a tourist attraction in New York—and we believe it is—there are two stores that ought to be on everyone's "must-see" list: Bloomingdale's and Macy's.

Bloomingdale's (705–2000), taking up the square block from 59th to 60th Sts. and between Lexington and Third Aves., is nothing less than a fashion showplace whether you're looking at designer dresses or sheets and pillowcases. The main floor, with its walls upon walls of mirrors and stark lighting, is a chic open bazaar half given over to makeup, perfume, and fast-buy women's items, the other half a complete men's haberdashery. Be sure not to miss its two-level gourmet food department, complete with special pasta and caviar sections. You can receive personal shopping help in over 10 languages, and there are special services available to blind and physically disabled customers. Bloomies also specializes in large purchase shipments abroad. Now open on Sunday.

Macy's (695–4440), also a full block square from 34th to 35th Sts. between Seventh Ave. and Broadway, is more the everyman's department store. At Macy's the brand names and merchandise are familiar; it's not so much what the store carries as the depth of stock in virtually everything. The basement-level Cellar is the most popular part of the store, overflowing with housewares in what has been designed as a series of integrated boutiques. The Cellar also has a wonderful cheese counter (relatively reasonably priced) and a full stock of tinned, bottled, and otherwise prepared gourmet items (not so reasonably priced, though you can't beat the selection), and a small grocery with first-rate produce (very highly priced, but you won't find a rotten apple, or mushroom, in the barrel). The children's floors are indeed a wonderland from Thanksgiving through the New Year, with free shows and a spectacular decorating job. The store also has one of the finest soda fountains in the city on the fifth floor. Macy's also features shopping assistance in French, Spanish, Italian, German, Japanese, and even Portuguese. Be sure to visit Macy's Visitors Center on the balcony or 34th St. side. Here customers receive a special welcome and assistance with everything from hotel arrangements to selecting the right gift to take back home.

By July 1989, the new *A & S Plaza* indoor shopping mall (on the site of the old Gimbel's) should be open. This sparkling new addition will feature a branch of the Brooklyn store along with other specialty shops and restaurants.

On 34th St. between Fifth and Sixth aves. there are a large number of shoe stores and one of the outlets of the chain called *The Gap,* selling men's and women's jeans and jeans-style fashions. Finally, at Fifth Ave., *B. Altman's* (679–7800) is the last of 34th Street's department stores. This is a favorite of the middle-income shopper—respectable, always-acceptable merchandise is sold here; there is a fully stocked menswear department, along with excellent furniture, china and glassware sections, and fine foods. The store also offers special personalized shopping assistance.

Fifth Ave. between 34th St. and 59th St. has long been known as a mecca for shoppers, although in recent years some of its more illustrious residents have folded their tents and been succeeded by less refined tenants. It is well to be suspicious, in fact, of several stores in this stretch selling cameras, electronics, carved "ivory," and such. But Fifth Ave. still offers an unusual number of fine shops of every description, and it remains a top attraction for visiting shoppers.

The traditional Fifth Ave. tour begins at 38th St., at *Lord & Taylor.* Here the Christmas-window decorations are a special treat, while the store itself is known for its fine clothing, especially that by American designers. They also offer special shopping services. The new *Lane Bryant* at 39th St. offers stylish clothes and accessories for the larger woman. At 50th St., *Saks Fifth Avenue* has long been a beacon of fashion and accessories. As you walk north along Fifth in the 40s and 50s, you'll notice that this is where many of the airlines have their offices, and also that this is good bookshop country (*Scribner's,* near 49th, and *Rizzoli* just west of Fifth Ave. at 57th St., are the most handsome). *Steuben Glass* has a showroom on Fifth Ave. at 56th St. American glass raised to an elegant art, at elegant prices. *Aquascutum,* at 54th and Fifth, carries traditional British garb for men and women as does *Burberry's* on E. 57th St., between Madison and Fifth.

Henri Bendel (pronounced BEN-del by those in the know) on 57th St. just west of Fifth Ave.; 247–1100, is a small pearl of a store—set up in aisles of boutiques—known for its trend-setting women's fashions and for its always beautifully designed displays and windows. (Note: *The Limited* has recently purchased this property, so there's a chance that this posh emporium might be moving.) Just opposite it, on the corner of 57th St. and Fifth Ave., is *Bergdorf Goodman* (753–7300), chic and expensive; and a little farther east on 57th St. is the new *Bonwit Teller,* reopened after an absence and much reduced in size. Don't miss the ultra-elegant multilevel shopping arcade in the new Trump Tower, 56th St. and Fifth Ave., featuring the best (and most expensive) in European fashions, jewelry, and *objets d'art.* (You can walk right through from Bonwit Teller.)

While in the neighborhood, consider *Alexander's* (593–0880), one block south of Bloomingdale's. This is another store noted for inexpensive clothing of all kinds, some of it very stylish; while it's somewhat chaotic and noisy, the values are good, offering special purchases and closeouts, some with famous labels, and Alexander's has a reputation for decent quality, if you are an aggressive shopper. It's also open most evenings until 9.

Farther uptown, on Madison Ave. at 72nd St., *Polo/Ralph Lauren* has opened in an elegant old mansion with just as elegant signature wear and accessories for men and women, antique gifts, and home furnishings.

Some of the stores we've named have branches scattered in other parts of the city. Shopping in midtown deserves some strategic thinking: Try to avoid the hours between noon and 2 A.M. (when office workers descend *en masse* to get their errands done) and weekends. Also crowded are the late-opening nights—usually Thursdays, when many of these stores will close at 9 P.M. If you prefer to avoid the midtown rush, find out if a branch is more convenient by calling the main office, or checking the ads in the newspapers, although stock and selection at the branches are rarely as good as at the flagship stores. Nearly all major stores (and even some of the smaller boutiques) extend their shopping hours for the Christmas season. If you happen to be in New York right after Thanksgiving, you'll find such stores as Bloomingdale's and Macy's open seven days a week, with shopping hours extended well into the evening. Lord & Taylor and Saks usually follow suit.

For a historical shopping and dining jaunt, head downtown to South and Front Sts. for the new South Street Seaport restoration complex. The old Fulton St. Fish Market is still in business, now as part of a multilevel plaza featuring stalls selling fresh local and exotic produce, snack areas, and a seafood restaurant. There are also branches of some interesting uptown stores such as *Ann Taylor* and *Caswell-Massey.* And definitely worth a look is the reborn classic, *Abercrombie & Fitch.* The *South Street Pavilion* features dozens of quality restaurants and shops on what used to be Pier 17. New York's Upper West Side and West 20s in the Chelsea district are also great places to discover the latest fashion (along with dining) trends. Columbus Avenue now rivals Madison as the city's number-one browsing stretch, and both Seventh and Eighth avenues in the upper teens and low 20s are beginning to fill up with trendy galleries, boutiques, and branches of uptown stores.

As enticing as the larger stores are, the hundreds of specialty stores are the signature of the city. The list below is partial, and concentrates on relatively "stable" stores that have been in business for some time. A further guide, as mentioned, is the Yellow Pages.

As you walk through the city, you may see some stores with the notation "To the Trade" on the door or window. Such stores sell goods at wholesale prices to business clients, and often do not accommodate the general public. However, some of them do occasionally open their doors for a special sale. Check the "Living" sections of the daily and Sunday papers or the "Sales & Bargains" column of *New York* magazine for announcements of the latter.

Sales tax in New York City at press time is 8¼%.

Women's Clothing

All of the well-known department stores previously mentioned dedicate much or all of their floor space and counters to wooing women. Competition is fierce; there are frequent sales and special offers, which are widely advertised in the local papers.

Generally speaking, the largest array of merchandise, and therefore the greatest range of choices, will be found in the larger department and specialty stores. *B. Altman's* (679–7800) on Fifth Ave. at 34th St., is best known for conservative styles, though it also offers fine traditional sport clothes. Very reasonable (and moderately modish) items are on the sixth floor. *Lord & Taylor* (391–3344) has a range of traditionally styled fashion which appeals to women of every age, including the young contemporary customer, male as well as female.

Saks Fifth Avenue (on Fifth Ave. and 50th St.) still touts the best in "carriage trade" fashion. It isn't cheap, but the labels are famous, and the store has a reputation for accessories. Recently, they've added several boutique annexes on E. 49th St., including an imaginative gift and gourmet department. There's also a chic active sportswear shop. *Bergdorf Goodman* (on Fifth Ave. at 57th St.) is indispensable for those who can afford its outstanding collection. It appeals to the young—and to their grandmothers.

It is only natural to center your shopping attention on the bigger stores; but you should also sample the fantastic range of boutiques around the city. Try walking along Madison Ave. between 60 and 78th Sts. or so, for a dazzling array of high-fashion shops nestled amid the galleries and salons. *Veneziano,* near 68th St. is a favorite of the members of the best-dressed list (prices are steep, as is to be expected in this area). *Ralph Lauren* has recently opened a new boutique at 72nd St. and Madison Ave. And at 760 Madison Ave., try *Ménage à Trois* for understated youthful high fashion clothes. Many well-heeled celebrities with slim figures shop here. *The Limited* at 62nd St. and Madison Ave. features hot designs and accessories at cool prices (for this neighborhood). More branches of this popular store are due to open in midtown.

Right nearby, near 69th St., is *Jaeger International Shop,* where the tailored look finds its finest expression in some stunning sportswear. (Another Jaeger outlet is to be found at 19 E. 57th St. near Madison.) And near 71st St. you'll find *Saint Laurent Rive Gauche,* for the best Paris has to offer.

Back a little farther downtown, for a change in manner, look at the sweetly English printed fabrics and home accessories of *Laura Ashley,* on Madison near 63rd St. Clothing can be found at their new boutique at 219 E. 57th St. Finally, a midtown shopping expedition is not complete without a stop at *Martha Inc.,* 475 Park Ave., one of the oldest names in New York fashion.

Barney's stunning new *Women's Store* (directly connected to the *Men's Store*) appeals to the well-heeled sophisticate who enjoys making a strong fashion statement. Along with the finest in day and evening wear, you'll find a vast array of elegant personal and home accessories, and even a selection of top-drawer children's clothing. Try the chic basement level restaurant for lunch or tea.

There are plenty of worthwhile places to visit besides the above shops, less mainstream both in style and in locale. On the Upper West Side try *Charivari for Women,* at Broadway and 84th St., for Italian and American clothes in the latest modes—very modern but also very handsome. *Charivari Sport,* at 201 W.79th St., offers once again very modern stylings; and the newest *Charivari* on W. 57th St. for some of each. Women in larger sizes will find beautiful clothes in natural fabrics at *Ashanti Bazaar,* 872 Lexington Ave. at 65th St.; also a good selection at the *Forgotten Woman* at 880 Lexington Ave. at 65 St. *Reminiscence,* in Greenwich Village on Fifth Ave. near 14th St., carries a range of now-fashionable "antique" clothing, as well as up-to-date stuff under its own label. For the truly young-at-heart (or those prepared to be a little outrageous), *Fiorucci* is truly entertaining, at 125 East 59th St. There are also *Benetton* sportswear stores in nearly every neighborhood.

For stylish lingerie at surprisingly moderate prices, nothing can beat the new two-tier *Victoria's Secret* at 34 East 57th St. between Madison and Park. Whether your taste runs to frills or slink, you'll get the latest here, probably for a bit less than you would at the top department stores. VS carries both its own high-quality label goods and famous makers like Christian Dior; there's also a men's corner with underwear, robes, and a selection of ties. This store has a smaller branch in **The Limited** on Madison Ave. High-priced, limited-edition silk lounge and sleepwear can be found at *La Lingerie* at 792 Madison Ave. Expensive but fashionable pantyhose from Switzerland can be found at *Fogal's* two Madison Ave. stores; bargain hosiery seekers should head to *Value Hosiery* at 1653 Second Ave. or *M. Steuer* at 31 West 32nd St. near Macy's. (They have discount bodywear, too.) For men's and women's hosiery with a British flair, try a branch of *Sock Shop;* there's a large one near Macy's in Herald Square.

Accessories and Such. For shoes, *Gucci* might be your first stop; it offers high styled, high-priced shoes and other accessories and leather goods, and there is a branch on Fifth Ave. (While the staff no longer takes the infamous noon until 2 P.M. siesta, don't expect them to be overly helpful or friendly; Gucci didn't make its name on service.) *Charles Jourdan,* in the Trump Tower at 56th St. and Fifth Ave., can't be beaten for the latest Parisian shoe and boot designs—once again at astronomical prices. For more modest budgets, there's *Chandler's,* across the street, and *I. Miller,* at 57th Street and Fifth Avenue. Though its name may be less well known than the Fifth Ave. stores, *Maud Frizon USA,* at 49 E. 57th St., is a true competitor, both in styling and in prices. *Raspberry* carries quality imports at reasonable prices.

Handbags, gloves, scarves, and the like can well be bought at the department stores that cater to women, for example Bonwit Teller or Saks. But one downtown handbag outlet is worth knowing about—*Fine & Klein,* at 119 Orchard St. The price range of the wide selection of bags here ranges from very low to very high, but even the very high items are somewhat discounted. *Artbag Creations* at 735 Madison Ave. near 65th Street is known for both its elegant handbags and superior repair work. *LaBagagerie* is just down the street and features trendy European bags, belts, and accessories at a variety of prices. *Lederer,* at 613 Madison Ave. near 58th St., also has a huge selection, and though these satisfy the most discriminating tastes, the prices are mostly within reach. A midtown bargain spot

Midtown Shopping

CENTRAL PARK

Columbus Circle

CENTRAL PARK SOUTH

Grand Army Plaza

BROADWAY

58TH ST.
W. 57TH ST.
56TH ST.
55TH ST.
54TH ST.
W. 53RD ST.
52ND ST.
W. 50TH ST.
49TH ST.
48TH ST.
47TH ST.
46TH ST.
W. 45TH ST.
44TH ST.
43RD ST.
42ND ST.
41ST ST.
40TH ST.
39TH ST.
38TH ST.
37TH ST.
36TH ST.
35TH ST.
34TH ST.
33RD ST.
32ND ST.
62ND ST.
61ST ST.
60TH ST.
51ST ST.

FIFTH AVE.
MADISON AVE.
SEVENTH AVE.
(SIXTH AVE.)
AVE. OF THE AMERICAS
EIGHTH AVE.
VANDERBILT AVE.

Rockefeller Center
Theatre District
Times Sq.
Bryant Park
N.Y. Public Library
Herald Sq.

The Big Stores

1) Bloomingdale's
2) Alexander's
3) F.A.O. Schwarz (toys)
4) Bergdorf Goodman
5) Tiffany
6) Saks Fifth Avenue
7) Brooks Brothers
8) Bonwit Teller
9) Henri Bendel
10) Lord & Taylor
11) A & S Plaza
12) B. Altman
13) Macy's
14) Trump Tower

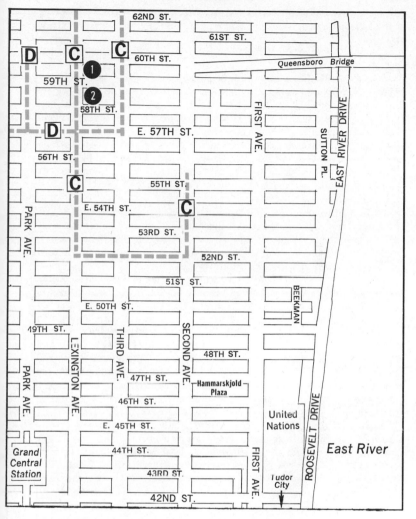

The Areas

A Fifth Avenue: clothing, accessories, jewelry, silver, design, luggage & leather,
  bookstores—all, except tourist-trap electronics and camera shops, are very up-
  market in both quality and price.
B Madison Avenue: boutiques of all description, men's clothes, leather & luggage—
  like Fifth Ave., all up-market. Also on some sidestreets. Art galleries above 57th St.
C Lexington & Third Avenues: boutiques and shops, but less prestigious than those of
  Fifth and Madison Avenues. Some antique stores on Second.
D 57th Street: boutiques, art galleries, antique specialists—most quite prestigious
  and expensive.
E 34th Street Area: clothing shops, but distinctly non-posh.
F Gems and jewelry.
G Hi-Fi.
H Musical instruments.
I Brazilian imports.

for top-quality handbags is *J.S. Suarez, Inc.* at 26 W. 54th St. *Dokkim,* at the Herald Center, offers unusual and durable designs in natural straw and leather. Purchasers of hats may enjoy *Whittall & Shon,* at 485 Seventh Ave., or *I.J. Herman,* 15 W. 38th St., one of the last establishments left that do hat blocking.

Henri Bendel has a small but luxurious fur section, but the fur district proper is on Seventh Avenue, where *Varriale* is one of the more widely known names (564–0284). When buying furs you should comparison shop as far as possible, since you're probably making a sizable investment; in the same stretch of Seventh Ave. as Varriale, in the high 20s and low 30s, you'll find several more furriers, including *Steven Corn,* at 141 W. 28th St., and *Aronowicz,* at 345 Seventh. Crossing town to the East Side, *Fred the Furrier,* at 581 Fifth Ave., is widely advertised and popular; the *Ritz Thrift Shop,* at 107 W. 57th St., offers fine used furs.

Bargain Shopping. Finally, there is the indescribable thrill of bargain shopping. Not just for a marked-down item (which can be a very good value at special season sales), but also for the designer dress you saw yesterday at an expensive midtown store and which you now find at a 50% to 75% reduction at a manufacturers' outlet.

Such shopping takes time and research. The advantage of an outlet, however, is that reductions occur at the very beginning of a fashion season. Often labels are cut out, but tags have code numbers veterans can identify as concealing a famous designer's handiwork. Stock can vary, and it may take several trips before you find precisely what you want. There may be slight irregularities in the stock, but *Loehmann's* (at Fordham Road and Jerome Ave. in the Bronx) and in Riverdale at Broadway and 236th St.) and *Bolton's* (on Madison at 86th St., and at several other locations) are fascinating because you never know what they'll have next. Loehmann's, the grandmother of all the popular discounters, also has branches in Queens and Brooklyn.

Resale stores carry "gently used" things culled from the best private wardrobes—some of their merchandise may never have been worn. One well-known shop is *Resale Dress Shop,* at 1041 Madison Ave., *Trishop,* at 1689 First Ave., and *Repeat Performance,* farther south at 220 E. 23rd St., are two charity shops which regularly receive donations of fashionable clothes (some good-quality seconds, some perfect); this is not secondhand stuff, but comes direct from the department stores—you should look the clothing over before buying, but there is little here that is unsatisfactory. The *Ritz Thrift Shop,* 107 W. 57th St., has used furs. For really high fashion at a discount, try *22 Steps* at Madison Ave. and 65th St. *Three Wishes* at 355 West Broadway in Soho carries a famous line of silk dresses and separates (we can't reveal the name) at less than wholesale; you'll recognize the prestige label. *Odd Job Trading* at 66 W. 48th St. near Sixth Ave. has close outs, special purchases, discontinued merchandise, household items, shoes, clothing, perfumes, toiletries, toys—the items change from week to week. *New Store,* at 289 Seventh Ave., near 27th St., has a large collection of designer lines and shoes at heavy discounts. Finally, if you're invited to a once-in-a-lifetime gala, try renting a spectacular designer gown from *One Night Stand* at 905 Madison Ave. British owner Constance Sayre can turn you into Princess Di for the entire weekend for as little as $150.

Men's Clothing

Barney's, Seventh Ave. and 17th St., calls itself the largest men's store in the world, and it's hard to see how it could have any competition. This is *the* center for menswear in the city—if only because so many different elements of gentlemen's garb are found here under one roof. Conservative styles, high-fashion tailoring, and the most modern fashions are all available, and in an enormous range of sizes. In addition, Barney's has occasional sales—very popular ones, and widely advertised. Very early on the first morning of a sale, the line of well-dressed men waiting for the store to open circles the block.

Brooks Bros. has been offering its wares to conservative New Yorkers since the beginning of the 19th century, and is still going strong at Madison Ave. and 44th St. The first floor contains an ocean of button-down shirts and striped ties, and the store is famous for its dignified high-quality suits; but you'll also find hats, haberdashery, sport clothes, and much else too. Still in the conservative vein are a series of stores in the same neighborhood, including *Chipp, Inc.,* at 14 E. 44th St., and the well-known name *Paul Stuart* (on Madison at 45th St.), for the slightly more adventurous. *F. R. Tripler,* on Madison Ave. at 46th St., is another long-established and reliable store.

Of course, all the major department stores have extensive men's sections.

In recent years, there has been a marked trend away from the stylish stores; the so-called "discount" men's outlet shops have taken a lot of the traffic away from their more impressive brethren. On Fifth Ave., in the area between 14th and 23rd Sts., you'll find a number of such places, of which perhaps the best known is *Rothman's* at Park Ave. and 17th St. Rothman's grandson, Ken Giddon, has given this venerable Manhattan institution a fresh, fashionable look. This is one of the few places in the entire country where you'll find famous brands of American suits whose retail prices are often in the $700 range. Salesmen will decipher the label codes and tell you what you're actually buying; in many cases you'll see the name on the suit sleeve; it's the real item. *Hampshire International,* nearby at 85 Fifth Ave., has similar stock at similar prices.

Part of the trend away from tradition has been toward stylish Italian clothes, such as those available at a variety of specialty stores on East 60th St. between Second and Third avenues. Many of these shops have frequent sales, so do some exploring before you buy. *Charivari for Men,* 2339 Broadway at 85th St., also offers very handsome modern men's fashions. On the less formal side, jeans, workshirts, and western wear are an increasingly important element in men's fashion these days, and for that matter in women's too. Both sexes are catered to at *The Gap,* where the selection of jeans and related accessories is among the most complete in the city. There are several branches, the largest of which is at 86th St. and Third Ave. Downtown, *Hudson's* (105 Third Ave. near 14th St.) is the granddaddy of the so-called Army & Navy stores, though the merchandise here encompasses a far wider range than just military surplus. *Canal Jean,* at 304 Canal St. and on Broadway near Spring St., and *Unique Clothing Warehouse,* on Broadway near 8th St., both offer wilder, funkier, more diverse variants of jeans-style fashions. Both are city institutions, for inexpensive, trendy clothes.

While on the subject of Western-style clothing, let's talk shoes—or, rather, boots. *To Boot,* at 72nd St. and Columbus Ave., has a large selection of very fine cowboy boots, ranging from the straightforward to the ornate, and to be sold to both men and women; unfortunately, while the denims and shirtings of Western stylings may be bought relatively inexpensively, the same cannot be said of the footwear. The elegant new *Cole-Haan* shop on Madison Ave. and 61st St. has a wide variety of traditional styles for men and women, including some English bench-made models at surprisingly good prices.

More usual types of shoes may be bought all over the city, at branches of such chains as *Florsheim* or *Coward.* For distinctive stylings, try *Church's Shoes,* on Madison Ave. at 49th St.; this is a branch of the famous London bootmakers and offers elegant traditional footwear, but the price you pay for these traditional, but *very* durable and handsome, items is high. *Susan Bennis/Warren Edwards,* at 440 Park Ave., offers unusual and fine-quality shoes for men and women, as does *Maud Frizon,* at 49 E. 57th St.; and *Barney's,* that great capital of menswear, has not one but two shoe departments. Lastly, *McReedy and Schreiber,* at 37 W. 46th St., is another popular shop.

A few expensive shops still specialize in what is popularly known as men's furnishings, and you had best visit these establishments with a thick wallet. Underwear, hosiery, ties, and shirts combine with sweaters, robes, and miscellaneous sportswear of the highest quality. *A. Sulka,* at 430 Park Ave., *Countess Mara,* at 110 E. 57th St., and *H. Herzfeld, Inc.,* at 507 Madison Ave., are good examples of this kind of store. On the Lower East Side, *The Tie Orchard* offers high-quality neckwear (mostly Italian) at pushcart prices.

In New York City, men don't take a back seat even when it comes to the matter of haute couture. Designer fashions for men exist in virtually every major department and specialty store, and there are also high-fashion boutiques solely for men. Famous among these are *St. Laurent for Men,* at 543 Madison Ave. near 55th St., and *Pierre Balmain,* at 795 Madison near 68th St. St. Laurent in particular has fine shirts. *Gianni Versace's* pricey but popular styles can be found at Madison Ave. and 68th St., and the male Francophile will be delighted with the new *Givenchy Gentleman* store in the same neighborhood. And finally, of course virtually every men's department in the big stores such as *Bloomingdale's* or *Saks* is highly rewarding.

For renting good-quality, conservative, traditional formal wear, *Baldwin Formals,* 40 W. 56th St., and *A. T. Harris,* upstairs on 44th St. between Madison and Vanderbilt Aves.

Children's Clothes

All of the major department stores have children's sections that reflect their positions on the adult fashion ladder. Thus *Bergdorf Goodman* has elegant clothes in both the ready-to-wear and made-to-order categories. *Saks Fifth Avenue's* children's section is only slightly less posh. *Bloomingdale's* has very interesting clothes in a wide assortment, and *Alexander's* is the inexpensive (though good) end of the spectrum. Of all these stores, however, *Macy's* rates as the top choice, if only because of the size of its selection.

A great many boutique-style stores specialize in nothing but children's apparel, and they too cover the full spectrum of prices and styles. *Space Kiddets* at 46 E. 21st St. has snappy original designs for the pint-size punk rocker, plus never-worn (all cotton) clothes from the 1950s at low prices. They also carry shoes from the '50s in the original Buster Brown boxes. *Cerutti,* at Madison and 68th St., received a measure of publicity from the patronage of Jackie Onassis, who reportedly purchased some of Caroline and John-John's gear there; the clientele is that affluent, and the prices reflect it. In a similarly priced but less conservative vein, *Petite Bateau* at 930 Madison Ave. offers the latest imported children's stylings. *Wendy's Store* is a delightful source of infant and toddler wear and toys, at 131 Wooster St. For bargains, *Goldman & Ostrow,* at 315 Grand St. on the Lower East Side, is the real McCoy, or you could go a few steps down the block to *Rice and Breskin* (323 Grand). Or cross the river to Brooklyn and visit *Natan Borlam,* at 157 Havemeyer St. At this discount shop name brands are available at very low prices; open only Sunday through Thursday.

Jewelry

Eye-catching, ready-to-wear, and conveniently centralized, high-fashion jewelry in New York clusters around 55th St. and Fifth Ave. Within a 10-minute walk, the shopper encounters Van Cleef and Arpels (at Bergdorf Goodman), the highly esteemed Tiffany & Co., Buccellati, Fortunoff, Harry Winston, and Cartier. Along with the dazzling adornments that have earned them reputations as dazzlingly expensive, these stores also sell attractive items everyone can afford.

Tiffany's, at Fifth Ave. and 57th St., is almost as elegant as the reputation that precedes it, though there really isn't anywhere here to have breakfast. Even more elegant is the fabled *Cartier's,* at Fifth and 52nd St., where the mantle of wealth and privilege hangs heavy over its gilt and plush decor, but even Cartier takes a backseat in high prices to *Harry Winston's,* at 718 Fifth Ave. *Fortunoff,* a relative newcomer, has been very successfully advertised by Lauren Bacall, and prides itself on discounting brand-name items and stocking a vast array of not-too-expensive trinkets that make very welcome gifts. *H. Stern,* across 51st St. from St. Patrick's, has beautiful precious and semi-precious stones, and jewelry.

If you could use a change from Fifth Avenue's typically cool and sophisticated sales transactions, shopping for jewelry can give you a great chance to do so. West 47th St., between Fifth and Sixth Aves., has been described more than once as the closest thing to a Middle Eastern bazaar to be found in New York—haggling included. This block is known as "the diamond district," and in shops packed with merchandise, where no time or expense has been wasted on decor, you can bargain over gems, gold, silver, and all kinds of semiprecious stones. Investigate *Bill Schifrin,* reputedly the world's largest purveyor of wedding rings, at Booth 86 of the National Jewelers Exchange. The whole block has an element of theater to it, and is well worth a visit, though the procedure of buying a stone here can be intimidating and chancy. It's best to go with a friend who knows diamonds. For glitter that isn't real gold, try the various branches of *Zoe*

Coste and *Ylang-Ylang.* Both feature opulent costume jewelry from around $25. All of the major department and jewelry stores carry a selection of watches. However, the greatest variety of wristwear can be found at *Tourneau Corner* on Madison and 52nd St. or at 34th St. and Seventh Ave.

Leather and Luggage

You will see any number of luggage shops tucked into the various corners of the city, and these are generally the best places to find bargains. *Innovation Luggage,* for example, has several branches, one of them at 42nd St. and Second Ave.; a walk down Orchard Street will furnish you with various displays of luggage, with *Altman's* (no relation to the department store), at 135 Orchard, among the better known. Sticking to the beaten path will involve higher prices, but willing buyers are apparently available in sufficient numbers to enable the more glamorous names to survive. *Gucci,* on Fifth Ave. at 54th St., has a worldwide reputation for its fine products, with prices to match. *Mark Cross,* just south of Gucci at Fifth and 51st St., is in the same class, as is *T. Anthony,* at 480 Park Ave. at 58th St. *Crouch and Fitzgerald,* at Madison and 48th St., is a handsome store that handles its own line of luggage, as well as *Louis Vuitton* bags (Vuitton also has its own outlet, on 57th Street near Madison); and *Dinoffer,* at 22 W. 57th St., is another of the city's reputable old names. The *Coach* company has opened its own boutique at 754 Madison at 65th St., where you can find the largest selection of their bags and portfolios. *Saks, Bloomingdale's, Macy's,* and *Alexander's* all have sizable luggage departments, too.

Cosmetics, Perfumes, and Toiletries

One of New York's finest toiletry shops is *Caswell-Massey,* on Lexington Ave. at 48th St. This is a place that combines a certain modern flair with extremely long-established quality (the store dates back to the eighteenth century); the variety of soaps and all kinds of other liniments and miscellany is a delight. Ask for a catalog; it's wonderful reading. *Cambridge Chemists,* famous for their lines of imported English toiletries and advance stocks of new French perfumes, has moved to fancier and larger quarters at 21 E. 65th St., off Madison. Down in Greenwich Village, the *Soap Opera,* at 51 Grove St., and the *Bath House* on Thompson St. have a wide range of soaps. The department stores are also where most New York women go to buy perfumes, but a better idea is *Scente,* on E. 36th St. just off Madison. This perfume boutique sells all the major brands, including some not always available in the United States, at discounts ranging from 10% to 40%. They carry men's fragrances, too. And you can reorder with their toll-free telephone service. They've been written up in *Good Housekeeping* and other major magazines. The *Love* chain of drug stores features popular brands at good discounts and *Block Pharmacy,* at 74th St. and Third Ave., has a variety of fine soaps and related bath items.

Beauty Salons

There are a few establishments that can't be neglected—*Georgette Klinger,* for example, with its beautiful engraved doors at 501 Madison

Ave. near 53rd St., is known for facials and skin care. They have opened a "total care" salon at 978 Madison Ave. near 76th St. *Christine Valmy,* at 767 Fifth Ave. (near 58th St.) is also popular. *The Make-Up Center* at 150 W. 55th is popular with models and actors because of its unusual cosmetics and skincare services. And of course there are both men and women who will go nowhere else but *Vidal Sassoon,* at 767 Fifth Ave. (58th St.) for their hair. Many of the department stores, including *Bloomingdale's* and *Saks,* have their own salons. And a less famous, but well-liked, salon is *Monique of the Waldorf,* at 301 Park Ave., at 49th St. The *Nardi* salon at 143 E. 57th St. is popular with those seeking high style at moderate prices. They often have good seasonal specials on cuts and perms.

Toys

The magnet for the majority of young and young at heart would have to be *F.A.O. Schwarz,* at Fifth Ave. and 59th St. in the General Motors building. Here, stuffed animals of a size that one would think would terrify a small person are instead immediate objects of delight; and every other conceivable game, toy, or member of a menagerie is available in some part of the store.

At least as famous is the toy department of *Macy's,* where most of the present crop of middle-aged, middle-class New Yorkers originally whet their acquisitional appetites. Shelf upon shelf, counter upon counter— while most of the other department stores have representative departments devoted to toys, this has got to be the definitive department. Two smaller stores that stock unusual toys at decent prices are *Geppetto's Workshop* at the South Street Seaport, and *The Laughing Giraffe* at 1065 Lexington Ave. near 76th St.

There are many dollhouse-and-miniature furniture retail stores in Manhattan; one is *Dollhouse Antics* on Madison Ave. near 92nd St.

Go Fly a Kite, at 1201 Lexington Ave., is devoted to kites—from very simple ones to very expensive ones that one can't imagine being flown. Several stores specialize in model trains, including *Madison Hardware,* at 105 E. 23rd St., the *Train Shop,* at 23 W. 45th St., and the *Red Caboose* at 16 W. 45th St. The *Compleat Strategist,* at 11 East 33rd St. and other locations, features a wide variety of adventure and fantasy board games.

Gourmet Foods and Equipment

Whatever tastes in foodstuffs the visitor to New York may have, he can sate them here, and if he's not careful he'll develop a whole range of new ones too.

Probably New York's favorite delicatessen, and certainly its most often discussed, is *Zabar's.* This establishment occupies three storefronts, on Broadway at 80th St. On Saturday nights the store is open until midnight, and is jammed with New Yorkers who have picked up the bulky Sunday *New York Times*—on sale around 9 P.M. Saturday—and are now waiting in line to buy the fixings for a luxurious Sunday breakfast of smoked fish, bagels, cheese, and croissants, all sold here. Zabar's also has fine kitchen equipment, often at the best prices anywhere. They have sold their Cuisinarts at such a low price that for a time the company refused to sell them any. The fish counter—for whitefish, smoked salmon, sable, sturgeon, etc.—is usually especially crowded, and you must "take a number," but you'll also find meats, a slew of canned and packaged delicacies, coffees, fresh pasta, and much more. While you're on the Upper West Side, *Murray's,* at 2429 Broadway near 90th St., and *Barney Greengrass,* at 541 Amsterdam Avenue, near 86th St., are also renowned for sturgeon, lox, and the like. On the Upper East Side, *Caviarteria,* unsurprisingly, specializes in caviar (at 29 E. 60th St.); a more diversified store is *E.A.T.,* at 1064 Madison at 80th St. While you're looking at galleries in SoHo, take a peak at *Dean & DeLuca's,* 121 Prince Street. This place isn't cheap, but you'll find a range of high-quality pastries, cheeses, pâtés, olive oils, sausages, and you-name-it, as well as impressive-looking kitchen equipment. Another such place in the Village is *Balducci's,* at Sixth Avenue and 9th Street, which in addition to all the exotica also stocks fine fruits and vegetables, meats, fish, and so on. *The Silver Palate* at 73rd St. and Columbus Ave. is the tiny but important gourmet shop that has launched a nationally available line of expensive but exquisite jams, condiments, and even pasta. Here you can buy fresh foods and baked goods as well.

Ninth Avenue is the city's grocery store, and by walking down it between, say, 40th and 50th Sts., you'll find all kinds of good-quality meats, vegetables, pasta, and ethnic specialties. The *International Groceries and Meat Market* at 529 Ninth Ave. (at 39th St.) is packed with open sacks of grains and spices, along with the usual assortment of Greek, Spanish, and Italian gourmet items at good prices. Italian foods are best located by strolling through Little Italy, in the area of Mulberry and Grand Sts., and stopping at any of several stores of which the *Italian Food Center,* at 186 Grand, is an example. Also, *Ferrara's* is nearby: for pastry and coffees. *Katagiri* at 224 E. 59th St. will provide you with Japanese foodstuffs; for Chinese, try any of the curious-looking stores on Mott Street or Mulberry Street south of Canal Street, in Chinatown. For Hungarian provisions, try *Paprikas Weiss,* at 1546 Second Ave. at 78th St., which not only has spices, jams, jellies, and imported candies, but can also provide such esoteric items as ready-to-use strudel dough. Indian spices can be found at a number of shops in "Little India," along Lexington Avenue between 26th and 30th Sts. In the way of coffee and teas, Zabar's has a famous name, and a very old but youthful-looking and expanding store is *Gillies 1840,* at Third Ave. and 84th St., plus other locations. Along Ninth Ave., try the tiny but well-stocked *Empire Coffee and Tea Company,* at number 592 between 42nd and 43rd Sts. In the Village at 109 Christopher St. near Bleecker, *McNulty's* has a wide range of teas and coffees too. The gourmet shops at *Bloomingdale's* and *Macy's* are also prime choices for fine and unusual spices, and their housewares departments are great places to find all kinds of cooking equipment. In cold meats, the store to measure all others by is *Schaller and Weber,* at 1654 Second Ave., near 86th St. Nearby, at 218 E. 86th St., is *Bremen House,* specializing in German foods. *Myers of Keswick* at 634 Hudson St. in the West Village is the model of an English high street grocer with imported British jams, scone mixes, Ribena, ginger beer, and piping hot fresh steak and kidney pies to take away. A good place for kitchenware is the *Cellar* in Macy's basement; alternatives are the chain of stores called the *Pottery Barn,* at several locations, which is noted for its good prices on a range of cooking equipment, and *Conran's,* at 54th St. and Third Ave., at a new giant store on Broadway at 81st St., and on Astor Place in the Village. This last is an interesting place—downstairs is a range of modern furniture, while on the second floor are fabrics, rugs, and such, and pots, pans, earthenware in unusual shapes, utensils, spices, serving ware, and all kinds of other things unexpected in this sleek, modern setting. New York's first *Williams-Sonoma* shop at 20 E. 60th St. has expensive (and attractive) cookware for the serious semi-pro.

Godiva, main shop at 701 Fifth Ave. near 55th St., makes well-known, beautifully packaged (and expensive) chocolate. *Teuscher Chocolates of Switzerland* has a branch in the Channel at Rockefeller Center and one at 25 E. 61st St., off Madison Ave. Both feature the famous chocolate truffles (flown in each week) and some of the prettiest packaging in town. *Huwyler's* at 510 Madison is another source of Swiss delights, while *Manon,* at 872 Madison Ave., has Belgian handmade delights. *Fifth Avenue Chocolatiere* at 575 Fifth Ave. near 47th St. has yummy hand-dipped fresh fruits and a variety of unusual molds and edible gift items. On Lexington Ave. and 54th St., you'll find New York's only *Perugina* shop. Along with those famous Baci, this Italian confectioner has beautiful ceramics filled with brightly wrapped chocolates and gelato made with imported flavorings. The best of the several chains of stores selling cookies is generally considered to be *David's Cookies,* at several locations, including Zabar's and Macy's, or *Mrs. Field's* at Bloomingdale's and citywide branches.

Tobacco

Village Cigars, at 110 Seventh Avenue South, is a crowded little shop that has been around a long time at this busy Greenwich Village corner (Sheridan Square). *Nat Sherman,* at 711 Fifth Ave. near 55th St., is celebrated as "tobacconist to the world," and offers every conceivable type of tobacco. *J. R. Tobacco,* at 108 West 45th St., calls itself "the world's largest cigar store"—nobody has been heard to argue, and in addition to the merits of the selection, the prices are reasonable too. And one of the most respected names in the tobacco world, *Alfred Dunhill of London,* has a store at 620 Fifth Ave. in Rockefeller Center, and branches in both Macy's and Bloomingdale's.

For pipes, two places are recommended—*Barclay Rex,* at 7 Maiden Lane, downtown, and midtown, *Connoisseur,* at 51 W. 46th St. Both have large assortments of pipes and pipe tobaccos.

Art and Galleries

There is really no easy way to compile a useful guide to New York's art galleries. You will have to do what New Yorkers do: once you've checked these listings in the *New York Times* (especially the Friday, Saturday, and Sunday editions), *New York* magazine, or the *New Yorker* and marked the ones that seem most interesting at the moment, you start walking, either down Madison Avenue from 86th St. or across 57th St. and up Madison to 86th, stopping as you go.

But in recent years New York has developed another art center downtown, for balance. This is SoHo, an area of beautiful cast-iron architecture that was once a manufacturing and warehousing district. As industry moved out over the last decade, leaving behind large "loft" spaces with

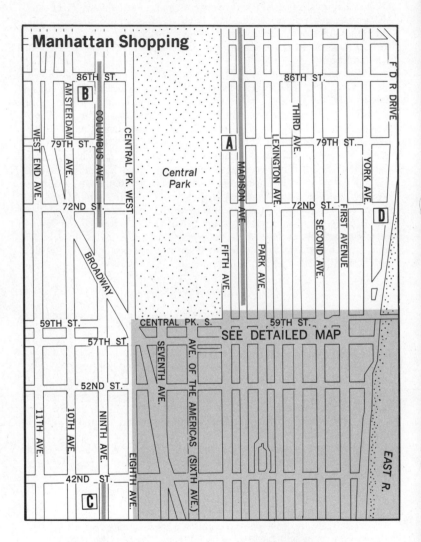

A   Art galleries, swank boutiques, fine antiques, antiquities.
B   Boutiques, ordinary antiques.
C   Foreign food specialties.
D   Sotheby Parke Bernet Decorative Arts Gallery.
E   Second-hand books, antiques, auction galleries.
F   Discount stores (clothes, accessories).
G   Antiques, boutiques.

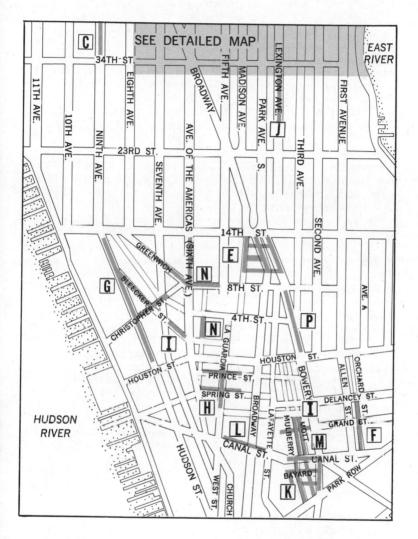

H Art galleries (contemporary), posters, boutiques.
I Italian specialties.
J Indian specialties.
K Chinese specialties.

L Tools and machinery.
M Jewelry.
N Clothing (trendy, funky, or casual).
P Restaurant equipment.

huge windows for plenty of light, artists began to move in; and it wasn't long before galleries followed them.

SoHo is now fashionable, handsome, and diverse, but the galleries are still there in quantity. In just one building, 420 West Broadway, you'll find five, including *Mary Boone, Leo Castelli,* and *Sonnabend.* Castelli alone has been associated with such modern figures as Jasper Johns, Robert Rauschenberg, Roy Lichtenstein, Andy Warhol, and Cy Twombly. Other galleries within these crowded few blocks include *O.K. Harris,* at 383 West Broadway, and *Vorpal,* at 465 West Broadway (Vorpal is known for its representation of prints by M. C. Escher, that proponent of visual paradox); but there is too much here, in the way of painting, sculpture, and other forms harder to find names for (but most of it super-modern), to list, and the best thing to do is simply explore this quite small, concentrated area.

Another, much more adventurous gallery scene exists east of Second Ave. around E. 10th and 11th Sts. in the East Village, where "dealer" doesn't always refer to art. These storefront galleries change frequently, so explore—during daytime.

Uptown, of course, the scene remains as strong as ever, and here too we can only name a few of the best known galleries. For contemporary art, for example, *Tibor De Nagy,* at 41 W. 57th St., *Marlborough,* at 40 W. 57th St., *Sidney Janis,* at 110 W. 57th St., and *Holly Solomon,* at 724 Fifth Ave., all have worthy reputations; they specialize in painting, but usually handle sculpture too. For older art (interspersed with recent work), try *Knoedler,* at 21 E. 70th St., or *Wildenstein,* at 19 E. 64th St., among many others. If you're interested in a somewhat newer art form, try the *International Center of Photography,* at 1130 Fifth Avenue, or *Photograph,* 724 Fifth Ave., between 56th and 57th Sts.

For those less interested in investing, but looking for something nice for their walls, the major museums, such as the Guggenheim, the Museum of Modern Art, the Metropolitan, and so on, all have fine in-house shops offering reproductions of works in their galleries. For the Metropolitan, particularly, this is big business, and the stock runs not just to posters, but also to pottery, jewelry, and so forth. *Poster Originals* is a well-stocked poster shop that, cannily, has two branches: one on the Upper East Side, at 924 Madison Ave. near 73rd St., and one in SoHo, at 386 West Broadway. Not all the stuff here is cheap, but all is handsome.

Off the beaten track, the *Aaron Faber Galleries* at 666 Fifth Ave. (53rd St.) has an impressive collection of artists' hand-crafted contemporary jewelry.

Contemporary prints (and some old prints) are the only offering at *Associated American Artists, Inc.,* 663 Fifth Ave. near 52nd St. For older prints, etchings, and illustrated books you might try, among many others, *Lucien Goldschmidt,* 1117 Madison Ave. at 83rd St., for the old-fashioned appeal of the shop if for nothing else. *Argosy Bookstore,* 116 E. 59th, near Bloomingdale's, has old prints as well as interesting old books.

Antiques

New York sports a huge variety of antique shops, and a lot of people spend a lot of time poring over a lot of objects, seeking finds. A word of warning: Prices in the city are usually higher than those offered in places farther outside the city; there are antiquers who make a point of not buying here, hoping to find better values elsewhere. But for both the serious collector and the amateur, there's simply so much in New York that browsing is worthwhile, and there's always the chance of a bargain.

The first place to start is at the auction houses. These are exciting, particularly if you've never been to one, and there's a rapid turnover of stock. Auction houses have sales on most days of the week, except Sunday. Check *The New York Times* for listings. As a general rule, Monday and Tuesday are exhibition days for midweek sales and Thursday for Saturday sales. No item, no matter how small, should ever be bought on the block without an examination at the exhibition. You may think you are getting a bargain on the silver vase from 40 feet away, but if on closer scrutiny you find an inscription from some sporting society on the other side, you have only yourself to blame, for there is ample time to examine each lot carefully. If you are bidding for the first time, don't hesitate to ask a staffer for advice.

Sotheby's is probably the most well known of the auction houses, at 1334 York Ave. (72nd St.). *Christie's*, at 502 Park Ave. (59th St.), is claimed by many to be as good. It has a branch for Americana and other specialties at 219 E. 67th St., and is planning to open a "contemporary art" showroom. Smaller houses are *Phillips*, at two Upper East Side locations, and *William Doyle*, at 175 E. 87th St., among others. Goods on display at these establishments fall into varied categories, which at any one time may include fine art, jewelry, all sorts of furniture, porcelain, antique toys, and much more. At some of these houses the *buyer* must pay a commission; terms change, so we leave you to check for yourself. The top houses are closed for viewing Mondays, and some are closed Sundays also.

Having tackled the auctions, explore a few specific areas. Most of the best (and most expensive) shops are along 57th St. east of Fifth Ave., and on Madison Avenue in the 50s, 60s, and 70s. Smaller and less fancy shops are scattered all over, but the general concentration is on Third Avenue between 45th and 70th Sts. and the surrounding streets; Second and First Aves. within the same boundaries can also prove rewarding. Another antiques area is the area bounded by Broadway and University Place and 8th and 14th Sts. in the northern part of the Village. For example, *Ace Galleries* on University Place near 11th St. is an active auction house—a step down from Sotheby's, to be sure, but fun and less costly. Go—and you'll be sure to buy *something*. Other such auction houses—and there are many more—are *Tepper* at 110 E. 25th St., *Lubin*, 30 W. 26th St., and *Manhattan Galleries*, 1415 Third Ave at 80th St.

The Consumer Yellow Pages has a lengthy list of antique shops broken down into specific categories, and this is worth consulting before you start exploring an area which is quite widely dispersed. Not to be missed is the new multistory *Place des Antiquaires* on E. 57th St. between Lexington and Park aves. This stunning building houses some of Europe's finest purveyors of antique jewelry, paintings, and other collectibles. Don't leave without seeing the French windup automatons on the lower level.

There are, in fact, antique shops all over the city. Greenwich Village has a large concentration of stores—try walking down Bleecker Street between Christopher Street and Hudson, or look at oak furniture on Hudson Street between Bleecker and Christopher (those street names are accurate; they all criss-cross the area!). Second Ave. also has a lot of oak furniture, for several blocks south of 26th St. A store that seems to have a wide range of period furniture—English, Oriental, French—is *Gramercy Galleries,* at 52 E. 13th St. Provincial French furniture is well served in the city by *Pierre Deux,* at 369 Bleecker, *Le Vieux Monde,* nearby at 94 Charles St., and *Howard Kaplan,* at 400 Bleecker St. *Pat Sales* at 390 Bleecker offers American country antiques. And *Inglenook,* at 529 Hudson Street, offers antique American furniture, with a particular emphasis on wicker.

James Robinson, at 15 E. 57th St., has a worldwide name for antique silver; another source is *Wyler,* at 713 Madison near 63rd St. Try *Carol Ferranti,* at 888 Madison near 72nd St., for glassware and pottery, or *Leo Kaplan,* nearby at 910 Madison. *Second Childhood,* at 283 Bleecker St., is much loved for its collection of antique toys, which may include multi-shaped coin banks, dolls, hoops, books for children, and toy trains at any one time. Look for toy soldiers there, too. *The Antique Doll Hospital of New York*'s name is a bit misleading: they also buy, sell and appraise dolls, at 787 Lexington Ave. near 61st St. On the more serious side of the scale, *André Emmerich,* at 41 E. 57th Street, offers very high-quality pre-Columbian objects and such (there are also exhibits of modern paintings here) while the *Asian Gallery,* at 1049 Madison near 80th St., offers Far Eastern art and antiquities. *Atikoth* (16 E. 71st St.) and *Moriah* (699 Madison Ave. between 62nd and 63rd Sts.) trade in antique Judaica. *Tuscany Galleries* at 1001 Second Ave. at 53rd St. specializes in antique clocks from here and Europe. They also have a wide variety of other objects, including glassware. The oldest autograph business in New York, at 25 E. 77th St., is *Charles Hamilton*; surprisingly, department store *B. Altman* also has a reputable autograph section. *Mitsukoshi,* on the northeast corner of Park and 57th, has fine Japanese pottery and other arts. *Fanelli Antique Timepieces,* 1131 Madison Ave. between 84th and 85th Sts., has a large selection of clocks and vintage wristwatches.

Griffin & Howe have both new and used hunting arms as well as antique firearms, 589 Broadway near Houston. *Centre Firearms,* 51 W. 46th St., is another such place. Specializing in antique firearms is *Robert Brooks,* 235 E. 53rd St. *The Soldier Shop,* 1013 Madison Ave., has antique firearms as well as books on the military and antique miniature soldiers. *Hunting World,* 16 E. 53rd, has every imaginable accessory for the hunter—as well as prints, etc.

There are many places for antique clothing—some of it tatty, some very fine. *Reminiscence,* at 74 Fifth Ave. near 14th St., and *Trash & Vaudeville,* at 4 Saint Marks Place, both sell old clothes (and new, too) in as-new condition, to fit with younger fashions. *Unique Clothing Warehouse,* 718 Broadway, is another source. Leaving the Village for the more sedate Upper East Side, pay a visit to *The Best of Everything,* at 307 E. 77th St., for clothing, jewelry, and accessories from the 20s through the 50s. On the Upper West Side, there are several possibilities on Columbus Avenue in the 70s and low 80s—a good place to browse, since there are also a number of pleasant antique furniture and memorabilia shops here (along with an increasing number of interesting places to stop for lunch).

Jacques Carcanagues, at 119 Spring Street in SoHo, offers beautiful Middle Eastern kilim rugs, and *Alexander,* at 130 W. 72nd Street, is good for Orientals.

The *Macklowe Gallery,* on Madison near 76th St., is one of several reputable jewelers where you can find both antique and contemporary stuff on and around Madison Ave., from the 40s through the 70s. Alternatively, you could visit the precious-stone and jewelry district along 47th St. between Fifth and Sixth Aves., where much antique gold, rings, and such are sold (although quality can vary widely).

You'll have to go through the Yellow Pages to find the shops that specialize in first-day covers, etc., but there are many good general stamp dealers, such as the long-established *J. & H. Stolow* at 989 6th Ave. (near 36th St.) and *Regal Stamp Co.* at 379 Fifth Ave. *Harmer,* 14 E. 33rd St., conducts auction sales. And there are dozens of dealers grouped together downtown on Nassau St. *Stack's,* 123 W. 57th St., and *Harmer Rooke,* 3 E. 57th St., are well-known dealers in coins (numismatics). *Macy's* at Herald Square (34th St.) has a good numismatic department; don't forget the auctioneers *Sotheby Park Bernet,* either, at York and 72nd on the Upper East Side.

One more recommendation before leaving the subject of antiques—the *Old Print Shop,* at 150 Lexington Avenue, near 30th St., for a fine display of collectible prints, maps, and other visual Americana. And a word of warning—some art and antique galleries limit their hours or close altogether during the summer months, so if you're visiting at that time it's wise to check ahead. And good hunting.

Books

New York is the capital of American publishing, and is blessed with an apposite number of bookstores. The chains—Dalton's, Waldenbooks—are represented here, but there are also countless more specialized establishments, some of them quite large; and even in the marketing of bestsellers, the chains have good competition.

An early stop for any book buyer should be *Barnes & Noble,* on both sides of Fifth Avenue at 18th St. The main branch, on the east side of the avenue, is known for its vast array of scientific and technical material, college textbooks, and general reference stuff, though you'll also find more entertaining matter here. Across the road, the Sale Annex has a huge selection of low-price remaindered stock in many categories; here, too, the current bestseller list is sold well below list prices. (Barnes & Noble branches throughout the city also offer this feature.) If the college books you wanted aren't at Barnes & Noble, try browsing through the several bookstores on Broadway in the area of 116th Street, near Columbia University.

Another good browsing place is Fifth Avenue from 47th St. to 57th St. Here you'll find not only branches of *Barnes & Noble* (discount) and *B. Dalton,* but also *Doubleday* (two branches), the *Antiquarian Booksellers' Center, Scribner's* (the most elegant shop), and more. Turn west on 47th St. and you'll come to the *Gotham Book Mart,* a store with a long and prestigious history, the home away-from-home to eerie illustrator Edward Gorey, and still a favorite of New Yorkers in search of poetry, modern thought, and literature, and the unexpected. *Coliseum Books,* Broadway and 57th St. for paperbacks. *Books & Co.,* 939 Madison Ave. and the *Madison Avenue Bookshop* at No. 833 near 70th St. have good selections of new and in-print titles. The *McGraw-Hill Bookstore,* in the McGraw-Hill Building plaza at Sixth Ave. and 49th St., has a wide selection of technical and business books. Medical books may be found at the stores associated with the city's large medical schools (Cornell, Mt. Sinai, New York University), and also at *General Medical Book Co.,* 310 E. 26th St.

A real clue to the importance of books in the life of the city is the number of bookstores devoted to seemingly limiting specialties; these are some of New York's great pleasures. For example, the *Drama Book Shop,* 723 Seventh Ave. at 48th St., 2nd floor and the *Theatre Arts Bookshop* at 405 W. 42nd St. for theater books; the *Ballet Shop,* near Lincoln Center at Broadway and 64th St., for coverage of dance—plus memorabilia. *Murder Ink,* at 271 West 87th St., and *The Mysterious Bookshop* at 129 W. 56th St., specialize in mysteries, as do the two branches of *Foul Play* (10 Eighth Ave. and 1465B Second Ave). *Eeyore's,* at 2212 Broadway and 25 E. 83rd St., is a children's bookstore, as is *Books of Wonder* at 132 Seventh Ave. at 18th St. *Womanbooks,* 201 W. 92nd St., sells books by, about or for . . . women. For the military buff, the *Military Bookman* is at 29 E. 93rd St. The moviegoer might go to *Cinemabilia,* at 611 Broadway. For books on music, try *Schirmer's* or *Patelson's* (see *Music*). Cooks and gourmets will do best at main branches of larger chains (Doubleday, Barnes & Noble, etc.), or at *Kitchen Arts and Letters* at 1435 Lexington Ave. near 94th St. *The Biography Book Shop,* 400 Bleecker St., specializes in biographies, letters, and travel memoirs.

There are a number of art bookshops, the best known of which are probably *Hacker,* at 54 W. 57th St., *Jaap Rietman,* 134 Spring St. in SoHo, *E. Weyhe* on Lexington Ave. near 62nd St., and *Wittenborn* at 1018 Madison Ave. (near 78th St.), 2nd floor. The museum stores are also worth trying for this specialty—especially the store at the Metropolitan Museum of of Art. The *Librairie de France* and the *Libreria Hispanica,* in Rockefeller Center at Fifth Ave. (and also downtown on Fifth, near the 18th St. Barnes & Noble) are probably the best sources for French and Spanish books. Books on the Orient are a specialty at *Paragon,* 14 E. 38th St. *Zen Bookshop* also has (popular) orientalia; Fifth Ave. between 43rd and 44th Sts.

For maps, globes, books on maps, nautical and navigation books, and charts: *Hammond,* 57 W. 43rd St., and *Rand McNally,* 10 E. 53rd St. *Argosy,* at 116 E. 59th St., has antique maps (as well as a general selection of used books and sets). *Weitz,* Lexington Ave. near 91st St., also carries sets and fine bindings. New York has a very fine selection of occult bookstores, among them *Mason's* at 789 Lexington Ave. (61st St.) and *Weiser's,* at 132 E. 24th St. The *New York Astrology Center,* 63 West 38th St., has books. See the Consumer Yellow Pages under "Book Dealers—New" for a complete guide to specialty bookstores by category.

Finally, older books. The *Antiquarian Booksellers' Center,* on Rockefeller Plaza, is a good place for the serious collector of rare books and first editions. See the Consumer Yellow Pages under "Book Dealers—Used & Rare" for a listing of other dealers and their specialties. The hub of the used-book market is along Fourth Ave. between 9th and 14th Sts.— though it is shrinking. The best of them all, and not shrinking, is *Strand,* at Broadway and 12th St.; books here include, besides some rare books and the over one million used books, mint-condition reviewers' copies (at half price) and remainders, including art books at much-reduced prices.

Several shops carry large stocks of back-issue periodicals; two are *Jay-Bee Magazines,* 134 W. 26th St., and *A & S Book Co.,* 274 W. 43rd St. Some of the shops also carry celebrity photographs and old movie posters; check the Yellow Pages. *West Side Comics,* 107 W. 86th St., has new, back-issue and rare comic books, as does *Supersnipe* at 222 E. 85th St.

The Complete Traveler, Madison Ave. at the corner of 35th St., specializes in travel guides and books about travel, as does *Travellers Book Store,* 22 W. 52nd St.

Records

Immensely large selections from all major labels are the rule in New York City; one place where this is an understatement is *Sam Goody,* with various locations. *Tower Records* on Broadway and 4th St. in the West Village and at Broadway and 67th St. is vast, and offers nonstop music and people-watching from 9 A.M. until midnight every day of the year. The uptown store is connected to a vast video outlet. *Colony Records,* Broadway at 49th St., isn't cheap, but they have a fabulous selection of pop and show records. If your needs are current releases—cheaper in the U.S. than just about anywhere else in the Western world—try *Discomat* or *J&R Music* (at several locations), which sells its stock at well below list prices—it's better for popular music than for classical, and most of what you'll find here is fairly current. Also for discounted current LP's and out-of-print recordings. Walk along 8th St. between Sixth Ave. and Broadway; this is "L.P. Alley," and there's good browsing at any of the several stores along here, especially for domestic and imported classical recordings. *The Record Hunter,* at 507 Fifth Ave., near 43rd St., also concentrates on classical music and foreign labels.

If old Beatles singles and pop esoterica strike your fancy, chances are that the *House of Oldies,* at 267 Bleecker, or *Bleecker Bob's* on MacDougal at 8th St., will too. *Dayton's,* at Broadway and 12th St. (across the street from Strand Bookstore), has a stock of reviewers' copies of records in mint condition, at low prices, and also of out-of-print records, at collectors' prices. Most of the stock is popular; for hard-to-get classical stuff, try *Darton,* at 160 W. 56th St. Other secondhand disk shops are *Free Being,* 129 Second Ave., *Gryphon,* 606 Amsterdam Ave. near 90th St., *Footlight Records,* 90 Third Ave., *Golden Disk Records,* 239 Bleecker St., *House of Oldies,* 35 Carmine St., and the *Jazz Record Center* at 133 W. 72nd St.

Music and Musical Instruments

First, walk along the section of 48th St. east of Seventh Ave., for about half a block. In this somewhat raffish environment, you'll find enough musical instruments, spread out over several shops, to equip dozens of orchestras—although the stock tends more toward brass instruments, electronic keyboards, guitars (both electric and acoustic), and the other necessities for rock and jazz than toward violins and cellos. They are here, too, though—specifically, at *Sam Ash,* 160 W. 48th St., one of the most well known and longest-established of these shops. Sam Ash also has stores at 155 and 166 W. 48th St. Secondhand items are available on this street, but even the prices of the new pieces are often good, and Sam Ash and other leading stores such as *Manny's,* at 156 W. 48th St., advertise their discounts.

Drummers World at 133 West 45th St. exists to service the drum community. *Charles Ponte,* at 142 W. 46th St., specializes in wind instruments, and has an amazing assortment of reeds and tools for same, including the classical wind instruments.

In pianos (many people travel to Manhattan just to pick one out, and have it shipped home), the great name is, of course, *Steinway;* the company's imposing showroom is at 109 W. 57th St. The saleshelp is friendly even to browsers, though, since there's a two year wait for many of their models. *Baldwin* is at 922 Seventh Ave., and Yamaha is at *Ostrovsky,* 10 E. 38th St., 2nd floor; Ostrovsky also has used and reconditioned pianos of all makes and ages. *Abe Tolchin* at 732 Broadway near 8th St. is among the best for rebuilt Steinways. *Jack Kahn,* at 158 West 55th St., has a variety of brands of pianos, including the Bosendorfer, and runs frequent sales. Zuckermann harpsichords (kits) are handled by *Harpsichord Service Cooperative* at 465 W. Broadway.

Havivi, at 130 W. 57th St., has classical string instruments—and there are other violin and bow dealers in the same building. *Jacques Français* also deals in (rather up-market) violins, violas, cellos at the same address. For brass and woodwind instruments, *Giardinelli,* 151 West 46th St.— same building as the Professional Percussion Center—has a wide assortment, including lots of brass mouthpieces. Fine acoustic or "classical" guitars are sold at many specialist shops or workshops, among them *Juan Orozco,* Sixth Ave. and Spring St., *Noah Wulfe,* 115 W. 57th St. (also lutes), *Gurian,* 100 Grand St., and *Matt Umanov* (also steel-string) at 273 Bleecker St. An unusual assortment of foreign and folk music instruments is to be found at *Music Inn* on W. 4th St. near Sixth Ave. in the Village; they have records too. Yamaha has a new electronic instruments showroom at 146 W. 57th St. in Metropolitan Tower.

Having the instrument, you also need music to play on it. One of the most popular sheet-music shops is *Joseph Patelson's,* at 160 W. 56th St.— all their music and books on music are discounted 10 percent. Many serious musicians stop in here (it is right behind Carnegie Hall). *Frank Music Co.,* at 575 Eighth Ave. has a wide selection of classical scores and parts, but there is no browsing and you must know what you want. Then, of course, there is also *Schirmer,* at 40 W. 62nd St. near Lincoln Center, which stocks the sheet music of most of the classical-music publishers, and has books too. *Carl Fischer* has a retail outlet at Cooper Square, South of 8th St. For up-to-the-minute rock stuff, there are the sheet-music departments of the various branches of *Sam Goody;* Schirmer has pop and some rock, too, as does *Colony Records* at Broadway and 49th St.

Photographic Equipment

A tip on buying cameras—buy the Sunday *New York Times,* and turn to the back few pages of the "Arts and Leisure" section. A number of discount camera stores regularly advertise here, and it's a simple matter to find where you can get the camera you want most cheaply—prices are included in the advertisements. Make sure, however, that you're not comparing apples and oranges—that the camera advertised at a certain price also comes with the lens you want, and so forth.

There are many discount shops—so many, in fact, that it seems almost criminal to pay list price for a camera. Not all the stores are reputable, however, so shop carefully. One absolutely solid name is *Willoughby's,* at 110 W. 32nd St. This large, long-established shop has good—if not the best—prices, and a great deal of varied stock. Some equipment is also available on a rental basis. For many New Yorkers, Willoughby's is New

York's photographic best bet. Another popular store is *Alkit Camera* at 866 Third Ave. near 53rd St. Many professionals use this and their other store at 222 Park Ave. South. They aren't the cheapest, but often have closeouts on film and photo accessories. Besides, you don't have to worry here about "gray goods" that do not carry U.S. warranties.

Hirsch Photo, at 699 Third Avenue at 44th St., discounts heavily and does a lot of developing work. *Fotomat,* with branches all over the city, is also popular for developing. *7 Hour Photo,* again with several branches, guarantees speed, whether it's color or black-and-white film to be processed. While on the subject of optics, *Dell & Dell,* at 19 W. 44th St., is an authorized dealer for Zeiss, Bausch & Lomb, and other fine makes of binoculars. Several manufacturers have showrooms, such as *Nikon's* in the "Channel" at Rockefeller Center.

Art and Craft Supplies

This is another field where much of your needs can be supplied at a few places. Go first to *Pearl Paint,* at 308 Canal Street. This five-story shop offers everything for the artist—canvasses, brushes, paper, pens, frames, easels, tables, stretchers, mats, and much more, including, of course, lots and lots of paint. The prices are good, and it's an interesting place to wander through, seeing the different kinds of people in the New York art community. Less exciting, perhaps, but equally good in their ways are such stores as *Sam Flax,* with several branches, *Arthur Brown,* at 2 W. 46th St. (this store advertises itself as having "New York's largest stock of artist materials"), *Lee's Art Shop,* at 220 W. 57th St., and *Charrette,* at 215 Lexington Ave. and other branches (Charrette aims particularly toward the architect or professional draftsman).

Joseph Torch, at 36 W. 15th St., handles handmade papers. *David Davis,* at 539 La Guardia Place, is also recommended for its variety of pigments and quality papers. *Baldwin Pottery,* nearby at 540 La Guardia, should have all you need for ceramic work. *Fezandie & Sperrie,* 111 Eighth Ave., is a treasure house of pure powdered pigments. For those whose hobby is jewelry-making (or whose business this is, for that matter), a well-known name is *Allcraft Tool & Supply* —the main office is in Hicksville, Long Island, but the showroom is at 22 W. 48th St. Knitters will find yarns at any of several stores, including *Coulter Studios,* at 118 E. 59th St.; Coulter also stocks equipment for a number of fabric-related activities, such as weaving, needlepoint, and such. *Ladies Hobby Shop,* at 2350 Broadway near 85th St., is a small and friendly Upper West Side yarn store; *Design Point,* at 15 Christopher St., is a Greenwich Village equivalent specializing in needlepoint. *Alice Maynard,* 120 E. 75th St., *Erica Wilson,* 717 Madison Ave. near 64th St., and *Joan's Needlecraft Studio* at 145 E. 27th St. near Lexington Ave., all sell supplies for the knitter or needlepoint worker. And finally, for glass-workers, the best game in town in probably *Glassmasters Guild,* 621 Ave. of the Americas near 19th St. selling not only glass and the tools to work it, but also some rather nice finished pieces.

Sporting Goods

A small number of New York stores will satisfy a large chunk of your sporting needs. Go to *Paragon* first. This store, at Broadway and 18th St., advertises itself as supplying equipment for tennis, hockey, camping, archery, squash, diving, golf, darts, skiing, skating (roller and ice), Ping-Pong, and more besides; the place is noisy and crowded, but that's only because it's popular, and because as a rule, the values are good. *Spiegel's,* at 105 Nassau St., and *Herman's World of Sporting Goods,* nearby at 110 Nassau and at various other locations such as 34th St. between Fifth and Sixth Aves., come similarly well equipped.

Try these stores before going to the more specialized places. *The Athlete's Foot,* and *U.S. Athletics* with a number of branches around town, have a large variety of running and other sport shoes, as well as various sweatshirts and pants, shorts, and such. Fencers can resort to *Frederick Rohde's,* at 169 E. 86th St., or *George Santelli,* at 40 W. 27th St.; a nice shop for fishermen is *Spiegel's,* at 105 Nassau St. All sorts of accessories and artifacts for and of interest to hunters are to be found at *Hunting World,* 16 E. 53rd St. If Paragon doesn't have all the camping gear you need, *Hudson's,* at 105 Third Avenue (13th St.), probably will, and *Kreeger,* at 16 W. 46th St., is another good source for backpackers; similarly, golfers may need to look no farther than Paragaon, but if they do they could try *Al Lieber's World of Golf,* at 147 E. 47th St. or *Richard Metz,* 35 E. 50th St. There are two important stores for riding equipment, quite close to each other— *H. Kauffman & Sons,* at 139 E. 24th St., and *Miller's,* at 123 E. 24th St.; both offer English and Western wear, saddles, boots, and all the necessary apparel. The *Scandinavian Ski Shop,* at 40 W. 57th St., is long established, and keeps selling skis all summer. *Peck & Goodie,* 919 Eighth Ave. near 55th St., has a superior line of ice skates and roller skates—and sells nothing else. *Goldberg's Marine* is the best-known of the city's suppliers of nautical and marine equipment for yachtsmen: 12 W. 37th St. *New York Nautical,* at 140–142 West Broadway, near Thomas St. in TriBeCa, is crammed with instruments (they also service), books, charts for the entire world, models, more. Besides general sporting shops (such as Paragon) which have diving equipment (scuba), there are a few specialists, among them *Richards Aqua Lung Center,* at 233 W. 42nd St. and *Scubaplus,* 201 E. 34th St.

And Everything Else

Finally, there's the large category of things that don't fit into any of our previous categories. A good entry to this field is *Hammacher Schlemmer,* at 145 E. 57th St. It's hard to describe this shop beyond saying that it sells gadgets—everything from the obviously useful to the intriguingly peculiar, from the clever corkscrew to the motor-powered surfboard. If anyone ever invents a better mousetrap, you'll find it at Hammacher Schlemmer.

While you're in the neighborhood, you might think about crystal. *Baccarat* is at 55 E. 57th St., and *Carole Stupell Ltd.* is at E. 73rd St., near Madison Ave. *Steuben* too is nearby at Fifth Ave. and 56th St., near *Tiffany's,* (which, in addition to its famous jewelry, also stocks crystal and gorgeous chinaware, some at surprisingly modest prices). At the more humble end of the china and glass scale, but still quite handsome and popular among New Yorkers for their good values, are the dinner services and barware stocked by the *Pottery Barn* chain, in several locations around town. There are regular sales, and the branch at 23rd St. and Tenth Ave. almost always has closeouts of good merchandise. *Pattern Finders* of Port Jefferson, among others, carries discontinued chinaware patterns; call 516–928–5158 for mail orders only. Discontinued silver flatware patterns are available at many places in the city; try *S. Wyler,* 713 Madison Ave. at 63rd St., or *Panken & Thorn Antiques,* 207 E. 84th St. *Robin Importers* at 510 Madison Ave. near 53rd St. carries a wide range of imported china, flatware, and giftware at discounts. Brands include Meissen, Mikasa, and Limoges. They have many sets of children's chinaware and silverplate at up to 50% off retail. *E.A.T. Gifts* at 1062 Madison Ave. (near its food store) has expensive but charming trinkets for children of all ages, including a full range of irresistible Babar the Elephant furniture, dishes, and even towels.

New York has many shops selling unusual collectibles, such as beautiful and interesting mineralogical and fossil specimens (try *Astro Minerals,* 155 E. 34th St.; *Crystal Resources,* 130 E. 65th St.), and seashells (*Collector's Cabinet*—they also sell butterflies—153 E. 57th St.; *Seashells Unlimited,* 590 Third Ave.; *Captain Hook's* at 10 Fulton St. *Maxilla and Mandible* at 453 Columbus Ave. near 81st St. sells an unusual assortment of decorative skulls and other animal bones. They have shells and preserved butterflies, too.

In addition to a whole range of gift ideas in the way of jewelry, china, and such, *Fortunoff* also stocks silverware (as, of course, does *Tiffany's*). You could go somewhere expensive for your linen, towels, sheets, drapes, and such, but why, when you can go to the famous *Ezra Cohen,* at 307 Grand Street on the Lower East Side? Many New Yorkers shop nowhere else for these goods. *Liberty of London,* at 229 E. 60th St., is the New York outlet for the famous English fabrics, scarves, and accessories, and *Tender Buttons,* with a large collection of antique and modern buttons, buckles, and cufflinks, is a good source for the trimmings. The millinery district, 38th and 39th Sts. between Fifth Ave. and Ave. of the Americas, has lots of outlets for wonderful ribbonry, silk flowers, beads, veils, trimming, and, of course, hats. *Sheru* on W. 38th St. (No. 49) is a good source of beads and crafts materials from around the world. *Simon's Hardware,* Third Ave. between 29th and 30th Sts., has one of the largest selections of decorative hardware in the country—so look here for those handles or hinges you can't find anywhere. There are good hardware stores all along Canal St. west of Chinatown; good selections of tools also at *Lilien Hardware,* 490 W. Broadway near Houston. Find fine Japanese tools at *O-zora,* 238 East 6th St., or *Garrett Wade,* 161 Ave. of the Americas, at Spring St., SoHo.

Star Magic, in the East Village at Broadway and Astor Place and on the upper West Side at 73rd St. and Amsterdam, has everything remotely connected with astronomy and the heavens.

Try *Capezio,* at several locations, for dance equipment. *Freeds of London,* an English firm, also has a boutique for dance gear (including toe and character shoes) at 922 Seventh Ave. The best-known cutlery store is probably *Hoffritz,* with various branches, including one at 203 W. 57th St.; this establishment also sells barware, gadgets, and such. There are plenty of pet stores, but it seems a shame not to take a kitten or puppy off the hands of *Bide-A-Wee,* at 410 E. 38th St.; this is an animal shelter, not a business, and the prices are token, and tax-deductible. For classier dogs, try *Pedigree Pups,* at 989 First Avenue (they have cats, too). *Fabu-*

lous Felines sells rare and unusual breeds: 657 Second Ave. And if you're not too far from home, you might be able to take away some tropical fish for your tanks at home; see *Fish Town USA,* Third Ave. near 34th St., and *Aquarium Stock Co.,* 31 Warren St., downtown, near City Hall. *Exotic Aquatics,* 1475 Third Ave., and Broadway at 73rd St. also has snakes, lizards, and other animals not known to us! *Bird Jungle* at 401 Bleecker St. has 100 different species of feathered friends from the classic parakeet to the exotic Amazon parrot. The flower district of the city is a few blocks of Sixth Avenue in the upper 20s—visit *King* at 643 Hudson St. for unusual plants, or *Bonsai Dynasty* for those tiny trees in pots. For floral (and flora-inspired) gifts, ranging from seeds to soap, try The New York Botanical Garden shop at the IBM Building at 590 Madison Ave.

Susan Kasen's *The Green Thumb* at 22 E. 65th St. is where many celebrities order elaborate baskets and arrangements. *William Fuss* at 218 E. 53rd St. has marvelous floral fakes for allergic friends or those who hate cleaning up fallen leaves. There are hundreds of florists throughout the city, but for that last-minute bouquet, nothing can beat the prices and selection found at the nearest Korean grocery.

There are several chess emporia in Greenwich Village; one of them is simply called the *Chess Shop,* at 230 Thompson St. near Bleecker. For a clock, go to *Tourneau,* at 500 Madison Ave. near 52nd St. *Bikes and Things,* at 377 East 23rd St., is an extremely well-equipped bicycle shop. A good, safe bet for stereo equipment is *Rabson's Stereo Warehouse* at 119 West 57th St.; there are a number of reputable hi-fi and advanced electronics shops on 45th St. between Fifth and Sixth aves. *Uncle Steve's* at 343 Canal St. has very good buys in electronic and hi-fi gear. Billiards fanciers can go to *Blatts* at 809 Broadway at W. 10th St.

New York has a considerable number of places selling herbs, herbal teas, and herbal preparations: *Aphrodisia,* 282 Bleecker St. in the Village (they also have books, as does *Samuel Weiser* at 740 Broadway); *Caswell-Massey* at 575 Lexington Ave.; *Good Earth* at Second Ave. and 72nd St.; *Kiehl Pharmacy,* 109 Third Ave.; *McNulty's, Paprikas Weiss,* and *St. Rémy* at 818 Lexington Ave., which also features French fabrics and crafts, (see *Gourmet Foods* for addresses). The *Kaufman Beverly Pharmacy* at Lexington Ave. and 50th St. is open 24 hours a day, seven days a week for sundries and prescriptions. *Cohen's Fashion Optical* stores around the city are reliable bets for replacing broken glasses and fitting contact lenses.

Inexpensive souvenirs of New York (T-shirts, mugs, buttons, calendars, etc.) can be found at a variety of small shops throughout the midtown area. *Hallmark* card shops are also a good source for similar items, as are *Azuma* stores. Many of the T-shirt stores will print personal slogans while you wait. A truly unique store is *Lost City Arts* at 339 Bleecker St., where you can find actual decorative pieces from old buildings for sale, along with smaller reminders of places gone by.

Finally, books, prints, drawings, photographs, and more on the ever-fascinating subject of New York City are to be found at *New York Bound Books and Urban Graphics,* 43 W. 54th St.

There's obviously an enormous amount that we haven't been able to touch, and that every visitor will discover for him or herself. But you'll find that no matter how well you know New York, there's always more to see. That makes tbe city tantalizing, but also somehow reassuring.

RESTAURANTS. As restaurant capital of the world, New York is a gourmet's heaven and a dieter's invitation to delicious disaster. Counting the city's renowned delis, hot dog stands, and pizza parlors, there are some 25,000 eating places in the Big Apple's five boroughs—serving every cuisine known in the world—and even the most insatiable restaurant critics admit to covering only a few hundred of them with any regularity. Furthermore, the restaurant scene is constantly in a state of flux. Scores of new places open every month; others fall victim to rising rents or site demolition and either relocate or close. Chefs (the highest-paid employees in the profession, who often name their own price) are lured away by other restaurants or encouraged to hang out their own shingles . . . at the drop of a *toque blanche.*

The wonder is that so many restaurants survive the competition and, indeed, are jammed with hungry customers every night. It helps to realize that the American people's interest in the culinary arts has never been more intense. It is also a fact that New York is increasingly a singles town, and even when they marry, both members of the couple work. Young professionals who slave over a hot computer all day don't want to fight a kitchen at night . . . so they eat out. Add to that crowd the city's 18 million annual visitors, who spend one-third of their Big Apple budget on food and drink, and you begin to realize that the end of the Fabulous Feast is nowhere in sight.

You can cover the globe gastronomically in New York, spending as much or as little as you like. You can feast on steaks at the *Palm* or *Christ Cella,* paying dearly for every succulent bite, or you can opt for a reasonable facsimile at *The Derby* in Greenwich Village or at trendy bistros like *Quatorze* or *Odeon* for far less money. You can be transported to the far reaches of India at the delicately appointed *Darbar* or *Shezan,* or you can head over to East 6th St. between First and Second Aves., where about a dozen friendly, inexpensive family-run eateries offer outstanding curries and tandoori specialties.

Most of the best restaurants in New York City center in Manhattan, and most of these are south of 86th St., so the bulk of our attention is focused on that area, although we have picked a few notables in the outlying boroughs for your additional consideration. Public transportation makes any corner of Manhattan Island, and most of the other boroughs, accessible, and the trip is frequently worthwhile. Enthusiasts of Middle Eastern cooking, for example, will do well to take a ride to Brooklyn's Atlantic Avenue section where there is a host of very good, modestly priced Lebanese restaurants (most owned by the Almontaser family, with the best of the lot, bearing the family name, at 218 Court St.; 718–624–9267). Similarly, many long-time natives swear that the *real* Little Italy of New York, with the best food at the cheapest prices, is on and around Arthur Avenue in the Bronx—at *Mario's, Amici's, Dominick's,* and *Pasquale's Rigoletto*—not on Manhattan's Mulberry Street. The partisans battle on forever.

Time was, in fact, when you *had* to go way downtown to Chinatown or Manhattan's Little Italy for a good Chinese or Italian meal. Not any more. There are those who tell you the East Side svelte belt (starting around the Grand Central Station area off Second Ave. and heading uptown) has the city's best Chinese cooking, or that the best is found on the upper West Side, near Lincoln Center. True, they are expensive, which is why Chinatown still has its supporters. (By Chinatown they mean the six to eight cluttered blocks bordered by Canal St. on the north and the Bowery on the east with the boundaries spilling over into Manhattan's Little Italy itself.)

You name the style of Chinese cooking you want and New York has it, be it Cantonese, Shanghai, Peking, Hunan, Szechuan, Fukien, Taiwanese, or Mongolian. The same holds true for Italian cooking, whether you're looking for the staples of southern Italian Neapolitan cooking or the delicate flavorings of Florentine or Roman chefs. And again you have a choice of the more expensive restaurants (with *Palio, Patsy's,* or *Parioli Romanissimo* considered among the best of this breed), the tourist spots (such as *Mamma Leone's*), or the moderately priced best of Little Italy (the *Grotta Azzura* taking top honors on that count for a savory balance between the quality of cuisine and price).

Indeed, the city is filled with ethnic pockets, and its restaurants spill over with the flavor of the Old World, Asia, the Orient. The far east 70s and 80s of Manhattan are known as the Yorkville area, and offer Slavic and German eateries galore. Greek and Thai restaurants have found a home north of the skin-flick houses on Eighth Ave. from 48th to 56th Sts. West 46th St., east of the theater district, has taken on a decidedly Brazilian flavor, and mid-Manhattan looks like Tokyo East, with the smell of fish and tempura coming out of just about every other doorway. Astoria, Queens, is Greek restaurant heaven.

By now you get the point that we have eschewed the normal geographic divisions of Manhattan in favor of trying to whet your appetite with some suggestions that you might otherwise miss—especially if you were concentrating only on those restaurants in the immediate vicinity of your hotel—for that is the best way to get a real taste of the Big Apple.

The range in price is as great as the variety of New York restaurant offerings—accounted for in matters of service, presentation, location, and decor as well as in who the chef is and what his or her capabilities are. This is so be the cuisine Chinese, Continental (that ill-defined hybrid of European and American influences), French, Indian, Italian, or otherwise. While a fine meal at an elegant restaurant can (and often does) extract a sultan's ransom from wealthy gourmands, it is also possible to have a nearly duplicate meal, served in more humble surroundings (and without a platoon of liveried attendants), at literally half the tariff.

In addition, there are a number of ways to dine at even the most expensive establishments without necessarily going bankrupt in the process. Many of the city's finest restaurants—and *The Four Seasons* heads the list!—offer special pre-theater dinners at prices that are a third to half less than the same meal ordered during prime serving periods. The menu selections are generally a little more limited, and you must usually be seated between 5 and 6 P.M., but service, preparation, and surroundings are at the same high standards for which these restaurants are noted.

Then, too, lunches are often 10 to 20 percent cheaper than the same dinners would be, so having a big midday meal at *Lutèce,* for instance, at a prix fixe for approximately $32 affords the opportunity to dine at what is generally considered the finest classical French restaurant in the city at a fraction of what a similar three-course meal would cost à la carte in the evening. Another suggestion: nowhere is it written that you must order courses as suggested on the menu at luncheon or dinner. If you are two or three people, for example, there is no reason why you can't order a selection of appetizers (which in at least some cases are scaled down portions of entrées), a salad, and a dessert—all to be shared. You get to sample several different items and the check—even if there is a "plate charge"—is within reason.

Remember that New York eats late; the better restaurants (except those near theaters or concert halls) don't get busy until 8 P.M., if then. If you insist on eating dinner as the second hand sweeps past six, you may be the only person in the place. Don't worry about going for dinner at 11 P.M.; lots of places will still serve. We've listed some that stay open much later.

In preparing the following lists of suggested restaurants, we've sought to provide a wide enough range of choices to fit every traveler's tastes and budget. And our listings do represent a *selection,* not a complete survey by any means, of places that will—we hope—enhance your visit to New York.

We regret, as you do, the prices that any meal costs everywhere these days, and the toll in New York is probably higher than anywhere else in the nation. But the following categories are the facts of life in today's dining out world, and we can only suggest that you mitigate each foray to some expensive temple of gastronomy with a visit to one of the city's more modest sub-temples. As a rule of thumb, the higher the price, the more necessary reservations become. Dress codes vary, so check when making a reservation.

The price categories we use are approximate; figure for an average three-course meal (appetizer, main course with vegetable, dessert) at a given establishment, per person. This does not take into account the suggestions offered above for lessening the blow to the pocketbook, **nor does it include wine or drinks, taxes or gratuities.** As of this writing, meals are taxed at 8¼ percent of the total bill; for average service, most New Yorkers simply double the tax as a tip. For outstanding service you may wish to tip 20%, with another 5% for the maître d' if he or she has been especially helpful.

Super Deluxe restaurants will cost $75 and up per person. **Deluxe** establishments will generally fit into the $50 range. **Expensive** dinners will usually cost about $35. **Moderate** meals should run about $20. A tab at an **Inexpensive** restaurant will cost an average of $15. Do not be misled, however, by traditional notions of super deluxe or deluxe. We have grouped the restaurants primarily by price category, and some very expensive places—particularly the *nouvelle cuisine* restaurants, and many establishments on otherwise abandoned SoHo streets—will hardly have the type of elegance one usually associates with such prices.

Today, credit cards, "plastic money," are a very acceptable commodity. Most—although not all—restaurants accept credit cards. These are indicated by the following abbreviations which appear at the end of the upcoming restaurant listings:

AE - American Express
CB - Carte Blanche
DC - Diners Club
MC - MasterCard
V - Visa

Where a listing says, for example, "No CB," that means that the restaurant in question accepts all credit cards except Carte Blanche. Because of the cost involved in processing credit card charges, a few establishments offer a cash discount of 5% to 10% for cash-paying customers; others may request that you tip in cash.

During the summer, many restaurants are closed for vacation for as much as a month; call ahead to check.

We have arranged the restaurants according to general stylistic categories first (American-International, Steakhouses, Seafood, etc.) and then by national or ethnic cuisine rather than geographically, although we have endeavored to make specific references if a particular place is especially convenient to, say, the theater district or Lincoln Center. And we have broken down the sections within each cuisine by price category with entries in alphabetical order. This should simplify your comparisons as well as facilitate looking up information about a restaurant whose name you may know. But before we go to the formal listings, here are a few notes on additional places that don't fit the regular categories.

Fast food. Croissanteries—serving a somewhat flat imitation of the buttery, multilayered French rolls, plain or with any number of fillings—have cropped up all over the city. In addition, such internationally renowned operations as *McDonald's, Brew Burger, Burger King, Tony Roma's, Arby's,* and *Roy Rogers* are alive and thriving all around New York City. *Kentucky Fried Chicken* and *Bojangles'* are similarly well entrenched, with listings in the White or Yellow Pages of the telephone directory the best way to find the locations nearest you. The best hot dog: *Nathan's,* Broadway at 43rd St.

Pizza seems to be a major staple of New York eating habits. *John's Pizzeria,* 278 Bleecker St. near Seventh Ave. in Greenwich Village, has what many insist is the best pizza in New York. They sell whole pies only, and there is almost always a wait for a table—they take no reservations. Wine and beer, however, are available. *Amalfi Pizza,* nearby at Bleecker on Seventh Ave. So., and *Famous Ray's,* 465 6th Ave. (both enormously popular), do sell slices. Every New Yorker has a different "best," it seems; try Sicilian style for a change.

Middle Eastern. Another very inexpensive and hearty fast-food alternative is the falafel stand—offering ground chick-peas deep fried and stuffed in a pita bread with shredded vegetables.

Chains. Other local chain-style operations with uniform outlets around the city include *Chock Full O' Nuts* (mostly in midtown office districts), *Bun & Burger, Houlihan's, Beefsteak Charlie's, McAnn's,* and *J.J. Mulligan's.* Some offer free all-you-can-eat salads with the modest price of a meal and represent a good value for the money when you need a quick bite.

Cafeterias. *Horn & Hardart* has one remaining coin-in-the-slot "automated" cafeteria at 200 E. 42nd St.

24-hour stops. People in New York do seem to be hungry at all hours of the day and night, and the selection among available offerings is only slightly less limited than normal if the time happens to be 4:30 A.M. or so. There are two reliable places on Second Ave. between 4th and 6th Sts.: *Kiev* (117 Second Ave.; 674–4040), an outstanding coffee shop great for hearty soups, blintzes, and fruit-filled pancakes that are almost like fritters; *103 Second Restaurant* (103 Second Ave.; 533–0769), which feels as though it were transplanted from SoHo, serving spicy, chunky chili, Continental meals and sandwiches, and breakfast at all hours. The *Empire Diner* (210 Tenth Ave., at W. 22nd St.; 243–2736) is a glorified candlelit boxcar with eggs and pasta and salads, at any time—and with the crowd worth the trip particularly in the wee hours. In the theater district the *Century Cafe* (132 W. 43rd St.; 398–1988) serves dinner until 1:30 A.M., with the bar open until 4 A.M. The *Green Kitchen* (1477 First Ave.; 988–4163) and *Silver Star* (1236 Second Ave.; 249–4250) both serve a little of everything—they're more than a few steps above a coffee shop in quality and very reliable. *Mamun's* (119 MacDougal St.; 674–9246) serves up falafel (mashed chick peas deep fried) and other mid-Eastern sandwiches from 10:30 A.M. to 5 A.M., while *Sarge's Delicatessen and Restaurant* (548 Third Ave.; 679–0442) has sandwiches right in midtown. *The Brasserie* (100 E. 53rd St.; 751–4840), a large but pleasant more-or-less French, well, brasserie, is open 24 hours a day, seven days a week. Among the places included in the listings below, the *Carnegie Deli* is open 6:30 A.M. to 4 A.M., while *Sardi's*, the *Oak Room* at the Algonquin, and others in the immediate vicinity of Broadway at least serve post-theater suppers. So, too, does *Four Seasons* with dessert and/or cheese in the bar area. Chinatown's *Hong Fat* is always open, and both *Palsson's* (158 W. 72nd St.; 362–2590) and the *Riviera Cafe* (225 W. Fourth St.; 242–8732) serve until 3 A.M. Throughout the city there are "Greek" coffee shops, known as such because so many appear to be owned by Greeks, not necessarily because they serve Greek food. They'll do well enough when it's a couple of scrambled eggs you want without having to travel very far.

Places with a view. There are lots of restaurants with good city views; we mention them in the individual entries. Here is a selection: *Top of the Tower,* Beekman Hotel, First Ave. at 49th St., offering drinks and music, has great views of the East River and the midtown skyscrapers. *Top of the Park,* Gulf & Western Bldg., Central Park West at 60th St., has a splendid view of Central Park. *Top of the Six's,* 666 Fifth Ave., is smack in the middle of the midtown building cluster, as is the *Rainbow Room* at the top of the RCA Building in Rockefeller Center—but the Rainbow Room is higher. *Windows on the World,* in the World Trade Center on the 107th floor, has the best city view of all—by far. As mentioned, Windows (or WOW) and the Rainbow Room offer fine cuisine as well as knockout views as does *The Terrace* in Butler Hall at Columbia University, at 119th St. a block from Broadway. The Terrace (French, dinner only) has a good view of the midtown skyline, chamber music, all in all, romantic. *Nirvana* has one location overlooking Central Park and a second perched high above Times Square. There are also good views of Manhattan from across the East River in Brooklyn, at the *River Café*. In contrast, the *Water Club,* on the East River faces Queens and Brooklyn.

Brunch. We mention good brunches in the individual entries. Places offering Sunday brunch—usually starting at 11 A.M. or noon—are legion in New York. Many offer chamber music too. Saturday brunches are less popular. Carry your *New York Times* into the restaurant and look as if you live here.

Dessert. Finally, if you turn to the last page of these listings, you'll discover our suggestions for desserts. These include notable ice cream parlors and pastry shops that just may lure you into forgetting lunch or dinner altogether.

If you are still undecided where to dine after looking over our extensive selection of restaurants listed here, you may want to try a free information service by phone. **New York Restaurant Hotline** offers service to some 200 restaurants via recorded messages. Most of the messages are, however, available only on a push-button phone. Four different phone numbers are available, depending on where you want to dine. For Upper East Side, with 59th Street as the dividing line the number is 838–6644; Lower East Side, 838–7020; Upper West Side, 838–6883; and Lower West Side, 838–7430.

American-International

Super Deluxe

The Four Seasons. 99 E. 52nd St.; 754–9494. One of New York's most beautiful, ambitious, and interesting restaurants. As seasons change, so do menus and decor. The main dining room is dominated by a large, shimmering reflecting pool. Art work includes a Picasso, and changing floral displays constitute a veritable botanical garden. But the heart of the restaurant revolves around a series of gastronomic "events," featuring famous chefs from around the world preparing their most famous creations. Best seats are thought to be near the pool in the formal dining room, where prices can reach the stratosphere. The outside Grill Room is a little less fancy and a lot less expensive. Knowledgeable New Yorkers who don't mind eating early or after the theater can take advantage of a pre- or post-theater dinner ($41.50 prix fixe, as of this writing, not including tax, tip, or drinks) served Monday–Saturday, and guests must be seated between 5 and 6:15 P.M. or 10 and 11:15 P.M. Entree choices are staggering in each case, as is the selection from one of America's most complete wine cellars. If the chocolate velvet for dessert is a once-in-lifetime experience, so is the restaurant itself. Closed Sundays. All major credit cards.

Sign of the Dove. 1110 Third Ave. at 65th St.; 861–8080. A complete townhouse with terraces and a winter garden. The Sanctorum is upstairs. One of the city's prettiest, most romantic restaurants, and the food has recently skyrocketed in quality. No lunch Monday. All major credit cards.

"21". 21 W. 52nd St.; 582–7200. Great social cachet among high-class fixers, celebrity-chasers of all ranks, and slightly aging "beautiful people," and therefore in a category of its own. Somewhat difficult to enter unless you have reservations. Frequented by business people at lunch and "society" at night. Handsomely furnished dining rooms, a well-packed, convivial bar. Most-sought-after tables are downstairs, along the left wall. Located in several former townhouses, decorated with turn-of-the-century elegance. Recently completely renovated, with imaginative new menu by the celebrated young chef Anne Rosenzweig. Excellent wine cellar. All major credit cards.

Windows on the World. 1 World Trade Center; 938–1111. A stunning and lavish restaurant with a wraparound view of the city that is suggestive of a ship's dining room—providing the ship is the *QE2* and she is perched atop the world's second tallest building, 107 floors up, where only the daringest crow would nest. The decor includes a rock-lined, mirrored reception chamber, a multitiered, multi-mirrored main dining room, a veritable acre of glass encompassing various dining rooms, cocktail lounges, and private rooms, lavish touches of brass, wood, plants, and fresh flowers, and waiters resplendent in white uniforms with gold epaulets. The neighboring **Hors d'Oeuvrerie,** on the same floor and run by the same management, is an internationally minded cocktail lounge and grill that can be inexpensive if you eat and drink lightly while enjoying the sights and listening to the piano music. Cellar in the Sky, windowless, concentrates instead on multicourse, multiwine, fixed-price menus. Reservations for Windows and Cellar, not required for Hors d'Oeuvrerie, although there is often a wait at the latter for seats. Men must wear jackets at the bar and restaurant and a tie in the restaurant; no jeans. All major credit cards.

Deluxe

American Harvest. 3 World Trade Center; 938–9100. The menu at the main restaurant in the Vista International Hotel is built completely on seasonal themes and the freshest of American meats, fish, and produce. Formal but not stiff, the restaurant also features an excellent selection of American wines by the glass or bottle. Note: For less extravagant times and lighter fare, the glass-roofed **Greenhouse** next door (overlooking the Trade Center plaza) shares the American Harvest's kitchen. Lunch weekdays only. *Tall Ships Bar* serves snacks and light fare, and *Vista Lounge* features a business buffet lunch. All major credit cards.

Christ Cella. 160 E. 46th St.; 697–2479. Perhaps the largest piece of roast beef around, ditto the steaks, and everything else is similarly served in oversized portions. Decor on two floors is simple, but who cares, for this is generally considered the best steak and roast beef house in town, although supporters of The Palm will give you argument there—and have for years in a rivalry reminiscent of the Yankees and Dodgers. Closed Sunday. All major credit cards.

The Coach House. 110 Waverly Place (the Village); 777–0303. A glowingly handsome English inn setting, where the best American dishes are served along with European classics in what many galloping gourmets consider the best all-around restaurant in the Big Apple. Specialties include black-bean soup, crab cakes, rack of lamb, house custard. Open at 5:30 P.M. on Saturday, 4:30 P.M. on Sunday, closed Monday. All major credit cards.

JW. 154 E. 79th St.; 772–6800. Formerly Jams, a celebrated temple of California nouvelle cuisine at steep prices, JW now features entrees in the $15–$19 range. Same owner/chef: Jonathan Waxman. All major credit cards.

Rainbow Room. 30 Rockefeller Plaza (Rockefeller Center); 632–5000. Beautifully restored, with a new menu (designed by restaurateur Joseph Baum) to match its 1930s art deco splendors. All major credit cards.

Sardi's. 234 W. 44th St.; 221-8440. The place to see theater world celebrities, sometimes. The stars (catch them at lunch and *after* the theater) generally sit downstairs, although the upstairs room is quite comfortable. Large dining room with convivial atmosphere has caricatures of the well-known as decoration. Cannelloni alla Sardi, crabmeat Sardi, steak tartare, chicken salad are specialties. No longer owned by Vincent Sardi. All major credit cards.

Top of the Park. Central Park West at 60th St. atop the Gulf & Western Bldg.; 333–3800. The view is terrific if you get a window table in the restaurant or the bar—the latter frequently noisy, ill-kept, overcrowded, and smoky. The food is not memorable because many of the items seem to be prepared in advance. Suitable if you want to look, eat, and run over to Lincoln Center. Dinner only. Closed Sunday. All major credit cards.

Water Club. 500 E. 30th St.; 683–3333. With 700 seats on a converted, anchored barge—all more or less with an East River view toward Queens and Brooklyn—the Water Club can hardly be termed intimate. Its popularity within months of opening, though, demanded reservations well in advance; service generally tends to be good, the food good if not great. Not a place for regular dining but perfect for a celebratory night (or weekend lunch) out. All major credit cards.

Expensive

Berry's. 180 Spring St., SoHo; 226–4394. One of the first, and consistently most rewarding, of the SoHo dining spots. Intimately lit Victorian decor and a light hand in the kitchen. The menu changes frequently, making for particularly fine seasonal offerings and the best of vegetable accompaniments. Excellent Sunday brunches, too. Reservations a must, and be forewarned that weekend evenings tend to be overcrowded and ear-shatteringly noisy. Even then, though, it's worth the trip. Closed Monday. All major credit cards.

Café Europa. 347 E. 54th St.; 755–0160. The festival Mediterranean setting makes up for only moderately interesting food that is nonetheless fresh and well prepared. The back room is also especially notable for the intimacy it affords. Closed Saturdays until 5 P.M. and all day Sunday. All major credit cards.

Café Un Deux Trois. 123 West 44th St.; 354–4148. A colorful, young, tremendously alive French-style bistro in the theater district, though the food goes considerably beyond French influences. As at so many places, the effort to develop a new concept frequently finds the kitchen staff overextended, but rarely is anything downright bad. Trendy among theater and advertising types—with paper tablecloths and crayons—but in a most friendly sort of way. Major credit cards.

Chelsea Place. 147 Eighth Ave. near 17th St.; 924–8413. From the outside, the antique store at this address gives no hint that there's an exceedingly popular singles bar and restaurant literally "through the looking glass." You enter the eatery through what looks like an oversized armoir. There's a very pleasant glassed-in garden for dining year-round—well-removed from the bustle of the bar scene. The food is good yet overpriced in its class, but the setting and atmosphere are unique. The Alex Room upstairs features jazz pianists. All major credit cards.

The Conservatory. 15 Central Park West at 61st St.; 581–1293. A relaxed, attractive spot for the Lincoln Center crowd. Diversified menu includes Mongolian lamb chops, shrimp scampi, and breast of capon piccata. All credit cards.

Elaine's. 1703 Second Ave. at 88th St.; 534–8103. The only legitimate reason for trying this restaurant, unless you know the proprietress, is to try to catch a glimpse of the large number of publishing and journalism notables or nonnotables who call it home. The food's ordinary at best, and mere mortals are treated shabbily, if not worse. A club, however, for the likes of Woody Allen, Gay Talese (who?), and visiting Hollywood pretty faces. Primarily Italian menu, some American dishes in what is more like a renovated saloon than a celebrity haunt. AE.

The Ginger Man. 51 W. 64th St.; 399–2358. Another favorite dinner locale among those attending performances at Lincoln Center. A well-decorated, pubstyle establishment that is noted for its spinach salad, omelets, daily fish specialties, chops, and steaks. All major credit cards.

Greene Street. 101–103 Green St. between Prince and Spring (SoHo); 925–2415. Good but not great food in delightful setting—plants, catwalks, lots of space—in the interesting SoHo area. Music, usually jazz, Latin, or cabaret, usually beginning around 11 P.M. All major credit cards.

Hurley's Steak & Seafood. 49th St. and Sixth Ave.; 765–8981. Jammed at lunchtime. Very popular with broadcasting and advertising folks—the NBC headquarters and studios are about thirty feet away. Major credit cards.

The Leopard. 253 E. 50th St., near Second Ave.; 759–3735. A fine, spacious dining room, with tables comfortably far apart, overlooking a plastic garden. Prix-fixe meals include all the wine you wish—and the wines are surprisingly good. The Continental-style food is not four-star, but neither are the prices. All major credit cards.

One If by Land, Two If by Sea. 17 Barrow St., between W. 4th St. and Seventh Ave.; 255–8649. In what was once a stable, this charming restaurant is a favorite more for its ambience and layout than for its food, though the food is all right if you stick to basics. There is no sign outside the place, so look for the street number. Not terribly casual in dress. All major credit cards.

Tavern-on-the-Green. Central Park West at 67th St. (just inside Central Park); 873–3200. This long-time New York landmark has six beautifully appointed rooms with views of the park, and outdoor dining when weather permits. Can't be beat for value-for-the-money on the $14.50 pre-theater dinner; à la carte you pay for the admittedly spectacular setting. Perfect for weekend brunch in any season. All major credit cards.

Terrace Five. 725 Fifth Ave. at 57th St., on fifth floor of Trump Tower; 371–5030. Emphasis is on lightness, with no flour or cream in the soups or the sauces for fine entrées. Lovely terrace overlooks the avenue. All major credit cards.

Texarkana. 64 W. 10th St.; 254–5800. Tex-Mex is something of a New York fad these days, and Texarkana caters to the trendiest of the faddists. Still, the seafood bisques and gumbos, suckling pig, chicken with honey butter, dirty rice, and black bottom pie are very fine. Reservations a must, and then expect a wait. AE, DC.

Toots Shor. 233 W. 33rd St. at Penn Plaza; 279–8150. A famous watering hole for New York's sporting fraternity, moved from its old midtown location to this relatively new spot opposite Madison Square Garden. Standard steak and chops fare, lively atmosphere. Closed weekends unless there are events of importance at the Garden. All major credit cards.

Top of the Sixes. 666 Fifth Ave. at 53rd St.; 757–6662. Provides a view of the city from its dining room and candlelit cocktail lounge. The menu is diversified with Continental overtones, but it is hardly haute cuisine. (In fact, most of the food tastes as though it were defrosted right from the Stouffer's freezer—which is the company that runs the restaurant.) All major credit cards.

Union Square Café. 21 E. 16th St. 243–4020. Chic and smart, spacious and softly lit, this handsome restaurant with a long eating/drinking bar serves an imaginative menu (vegetable pastas, seafood risottos, numerous oyster dishes, grilled fish and meats, luscious desserts) to a young, well-heeled crowd. Savvy, concerned service. All major credit cards.

Moderate

America. 9 E. 18th St. between Fifth Ave. and Broadway; 505–2110. A cavernous restaurant with a huge skylit bar area for mingling. The best of the large, big-menu, big-portion establishments that seem to be taking over the city. The emphasis is on "Mom food," but with pastas, eggs, steaks, burgers. Fun if you can bear the noise and great for a weekend brunch or early dinner. Reservations are a very good idea. All major credit cards.

American Festival Café. Rockefeller Center, 2 W. 50th St., 246–6699. Stunning new restaurant, filled with sunshine and authentic American folk art, facing Rockefeller Center's Lower Plaza (an ice-skating rink in winter, an outdoor garden restaurant in summer). Regional specialties include corn/crab chowder, Maryland crab cakes, grilled North Atlantic salmon, huge Texas Gulf shrimp, and the finest key lime pie this side of Key West. All major credit cards.

B. Smith's. 771 Eighth Ave. at 47th St.; 247–2222. Hot new spot in the Broadway theater district. High-tech, slick, spacious and minimalist, yet extremely comfortable and relaxing. B. (for Barbara) Smith, an elegant young black woman, is your hostess, and her cadre of waiters (dressed and styled by the trendiest East Village boutiques) could not be friendlier or more helpful. The ambitious, imaginative menu of small dishes, from appetizers to desserts, invites "grazing." Suggestions: roasted-tomato soup, Gulf shrimp, a salad topped with succulent slices of chicken breast, duck sausage, white-chocolate ice cream with white-chocolate chunks served in a crisp coconut pastry shell. All major credit cards.

Bridge Café. 279 Water St.; 227–3344. Near the South Street Seaport and convenient to the financial district, though the restaurant itself is well hidden beneath the Brooklyn Bridge (on the Manhattan side). The kitchen experiments with unusual combinations and there are superior soups and seafood. Very congenial, a little noisy, and excellent for Sunday morning brunch. AE.

Century Café. 132 W. 43rd St.; 398–1988. The Art Deco neon movie-house sign over the bar sets the stage for this popular theater district restaurant. Among the outstanding entrees are: mesquite-grilled veal chops and filet mignon, duck accompanied by a seasonal fruit sauce, and such oddities as chicken hash with mushrooms, along with a good, reasonably priced wine list and an accommodating if sometimes harried staff. Closed Sundays, otherwise one menu from 11:30 A.M. to 1:30 A.M. All major credit cards.

Charley-O's. 218 W. 45th St.; 563–7450. Fronts on famed Shubert Alley. You can order your choices via the phone at your table. Good for pre- or post-theater dining. All major credit cards.

P.J. Clarke's. 915 Third Ave. at 55th St.; 759–1650. The most chic hamburger joint in town. A legend that is the special province of NYC's advertising and publishing set, this venerable saloon was the setting of scenes in the film classic, *The Lost Weekend.* Good chili served in the bar area. AE, DC.

Crawdaddy. 45 E. 45th St.; 687–1860. New Orleans in New York; Creole dishes, gumbos, cheerful decor, live music evenings. Closed Saturday/Sunday. All major credit cards.

Fraunces Tavern Restaurant. 54 Pearl St., downtown; 269–0144. Original building dates from pre-Revolutionary days (the present one only to 1907). Behind the white portico there's a restaurant for lunch and dinner and a museum filled with Early American memorabilia. It was here that George Washington bade farewell to his troops in 1783. Quite convenient to Wall St. and for George, who loved the roast oysters, chicken à la Washington and fresh fish—and so will you. Closed Saturday and Sunday. All major credit cards.

Harvey's Chelsea Restaurant. 108 W. 18th St.; 243–5644. An elegant old New York town house turned into a handsome but informal neighborhood bar/restaurant. Basic American dishes: chicken pot pie, prime ribs, fresh seafood. A bargain for Sunday brunch. AE.

Joe Allen's. 326 W. 46th St., in the theater district; 581–6464. A longtime theatrical hangout for Broadway's "gypsies" (chorus dancers) before they moved to **Charlies'** (263 W. 45th St.; 354–2911). Allen's now attracts customers from the *other* side of the footlights. MC, V.

Lion's Rock. 316 E. 77th St.; 988–3610. Very good Continental-type food in a casual atmosphere, with an attractive open garden (dominated by a huge rock) at the rear. Major credit cards.

Martell's. 1469 Third Ave. at 84th St.; 861–6110. French farmer's sandwich is a specialty at this Upper East Side boite, which advertises its "spirituous liquors." Sidewalk café in good weather. Good bar scene. All major credit cards.

Jim McMullen's. 1341 Third Ave. near 77th St.; 861–4700. Natural brick walls, no reservations. A hangout for models—Jim was one himself—the beautiful people and the sports crowd. Good seafood, first-class steaks. AE.

J.G. Melon. 1291 Third Ave. at 74th St.; 744–0585. This is fast food for the Beautiful People. The bar is a regular meeting place for New York's informal chic set. Hamburgers are fine, as are the Monte Cristo sandwiches. No credit cards. Also a West Side branch at Amsterdam Ave. and 76th St. (874–8291). V, MC with $20 minimum

Palsson's. 158 W. 72nd St.; 362–2590. This extremely comfortable Upper West Side bar and restaurant is supposedly Icelandic, but the manager-owner is from a Romanian Jewish family and the chef is Chinese—but the food is good and reasonably priced: chicken tarragon or whatever, fish smoked to order, a few other well-chosen dishes—and the place really gets busy after 11 P.M. *Forbidden Broadway* cabaret upstairs. Major credit cards.

Tastings. 144 W. 55th St.; 757–1160. An offshoot of the International Wine Center, Tastings usually offers upwards of 20 different wines for sampling by the glass or half-glass (for those who are really serious) on any given night. Best approach here is to create a meal from a variety of appetizers—either at the bar or in the modern, wood-plants-and-Italian-lamps dining room—and to let the liquid refreshment serve as the focus. AE, V, MC.

West Bank Café. 407 W. 42nd St.; 695–6909. Good ribs, chicken, salads, and quiches in the Manhattan Plaza apartment complex—excellent for after theater (be sure to have reservations). No DC.

Inexpensive

Amsterdam's Bar/Rotisserie. 428 Amsterdam Ave., between 80th and 81st sts.; 874–1377 and 454 Broadway, between Grand and Howard sts.;

925–6166. Good basic rotisserie fare, with chicken the mainstay and fresh fish of the day generally a good bet. Most entrees are under $15 with a salad and vegetable and that—along with the fact that it's good—means there are always lines. Reservations for larger parties only. All major credit cards.

Elephant & Castle. 183 Prince St. and 68 Greenwich Ave.; 260–3600 and 243–1400. The Prince St./SoHo outpost is the newer, brighter, and livelier of the two, the Greenwich original a uniquely Village hole in the wall with great charm. Burgers, salads, and omelettes are what to count on—the kitchen isn't as adept at more complicated fare—with bar in SoHo, BYOB invited in the Village. Nice for brunch. All major credit cards at both.

Hamburger Harry's. 157 Chambers St.; 267–4446, also at 145 W. 45th St., between 6th Avenue and Broadway, 840–0566). Many burger experts consider these two comparatively new pit stops the very best places for America's favorite snack. No reservations. AE.

Hard Rock Café. 221 W. 57th St.; 489–6565. If you are a teenager (or have one in tow), this is a must stop—so don't fight it. Sure the music's loud and the place looks like a Western saloon decorated by Bruce Springsteen, but the food (burgers, sandwiches, guacamole, shrimp, and other light snacks) is surprisingly fresh and tasty. (Post-teens should bring ear plugs.) All major credit cards.

Manhattan Island. 482 W. 43rd St.; 967–0533. A dazzling new beauty on the third floor of the towering Manhattan Plaza apartment complex opposite Theater Row on West 42nd St. Several dining areas, including an outdoor patio, overlook the Plaza's health club and pool. Tasty (and healthy) salads, grilled meats and fish (the crab cakes are superb!), and succulent desserts like peanut-butter pie and lemon tart. AE, MC, V.

Smoke Stacks Lightnin' Bar. 380 Canal St.; 226–0485. Good hamburgers, salads, and quiches. Borders on SoHo and on TriBeCa punk-rock territory (the regulars are a colorful lot), but friendly. All major credit cards.

Ye Waverly Inn. 16 Bank St.; 929–4377. A Village landmark with three low-ceilinged, candlelit dining rooms—two with fireplaces—and a backyard garden. Down-to-earth American cookery that has been tired in recent years, though the pies and cakes are still homemade. All major credit cards.

Steak Houses

Super Deluxe

Joe & Rose. 747 Third Ave. near 46th St.; 980–3985. They built an entire skyscraper around this humble-looking eatery. Food is hardly humble, though, and the steaks and corned beef and cabbage are specials. Like The Palm and Pietro's, this is a New York phenomenon, where the service and surroundings belie the prices—the food doesn't. AE, DC, V.

The Palm. 837 Second Ave. near 45th St.; 687–2953. For the roughly two hundred ten million Americans who've been weaned on "New York cut" steaks, it's going to come as a rude awakening to discover that such a description has no meaning in NYC. But if you are looking for just about the best piece of sirloin in town, this is the place. You should know that it's a madhouse at the prime dinner hours, and because of a non-reservation policy, an hour's wait is not the least unusual. We should also mention that the noise level is high and that the walls are decorated in a way that can only be described as vintage graffiti and the waiters will do their best to antagonize you and get you in and out quickly. Yet beef lovers queue up gladly, and the double sirloin is a total delight. The cottage-fried potatoes and crisp onion rings are unequaled in the city, and the double lobster (carrying a tariff that may require payment in 30-, 60-, and 90-day notes) is simply splendid. A branch called **Palm Too,** 697–5198, directly across the street and serving the same food, tries to handle the overflow. Closed Sunday. All major credit cards.

Pen & Pencil. 205 E. 45th St.; 682–8660. Another steak house with an established (and highly vocal) group of supporters among the journalistic and entertainment crowd. In addition to grilled steaks and chops, a few Italian specialties can be ordered. All major credit cards.

Ponte's Steakhouse. 39 Desbrosses St., corner of West St.; 226–4621. Imagine a Hollywood set for a New York steak house—deserted warehouse neighborhood, '50s lounge-like decor, older men with big pinky rings and long cigars at half the tables, younger men with dates to impress at the others—and you'll recognize Ponte's immediately. The management is Italian, but the specialties are large steaks and chops. Lunch and dinner weekdays, dinner only on Saturdays. Closed Sundays. Free valet parking. All major credit cards.

The Post House, 28 E. 63rd St.; 935–2888. One of New York's newest and most comfortable steak houses. All major credit cards.

Smith and Wollensky. 201 E. 49th St.; 753–1530. Steaks, chops, roast beef, and lobsters are the basic items, and flank steak surrounded by vegetables is a feature. The Grill is somewhat less formal than the clubby main dining room, and there's a sidewalk cafe in summer. All major credit cards.

Sparks Steak House. 210 E. 46th St.; 687–4855. Prime aged beef, huge lobsters, fresh seafood, and an award-winning wine cellar (one of the best in town). Closed Sundays. All major credit cards.

Expensive

Ben Benson's Steak House. 123 W. 52nd St.; 581–8888. Classic New York steak house in heart of midtown business district and near upper Broadway-area theaters. Valet parking after 6 P.M. All major credit cards.

Broadway Joe's Steak House. 315 W. 46th St.; 246–6513 or 974–9832. This well-known old-timer has an open kitchen. Waiters recite the menu. All major credit cards.

Elmer's. 1034 Second Ave. near 55th St.; 751–8020. With a name like that, it has to be good—and it is. All major credit cards.

Frankie & Johnnie's. 269 W. 45th St. off Eighth Ave.; 997–9494. Well worth the short climb to the second-floor dining room. Great steaks and potatoes served—but open (until midnight) for dinner only. All major credit cards.

Frank's. 431 W. 14th St.; 243–1349. A little-known, first-rate steakhouse that also happens to have exceptional veal chops and hearty pastas—all in the most unprepossessing surroundings in the heart of what's left of the 14th Street meat market. By day this a hangout for market personnel. At night they pull out the tablecloths, throw some fresh sawdust on the tile floor and go upscale. Funky atmosphere, then, and great food.

Take a cab, and have the restaurant phone one for you when leaving. All major credit cards.

Gallagher's Steak House. 228 W. 52nd St.; 245–5336. Near the theaters, it has a rugged, comfortable air, red-checked tablecloths in the several dining rooms, and a large bar. As you enter, you can see your steak hanging in the glass-enclosed "aging box." All credit cards.

Kenny's Steak Pub. 565 Lexington Ave. near 51st St.; 355–0666. Favorite of the NYC professional footballer, who appreciates the generous portions of steak and prime ribs. The noise can sometimes sound like being in a stadium. Banana layer cake a treat. Open every day. All major credit cards.

Le Steak. 1089 Second Ave. near 58th St.; 421–9072. Red meat prepared lusciously in the French style. Steak sautéed in garlic butter is indescribably good. A unique steakhouse open for dinner only. All major credit cards.

Old Homestead Steak House. 56 Ninth Ave. near 14th St.; 242–9040. The oldest steakhouse in NYC, established 1865, in the heart of the wholesale meat market. If you're especially lucky, you may hit them on the day each year when they roll back prices to those offered on the date of founding. Oversize steaks and lobster, and home-fried potatoes are the specialties. Hot shrimp balls are an unusual appetizer. All major credit cards.

Slate Steak House. 852 Tenth Ave.; 581–6340. Near the CBS studios, so of course big with the TV crowd. All major credit cards.

Moderate

Blue Mill Tavern. 50 Commerce St. in the Village; 243–7114. Tucked away amidst century-old buildings, and within walking distance of many Off-Broadway Village theaters. The management is Portuguese, and the food is good. AE, MC, V, DC for dinner only.

The Cattleman Palace. 5 E. 45th St.; 661–1200. Has to be seen to be disbelieved. A jam-packed bar, one room with an 1890 dining-car interior, another looking like a very elegant Crazy Horse Saloon, and steaks, prime ribs, and daily fish specials. All this, and a stagecoach to take you to the theater after dinner! Miss Grimble's cheescake. Bring appetite because portions are enormous. But quantity has little to do with quality. All major credit cards.

Derby Steak & Seafood House. 109 MacDougal St.; 475–0520. Long-established and family-run (Andrew Scarsi is your host), this cozy, comfortable, convivial bar/restaurant is steeped in Greenwich Village atmosphere and charm. All meats and fish are cooked to order on the open grill. Just steps away from a dozen off-Broadway theaters. All major credit cards.

Inexpensive

Beefsteak Charlie's. Various midtown locations. Singled out mostly because of its low prices and "Small Fry" meals, which mean bargain prices for the kiddie korps. All major credit cards.

Seafood

Super Deluxe

Gloucester House. 37 E. 50th St.; 755–7394. Among the most extensive (and expensive) seafood menus in New York. New England decor; scrubbed table tops. Fabulous homemade biscuits. If you have an expense account, this place will use it up for a month. All major credit cards.

The Sea Grill. 19 W. 49th St., off Rockefeller Center's Lower Plaza; 246–9201. Stunning new seafood restaurant on two levels overlooking the center's skating rink (in winter) and outdoor dining area (in summer). The catches of the day are the freshest and the preparation impeccable. Suggestions: fresh oysters, broiled salmon, crab cakes, seafood pasta, key lime pie. Fine white wines. Reservations (as far in advance as possible) are a must. Pre- and after-theater menus; Saturdays and Sundays brunch. All major credit cards.

Deluxe

John Clancy's. 181 W. 10th St. in the Village; 242–7350. Seafood, all fresh and all excellently prepared. Broiling is done over mesquite charcoal, à la Texas and West Coast. Must reserve days in advance. Dinner only, 6–11 P.M. Major credit cards.

Oyster Bar of the Plaza. Plaza Hotel, Fifth Ave. at 59th St.; 759–3000. If you want to combine Edwardian elegance with excellent seafood, this is the place. Full-course dinners will run high, but you can snack heartily very reasonably at the bar, as many New Yorkers do at lunch and after work. All major credit cards.

Expensive

The Captain's Table. 860 Second Ave. near 47th St., 697–9538. Selections are broad and simple and the fish is fresh. AE, MC, V.

Joe's Pier 52. 163 W. 52nd St.; 245–6652. Huge, sprawling; music in lounge. If you're going to the theater—and crave seafood—this couldn't be more convenient. All major credit cards.

King Crab. 871 Eighth Ave. at 52nd St.; 765–4393. Gas lamps, track lighting, young plants, old furniture and fresh fish, crabs, and interesting seafood combination. Open 7 days a week, dinner only Saturday/Sunday. AE, DC.

Manhattan Ocean Club. 57 W. 58th St.; 371–7777. Attractive two-level restaurant convenient to Carnegie Hall, the TV networks' executive offices, Central Park South, and midtown shopping. The speciality? Seafare, grilled to perfection. Dinner served until 11:30 P.M. All major credit cards.

Marylou's. 21 W. 9th St. in the Village; 533–0012. A very handsome place on one of the Village's handsomest streets. The fish dishes are almost uniformly excellent. The clientele is often from the photography/fashion world. No lunch Saturday; only brunch on Sunday. Major credit cards.

Oscar's Salt of the Sea. 1155 Third Ave. near 67th St.; 879–1199; also the Citicorp Atrium, 371–2201. Stuffed lobsters are a particular specialty of this exceptional seafood restaurant, and virtually everything on the extensive menu is prepared perfectly. The only discordant note is the inevitable wait (often quite long) for a table. All major credit cards.

Pesca. 23 E. 22nd St.; 533–2293. A beautiful, simply appointed restaurant with an open feeling. Some very unusual seafood dishes. The preparation tends to Latin-style—Italian and Portuguese. The waiters all started work today. AE.

Sweet's. 2 Fulton St. South St. Seaport; 344–9189. A landmark from the old clipper-ship days. Exceptional fish prepared in the traditional manner and considered the best seafood place in town—even though it takes no reservations and is usually crowded. It's in the Fulton Fish Market area and seems to get its fish fresh off the hook. Closed Saturdays, Sundays, holidays. AE, MC, V.

Moderate

Broadway Bay. 2178 Broadway, corner Broadway and 77th St.; 362–4360. Italian seafood specialties in a very casual Upper West Side atmosphere. The bar is especially casual—unprepossessing would be an understatement. All major credit cards.

Claire. 156 Seventh Ave. (near 19th St.); 255–1955. Key West decor and atmosphere, with revolving fans, hanging plants, lattice-work panels, snake-skin bar, airy rooms (the site was formerly a furniture showroom) along with slightly trendy, always pretty, and usually successful seafood and fish. Some meat dishes available for landlubbers. AE, MC, V.

Dobson's. 341 Columbus Ave. at 76th St.; 362–0100. This very large and understated restaurant is representative of the newly stylish Upper West Side, a dozen blocks north of Lincoln Center. The fish is fresh, the atmosphere casual—but not overly so. AE, MC, V.

Docks. 2427 Broadway, near 90th St.; 724–5588. The freshest seafood in a most attractive art deco setting.

Hobeaus. 52nd St. and Second Ave.; 421–2888. Hobeaus got gussied up when it moved from First to Second Ave., but it still has the park bench out front to make life a little easier while waiting on line to get in. The new quarters are larger than the old, and the lines less unwieldy, but even with somewhat higher prices the place is still notable for good food for a reasonable amount of money. Because of the prices you may feel guilty lingering, but you won't be pushed out the door. Note: nothing for landlubbers here. MC, V, AE.

Jane Street Seafood Café. 31 Eighth Ave. two blocks south of 14th St.; 242–0003 or 243–9237. Narrow, intimate West Village setting with exposed brick and natural wood—and a gourmet touch in the kitchen. AE, MC, V.

Janice's Seafood Place. 570 Hudson; 243–4212. Seafood with fresh vegetables—all handled with an Oriental flair. AE, MC, V.

Manhattan Brewing Co.—Ocean Grill. 40 Thompson St., between West Broadway and Sixth Ave.; 219–9250. Yes, this is a real brewery, with long camp-style tables, peanuts at every table (peanut shells on the floor), and snacks/light meals along with the beer on one floor and a grill restaurant on the balcony overlooking gleaming copper brewing vats. A fun, reasonably priced place where the collegiate atmopshere compensates for shortcomings in the food and service. No CB.

Oyster Bar. Inside Grand Central Station, off 42nd St. at Vanderbilt Ave., 490–6650. The freshest fish, impeccably prepared. NYC's most famous seafood restaurant does a booming business in its vaulted main room, in the quieter Saloon (490–6653 or 532–1358) and the first-come, first-served sit-down counter. Several kinds of oysters, clams, and crabs at any given time, plus specials that include fish not seen often enough in New York. Budget gourmets should try the clam chowders and she-crab soup, plus the superb desserts. Main room is noisy but exhilarating. Closed Saturday/Sunday. All major credit cards.

Dairy

Inexpensive (See also *Health Food*)

Boychik's. 19 W. 45th St.; 719–5999. Kosher pizzeria (the pizza's pretty good, though high, at $1.25 a slice); good dairy platters built around Middle Eastern salads. Also: fried-fish sandwiches and quiches, but pass these up for the far better (and substantial) knishes. Closed Friday after sundown and Saturday until sundown. No credit cards.

Ratner's Dairy Restaurant. 138 Delancey St., near Essex; 677–5588. A legend in its own time on the Lower East Side for East European Jewish dairy cooking. No credit cards.

Delicatessen

Deli in New York is unique unto itself. A genuine deli sandwich here, as opposed to the kind that merely comes out of coffee shops, carries with it an entire set of expectations—pickles, peppers, and cole slaw not the least among them. The best corned beef or pastrami on rye in midtown will run an easy $7, while special triple-decker combinations such as chicken, salami, and roast beef, or tongue, turkey, and pastrami command $9.50 and up. That's expensive for a sandwich, but consider that one such sandwich at the Carnegie Deli (see below) will easily suffice for two people—and add a similarly shared side order of potato salad and you've got a feast.

Expensive

Kaplan's at the Delmonico. 59 E. 59th St.; 755–5959. Classiest of the lot, with fantastic deli sandwiches. All major credit cards; $10 minimum. Kosher.

Inexpensive

Carnegie Delicatessen. 854 Seventh Ave.; 757–2245. By far the best deli in the city, according to deli maven Herb Hartig—and therefore in the world. The corned beef hash—always freshly prepared—is a minor New York miracle. The sandwiches are beyond overflowing, and all ingredients are first rate. Forever crowded and forever bustling and always worth a visit. An excellent choice for breakfast, too, if you're staying at the Sheraton Centre, Hilton, or other midtown/Broadway hotels. Open 6:30 A.M. to 4 A.M. No credit cards.

Fine & Schapiro. 138 W. 72nd St.; 877–2874. An easy walk to and from Lincoln Center—especially worthwhile on matinee days. Also Kosher Chinese delicacies. AE; $10 minimum.

Golden's Madison. 1175 Madison Ave. at 86th St.; 369–6670. Convenient to Upper East Side museums, this large, informal delicatessen restaurant offers a variety of sandwiches as well as appetizers, soups, smoked fish, dairy dishes, hot main courses, and Danish pastries. No credit cards.

Katz's Delicatessen. 205 E. Houston St.; 254–2246. A Lower East Side institution—cafeteria-style self-service that's a perfect treat after bargain-hunting on Orchard St. downtown. No credit cards.

Nathan's Famous. Broadway at 43rd St.; 382–0620. Having acquired fame and reputation at Coney Island, Nathan's in Manhattan now dispenses the same clams, clam chowder, pizza, barbequed beef sandwiches, and chow mein on a bun as at the original (still open) location. But Nathan's earned its nickname—"Famous"—with great hot dogs and French fries. Free sauerkraut, mustard, and catsup with the dogs and fries. Eat at stand-up counters, cafeteria-style at communal tables, or downstairs in the dining room. No credit cards.

Pastrami & Things. 666 Fifth Ave.; 581–6300. Another Jewish delicatessen with a dining room and counter. The pastrami sandwiches are unsurpassed, and were chosen by *New York* magazine as the best in the city. Popular and crowded. All major credit cards.

Reuben's. 244 Madison Ave. near 38th St., 867–7800. "From a sandwich to an institution" is its boast, and justly so. No credit cards.

Second Ave. Kosher Delicatessen. 156 Second Ave. at 10th St.; 677–0606. Real kosher-style deli with all the trimmings—free pickles, cole slaw, waiters who invariably know what you want better than you do—and the unique offer of half sandwiches at half price. Easily among the best of the lot, and a relative bargain because of its out-of-the-way location. No credit cards.

Stage. 834 Seventh Ave. near 54th St.; 245–7850. This restaurant attracts a large after-theater crowd, but is nearly always bustling and noisy. Their sandwiches are packed with meat, the rye bread is superb, their appetizers tantalizing, and there is a variety of hot dishes, salads, and fish platters. Tables are for four, so if you're a couple expect company and surly-at-best service. Open 6:30 A.M. to 1:30 A.M. No credit cards.

West Park. 1802 Broadway (at 59th St., across from Columbus Circle), 245–5898. Perfect for picking up a delicious and inexpensive lunch for taking to a bench in Central Park. Have a soup (pea, beef barley, or clam chowder), whitefish salad sandwich on pumpernickel, a sour pickle slice, tapioca pudding, and milk—all for about $6. No credit cards.

Health Food

Inexpensive

Au Natural. 1043 Second Ave.; 832–2922. Beautiful fresh salads, fruit and vegetable drinks and some sandwiches—perfect for lunch fare and light snacking. No credit cards.

Great American Health Bar. 35 W. 57th St.; 355–5177. Popular among diet-conscious shoppers stalking the exclusive women's department stores (Bendel, Bergdorf, Bonwit Teller) in the area. No credit cards.

Greener Pastures. 117 E. 60th St.; 832–3212. The salads and platters are a little more original than is usually the case, and the location is perfect when shopping at Bloomingdale's or catching an Upper East Side movie. No credit cards.

Healthworks! 153 E. 53rd St.; 838–6221. Flagship branch in Citicorp Center features salads galore plus yogurts, quiches, and other light, interestingly prepared dishes. Also takeout. No credit cards.

Spring Street Natural Restaurant. 62 Spring St.; 966–0290. One of the earlier revitalized SoHo outposts with something of a rustic, artsy New England feel to it, despite words like "macrobiotic" on the menu. Everything, however, is homemade. All major credit cards.

Zucchini. 1336 First Ave. at 72nd St.; 249–0559. Salads, soups, home-baked goods in a cheery Upper East Side setting. No DC, CB.

Southern

Expensive

The Ritz Cafe. 2 Park Ave. (entrance on E. 32nd St.); 684–2122. One of the new-wave, brightly lit, pinkish-hued places specializing in Southern regional cuisine. On the menu you'll find such delectables as Carolina corn and crab chowder, Texas meatloaf, Mississippi catfish with jalapeno cilantro sauce, or Flordia snapper stuffed with crabmeat. Closed Sundays. No DC.

Inexpensive

Acme Bar & Grill. 9 Great John St.; 420–1934. Located in the NoHo ("North of Houston") section of Lower Manhattan, this casual place serves up some mean Cajun food. Included are panfried, blackened, or spicy crabcakes, chicken fried steak, and Cajun chicken. A shelf runs the length of the restaurant, stocked with an amazing variety of hot sauces. No credit cards.

Sylvia's. 328 Lenox Ave., 534–9348. In the heart of Harlem, near 125th St. (take a taxi to and from, although the A train on the subway stops on 125th St. just a few blocks from the restaurant). Sylvia and her staff serve what has been called the finest soul food in the city. A regular stop for top stars, business execs, and politicians (Jesse Jackson was a recent visitor), who love the Southern-fried chicken, smothered chicken, corn bread and greens, and stuffed pork chops. It's very popular during peak breakfast, lunch, and dinner hours, so go early or late for immediate seating. No credit cards.

Cuisine by Nationality

Brazilian

Moderate

Amazonas. 492 Broome St.; 966–3371. Live, Brazilian music accompanies the exotic Brazilian specialities, which are served in a tropical decor. Every day for dinner: noon to 3 A.M. Sat.–Sun. All major credit cards.

Brazil 2000. 127 W. 72nd St. (near Broadway); 877–7730. Colorful, inviting place in the heart of the Yuppie West Side. Great place for steak, black beans, and rice. AE.

Brazilian Pavilion. 316 E. 53rd St., 758–8129. Although the setting is modern, the interesting cuisine is traditional Brazilian with steaks Portuguesa (garlic!), shrimp Paulista, and Portuguese fish stew. The black bean soup is excellent; so is the dried codfish. Closed Sunday. All major credit cards.

S.O.B.'s. 204 Varick St., in the South Village, near SoHo; 243–4940. This spare, high-tech restaurant is the best place in New York to enjoy a double dose of Brazilian food and music (there's a different band every night starting at 10:30). The initials? Sounds of Brazil, of course. All major credit cards.

Via Brasil. 34 W. 46th St.; 997–1158. On Manhattan's Brazilian street. The decor is a touch off-beat, but the grilled meats, especially the Brazilian-style marinated steaks, are superb. Major credit cards.

Inexpensive

Brazilian Coffee Restaurant. 45 W. 46th St.; 719–2105. In the heart of the theater district. *Feijoada* is on the menu every Wed. and Sat. Excellent Latin American specialties are available at all times. Appetizers may dissappoint but shrimp dishes and codfish are good. So is the guava compote with white cheese. The service is as informal as the ambience. Expect to see many Brazilians eating here at lunch. Closed Sun. All major credit cards.

Cabana Carioca. 123 W. 45th St.; 581–8088. Pleasant, friendly, and anything but elegant, but the food is good and cheap by today's standards—especially the *caldo verde* (vegetable and potato soup) and shrimp dishes. Open seven days a week for lunch and dinner. Service can be erratic. All major credit cards. **Cabana Carioca II** is located at 133 W. 45th St.; 730–8375.

British

Deluxe

Bull and Bear. Lexington Ave. and 49th St.; 872–4900. It's in the Waldorf-Astoria so expect it to be expensive. Everything is à la carte at both lunch and dinner, but the menu is large and so are the portions. Specializes in steak, chops, and seafood. Open seven days a week for lunch and dinner. All major credit cards.

Cheshire Cheese. 319 W. 51st St.; 765–0616. Owned by two chaps from England, who also decorated their small pub most attractively. Small, candlelit dining room, jolly bar. Steak and kidney pie, roast beef with Yorkshire pudding, and imported Dover sole are headliners. À la carte. Closed Sunday, Monday, July, and August, and all major holidays. Convenient to theater district. Excellent service. AE, DC, MC, V.

Expensive

Charlie Brown's Ale & Chophouse. At 45th St. and Vanderbilt Ave. inside the lobby of the Pan Am Building; 661–2520. This pleasant pub, named after an old English inn, is handsome and has steak and kidney pie, mutton chops, Dover sole. Try a yard of ale here. Lunch, dinner, and after-theater à la carte. Closed Saturday and Sunday. All major credit cards.

Moderate

Angry Squire. 216 Seventh Ave.; 242–9066. Best known for the jazz duos and trios that take to the bandstand around 10 P.M. most nights, the Squire turns out respectable shepherd's pie and traditional pub fare, along with plenty of cold beer. All major credit cards.

Charley O's. 33 W. 48th St.; 582–7141. As much Dublin pub as London Tavern on an immense scale, it is one of the best restaurants in the Rockefeller Center area. The stand-up bar serves sandwiches, clams, oysters. The main dining area offers immense portions of ham, steaks, roast beef, pigs' knuckles, and more. There are branches in various other midtown locations. All major credit cards.

Cambodian

Moderate

Indochine. 430 Lafayette St., between Astor Place and W. 4th Street; 505–5111. Looks like the lobby of a Beverly Hills hotel, but the food is as much fun as the furnishings—and the crowd is a riot: East Village punks, soap stars, Off-Broadway actors, uptowners from the Public Theater across the street. Graze here. Have a soup (the shrimp with everything is hard to beat) and then ask your waiter to recommend a small assortment of specials from the impossibly long list of goodies. Drink beer or white wine. Reservations necessary. No credit cards (cash or backed-up check).

Chinese

Super Deluxe to Expensive

China Grill. 60 W. 53rd St.; 333–7788. Located in the spacious, ground-level area of the CBS Building ("Black Rock"), this new and lively spot serves the choicest, trendiest Chinese fare in town. Try grilled scallops with red peppers and ginger coulis, Beijing oysters, and "sizzling whole fish" and you'll see what we mean. AE, MC, V.

Mr. Chow. 324 E. 57th St.; 751–9030. Part of the international chain where elegance takes precedence over cuisine. A place to go for impressive trappings, not for food. Lunch weekdays, dinner daily. All major credit cards.

David K's. 1115 Third Ave.; 371–9090. The old Safari Grill has gone Oriental, and this is the place to pick if you want your Chinese food served in smart Upper East Side surroundings. Spicy chicken dumplings, lemon lobster, and "jumping shrimp" are among the winners. AE, DC.

Pearl's Chinese Restaurant. 38 W. 48th St.; 221–6677. Fairly small, with simple decor, it is a media favorite, especially with the publishing and broadcasting crowd who slurp up selections from 12 soups (the soup is almost a meal in itself). Best bets include the braised fish in sweet and sour sauce, the *moo shu* pork, and a variety of those steamed dumplings called *dim sum*. The food is filled with Cantonese nuances, from lemon chicken to pike. Closed Saturday, open for dinner only Sunday. No credit cards.

Shun Lee Palace. 155 E. 55th St.; 371–8844. Decorated in what might be called Chinese Chippendale, the main room is a quietly lit and subdued Chinese/Hollywood set made up of alcoves, quiet corners, and large spaces, with amalgam of Mandarin, Szechuan, Hunan, and Shanghai dishes. Indeed, all the Chinese classics are cooked here with finesse, from Peking duck through fried dumplings to baby spareribs. The chef will even produce Cantonese favorites on request. This branch of the Shun Lee chain is open seven days a week. CB, AE, DC. The latest branch—**Shun**

Lee West at 43 W. 65th St., opposite Lincoln Center, 595–8895, has a dim sum cafe. AE, MC, V.

Tse Yang. 34 E. 51st St.; 688–5447. A beautifully decorated if somewhat dark hideaway on the same block as the Helmsley Palace Hotel, Tse Yang ("Paris—New York—Frankfurt") offers superb dishes from various Chinese regional cuisines, including some spicy ones, though it centers on Shanghai and Peking. At lunch there is a *prix fixe* selection only, at $19.50 per person. Lunch and dinner seven days. All major credit cards.

Moderate

China Pavilion. 200 W. 57th St. near Carnegie Hall; 765–4340. Paintings, fresh flowers, fine food. All major credit cards.

Dumpling House. 207 2nd Ave. at 13th St.; 473–8557. There's only one variety of dumpling here—with a forcemeat filling—and they are *very* good, as is most of the Szechuan-dominated menu. You can even watch the chef prepare your dinner on a television monitor that hangs over the bar. At this friendly East Village restaurant, there's a very pleasant balance between the informality of most Chinese restaurants and the niceties of dining out. In other words, Chinatown-style food (with full bar) in a setting that is most relaxing. All major credit cards.

First Wok. Actually, this should read "First Woks," for there are four of these franchised restaurants serving reasonably priced Szechuan and Hunan food on the East Side: 1384 First Ave. at 74th St., 535–8598; 582 Second Ave. near 33rd St. 689–6786; 1374 Third Ave. at 68th St., 861–2000; and 1570 Third Ave. near 88th St., 410–7747. All major credit cards.

Foo Chow. 1278 Third Ave. at 74th St.; 861–4350. This Upper East Side Mandarin restaurant offers over 100 entrees, but try the *moo shoo,* a delicious dish of shrimp, meat, bamboo shoots, and vegetables wrapped in a kind of pancake. Peking duck is available within 24-hour notice. All major credit cards.

Fortune Garden. 1160 Third Ave. at 68th St.; 744–1212. Divided into two sections, a cheerful front half and a squarish second half, the restaurant captains Cantonese-style, although the dishes can be spiced up Szechuan-style upon request. The kitchen is usually successful with beef and steak dishes, turns out interesting fish dishes—espcially the whole sea bass in ginger sauce—and an excellent pork and pickled soup. The spring rolls and spareribs are exceptional. Open seven days a week. All major credit cards.

G. Fung Dynasty. 511 Lexington Ave.; 355–1200. This pleasant spot, located on the second floor of the Hotel Lexington, offers such specialties as minced squab and water chestnuts steamed in a bamboo container for six hours; just one reason to go—the very popular "Dragon and Phoenix" (lobster and chicken) is another. On Saturday and Sunday, *dim sum* at lunch can be inexpensive. The two main rooms can be noisy. AE, DC.

HSF (for Hee Seung Fung). 46 Bowery; 374–1319. Excellent *dim sum* and other small delights are passed on trays so you can have a look before selecting (wise for the novice because the delights can include such exotica as chicken feet and squid). No credit cards.

Pig Heaven. 1540 Second Ave., between 80th and 81st sts.; 744–4887 (or PIG-IT-UP). The food gets mixed notices, but most diners are so taken by the fairy tale-like all-pig environment that they barely notice. Great for kids or a small group, providing you can (a) get reservations and (b) have the reservations honored. Still, worth seeing once. All major credit cards.

Silver Palace. 50–52 Bowery; 964–1204. Billed as the largest Chinese restaurant on the East Coast, this popular place has been visited by everyone from Mayor Koch to President Carter, who come for the Cantonese specialties (and *dim sum* on weekends at Sat./Sun. brunch). All major credit cards.

Siu Lam Kung. 18 Elizabeth St. (south of Canal); 732–0974. Very crowded and noisy, but outstanding and often very unusual dishes. One of the city's best. No credit cards. Also at 499 Third Ave., between 33rd and 34th sts. All major credit cards.

Inexpensive

Most of the restaurants listed below do not have liquor licenses, so you are welcome to bring your own wine or beer. However, it is advisable to call ahead to make sure this is the case, because the situation changes as pending licenses are granted.

Chi-Mer. 11–12 Chatham Square; 267–4565. Excellent food, typically Chinatown atmosphere. One of the few places where you can get Peking duck without calling up in advance. All major credit cards.

China Bowl. 152 W. 44th St.; 582–3358. Serves most of the well-known Cantonese dishes and has moderately priced family dinners. Also American food. Pleasant surroundings and handy for theater-goers. AE, DC, CB.

Empire Szechuan Gourmet. 2574 Broadway at 97th St.; 663–6004. Exotic Chinese food cooked Szechuan and Hunan style in what is basically a storefront with red wallpaper, minimal decor, and a glass-enclosed alcove that extends onto the sidewalk. But the food—especially the shrimp, pork, and chicken dishes—make this a great favorite with both the Columbia crowd and Upper West Siders. No credit cards.

Hong Fat. 63 Mott St.; 962–9588. This little Chinatown hole-in-the-wall specializes in noodles in many different forms. Many consider this New York's best Cantonese restaurant. Open 24 hours. No credit cards.

Hunan Balcony. 2596 Broadway at 98th St.; 865–0400. If you're in the neighborhood for a service or performance at Cathedral of St. John the Divine, for jazz at the West End Cafe, or visiting Columbia or Barnard, this is the place for great, inexpensive, and well-spiced fare. Open seven days, usually to the wee hours. All major credit cards.

Hunan House. 45 Mott St., Chinatown; 962–0010. Subterranean but with two dining rooms and excellent pan-fried dumplings, orange-flavor chicken (not the usual sweet-and-sour concoction) and similar fare. You must emphasize if you want your dishes hot, though. AE, DC.

Hunan Royal. 485 Avenue of the Americas at 12th St.; 691–6061. One of the most consistent neighborhood Chinese restaurants in the city—and one that's convenient to the center of Greenwich Village. Pleasant, accommodating, and the food is reliably fresh. Open daily. All major credit cards.

Hwa Yuan Szechuan Inn. 40 East Broadway; 966–5534. A long-time favorite—and that means long, long lines at prime dining hours. The restaurant is large, though, and the lines move fast. So do the waiters. But what they bring is first-rate. Open daily. All major credit cards.

Peking Duck House Restaurant. 22 Mott St. in Chinatown; 962–8208. The house specialty—Peking duck—doesn't have to be ordered 24 hours in advance as at most places. It is priced around $25—a relative bargain because it compares favorably with the same dish at higher priced restaurants. Mayor Koch eats here and has been photographed doing so! AE.

Say Eng Look. 5 E. Broadway; 732–0796. Our Peking (Mandarin) choice is a particular favorite with those who know their way around NYC's Chinatown. The name means "4, 5, 6" and refers to a particularly fine hand in Mah Jong. You'll notice that most of the patrons are Oriental, and we consider that an expert recommendation. It is also a favorite of NYC Mayor Ed Koch. Again, the decor is unimposing, the overall space small, and the atmosphere on the noisy side. But no lack of ambience can really detract from the *moo shoo* pork, Tai-Chien Chicken, or the deep-fried fish wrapped in bean curd or seaweed. There's also a whole pork joint in an incredible brown anise sauce. The specials are the dishes to go for here. So popular has this restaurant become that they've opened a branch across the street—1-2-3—to handle the overflow. Tell your waiter if you want your meal served in courses, however, or all selections will arrive simultaneously. Beer and wine available. AE, MC, V.

Szechuan Cuisine. 33 Irving Place near Union Square (15th St., a block from Park Ave.); 982–5678. Gutsy, spicy food, where two can have a fiery meal for under $12, with choices including dried sautéed beef, kidney, ginger shrimp, and bean curd. No credit cards.

Szechuan State. 55 Chatham Square; 619–1435. Owned by the same people who formerly had the Szechuan Taste right next door. The new restaurant is brighter and modern, with essentially the same menu. More care is taken in the kitchen here, though, than at most—even when the Friday-Sunday crush is on. AE, MC, V.

Szechuan West. 2656 Broadway near 101st St.; 663–9280. One of the original Empire chefs has branched out on his own—and very well. His crispy fried flounder tops a list of virtually uptoppable hot dishes at bargain-basement prices, in a simple storefront where the grandeur is in the food. No credit cards.

Ying. 220 Columbus Ave. at 70th St.; 724–2031. Outstandingly spicy Szechuan food of unusual variety and taste—and reasonably priced. Often crowded. Near Lincoln Center. AE.

Yun Luck Rice Shoppe. 17 Doyers St.; 571–1375. The Cantonese style of cooking doesn't have the heat of the Szechuan or Hunan provinces, but that doesn't give it any less character. Possibly the most popular Cantonese restaurant in Chinatown, so go before you're absolutely ravenous—you'll have plenty of time to work up an appetite on line. Open daily. No credit cards.

Czechoslovakian

Moderate

Vasata. 339 E. 75th St.; 650–1686. Owned by the Vasata family, it has a devoted following for the crisp roast duck, chicken paprikash, and game in season. Neat, pleasant dining room and small bar. Imported wines. Complete à la carte dinner starting from 5 P.M. six days a week from Tuesday through Saturday and from noon on Sunday. All major credit cards.

French

Super Deluxe

Aurora. 60 E. 49th St., between Madison and Park aves.; 692–9292. An "in" place as soon as it opened in the mid-'80s, with outstanding classic French cuisine and a jet set-and-advertising crowd with generous expense accounts: prices are in the stratosphere. All major credit cards.

Bouley. 165 Duane St.; 608–3852. This gorgeous place (you'll think you're in a château overlooking Lake Geneva) may be on its way to becoming New York City's finest restaurant, once glitches in service and the occasional lapse in preparation are eliminated. Try the velvety butternut squash soup, the elegantly sauced oysters, the langoustines, the rack of lamb, and the venison, which is (surprise!) both rare and tender. All major credit cards.

La Caravelle. 33 W. 55th St.; 586–4252. Elegant decor, top-notch wine cellar, attentive service, the latter especially so if you are known. Closed Sunday and the month of August. All major credit cards.

La Côte Basque. 5 E. 55th St.; 688–6525. Its reputation was made by its late founder, Henri Soulé, once also of the now legendary and defunct Le Pavillon. Stunning Bernard Lamotte murals enhance a totally handsome dining room. The cuisine is classic and can be superb. The service is a model of perfection. Closed Sunday. All major credit cards.

La Grenouille. 3 E. 52nd St.; 752–1495. A sublimely beautiful setting that complements a superb kitchen. The "in" place for lunch for expense-account diners. Classic French food as good as it exists in the city. Closed Sunday and holidays. AE, DC.

Le Bernardin. 155 W. 51st St.; 489–1515. A newcomer to the ranks of New York's four-star restaurants, with prix fixe lunches at $35 and dinners at $55 (plus supplements for special items) or à la carte. This all-seafood restaurant is a sister establishment to one with the same name in Paris, the New York version catering to business clientele. Excellent for discreet, formal conversation as well as for first class dining. Reservations required. All major credit cards.

Le Chantilly. 106 E. 57th St.; 751–2931. Large, stately, classical, and pretentious, but you can tell *toute le monde* it delivers when it comes to fish, lamb, veal, and desserts. Indeed, from soup to nuts, it is hard to beat—but at those prices, it should be. Open Monday to Saturday for lunch and dinner, closed Sunday. All major credit cards.

Le Cirque. 58 E. 65th St.; 794–9292. Plush, haute cuisine restaurant with animals painted as humans in interesting circusy mural. Offers excellent service and meals to match from a menu that draws the beautiful people. The cognoscenti order a traditional yet offbeat specialty (traditionally not listed on the menu) of spaghetti primavera—one of the city's better versions of this trendy dish. The restaurant is located in the Mayfair Hotel. It is closed Sun. AE, DC, CB.

Le Cygne. 55 E. 54th St.; 759–5941. This is the best of the newer restaurants spawned by La Caravelle. Its imaginative and well-executed dishes include an unusual appetizer of mussels in mustard sauce and whole braised pigeon. The desserts, too, are excellent. The atmosphere can be somewhat stuffy. Closed Sunday and month of August. All major credit cards.

Lutèce. 249 E. 50th St.; 752–2225. Probably the most ambitious and elaborate French food served in the United States. And almost as important, the pinnacle of perfection that has been achieved has not engendered the sort of pompous rudeness that is so much a part of the scene at other New York restaurants of this genre. The staff is almost uniformly pleasant, and aids immeasurably the consummate enjoyment of a unique dinner. The setting, in a former townhouse, is intimate and exquisite. If you only have the time (or budget) for one foray into fine French gastronomy, let us recommend Lutèce. Closed Saturday during the summer, closed Sunday throughout the year. AE, CB, DC, V.

The Quilted Giraffe. 550 Madison Ave. (in AT&T Building at 56th St.); 593–1221. The name is whimsical and its reputation is rather forbidding (reservations are *very* difficult to come by), but this is one of NYC's very few four-star restaurants. Dining here, in what feels like an elegant high-tech salon, is an *event,* and you should give it the better part of an evening—don't try to rush off to the theater or a concert. Some of Barry and Susan Wine's sublime concoctions include caviar beggar's purses, lobster with basil and fennel, and hot chocolate soufflé with ice cream. Worth every one of the pretty pennies you will spend. All major credit cards.

Restaurant Raphael. 33 W. 54th St.; 582–8993. Considered by many to be the best argument for the *nouvelle cuisine.* Raphael hides behind elegantly understated doors, and is strictly by reservation only. Closed Saturday and Sunday. Also closed the month of August. All major credit cards.

Deluxe

Chanterelle. 89 Grand St. in SoHo; 966–6960. Don't let the location—a seemingly deserted warehouse corner in SoHo—scare you off, because Chantarelle is celebrated as one of the most adventurous and interesting of *nouvelle cuisine* haunts—even if some of the more experimental taste combinations don't always work. Fixed-price meals (one, a tasting menu, has nine courses!) are served at ten tables in a spare but elegant room under a high, pressed tin ceiling. The staff is both helpful and unobtrusive, and the ambience is one of the quiet refinement. Dinner only Tuesdays through Saturdays. Reservations are very hard to come by, but persevere. AE, MC, V.

Le Coq d'Or. 5 Mitchell Pl. (just off First Ave. at 49th St.); 826–1084. Formerly La Petite Ferme, this quietly elegant restaurant in the UN's backyard has already made a name for itself with dishes like a smoky grilled-fish salad, grilled salmon on a bed of vegetables, and a succulent navarin of lamb. All major credit cards.

La Colombe d'Or. 134 E. 26th St.; 689–0666. Informal country atmosphere in a small establishment featuring *bouillabaisse, cassoulet,* and other Provençal specialties. The chairs are killers. Dinner only Saturday. Closed Sunday. AE, DC, MC, V.

Hubert's. Park Ave. and 63rd St.; 826–5911. This nomadic restaurant has moved again (their fourth location!), and the good news is that Hubert's is bigger (the place) and better (the food) than ever. AE, MC, V.

La Petite Ferme. 973 Lexington Ave. at 70th St.; 249–3272. The owner/chef is the scion of Burgundian restaurateurs and hoteliers, and the food is simple and well-prepared. Reserve well ahead for a table at what looks like a prosperous farmhouse with a garden to boot. Lunch and dinner, Monday-Saturday, dinner Sunday. All major credit cards.

La Tulipe. 104 W. 13th St.; 691–8860. Housed in the street level of a brownstone on a tree-lined Greenwich Village block overflowing with Continental restaurants. This rather small, trendy place, however, surprises with its emphasis on good *nouvelle cuisine.* Try the foie gras, rack of lamb, and dessert soufflé. Dinner Tuesday through Sunday. All major credit cards.

Lafayette. 65 E. 56th St., in Drake Hotel; 832–1565. Plush, handsome, subdued new four-star restaurant specializing in the imaginative seafood dishes of Louis Outhier (of l'Oasis fame on the French Riviera). Crayfish/salmon mousse/oysters appetizer is pure heaven, and the John Dory fish in a sweet wine sauce is close to divinity. Desserts are dazzling, and the waiter will bring a number to your table to tempt you—and you'll lose! Since Lafayette is Swiss-run, try a Swiss wine. Reservations required. All major credit cards.

Laurent. 111 E. 56th St.; 753–2729. Grand food in the grand French style of *haute cuisine,* with prices to match. All major credit cards.

Maurice. 118 W. 57th St.; in the Parker Meridien Hotel; 245–7788. The first of the new wave of great hotel restaurants and still one of the finest. The stately high-ceilinged room is gorgeously appointed and decorated, and fresh flowers are everywhere. A favorite meal, unsurpassed anywhere in New York: scallop-stuffed ravioli, firm yet tender Dover sole; an unbelievably rich lemon tart with raspberry puree. Reservations generally necessary. All major credit cards.

Melrose. 48 Barrow St. (west of Seventh Ave. just below Sheridan Sq.); 691–6800. This lovely Greenwich Village hideaway is one of the hottest new spots in town, and its California-French cuisine is memorable. First-timers must have the oysters in curry cream followed by the grilled chicken in a choice of several sauces. Sit in either the cozy front room or the lively enclosed garden. All major credit cards.

Montrachet. 239 West Broadway (in TriBeCa, near White St., just below Canal); 219–2777. Difficult for outsiders to find, but a gastronomical Nirvana rewards the diligent! Owner Drew Nieporent and his personable staff are perfect hosts—warm and hospitable to everyone—and the kitchen's creations are inspired. Start with vegetable and chevre terrine or parsley soup with belon oysters, proceed to succulent roast duck or rack of lamb, and end with the incomparable crème brûlée or twin soufflés with ice cream. Let Drew select your wines; just tell him what you like and how much you wish to spend; he's very perceptive. The mayor sits up front in the bar area at the round table, but you'll be happy in any of the three spare but tastefully decorated rooms. A place to savor again and again! Now open for lunch Fridays as well as for dinners Mondays through Saturdays. AE.

Le Périgord. 405 E. 52nd St.; 755–6244. One of the finest midtown restaurants. *Gratin de langoustines*—crayfish in a cheese sauce—is one of the specialties on the varied menu. Closed Sunday, dinner only Sat. All major credit cards.

Raoul's. 180 Prince St. in SoHo; 966–3518. The spirit of a genuine French bistro despite the neon beer signs in the window and the falling-apart-at-the-seams decor (that contrasts sharply with the high prices). Friendly place where you can eat at the bar or at tables in the bar. A lovely enclosed garden area has been added in the back. Dinner only. No DC, CB.

The Terrace. 400 W. 119th St. and Morningside Drive; 666–9490. On the top of Columbia University's Butler Hall, very good view of New York skyline, with good food and (usually) live chamber music. Good place for a romantic dinner. Lunch Tuesdays through Fridays, dinner Tuesdays through Saturdays. All major credit cards.

Expensive

The Black Sheep. 344 W. 11th St.; 242–1010. Everyone's idea of that perfect little West Village hideaway, with brick walls, soft lighting, flowers and hanging plants, and cheerful young waiters. The complete dinner consists of crudités and hard-boiled eggs with aioli dip, soup, pâté, entree, salad, dessert, and coffee—so go when starved! Fine (and reasonable) wine list, with daily specials. Ten percent off bill if you pay cash. All major credit cards.

Café des Artistes. 1 W. 67th St.; 877–3500. Amusing 1930s decor and famous Howard Chandler Christy murals on the wall may transport you to another time and place, though the food is at its best when most simply prepared. Try the duckling with pear, the gravlax, or the desserts bearing not too-fancy names. Reserve days ahead for dinner, but this restaurant has lots of regulars, so don't be surprised if even then you have to wait. However, no one will raise so much as an eyebrow if all you want is an appetizer and a salad—which often suffices here—or if you'd care to eat at the small but cozy back-room bar. Open seven days a week, with brunch on weekends. All major credit cards.

Café 58. 232 E. 58th St.; 758–5665. On a street lined with overpriced, overpublicized restaurant, this one stands out for its quiet value. A classic bistro offering blood sausage, pâtés, brains, and other "traditional" favorites, Café 58 also features daily *prixe fixe* dinners that can help you keep the final bill to under $30 per person and satisfy your hunger more than admirably. All major credit cards.

Cafe Loup. 18 East 13th St.; 255–4746. Charming, tiny neighborhood French bistro with wood tables, chalkboard menu and much French spoken by the regulars. Fresh fish and seafood are the specialties, though there are the requisite grilled meats. Closed Sundays; lunch and dinner weekdays, dinner only on Saturdays. All major credit cards.

Café Luxembourg. 200 W. 70th St.; 873–7411. Bubbling with high spirits, this chic art deco bistro (the best restaurant on the Upper West Side) serves superb dinners, suppers, and weekend brunches to a celebrity-studded crowd of beautiful people, rockers, punks, music lovers (the Metropolitan Opera's James Levine is a regular), and neighborhood achievers—all of whom dote on the tasty pastas, pâtés, fish and chicken specials, liver (with macadamia nuts, yet!), and an irresistible lemon tart. Wild and crazy at dinner; better at late supper (but never relaxed). Probably the most imaginative Sunday brunch in town. AE, MC, V.

Jean Lafitte. 68 W. 58th St.; 751–2323. Stylish and Parisian, this popular midtown restaurant is both a business and celebrity hangout. Everything's fine, but be adventurous and order the fresh oysters and steak tartare. Tarte tatin, with clouds of whipped cream, is a perfect finish. Daily, noon to 12:30 A.M. All major credit cards.

La Grillade. 845 Eighth Ave. near 51st St.; 265–1610. Its owners are all from Brittany, assuring authenticity in their many Breton dishes. The duck, as well as the roast lamb with flageolets, are especially good. Friendly service. Lunch and dinner daily. All major credit cards.

La Petite Auberge. 116 Lexington Ave. at 28th St.; 689–5003. Pleasant inn-like surroundings. Standard bourgeoise cuisine, but good; nice specials. The management came from the nearby Mon Paris. AE, DC.

Le Cheval Blanc. 145 E. 45th St.; 599–8886. The food is excellent at this family-run restaurant, and its bargain status at lunch generates quite a crowd. It's best, therefore, to sample the fare at odd hours. Charming back room. Must reserve. Be prompt, with no one missing from your party. Not so much of a bargain at dinner. Closed Sunday, most holidays. All major credit cards.

Le Vert Galant. 109 W. 46th St.; 382–0022. Very friendly, unhurried service in an elegant setting. Divine cheesecake, tender veal *piccata* and other house specials. Closed Sunday. All major credit cards.

Les Pyrénées. 251 W. 51st St.; 246–0044. Has a pleasant Gallic atmosphere and serves provincial French food. Though the menu is familiar, *quiche Lorraine* and ham in aspic are worth trying. A good choice for theater-goers. Closed Sunday. All major credit cards.

Mon Paris. 111 E. 29th St.; 683–4255. Small, unpretentious, and popular. Serves that relative rarity these days: unabashed *cuisine bourgeoise*. Closed Sunday. All major credit cards.

Paris Commune. 411 Bleecker St.; 929–0509. While the food here is always reliably good, the single most distinctive aspect of this restaurant is that it serves a superior breakfast daily (except Monday, when it is closed all day) beginning at 8 A.M. That fact is part of why the Paris Commune is also a throwback to what Greenwich Village was in its heyday—nothing fancy, slightly artsy, a hangout, cooking a touch out of the ordinary, and reasonably priced. You don't find that combination often for lunch or dinner. And certainly not for breakfast, be it romance or business you're conducting. AE, MC, V.

Quatorze. 240 W. 14th Street, between Seventh and Eighth aves.; 206–7006. Of the string of new French bistros in town, this is probably the most stylish, from the red entrance with gold lettering to the posters on the walls. Not a spot for lingering—it's too noisy and crowded—but fine for just about any other mood. All major credit cards.

Moderate

Crêpe Suzette. 363 W. 46th St.; 581–9717 or 974–9002. A little bistro that couldn't be plainer, but the food is well-prepared and portions ample. Breton crêpes are a specialty. Tiny bar, small wine list. Dinner only on Sunday. All major credit cards.

La Biarritz. 325 W. 57th St.; 757–2390. An unprepossessing restaurant with copper cookware on the walls and fresh flowers at each table, and where the kitchen turns out excellent salads, gigot and seafood. The seafood-stuffed crêpe Biarritz is superb. Closed Sunday, dinner Saturday from 5 P.M. AE, DC, V.

Le Café de la Gare. 143 Perry Street; 242–3553. The cassoulet is authentic, piping hot with a wonderfully fragrant garlic sausage, as is the general bistro atmosphere in this tiny (maybe a dozen tables) storefront. Bring your own wine and settle in for a most relaxing evening topped off with a fresh fruit tart. No credit cards.

Marie Michelle. 57 W. 56th St.; 315–2444. Your hostess is the eponymous Marie Michelle, and she is dazzling. She is determined that you will have a good time and a fine meal—and you will. Everything is fine, but the soups and salads are outstanding, as is the orange-flavored chocolate mousse in a pool of sculpted crême anglaise. Reservations. All major credit cards.

Mme. Romaine de Lyon. 29 E. 61st St.; 758–2422. Would you believe 500 different kinds of omelettes? Also fine salads and fresh croissants. Open Tuesday–Friday, 11 A.M.–8 P.M.; Saturday–Monday, 11 A.M.–3 P.M. Closed last two weeks of July. All credit cards with $30 minimum.

The Odeon. 145 West Broadway at Thomas St.; 233–0507. Still downtown's hottest, busiest, most exciting restaurant/bistro, even though Chef Patrick Clark has departed to establish his own Upper East Side place. Go for lunch (quiet), brunch (almost as quiet), dinner (bustling), or late supper (wild) to savor either simple bistro fare or an elaborate meal. The house white and house red wines are great buys. Some drop by just to cruise the lively bar. AE, V.

Le Parisien. 1004 2nd Ave. at 53rd St.; 355–0950. Simple, unpretentious, and very pleasantly French, popular among the young business set for lunch, afterwork drinks, and late-evening suppers. Broiled entrées work best, topped with light sauces and accompanied by invariably excellent potatoes. All major credit cards.

Pierre Au Tunnel. 250 W. 47th St.; 575–1220. Has unusual decor resembling an actual tunnel. It's small and unpretentious, and has the familiar French menu with different specialties added each day. Good choice when heading to the theater. Closed Sunday. AE.

Succes La Côte Basque. 1032 Lexington Ave. (Upper East Side); 535–3311. Light luncheon fare delicately prepared. Pâtés, salads, and the like—along with outstanding baked goods. AE, DC.

Au Trouquet. 328 W. 12th St., between Ninth and Tenth aves.; 924–3413. An out-of-the-way "find" tucked in among the meat packing houses. A well-prepared bistro menu and very friendly, to boot. No credit cards.

German

Moderate

Café Geiger. 206 E. 86th St.; 734–4428. A retail bakery in front. Continental-style café and restaurant in back. All major credit cards.

Harvey's Chelsea Restaurant. 108 W. 18th St.; 243–5644. The look of a Victorian mansion, but the specialties of the house lean toward sauerbraten, knockwurst, and the like. There's nothing exciting about the preparation but reliability is the key reason why reservations are almost always necessary at this otherwise "local" establishment. Very pleasant for brunch. AE.

Kleine Konditorei. 234 E. 86th St.; 737–7130. Simple, homey dinner with everything from steak smothered in fried onions to different veal schnitzels ordered à la carte or as a dinner. Huge portions come adorned with several side dishes; friendly, informal service. AE, DC.

Inexpensive

Ideal Lunch and Bar. 238 E. 86th St.; 535–0950. While this place looks like a shoe-repair shop converted to a lunch counter, it is by far the best food bargain on the Upper East Side "Since 1932." No credit cards.

Greek

Moderate

Avegerinos. Citicorp Building, Lexington Ave. at 54th St.; 688–8828. A bit overpriced when compared to what you get elsewhere for the same money, but the setting is far more pleasant than at most Greek restaurants, and the service is attentive and unhurried. Pre- and after-theater menu. All major credit cards.

Cafe Greco. 1390 Second Ave., between 71st and 72nd sts.; 737–4300. The name is deceptive, for this relatively new, comfortable, and informal restaurant features not only Greek food, but the cuisines of other Mediterranean countries as well, including France, Italy, and Morocco. Especially favored are swordfish with rosemary mayonnaise, grilled halibut, and roast chicken with couscous. Reservations suggested. All major credit cards.

Estia. 308 E. 86th St.; 628–9100. One of the best and most authentic. Fresh and simple Greek food, live music at 10:30 or so. All major credit cards.

Inexpensive

Delphi. 109 W. Broadway; 227–6322. The turnover here from noon to mid-night is such that with the exception of casserole dishes, everything is prepared to order. Exceptionally friendly, and a little out of the way (except perhaps for those at the World Trade Center), Delphi is the sort of place those who know return to again and again. No credit cards.

Z. 117 E. 15th St.; 254–0960. You might begin with the cheese-and-spinach appetizer—*spanakopita*—which is excellent at this pleasant, unassuming Greek restaurant where everything is served à la carte. The salads are superbly fresh and the lamb typically well prepared. Sandwiches, too, are offered and, weather permitting, there is dining in the garden. It happens also to be a favorite among budget-watching gourmands. AE.

Hawaiian

Moderate

Hawaii-Kai. 1638 Broadway near 50th St.; 757–0900. Polynesian, Chinese, American cuisine in touristy South Sea setting. All major credit cards.

Hungarian

Moderate

Csarda. 1477 Second Ave. near 77th St.; 472–2892. Bright, clean, uncluttered, with good food served tavern-style. Lunch Saturday and Sunday only; dinner seven days a week. AE.

Green Tree. 1034 Amsterdam Ave. at 111th St.; 864–9106. Hungarian food with a Columbian accent—Columbia University, that is—is served at this family-style place where the decor is virtually nonexistent but the meals are substantial. If you are looking for home-style chicken *paprikàs,* stuffed cabbage, or noodles stop by—but never on Sunday, when it is closed. No credit cards.

Red Tulip. 439 E. 75th St.; 734–4893. Small, simply decorated, crowded, and offering live music with dinner, this is a good spot for stuffed cabbage, chicken, varied paprika dishes and strudel. Closed Monday and Tuesday. AE

Inexpensive

Magic Pan. 149 E. 57th St.; 371–3266. Both Hungarian and French crêpes served. Soup, salad, and steak kebab are also available. Lunch is liable to be crowded but the dinner hour is much quieter. AE, V, MC.

Indian/Bangladesh

Expensive

Mogul 57. 327 W. 57th St. (between 8th and 9th aves.), 581–1774. Elegant cuisine to match the elegant atmosphere. Within walking distance of Lincoln Center, Carnegie Hall, upper Broadway-area theaters. Pre- and post-theater menus. All major credit cards.

Nirvana. 30 Central Park South; 486–5700; also at 1 Times Square, 486–6868. The view from this penthouse restaurant overlooking Central Park is nothing short of spectacular. The window tables are romantic beyond belief but all are set beneath *shamianas,* multicolored tents, where you can feast on Indo-Bengali delights including tandoori and curries. The fare is likely to be no less spicy than the place is colorful so beware if yours is a tender palate. Unfortunately, spicy or not, the food is not up to the surroundings. All major credit cards. A second branch has the peculiar distinction of overlooking Times Square. While the view might sound noteworthy, it is easy (and you'll likely want) to ignore it in favor of the draped ceiling, the Indian artifacts, and the heavenly aroma of curry spices. The fixed-price luncheon menu is reasonable; at dinner, even ordering a set meal, you're paying more for the location than the food. Still, convenience and the odd juxtaposition of settings are alone worth a visit when headed to the theater. All major credit cards.

Raga. 57 W. 48th St.; 757–3450. One of the most beautifully decorated Indian restaurants in America, occupying the site of the old Forum of the Twelve Caesars. Most well-known Indian specialties, including a superb assortment of breads, stuffed or otherwise. Ancient musical instruments are part of the decorative charm. Live Indian music some evenings. All major credit cards.

Shezan. 8 W. 58th St.; 371–1414. Lots of mirrors, chrome, glass bricks, and carpeted walls (from the designers who created the Four Seasons) meet you when you descend a flight of steps at the New York address for this famed London and Indian mini-chain. The food is uneven—too often prepared ahead and heated upon your arrival—but if you make your wishes known, the Pakistani-Indian cuisine will come out first-rate. Waiters will also gladly oblige to help you order and share the likes of the shrimp and vegetable curries, tandoori chicken, and lamb kebabs. Closed Sunday. Dinner only on Saturday. All major credit cards.

Tandoor. 40 E. 49th St.; 752–3334. Both pre- and after-theater menus are offered in this Indian restaurant—even though the curries are toned down to suit the American taste. Try the tandoori chicken, Indian breads, *pakhoras* (vegetable fritters), and *samosas* (sweetened pastries). Lunch features an economical buffet. All major credit cards.

Moderate

Akbar India. 475 Park Ave. at 58th St.; 838–1717. Tandoor (clay-oven) items are featured at this attractive restaurant serving food from the northern part of the country. They tone down the spiciness to suit the American palate but will spice the dishes up upon request. A mixed plate offers opportunity to sample a little bit of everything. Open seven days a week, dinner only on Sunday. All major credit cards.

Annapurna. 108 Lexington Ave. at 28th St.; 679–1284. A quiet, gracious restaurant serving a variety of authentic Indian dishes with chicken as a specialty. Major credit cards.

Bombay Palace. 30 W. 52nd St.; 541–7777. A large midtown restaurant quite popular with Indian businesspeople. There is a buffet lunch available as well as à la carte dishes. All major credit cards.

Indian Oven. 285 Columbus Ave., 362–7567; and **Indian Oven II,** 913 Broadway at 20th St., 460–5744. Northern Indian tandoori specialties: tandoori chicken, shrimp kabobs, biryanis. All major credit cards.

Shalimar of India. 39 E. 29th St.; 889–1977. A wide selection of Indian cuisine ranges from hot curries *(vindaloo)* to mild cream-style curry *(murghum masala),* from *mulligatawny,* a curried chicken soup, to a delicately flavored coconut soup. And the Indian breads are excellent. All major credit cards.

Inexpensive

Darbar. 44 W. 56th St., 432–7227. One of the city's best, with a buffet lunch that is a particularly good value. Good service (which can be a serious problem at other fine Indian restaurants) as well as outstanding cooking. All major credit cards.

India Pavilion. 325 E. 54th St.; 223–9740, and 240 W. 56th St.; 489–0035. The downstairs East Side original has all the ambience of a subway car but offers attentive service; the newer West Side location, just behind Carnegie Hall, is bright and attractive—but getting served has been a problem since the first week it opened. Nonetheless, the crisply fried vegetable appetizers, the curries, the tandoori specialties, and several unusual duck dishes are uniformly outstanding. Suggestion: Order one full meal and just one extra main dish for two people—portions are more than ample. Closed Sundays. All major credit cards.

Mitali. 334 E. 6th St.; 533–2508. One of about a dozen small, family-run Indian restaurants on the block (there are many more on First and Second aves.), with excellent curries, typically ethnic decor and recorded music, and friendly, attentive service. AE, MC, V.

Mughlai. 320 Columbus Ave., at 75th St., 724–6363. More expensive than the 6th St. Indian restaurants. Still, the food is rich in fragrance and flavor, and the setting is pretty, with window seats perfect for watching the action on Columbus. All major credit cards.

There are a number of very inexpensive but—for the price—quite good Indian fast-food shops on or around Lexington Ave. from 26th St. to 29th St., in "Little India." While some of them are quite shabby-looking, don't be put off, as they offer some of the best food bargains in Manhattan, among them **Shaheen Sweets** at 99 Lexington Ave. at 27th St.; 683–2139.

Irish

Moderate

Eamonn Doran. 988 Second Ave. near 53rd St.; 752–8088. Muzaked and carpeted, an Irish pub gone Continental. Exhaustive list of imported beers, pleasant food, good service. All major credit cards.

Tommy Makem's Irish Pavilion. 130 E. 57th St.; 759–9040. Folksinger Tommy Makem has taken over the Pavilion, gutted it, and decorated it with the work of contemporary Irish artist Jim Fitzpatrick and a gallery of portraits of famous Irish literary figures. The food is on the bland and overcooked side, and the menu is slim on Irish fare—but the draught beers are excellent and the ambience is warm indeed. Shows by Irish folk musicians and those of other nationalities are presented most nights at 9 and midnight. All major credit cards.

Landmark Tavern. 626 Eleventh Ave. near 46th St.; 757–8595. With a pot-bellied stove and mahogany bar, this century-old tavern offers charm and an unpretentious bill of fare. Dine heartily on homemade soda bread, shepherd's pie, and Irish potato soup. On the *far* West Side near the docks—take a cab. AE.

Inexpensive

Costello's. 225 E. 44th St.; 599–9614. Renowned with the newspaper crowd for good food, conversation. (This is a new location for the famous old joint with the Thurber murals.) All major credit cards.

Limerick's. 573 Second Ave. near 32nd St.; 683–4686. Brick walls and decor that might best be described as Irish miscellaneous make this an American idea of a typical Irish pub. But they do feature corned beef and cabbage and authentic Irish soda bread. Open seven days for lunch and dinner. All major credit cards.

Londonderry Pub. 134 W. 51st St.; 974–9077. Hearty pub atmosphere. All major credit cards.

McBell's. 359 Sixth Ave. near W. 4th St., in the Village; 675–6260. Red-checkered tablecloths, brick walls, and antique lights make this not quite Dublin but more than just another Irish pub, especially if you stick to the simple fare such as Irish ham and bacon and stew served in a congenial atmosphere. Rich soups and great burgers, too. No credit cards.

McSorley's Old Ale House. 15 E. Seventh St. near Third Ave.; 473–9148. One of New York's oldest landmarks, a drinking and dining institution for over 125 years. In the 1970s women were permitted to enter. Dormitory-style rowdy in the extreme. Fine ales on draft. No credit cards.

Rosie O'Grady's. 800 7th Ave. at 52nd St.; 582–2975. Irish and Continental specialties with kitchen open 'til 2 A.M., music seven nights. All major credit cards.

Italian

Deluxe

Barbetta. 321 W. 46th St. in the theater district; 246–9171. The most luxurious of the Italian restaurants, with its 18th-century furnishings and gorgeous crystal chandelier. Northern Italian cuisine, from the Piedmont area, can be sublime (and can be very expensive). Among the incredibly delicious dishes are *pasta al pesto* (redolent with fresh basil), lightly broiled fish dishes, veal in lemon-butter sauce, *vitello tonnato* (sliced veal with tuna/caper sauce), *zuppa inglese* (literally English soup but an Italian custard/cake combination), and the richest chocolate mousse in the world. A beautiful bar/lounge for waiting, and do request the charming outdoor garden, with splashing fountain, if the weather is fine. Closed Sundays. Major credit cards.

Canastel's. 19th St. and Park Ave. South; 677–9622. This is a picture postcard of a place, with pink lights (spectacular at night but pretty even in the daylight), giant flower arrangements, spacious tables set far apart. Serving several hundred diners at a sitting in the heart of the new advertising and publishing district, the oversize menu offers scores of choices that are almost surprisingly well prepared (given the number of meals that must be turned out). A pasta here will run $15–25 so be forewarned, though meat and fish dishes are in the same range. All major credit cards.

Erminia. 250 E. 83 St., 879–4284. With a mere dozen tables, Erminia is best for twosomes—four at most. Meats are seared on an open wood fire while pastas are exceptional and original. A mite haughty (espresso only at dessert, no exceptions) but the food is first-rate. Reservations absolutely necessary, as is cash; no credit cards, no checks.

Giambelli Madison. 238 Madison Ave. near 37th St.; 685–8727. The food is Northern Italian, delicate, refined, cooked with butter instead of olive oil, and light on garlic and tomatoes. The result is excellent pastas. Closed Sunday, and during the summer months. Sat. as well. All major credit cards.

Giambelli Fiftieth. 46 E. 50th St.; 688–2760. Good veal, fish, and pastas—but as expensive as the restaurant is ornate. Yet this Giambelli's is so big with visiting Italian dignitaries and brass from Italy's tourism office, so they must be doing something right. Closed Sun. All major credit cards.

Girafe. 208 E. 58th St.; 752–3054. On two levels, connected by a long-thin spiral staircase so it resembles its namesake, this restaurant provides a supper-club setting for savory pastas, especially the fettucine and carbonara. Closed Sunday. All major credit cards.

Nanni Al Valletto. 133 E. 61st St.; 838–3939. An offshoot of the excellent original Nanni's at 146 E. 46th St. (697–4161), and somehow Nanni manages to keep on top of both places—but Il Valletto is much the posher of the two and less noisy (and with less character). Closed Sunday. All major credit cards.

Orsini's. 26 E. 63rd St.; 644–3700. The fashionable restaurant on W. 56th St. has moved to Quo Vadis's elegant former home, and the food is now as classic as its surroundings. For example: *bresaola* (dried, salted beef over greens), pappardelle noodles in porcini mushroom sauce, and superb risottos. AE, MC, V.

Palio. 151 W. 51st St. (in new Equitable Center complex); 245–4850. By far the most elegant, most sophisticated of the new North Italian restaurants. Ground-floor bar area contains Sandro Chia's spectacular mural of the famous Siena horse race, and the upstairs dining room (spare and sophisticated—almost Japanese in feeling) serves such delicacies as ricotta dumplings with truffles, risotto with quail, and freshly made gelato. If you ask, Tony May, your suave host, will guide you to other delicacies. All major credit cards.

Parioli Parioli, Romanissimo. 24 East 81st St.; 288–2391. Small, gaudy, exhorbitant but terrific cannelloni and tortellini. Closed Sundays and Monday. AE, DC.

Pietro's. 232 E. 43rd St.; 682–9760. The steaks and seafood here are as good as in any house and the Italian dishes also rank with the best. AE.

Remi. 323 E. 79th St.; 744–4272. New, sleek, smart, and chic. A Venetian-flavored place (the name means oars) with superb pastas, risottos, and small, light *gnocchi* (potato dumplings). AE, MC, V.

Romeo Salta. 30 W. 56th St.; 246–5772. This remarkable restaurant in a spacious former mansion is handsomely decorated. The extraordinary pastas are conscientiously prepared and the veal Villa d'Este with eggplant is outstanding. A large menu offers a wide choice of carefully prepared and attentively served dishes. Closed Sunday. All major credit cards.

San Marco. 36 W. 52nd St.; 246–5340. Northern Italian cuisine in a small, smart room decorated with a display of wines. Veal and chicken dishes and made-at-the-table *zabaglione* are special, as are the sweetbreads in white wine. Closed Sunday. All major credit cards.

SPQR. 133 Mulberry St.; 925–3120. Elegant but hardly understated turn-of-the-century dining room in the heart of Little Italy, where classic Northern and Southern Italian cuisine is served for lunch and dinner. Initials stand for *Senatus Populus Que Romanus* (the senate and people of Rome). Valet parking for dinner. All major credit cards.

Toscana Ristorante. 200 E. 54th St. (in the controversial "Lipstick Building"); 371–8144. A marvel of ultramodern, northern Italian design serving such delicate Tuscan dishes as cheese-filled ravioli, angel-hair pasta with a basil-flavored tomato sauce, and spinach fettucine with scallops. All major credit cards.

Tre Scalini. 230 E. 58th St.; 688–6888. The mural of the Piazza Navona makes you feel as though you were in Rome, the pastas makes you think you *are* there. It is a flashy dining room for Northern Italian cuisine that could hold its own on the Via Veneto. Closed Sun. All major credit cards.

Expensive

Amalfi. 16 E. 48th St.; 758–5110. Established 1927 and as Italian as the Amalfi Drive. All major credit cards.

Antolotti's. 337 E. 49th St.; 688–6767. Established in 1950 and improving with age. A conventional Northern Italian menu, generally well prepared. Good and friendly service. Superb veal parmigiana. No lunch Sat. and Sun. All major credit cards.

Bruno. 240 E. 58th St.; 688–4190. Simple modern dining room with a country atmosphere—and outstanding pastas, from linguine matriciana with tomato sauce, prosciutto and onion, to trenette in pesto (basil) sauce. Dinner only Saturday, closed Sunday. All major credit cards.

Capriccio Ristorante. 33 E. 61st St.; 759–6684. Family operated, featuring fuzi Angela—a flat pasta that is chief among the many pasta specialties. Closed Sunday, no lunch Saturday. All major credit cards.

Cent'anni. 50 Carmine St. in the Village, off Bleecker St.; 989–9494. A storefront restaurant, with tasteful, minimalist/modern decor. Because the restaurant is so hospitable and the host so gracious, no one wants to leave and so you may have to wait at the door or the stand-up bar, even with a reservation. Florentine cooking—a rare cuisine in these parts—makes up for all. Light and fragrant is the best general description, with fish and veal the main features on the menu. And do ask for the pasta combination plate to start. Dinner only. AE.

Da Silvano. 260 Sixth Ave. south of Bleecker in the Village; 982–2343. Smartly trim storefront with excellent pasta dishes, from quill-cut penne in a Bolognese sauce to tortellini with a spicy meat filling. Reserve. Dining out front in good weather. AE.

Eleonora Ristorante. 117 W. 58th St.; 765–1427. Northern Italian cuisine in a lavish theatrical setting celebrating the great Duse. After-theater suppers a specialty. Closed Sunday. All major credit cards.

Gian Marino. 221 E. 58th St.; 752–1696. Fair food from six provinces of Italy; popular among show-business folk. Closed Monday. All major credit cards.

Gino's. 780 Lexington Ave. near 61st St.; 223–9658. The food is good, though hardly extraordinary, yet this restaurant is very fashionable for models, fashion buyers, photographers, and their camp followers. Being seen is obviously more important than the quality of the cuisine. No reservations. No credit cards.

Giordano's. 409 W. 39th St.; 947–9811. Northern Italian cuisine served in a supremely refined setting, with romantic alcoves for when the occasion demands, or a lone terrace table for when spring arrives (though the air here, given the restaurant's proximity to the Lincoln Tunnel, is particularly noxious). The pastas and veal come most highly recommended. All major credit cards.

Grotto Azzurra. 387 Broome St.; 925–8775. One of the most popular Little Italy haunts, though some are put off by the prices relative to the simplicity of the décor and the sawdust on the floor. Still, the food is superior, though the best time to go is on a weeknight, when neither the kitchen nor the diners are quite so rushed. No credit cards.

Il Cantinori. 32 E. 10th St.; 673–6044. A Village version of the pricey Upper East Side northern Italian restaurants with fancy pastas in the $9–$15 range and meat and fish entrees about $20. All major credit cards.

Il Monello. 1460 Second Ave. near 77th St.; 535–9310. A restful setting for some of the best pasta on the East Side, especially the green lasagne, tortellini, and thin pasta strands in a Bolognese meat sauce. Closed Sunday. All major credit cards.

Il Mulino. 86 W. 3rd St. (in the Village); 673–3783. Not on the busiest thoroughfare, but one of the best Italian restaurants in the city. Great pastas—especially the mildly spicy ones—and unusual wine labels. The daily specials are truly special. A very European atmopshere. Closed Sundays. AE.

Il Nido. 251 E. 53rd St.; 753–8450. A stylish and currently very fashionable restaurant with provincial overtones—and some of the best ravioli and fettucine this side of Tuscany. The back room is noisy. Closed Sunday. All major credit cards.

Il Pescatore Veneto. 56 W. 56th St.; 586–7812. This restaurant does not, as you would expect from the name, specialize in seafood—nor even Venetian cuisine. Instead, this is a solid but middle-of-the-road Northern Italian place on the 56th Street restaurant row. Very comfortable and unthreatening. Closed Saturday lunch and Sunday; also, no Saturday dinner in summer. AE, V.

Il Tinello. 16 W. 56th St.; 245–4388. As comfortable as a living room, Il Tinello (the little room) is a refreshing respite from bustling midtown Fifth Avenue, a few steps away. Proprietor Mario Fabris knows how to make you feel at home, too, in this elegantly appointed dining room, which offers a fine balance between northern and southern Italian cuisine. Try the *tre colore* (three-color) pasta or the saltimbocca Florentine. Closed Sundays. All major credit cards.

Isle of Capri. 1028 Third Ave. near 61st St.; 223–9430. Generally acknowledged as one of the best Italian restaurants in the city, though it can be very uneven. A "trattoria"-style operation where the food's the thing. Sidewalk café. Closed Sunday. All major credit cards.

Italian Pavilion Café. 24 W. 55th St.; 586–5950. An old reliable, a favorite for midtown business lunches. Closed Sunday. All major credit cards.

La Strada East. 274 Third Ave. near 22nd St.; 473–3760. Friendly, informal atmosphere where you may enjoy well-prepared food that includes all manner of pastas, veal, beef, and some unusual dishes. Dinner only Saturday and Sunday. All major credit cards.

Marchi's. 251 E. 31st St.; 679–2494. In an old brownstone, has a long-time reputation for its many-course dinner ($26.50 fixed price at this writing). You eat whatever the host has selected for the day. Reservations accepted Monday through Friday only, closed for lunch and on Sunday. AE.

Nanni's. 146 E. 46th St.; 697–4161. Excellent Northern Italian cuisine that reaches its highest standards in the tortellini and chicken Valdostana. The same owner runs Nanni Il Valletto. Closed Sunday. All major credit cards.

Orso. 322 W. 46th St.; 489–7212. The current darling of the after-theater set, this sassy Roman trattoria serves some of the freshest, most appealing Italian food in town. Pastas are imaginative and change daily. The small pizzas make perfect light suppers, and the chef knows exactly what to do with fish: *lightly* grill it. The carafes of house white and house red are bottomless, so order a half-carafe unless you're bone dry. No credit cards. Reservations a must.

Il Palazzo. 18 W. 18th St.; 924–3800. The fashion set and the downtown advertising and publishing honchos flock to this high-ceilinged loft space for creative salads and imaginative pastas. Packed at both lunch and dinner. All major credit cards.

Parma. 1404 Third Ave. at 80th St.; 535–3520. With its no-nonsense decor, Parma sets an informal mood that lets one get down to the serious business of wrestling with some of the best pasta this side of, well, Parma. Dinner only, daily. AE.

Patsy's. 236 W. 56th St.; 247–3491. Noted for its Neopolitan food and friendly atmosphere. Simple, cheerful surroundings. Many different pastas, but the stuffed shells are unusual in this bright, two-story restaurant that offers choice of 35 main courses. Closed Monday. No CB.

Per Bacco. 140 E. 27th St.; 532–8699. Possibly because it is a bit out of the way, this Northern Italian restaurant (the Trieste region) is one of the unsung stars of dining out in New York; the daily specialties are the thing. Major credit cards.

Piccolo Mondo. 1269 First Ave. near 69th St., on the Upper East Side; 249–3141. Reliable Italian fare. The fish and scampi are among the best in the city. All major credit cards.

Poletti's. 2315 Broadway at 84th St.; 580–1200. If there is such a thing as an Upper West Side style, this restaurant—along with Teacher's—exemplifies it. Pastas are made on the premises, and the pastas are what you should go for here—rather than the main dishes. All major credit cards.

Primavera Ristorante. 1578 First Ave., 81st St.; 861–8608. One of the best of the First Ave. storefront restaurants, especially the tortellini and fish dishes. All major credit cards.

Roma di Notte. 137 E. 55th St.; 832–1128. Appeals to the eye. Stunning Roman decor in bar and cocktail lounge and dimly lit dining room. Dazzling array of appetizers, chicken Nero, rollatine of veal, fettucine are among many choices. They do a lot of cooking over a flaming rotisserie—none of which is terribly distinguished. AE, DC, CB.

Rosemarie's. 145 Duane St. (north of Charles and West Broadway); 285–2610. A bright and shining new star on TriBeCa's Duane St. Restaurant Row (nearby are Le Zinc, dal Barone, Tapis Rouge, Country Fare, and Bouley). It's an elegant beauty—with its brick walls, ceramic tiles, Italian mural, blue-sky ceiling with clouds, and fresh flowers and candles on the handsomely appointed tables—but it's anything but stuffy. Romantic and relaxing, that's Rosemarie's (named for the eager young woman who serves as chef/host and who is always on hand). Try the tomato and mozzarella salad with extra-virgin olive oil, the *vitello tonnato* (cold thin veal slices in tuna mayonnaise), the lasagne with pesto and cheese, the superb lamb chops, and *tiramisu* ("pick me up," made with rum-and-coffee-soaked cake, mascarpone cheese cream, whipped cream, and chocolate shavings) for dessert. Needless to say, a find!. AE.

Sal Anthony's. 55 Irving Place near 17th St.; 982–9030. Go up a few stairs into a large, spacious, and well-decorated room and you enter a restaurant that serves as delicate a tomato sauce as can be found this side of Florence. Excellent pastas and eggplant. All major credit cards.

Salta in Bocca. 179 Madison Ave. near 33rd St.; 684–1757. A pleasant if undistinguished-looking dining room, where the excellent pasta is what catches your attention, especially the green-and-white fettucine casalinga. Very noisy, with tables close together. Closed Sun. All major credit cards.

Trastevere. 309 E. 83rd St.; 734–6343. Small, intimate, rushed, named for a section of Rome renowned for its restaurants—and lives up to its name. AE.

Villa Berulia. 107 E. 34th St. near Park Ave.; 689–1970. Cavelike decor and excellent northern-Italian dishes (the staff are Yugoslavian-Americans). Near the Morgan Library and Altman's. All major credit cards.

Moderate

Alfredo the Original of Rome. Citicorp Center, 54th St. at Third Ave.; 371–3367. The name tells the whole story, but surprisingly, the pasta is excellent. Slightly hectic service at lunch, so try in evening. All major credit cards.

Angelina's. 41 Greenwich Ave. in the Village; 929–1255. A homey sort of place, unpretentious as far as decor and menu. The same à la carte menu is used for lunch and dinner. Veal parmigiana, shrimp marinara, and breaded pork chops are popular entrées. AE, DC.

Angelo of Mulberry Street. 146 Mulberry St.; 966–1277. Deep in the heart of "Little Italy." The pastas are a specialty, as is fish stew *(zuppa di pesce)*. President Reagan ate here. All major credit cards.

Asti. 13 E. 12th St.; 242–9868 or 741–9105. A sing-along place, with waiters and customers getting into the act, whether opera or musicals. Also features a "Flying Pizza" act. Italian-style cuisine, but who's to notice? No Lunch. Closed Mondays and July and August. All major credit cards.

Beatrice Inn. 285 W. 12th St.; 929–6165. From the outside this downstairs restaurant looks foreboding, but this is a genuine family-run affair in a surprisingly decorous setting—fresh flowers, brightly lit, and exceedingly friendly. The manicotti is outstanding, and the veal, chicken, and seafood dishes are on par with those at far more expensive establishments. Closed Sundays. All major credit cards.

Bianchi and Margherita. 186 W. 4th St. in the Village; 242–2756. If you enjoy music, especially opera, and don't care too much about its quality, you'll love this place, where waiter, proprietor, bartender, and customer join together (with luck) to sing duos, trios, quartets, sextets, even solos. The food is like the music—enjoy it and stop fussing. Closed Sun. All major credit cards.

Chelsea Trattoria Italiana. 108 Eighth Ave. (near 16th St.); 924–7786. Charming spot in booming yuppie neighborhood. Perfect pastas, succulent seafood, fabulous fegato (liver), and many other specialties to challenge hearty appetites. All major credit cards.

Forlini's. 93 Baxter St. in the vicinity of Canal St.; 349–6779. Red sauce cooking with finesse. All major credit cards.

Il Gattopardo. 49 W. 56th St.; 586–3978. Just as you'd expect a restaurant in Milan or Turin to look. Excellent service, very good food. Closed Sunday. All major credit cards.

Mamma Leone's. 261 W. 44th St.; 586–5151. She's back! This time she's moved to the Milford Plaza Hotel, and the old place (which looks the same: massive oil paintings, marble statues, ornate mirrors, stucco walls, and Mamma's portrait at the entrance) is better (if not bigger) than ever. Tons of food—the perfect place to take starving kids. All major credit cards.

Minetta Tavern. 113 MacDougal St., at Minetta Lane in the Village; 475–3850. Generations of poets, playwrights, artists, writers, and college kids have grown up here, and some have produced some of their best work over plates of pasta and herb-scented chicken, veal, and seafood. (Franz Kline left an invaluable set of pen and ink portraits in the bar.) Convivial bar (with tables and booths) and lively back dining room. All major credit cards.

Patrissy's. 98 Kenmare St. in Little Italy; 226–8509. Friendly, informal, long-established Neopolitan restaurant, where everything is à la carte and you need a cart to carry off what you can't finish from thier first-rate pastas. All major credit cards.

Pete's Tavern. 129 E. 18th St.; 473–7676. The manicotti is the best thing on the menu, the tomato sauce not the most subtle. This is the tavern made famous by O. Henry. Very simple setting, with outdoor café in summer. Wonderful old-fashioned bar.

Ponte Vecchio. 206 Thompson St.; 228–7701. Very popular among Villagers for its simplicity as well as its freshly prepared pastas, veal, and seafood and its reasonable prices. Always crowded and always noisy—though if you don't mind eating in the bar area, you can usually be seated immediately. AE.

Pronto Ristorante. 30 E. 60th St.; 421–8151. Pasta made in front of your eyes; ultra-modern restaurant design and good Northern Italian dishes. Can be expensive. All major credit cards.

Rao's. 455 E. 114th St.; 534–9625. So out-of-the-way it is located in one of the city's most broken-down neighborhoods, but so "in" that the cognoscenti make the trip by car for some of the city's best homemade pastas. You can look into the kitchen on your way to a table. Dinner only. No credit cards.

Rocco. 181 Thompson St. in the Village; 677–0590. Neapolitan food, and very good—though the restaurant itself doesn't look very promising at first glance. Go here if you want the flavor of the Little Italy of times gone by. Major credit cards.

Trattoria. In the Pan Am Building. 45th St. between Vanderbilt and Lexington Aves.; 661–3090. Informal, though strikingly decorated with Italy's colors and posters. Closed Sunday. All major credit cards.

Uzie's. 1442 Third Ave. near 82nd St.; 744–8020. Giancarlo Uzielli holds forth for pasta-eating beautiful people—but the food *is* good, if your ego is strong. All major credit cards.

Inexpensive

dal Barone. 131 Duane St.; 732–9770–1. Delightful and airy shrine of *cucina Italiana* on TriBeCa's Duane St. Restaurant Row. Pick your first course from the enticing spread on the hall table, then go on to a pasta special or one of the superbly prepared fish or meat dishes. AE.

Guido's. 511 Ninth Ave., at 39th St.; 564–8074. Hidden behind the storefront Supreme Macaroni Company (where you can indeed buy freshly made pasta), this is a family-style southern Italian cooking—festive, well-prepared and served with a friendliness that is rare indeed. Don't be misled by the minimum $7.50 charge at dinner, because you'd really have to stuff yourself to surpass it by much. Great before theater, but be sure to have a reservation. No credit cards.

Luna. 112 Mulberry St.; 226–8657. From noon to midnight, this is possibly the most inexpensive *and* (relatively speaking) high-quality—and friendly—Southern Italian restaurant in the city. Don't expect to eat anything delicate or to while away the night lingering over a bottle of wine (the prices are low because the turnover is high), but do go for more-than-ample portions at very reasonable prices. And do go with the expectation of waiting on line for a table, as you may have to do. No credit cards.

Manganaro's. 492 Ninth Ave. near 38th St.; 947–7325. The best place in New York for overstuffed hero sandwiches—eggplant parmigiana, mixed cold cuts, sausage and peppers. Bustling at lunch and closes at 7:30 P.M. but always worth the trip. Closed Sun. No credit cards.

Monte's. 97 MacDougal St. in the Village; 674–9456. Down half a flight of steps from street level, this restaurant has provided good, solid, bountiful, and unpretentious Southern Italian fare to the local Italian-Americans, New York University faculty and plenty of other New Yorkers for a long time—and at better than reasonable prices. Closed Tuesday. No credit cards.

Pasta Presto. 613 Second Ave. near 34th St.; 889–4131. This new small place squeezes them in before and after a movie at one of the E. 34th St. cinemas. Patrons don't mind, for the pasta in all varieties is quite good, prepared by an Italian-Japanese chef. Accompanying crisp salads are excellent. Small backyard garden open in warm weather. All major credit cards.

Perretti. 270 Columbus Ave., at 72nd St.; 362–3939. Bright, glass-enclosed neon-lit dining room popular among neighborhood denizens and those headed to Lincoln Center. No reservations, so be prepared to wait. Pizza also served. AE, MC, V.

Prego. 1365 Avenue of the Americas; 307–5775. Pastas—in every shape, size, and sauce—are the specialties here. The place is appealing, the food very fine, given the price and the location (convenient to the communications giants such as ABC, CBS, MGM, etc., Carnegie Hall and midtown shopping). Good for quick snacking while on the run.

Puglia's. 189 Hester St. in Little Italy; 226–8912. This is the place for partying. Seating is at long, camp-style tables, the homemade wine served by the bottle (beer by the pitcher), the hearty Southern fare a mite greasy at times—but once the little old lady begins her sing-along routines (weekends only) you won't even notice. No credit cards.

Tutta Pasta. 26 Carmine St. (between Sixth and Seventh aves. in Greenwich Village); 242–4871. Very informal, very delicious, and totally charming. The flawless pastas are made on the premises (there is a take-out store attached) and you bring your own wine or beer. The fried calamari, the chicken dishes, and the spinach loaded with chopped garlic are also superb. No reservations, no credit cards; appetites required.

Umberto's Clam House. 129 Mulberry St. in Little Italy; 431–7545. Site of the infamous Joey Gallo underworld murder but a favorite fresh seafood place. Very informal, with sidewalk tables in summer and open very late. No credit cards.

Vincent's Clam Bar. 119 Mott St. in Little Italy; 226–8133. The home of hot and spicy tomato sauce. Try your spaghetti with it, with scungilli or calamari—and you get one roll. Informal. No credit cards.

Jamaican

Moderate

Carlos One. 432 Sixth Ave. near 10th St. in the Village; 982–3260. What you might expect, featuring a kind of Jamaican bouillabaisse, and all the trimmings, including plantains. All major credit cards.

Inexpensive

Sugar Reef. 93 Second Ave.; 477–8427. Funky and fun, filled with nearby college kids and other denizens of the Lower East Side who come for the unusual and irresistible garlic bread, the asopao rice stews, jerk chicken, and Bajan kingfish. Insane-looking drinks to match the spray-paint decor. No credit cards.

Japanese

Expensive

Benihana of Tokyo. East: 120 E. 56th St.; 593–1627. Also **West:** 47 W. 56th St.; 581–0930. The show is what counts here, with a chef attending to every party (though parties are often grouped together) chopping, seasoning, and stir-frying over an open gas-heated grill. There's certainly better and more seriously traditional food around, but the spectacle involved is entertaining. All major credit cards.

Gibbon. 24 E. 80th St.; 861–4001. Combination of French and Japanese cuisines in a remodeled private house, with some dining on street level, but the main dining area is one flight up. Features good fish dishes. Open for lunch Monday through Friday, dinner Saturday. Closed Sunday. All major credit cards.

Hakubai. 66 Park Ave. at 38th St. (entrance on side street); 686–3770. In New York's only avowed Japanese hotel, the Kitano. Very comfortable, uses very best raw materials for all dishes (the key to Japanese cuisine); everything is good here. All major credit cards.

Hatsuhana. 17 E. 48th St.; 355–3345. Very busy, specializing in raw-fish preparation and seafood. Totally authentic, but is having trouble managing its success after being given four stars by the *New York Times*. All major credit cards.

Inagiku. 111 E. 49th St. in the Waldorf Astoria; 355–0440. Excellent, authentic food in handsome restaurant, decorated in Japanese style—though a bit overstated. Some dishes available in three different areas—a special bar, grill room, and main dining room, with prices escalating accordingly. *Tempura, sukiyaki,* and seafood do Japan proud. Dinner only Saturday and Sunday. All major credit cards.

Kabuki. 115 Broadway, downtown; 962–4677. This financial district restaurant typically attracts large Wall Street crowds for lunch, but the dinner is quiet, almost intimate. There are tatami rooms along one wall and regular Western tables in the center. Special banquet-style dinners and *donburi* lunches are offered. Serves lunch and dinner Monday through Friday. All major credit cards.

Kitcho of New York. 22 W. 46th St.; 575–8880. A favorite of the Japanese themselves. In addition to the usual *sukiyaki* and *tempura* fare so popular with Americans, there are a number of unusually prepared delicacies. Southern Japanese cuisine. Gentle, attentive service. Closed Saturday. Open 5 P.M. Sunday. AE, DC.

Kurumazushi. 18 W. 56th St.; 541–9030. Outstanding, if pricey, sushi bar. All major credit cards.

Mitsukoshi. 461 Park Ave., at 57th St.; 935–6444. Absolutely stunning restaurant that specializes in sushi but does offer cooked foods as well. This is like dining in a museum. All major credit cards.

Nippon. 155 E. 52nd St.; 355–9020. Probably New York's most famous Japanese restaurant. Like a Japanese garden, complete with a stream. Tatami rooms or regular tables in an attractive setting. Unusual Japanese dishes are featured along with familiar *sukiyaki*. Cosy bar and cocktail lounge. *Tempura* and *sushi* bar for light meals. Closed Sunday. Dinner only on Saturday. All major credit cards.

Sagano. 3 E. 44th St.; 986–1355. Elegant and stylish décor—and very authentically Japanese—with elegantly served food in the Japanese style. With allegiances to Kyoto (southern Japanese) cuisine, there is the usual tempura, teriyaki, etc., but all of it top-flight. Closed Sunday; no Saturday lunch. Major credit cards.

Seryna. 11 E. 53rd St.; 980–9393. Steak as well as fish in a neighborhood generally given over to classical French fare. All major credit cards.

Shinbashi. 280 Park Ave. at 48th St.; 661–3915. Tatami rooms where you sit on the floor, kimono-wearing waitresses, and Western-style items to go along with good Japanese beef or seafood grilled with vegetables make this large, somewhat austere place an interesting choice. Closed Sunday, dinner only on Saturday. All major credit cards.

Takesushi. 71 Vanderbilt Ave. at 45th St.; 867–5120. Yes, a sushi restaurant, and one of the very best in the city. Must reserve. Closed Sundays. Major credit cards.

Moderate

Japonica. 90 University Pl.; 243–7752. A cozy place in the heart of Greenwich Village, popular with actors and artists as well as local clientele. Soothing decor with warm ambience. For a special sushi, try the Japonica Invention, raw tuna wrapped with seaweed and rice and accompanied by caviar and thinly sliced avocado. Reliable, too, are the sashimi, tempura, and teriyaki. Open seven days. No reservations. AE, CB, D.

Nakagawa. 7 W. 44th St.; 869–8077. Authentic in decor and atmosphere. Divided into two sections, with a *sushi* counter and small tables up front and, down a few steps, more tables—but slightly larger. The food is authentic Japanese. AE, MC, V.

Tatany. 388 Third Ave., between 27th and 28th sts.; 686–1871. Have you ever tried "Japanese bouillabaisse"? You can have it under the name of *yosenabe* at this cheerful restaurant whose version of the French seafood stew is delicious. Chefs here also slice up a large assortment of sushi and sashimi that delights the eye as well as the palate. Of course, there's the wide array of teriyaki and tempura, among other dishes, to choose from too. Dinner only Saturdays and Sundays. All major credit cards.Also at 62 Greenwich Ave.; 675–6195.

Inexpensive

Dan Tempura House. 2018 Broadway, at 69th St.; 877–4969. From the outside it looks like a tacky Japanese coffee shop, but inside is a consistently satisfying restaurant most popular for (obviously) its *tempura* and seafood casserole-type dishes. For dessert: deep-fried ice cream—and it's wonderful, not just a gimmick. Convenient to Lincoln Center. AE.

Dojo. 24 St. Marks Place; 674–9821. Somewhere between Japanese and health food—everything's grilled, the portions are larger than for typical Japanese restaurants, and the atmosphere is East Village fun. No credit cards and, take heed, no air conditioning (and with an indoor barbecue . . .).

Dosanko Larmen. 423 Madison Ave. at 48th St., 688–8575; 10 E. 52nd St., 759–6361; 135 E. 45th St., 697–2967; 19 Murray St. near City Hall, 964–9696; plus other locations. Noodles in hot broth, with various trimmings, light and healthful. Super cheap. No credit cards.

Fuji. 238 W. 56th St.; 245–8594. Very convenient to Carnegie Hall, also especially popular among music industry executives at lunch. Highly reliable if unspectacular. All major credit cards.

Genroku Sushi. 366 Fifth Ave. near 34th St.; 947–7940. Sit around an enormous counter and pick your dishes off a perpetually moving conveyor belt. In addition to *sushi,* you can choose Japanese curry noodle and rice dishes, *tempura, sashimi, gyoza,* fried chicken, even soups and desserts. You are charged by the number of plates you take. Open seven days. Very cheap. No credit cards.

Hasaki. 210 E. 9th St.; 473–3327. This clean and serene downstairs refuge in the East Village is painted in cool shades of blue to complement the natural woodwork. Filled with Japanese (students, doctors, business people, punks, musicians) who dote on the sushi, sashimi, tempura, seafood specials, and a dessert made with ice cream and lentil beans! No reservations. AE.

Taro. 20 E. 47th St.; 986–7170. A kind of Japanese McDonald's with noodles, filling the need for simple, tasty, low-priced meals served at round counters. It follows the concept of hundreds of similar restaurants in Japan, and serves *larmen* (noodle dishes) that come in soup, in fried dishes, or broiled with fish, chicken, or meat. Closed Sunday. No credit cards.

Jewish/Kosher
(See also *Delicatessen*)

Expensive

Kaplan's at the Delmonico. 59 E. 59th St.; 755–5959. Kosher deli with cozy, informal atmosphere. Pastrami, corned beef, potato pancakes, chicken-in-the-pot, and goulash are among the treats. Good for brunch. All major credit cards.

Lou G. Siegel. 209 W. 38th St.; 921–4433. Serves authentic Jewish food under rabbinical supervision. The menu has *lungen* and *miltz* stew, stuffed derma, stuffed cabbage, meats, and poultry. Separate bar. No smoking after sundown Friday, closed Saturday. All major credit cards.

Moshe Peking. 40 W. 37th St.; 594–6500. A handsome restaurant only New York could spawn, featuring kosher Chinese cuisine, including Peking duck, beef and veal. Closed Fri. sundown to Sat. sundown. All major credit cards.

Sammy's Famous Roumanian Restaurant. 157 Chrystie St. on the Lower East Side; 673–5526 or 673–0330. The waiters think they're comedians but from the bowls of pickles and roast peppers on every table to the delicious mushroom-barley soup, stuffed derma, sliced brains, Romanian tenderloin steak and Romanian beef sausages *(karnatzlach)* the food is not a joke. An experience, to put it mildly. Kosher-style, but not kosher. (One critic recommends ending with "lots of hot tea and Alka Seltzer.") AE, DC,CB.

Moderate

Edible Pursuits. 325 Fifth Ave. at 32nd St.; 686–5330. Dairy and fish dishes in a pleasing, modern setting. This is the youthful nouvelle-ish version of a kosher restaurant, busiest at lunch and very calm for dinner. Closed Friday night, Saturday lunch, Jewish holidays. All major credit cards.

Levanas Café. 141 W. 69th St.; 877–8457. Fish, vegetables, pasta, and excellent babkas (dry cakes) and danish within walking distance of Lincoln Center. Very simple, very friendly, with the staff's earnest good cheer compensating for a chef who knows not of the term delicate. Closed Friday evening through sundown Saturday. AE.

Marrakech West. 149 Bleecker St.; 777–8911. Kosher Moroccan cooking in a suitably ethnic setting that could be a throwback to the '60s given the Village location. All major credit cards. Closed Friday night. AE, MC, V.

Inexpensive

Ratner's. 138 Delancey St. on the Lower East Side; 677–5588. Strictly kosher dairy (and listed under that heading, too). Sunday breakfast is the best time for a visit. A great place to take the kids. No credit cards.

Korean

Moderate

Arirang House. 28 W. 56th St.; 581–9698. If you like spicy grilled beef and the sourest of pickles, this is the place for you. Best example of Korean cooking in the city, but the atmosphere within is darkly mysterious. All major credit cards.

Myong Dong. 42 W. 35th St.; 695–6622. Long bar, semicircular banquettes, and all kinds of banquets, from soups, *sirhas mandoo gook,* to *jeyook kooi* (slices of pork). All major credit cards.

Woo Lae Oak of Seoul. 77 W. 46th St.; 869–9958. Perhaps the largest menu of all the city's Korean restaurants. *Bool koki*—strips of marinated beef cooked over small fire—pork ribs, baked short ribs, noodles, and all kinds of fish. No CB.

Middle Eastern

Moderate

Ararat. 1076 First Ave. near 59th St.; 686–4622. Beautifully decorated establishment specializing in Armenian cuisine to match. All major credit cards.

Balkan Armenian. 129 E. 27th St.; 689–7925. One of the oldest and most popular Armenian restaurants, offering such typical fare as stuffed grape leaves, egg-lemon soup, and a most unusual mushroom kebab. Short on frills. Closed Sun. All major credit cards.

Cedars of Lebanon. 39 E. 30th St.; 725–9251. A variety of interesting and absolutely authentic Lebanese dishes in cavernous and poorly decorated surroundings. All major credit cards.

Russian

Deluxe

Russian Samovar. 256 W. 52nd St.; 757–0168. A menu similar to that of the Russian Tea Room, but at reduced prices. Borscht, eggplant samovar, Georgian dried beef, pelmeni, chicken Kiev, and two spectacular cakes: Anna Pavlova and Kiev. Convenient to many upper Broadway-area theaters. Closed Mondays. AE, V, MC.

Russian Tea Room. 150 W. 57th St.; 265–0947. A landmark right next to Carnegie Hall, and a favorite among musicians, dancers, movie celebrities, and other show-biz folk. Perhaps the city's richest food, and Christmas decorations all year long. Borscht, *blini* (pancakes with caviar), chicken Kiev, and (on Wednesday only) the legendary Siberian *pelmeny*. Russian cream for dessert if you can handle it. Watch out for the lethal concoctions brewed by the "Cossack' bartenders. All major credit cards.

Scandanavian

Super Deluxe

Aquavit. 13 W. 54th St.; 307-7311. A stunning new addition to the city's restaurant scene. Located in a former Rockefeller town house, the two-level Aquavit consists of a lively and attractive bar/cafe area and a more formal dining room located in a soaring eight-story atrium (actually the enclosed garden area), which is decorated with tall birch trees and a sloping waterwall. The design, Scandinavian modern, is superb; the table settings tasteful and elegant; and the service by young, intelligent waiters is both helpful and friendly without a trace of attitude. The cuisine (by Swedish chef Christer Olsson) is spectacular: the gravlax with a dill-and-mustard sauce is perfection, all salmon dishes are flawless (try the one-side sautéed version), the Arctic venison tender and juicy, the medallions of veal sublime, and the desserts (especially the Swedish pancakes with vanilla ice cream) are irresistible. Reservations are difficult to obtain but make a real effort: this place is worth every penny of the sizable bill you'll receive. AE, MC, V.

Spanish

Expensive

Café San Martin. 1458 First Ave. (at 76th St.); 288-0470. Spanish as opposed to Mexican, with *paella* abundant in sausage, scallops, mussels, shrimp, and peppers. All dishes are freshly prepared, and if you have the time a chicken roasted to order is worth the wait. All major credit cards.

Fonda La Paloma. 256 E. 49th St.; 421–5495. Hot and spicy Mexican dishes here are all prepared to order and courteously served in a pleasant atmosphere. The guacamole is without peer. Fine bar on ground floor. Open seven days but only from 5 P.M. on Saturday/Sunday. All major credit cards.

Plaza España. 130 W. 58th St.; 757–6434. Authentic dishes in traditional surroundings. Try the garlic chicken. Closed Sunday, open for dinner only Saturday. AE, MC, V.

Victor's Café. 240 Columbus Ave. at 71st St.; 877–7988. The place to go for the finest Cuban food in the city. The soups are excellent, fried beef with garlic and onions, and rice with seafood or chicken are equally delicious. Unusual on Sunday are Cuban hero sandwiches and roast suckling pig. Victor's is so popular it now has a theater district offshoot called **Victor's Cafe 52,** 236 W. 52nd St., 586–7714. All major credit cards.

Moderate

Olé. 434 Second Ave. near 24th St.; 725–1953. Some aficionados say this authentic Spanish restaurant has the best *paella* and *mariscadas con* *salsa verde* (mixed seafood with green sauce) in town. Also good are the meat dishes and special-priced lobster, but pass up the nondescript salad that goes with the meal. Service is attentive and dinners are accompanied by a guitar-strumming tenor. All major credit cards.

Swiss

Expensive

Chalet Suisse. 6 E. 48th St.; 355–0855. A pleasing but pricey place for Swiss cheese fondue or fondue bourguignonne (cubes of beef you cook yourself in hot oil at the table). Other specials: onion and cheese pie, veal dishes, and roesti potatoes. Complete dinners and à la carte. No CB.

Inexpensive

La Fondue. 43 W. 55th St.; 581–0820. As the name suggests, cheese dishes, and fondue in particular, are featured here. For those who demand meatier fare there is filet mignon. A charming, casual atmosphere, but luncheon eating is liable to be crowded and rushed. No credit cards.

Tex-Mex

Moderate

Cantina. 221 Columbus Ave. at 70th St.; 873–2606. Not slavishly authentic food, but a very popular Upper West Side hangout. Try the Mexican kitchen casserole if you are very hungry. No CB, DC.

Caramba. 918 8th Ave.; 245–7910, and 684 Broadway, at 3rd St.; 420–9817. Among the vanguard in the Tex-Mex craze and still wildly popular. Famous for birdbath-size margaritas. Bright and lively. Expect to wait even if you have a reservation. All major credit cards.

Cinco de Mayo. 349 West Broadway, between Grand and Broome Sts.; 226–5255. The trendy side of Soho, with consistently fine food as well as crowds (expect to wait for a table any night of the week). Good for partying. Now a branch at 45 Tudor City Place; 661–5070. All major credit cards.

El Coyote. 774 Broadway, 9th St.; 677–4291. Mexican cantina decor and best-selling combination platters. After 7 P.M. there can be a considerable wait at the bar. No CB, DC.

El Parador. 325 E. 34th St.; 679–6812. Small, plain restaurant that has been an East Side institution for years, and the Mexican and Spanish cuisines are hailed by Latins. Try a margarita during the inevitable wait at the bar (that's the purpose, of course), which is a low-key singles scene in and of itself. Spanish wines and Mexican beers. Dinner only, à la carte. Closed Sunday. AE.

El Rio Grande. 160 E. 38th St., at Third Ave.; 867–0922. El Rio Grande consists of two separate bright, glass-walled dining rooms—"Texas' on the north side and "Mexico' on the south, sharing the same kitchen—on the plaza of a new apartment building, up and away from the street. Both bars and both rooms are very lively. Stay away from the dishes with a lot of cheese on them. All major credit cards.

Los Panchos. 71 W. 71st St. east of Columbus; 874–8006. Very accommodating neighborhood restaurant with outdoor garden for summer dining and a life-size stuffed burro at the bar. Food is simple but well prepared. All major credit cards.

Pamplona. 822 Avenue of the Americas near 29t St.; 683–4242. This bright, unimposing restaurant is among the best of those serving Spanish cuisine. Black bean soup is delectable, chicken dishes also commendable. Convenient to Madison Square Garden. Closed Sunday. All major credit cards.

Rosa's. 303 W. 48th St.; 586–4853. You won't get a kinder, more gracious welcome than the one Rosa and her staff will offer you. Consequently, you start off with a rosy glow that only increases with the giant frozen margaritas, the salsa, the cheese nachos, the guacamole, the enchiladas suizas, and the tacos. (All entrees come with black beans, rice, and salad.) Reservations are becoming necessary. Major credit cards.

Santa Fe. 72 W. 69th St.; 724–0822. The competition is stiff, but Santa Fe is holding its own. Fun, good food and a little more laid back than at other spots. All major credit cards.

Zapata's. 330 E. 53rd St.; 223–9408. Narrow, dim, dominated by a portrait of the revolutionary, but viva the good, heaping food portions that are reasonably well-seasoned. All major credit cards.

Inexpensive

Anita's Chili Parlor. 287 Columbus Ave. at W. 74th St.; 595–4091. Tex-Mex food inside, or at sidewalk tables to watch the Columbus Avenue madness. Service indifferent at best. AE, MC, V. $10 minimum.

Cadillac Bar. 15 W. 21st St.; 645–7220. A wild and crazy place (the NYC outpost of the Houston bar) and wildly popular with the young and uninhibited set. Mesquite fajitas, cabrito, frog's legs. Open very late. Sunday brunch. AE, MC, V.

El Charro. 4 Charles St. in the Village; 242–9547. Full selection of spicy Mexican fare available in this homey restaurant. The combination plates let you sample the usual variety of dishes such as *tortillas, tostadas, enchiladas,* and *tacos.* All major credit cards.

Cottonwood Cafe. 415 Bleecker St.; 924–6271. The Cottonwood got the Tex-Mex ball rolling in New York with its inexpensive storefront fare. The cooking is reliable, the checkered tablecloths are plastic and the check is cheap. What more could you want? A guitarist? That too some nights after 11:30 P.M. No credit cards.

El Faro. 823 Greenwich St., Horatio St. in the West Village; 929–8210. Don't be put off by the unappetizing exterior—or by the small, dark interior for that matter—for this is absolutely NYC's finest Spanish kitchen. Besides the obligatory *paellas,* there is a raft of other shellfish dishes called *mariscadas.* The sangria is the genuine article, and *natilla* is a special treat for dessert. Huge portions. Again, no reservations; can mean a lengthy wait. AE, MC, V.

Rincón de Espana. 226 Thompson St. in the Village; 260–4950. Dinner only. And at **Rincón de Espana II,** 82 Beaver St., 344–5228, dress is as informal as food, which is good. Beaver St. closed Saturday/Sunday. All major credit cards.

Tío Pepe. 168 W. 4th St.; 242–9338. From your vantage point on the sidewalk of this pleasant café you can watch the Village denizens while enjoying creditable Spanish fare and the music of a flamenco guitarist. Or choose the more intimate candlelit dining inside. All major credit cards.

Thai

Moderate

Bangkok 54. 261 W. 54th St., off Eighth Ave.; 582–6640 Rather spacious, friendly, and casual, with a wide range of Thai dishes. If you like super-spicy, best ask for it. All major credit cards.

Siam Inn. 916 Eighth Ave. near 55th St.; 974–9583. Dozens of beguiling Thai specialties are skillfully presented by a shyly gracious and efficient staff in a cheerful modern dining room with decorative Thai accents. Close to the theater district, Columbus Circle, and Carnegie Hall—and gets very crowded during the pre-theater hours. AE, DC.

Inexpensive

Bangkok Cuisine. 885 Eighth Ave. near 53rd St.; 581–6370. Rice with duck, pork with pepper, fish with curry. The usual mixtures which make Thai cuisine so delicious, yet hard to define, as though it were simply a mixture of Chinese and South Asian (yet it is more than that). No DC, CB.

Pongsri Thailand. 244 W. 48th St., 582–3392. Within a month of opening became one of the most popular of Thai restaurants because of its spaciousness, gracious staff, modern theater-district setting and, especially, its seafood offerings. All major credit cards.

Thailand. 106 Bayard St. in Chinatown; 349–3132. The best of the lot, and one of the cheapest. Nobody does it better than they do here—but you'd better specify how hot you want your food done. Curries are authentic, fried fish and crab dishes outstanding, but the looks of this small, unpretentious restaurant leave a lot to be desired. Reservations a must. No credit cards.

Ukrainian

Inexpensive

Ukrainian Restaurant and Caterers. 132 Second Ave.; 533–6765. This is the modernized version of what used to be situated up the block in an old meeting hall. The look is cleaner, but there was something about just how funky the old place was that made it really special. In its new home the run-of-the-mill pirogi (dumplings stuffed with potato or cheese), blintzes (pancakes stuffed with cheese or blueberries or cherries), and stews just aren't as interesting. No credit cards.

Yugoslavian

Moderate

Dubrovnik. 88 Madison Ave. near 29th St.; 689–7565. Named for the resort town on Yugoslavia's Dalmatian coast, this pleasant restaurant offers an interesting though limited selection of Yugoslavian specialties such as *brudet* (a sort of chowder), and *cevapcici* (flavorful ground meat sausages). American and Continental dishes fill out the menu. Closed Sunday, dinner only Saturday. All major credit cards.

Portoroz. 340 Lexington Ave. near 39th St.; 687–8195. Rough brick areas, white walls. The restaurant is named for a resort area, looks like a country inn—near Grand Central Station—and serves good *sarma* (stuffed cabbage), interesting ground beef and pork dishes, and even some Italian main courses. Closed Sun. All major credit cards.

Other Boroughs

Bronx

Expensive

Thwaite's Inn. 536 City Island Ave.; 885–1023. This old eatery dates from the Gilded Age, and is doing a roaring trade nowaways since New Yorkers are once again getting curious, then proud about the diverse neighborhoods that make up their city. In this case, City Island, jutting into Long Island Sound from the extreme northeast Bronx, is being redis-covered as a tiny relaxed fishing "village." Thwaite's helps its own cause by turning out superb dinners, with lobster the logical and palate-pleasing specialty on this island that is a little bit of Cape Cod in the Bronx. All major credit cards.

Lobster Box. 34 City Island Ave.; 885–1952. A little "inland" from Thwaite's, this is also a focal point for City Island day-trippers. After all, who else but Lobster Box is going to offer a choice between fifteen or more preparations of lobster or shrimp? The baking is their own. If you can find a table on the terrace, a view of Long Island Sound is yours along with a scrumptious meal, although the nearby honky-tonk atmosphere of fast-food restaurants, custard stands, and an arcade gives the area a bit of Coney Island atmosphere. All major credit cards.

Anna's Harbor Restaurant. 565 City Island Ave.; 885–1373. A large restaurant, with Italian seafood specialties such as lobster fra diavolo (hot and spicy), AE, MC,V.

Between Thwaite's, near the beginning of City Island, and the Lobster Box, virtually at the farthest tip, are several seafood restaurants of slightly lesser quality—and slightly less expensive. These include the **Sea Shore,** (885–0300) and the **Crab Shanty** (885–1810), both on the same main street from end-to-end of the island. AE, MC, V.

Moderate

Amerigo's. 3587 E. Tremont Ave.; 792–3600. Began life as a pizzeria nearly half a century ago, now boasts two dining areas—one decorated in a Roman motif, the other with a back wall that becomes a waterfall. But it is the sauce, soups, pastas, and veal that make it Amerigo the beauti-ful—and one of the best in the North Bronx. All major credit cards.

Il Boschetto. 1660 E. Gun Hill Rd.; 379–9335. Unpretentious, small white building just off the New England Thruway—but as close to haute cuisine, Neapolitan-style, as you can get in the Bronx—especially the fish and veal dishes. Favorite of Bronx politicians noshing pasta. All major credit cards.

Mario's. 2342 Arthur Ave.; 584–1188. First-rate, unpretentious and ad-venturous Neapolitan cookery served up by the Migliucci family since

1919 in a style that has become famous throughout the Little Italy section of the Bronx and beyond. A favorite of *Times* gourmet writer Craig Claiborne. Octopus salad, *spiedini* (deep-fried mozzarella appetizers), striped bass, and beef and veal scaloppine among best dishes. Pizza may be the best in town, right up there with John's of Bleecker St. Ornate Bronx Renaissance decor. All major credit cards. Valet parking.

Within roughly 100 yards of Mario's, in the famed Arthur Ave. Italian shopping district, are three of the area's best Neapolitan restaurants—

Dom's (no reservations, noisy, really little more than a bar but with a veal Francese dish and a spaghetti and shrimp concoction that has regulars lining up from all over the city), the **Full Moon** (scungilli, calamari, pastas in what looks like a fast-food pizzeria), and **Ann and Tony's,** a family-style trattoria. No credit cards at any of these three restaurants—but good eating. And all within easy walking distance of the Bronx Zoo.

Stella D'Oro. 5806 Broadway near 238th St.; 548–2245. Family dinners Italian-style, with spaghetti à la Stella D'Oro the masterpiece, are graced with homemade pastas. The aromas from their nearby bakery may entice you to try some of their well-known egg biscuits. The restaurant is very near Van Cortlandt Park, so a visit to the area could also include a mansion tour, a Gaelic Football match, or some horseback riding. All major credit cards.

Brooklyn

Super Deluxe

Peter Luger. 178 Broadway, near Bedford Ave.; 718–387–7400. Many insist Luger, lying in the shadow of the Williamsburg Bridge, convenient to Manhattan and the Brooklyn-Queens Expressway, is the city's most venerable steakhouse. There's no menu, and the waiter recites the day's offerings, but everyone orders steak or chops with perhaps a tomato and onion salad to start. A subway stop is nearby (Marcy Ave. on the "J" or "M" line), but it's also an easy cab ride across the Williamsburg Bridge (if not closed). No credit cards.

River Café. 1 Water St., Brooklyn; 718–522–5200. A unique New York City dining experience and one to mark very special occasions. The view of the Manhattan skyline (from the sleek barge-restaurant moored at the Brooklyn end of the Brooklyn Bridge) is spectacular, the lovely dining room softly lighted (so as not to compete with the backdrop), and the American-inspired Continental cuisine is sublime. Feisty owner Buzzy O'Keeffe has had celebrated arguments with various critics (and this has affected reviews), but the *New York Times*'s Bryan Miller gives River Café a well-deserved three-star rating. Reservations are difficult to make, but worth fighting for. Take a cab to and from the front door; valet parking available. All major credit cards.

Deluxe

Gage and Tollner. 372 Fulton St.; 718–875–5181. The unhurried pace of Brooklyn, before it surrendered its independence to New York City, is preserved here. The menu changes with the seasons, and you can expect delightful specials that follow nature's calendar. Try the crabmeat Virginia, the soft clam bellies, the cole slaw. The owners have preserved the 1879 landmark building's original decor, too. All major credit cards.

Expensive

Ferrybank. One Front St.; 718–852–3137. Seafood and southern American fare are the specialties at what was, in fact, once the bank by the Brooklyn/Manhattan ferry. Elegantly brassy, with tables on the main floor and an over-hanging balcony. Ferrybank was started by waiters from Gage & Tollner's. All major credit cards.

Moderate

Bamonte's. 32 Withers St. in Greenpoint section; 718–384–8831. In business over 80 years, so whither thou goest, this is one of the city's best Italian neighborhood restaurants. MC, V.

Bay Ridge Seafood Center. 8618 Fourth Ave.; 718–748–2070. Where the men and women who work at the Fulton St. Fish Market go for seafood. Need more endorsement? Just be prepared for a wait despite the restaurant's size. All major credit cards.

Carolina. 1409 Mermaid Ave.; 718–266–8311. A landmark in Coney Island since the turn of the century for good Neapolitan home-style cooking. Large portions, everything saturated in garlic and best ordered family-style. Fresh seafood, good pastas, and a veal parmigiana that's the picture of what you want veal parmigiana to be. They've tripled the size of the restaurant in recent years, but you'll still have to wait for a table. No reservations, but fun for the family after the beach or the nearby aquarium. AE, MC, V.

Henry's End. 44 Henry St.; 718–834–1776. Popular Brooklyn Heights spot with solidly prepared Continental dishes as well as better-than-usual hamburgers and salads, and excellent desserts. All major credit cards.

Gargiulo's. 2911 W. 15th St., Coney Island; 718–266–0906. A wide, spacious setting for some of the city's best Neapolitan cooking—in which pasta in the noodle category is homemade. Ravioli and fettucine dishes are classics, veal is good. Italian politicians love it as much as votes. Great atmosphere for kids, too. All major credit cards.

McFeely's. Union Street at Seventh Ave.; 718–638–0099. A Victorian saloon and restaurant in Park Slope—which abounds with Victorian brownstones—and an offshoot of the former similarly themed spot in Manhattan. Fresh fish is the house specialty, though duck comes crisp as ordered and there are excellent hamburgers and omelets. Expect a 20-minute to half-hour wait with or without reservations. Dinner only seven days, plus Sunday brunch. All major credit cards.

Raintree. Prospect Park W. at 9th St.; 718–768–3723. A bit of SoHo comes to Park Slope by way of the restoration of a one-time soda fountain—the marble fountain counter has been converted to a bar—into a casually elegant Continental eatery. Piano music weekend evenings. Take the F train (subway) to Seventh Ave./Prospect Park. AE, MC, V.

Inexpensive

Junior's. Flatbush & Dekalb Aves.; 718–852–5257. Best-noted for its prize-winning cheesecake, Junior's is a wonderfully gaudy orange-and-white deli, serving overstuffed sandwiches, charcoal broiled hamburgers, and dozens of desserts. Not as good as it used to be, but what is? Convenient to Brooklyn Academy of Music. No CB.

Brooklyn's Atlantic Ave. and Court St. (the two cross each other) have a big concentration of Middle Eastern restaurants, most owned by the Almontaser family and its various offshoots. Among the best, all serving essentially similar menus heavy on lamb and curry dishes, are: **Almontaser,** 218 Court St., 718–624–9267; **Adnan,** 129 Atlantic Ave., 718–625–8697, **Near East,** 136 Court St., 718–624–9257. Also of note is **India House,** at corner of Atlantic and Court, 718–852–3486, and also at 293 Seventh Ave.; 718–768–8550; excellent Indian and Pakistani specialties, freshly prepared.

Queens

Moderate

La Stella (102–11 Queens Blvd., 718–459–9511, closed Monday, all major credit cards) is to many the borough's best Italian restaurant, but don't rule out **Manducatis** (13–27 Jackson Ave., 718–729–4602, no credit cards), a Long Island City neighborhood restaurant that is as good as most Neapolitan trattorias—and reason enough to consider masking a culinary pilgrimage to Queens.

Jahn's. 117–03. Hillside Ave.; 718–847–2800. In the residential Richmond Hill area not far from Kennedy Airport or Forest Hills tennis, this beloved landmark is famous for old-fashioned ice-cream desserts. Every sweet tooth in Queens is enthralled by it, and you get a free ice cream soda on your birthday, no matter what your age. No credit cards.

Steinway Brauhall. 28–26 Steinway St.; 718–728–9780. Hearty German food served up off Northern Blvd., near the Steinway piano factory. Closed Monday. AE, MC.

Staten Island

Inexpensive

Jade Island. 2845 Richmond Ave.; 718–761–8080. Don't let the shopping-center location fool you: the food's excellent and invitingly served. There's a smorgasbord Monday and Tuesday, but the main efforts go into the Polynesian and Chinese items. After other mall stores close, parking should be a breeze. All major credit cards.

DESSERTS. Perhaps inevitably, the best ice cream sundaes in New York are the biggest nuisance to obtain, and the prices are equal to those for a meal. Nonetheless, who can resist when the craving strikes? For quick refreshment, definitely consider an egg cream. An egg cream, you ask? Nothing more than chocolate-flavored syrup, milk, and seltzer.

Among the chain operations, there is a **Howard Johnson's** at 46th St. and Broadway, but it has been joined by dozens of **Baskin-Robbins, Haagen-Dazs, Seduttos,** and **Bassetts** specialty shops, while the California **Swenson's** chain has an outlet on 65th and Second Ave. (expensive, and the service is deplorable). It's getting so you can't go around the corner in New York without tripping over one or more of these ice-cream supermarkets, and the choice of flavors is mind-boggling, as can be the prices. Don't be surprised by $1.50 for a one-scoop cone!

Agora. 87th St. and 3rd Ave.; 369–6983 is an old-fashioned ice cream parlor in elaborately Art Deco setting that is attached to a clothing boutique. Sundaes and ice cream sodas are especially good, served with mounds of real whipped cream. The "Flatiron Building" is a specialty—pound cake, chocolate ice cream, hot fudge, and whipped cream prepared in the shape of its namesake. Other food is available, but why bother? All major credit cards.

Macy's The Fountain. 34th St. and Seventh Ave.; 695–4400. Yes, the world's largest department store happens to have one of the best ice-cream parlors in the city on the fifth floor. Beautiful green-and-white patio setting and great sodas. AE or Macy's.

Rumpelmayer's. 50 Central Park South in the St. Moritz; 755–5800. More of a tradition than a good ice-cream parlor, the stuffed animals and bright setting are always pleasing for kids. All major credit cards.

Serendipity. 225 E. 60th St.; 838–3531. A celebrity ice-cream-parlor-cum-boutique, where you're likely to encounter Barbra Streisand or Cher slurping and splurging. Expensive even by New York standards (a banana split for $7!), but most preparations are enough for two or three. All major credit cards.

In the boroughs, look for **Jahn's** various branches in Brooklyn and Queens; *Once Upon a Sundae,* 7702 Third Ave.; 718–748–3412 (with original 1890s set-up) in Brooklyn; and **Hoft's,** 3200 White Plains Road, 654–5291, in the Bronx. (Hoft's closes at 6 P.M. and on Sundays.)

Moving briskly from ice cream to pastry, first and foremost is **Ferrara's,** the bastion of Italian sweets nestled at 195 Grand Street (226–6150) in the middle of "Little Italy." All sorts of specialties are available (most served with piping-hot cups of espresso or cappucino), and there are some nifty items to take away with you. The line for tables is long on weekends, but the setting is uniquely festive. Also strikingly attractive with brick and glass walls, marble counter and enclosed garden, and with outstanding cheesecake, is **Café Biondo,** 141 Mulberry St., 226–9285, around the corner from Ferrara's.

Another, more imaginative, way to enjoy great desserts in a civilized manner is to go to some of the best restaurants—**Four Seasons,** for example—later in the evening, such as after a concert or the theater, and tell the maître d'hôtel that you want only dessert. This particular restaurant even encourages dessert-only patrons. At others, if business is tapering off, they'll be happy to oblige. **Eclair,** 141 W. 72nd St. (873–7700) is part restaurant, but the real lure is the outstanding Austrian pastries. Similarly, **Cakemasters** at Third Ave. and 65th, 759–7212, is a bakery-cum-café. Up by Columbia University (diagonally across from the Cathedral of St. John the Divine) is the **Hungarian Pastry Shop,** 1030 Amsterdam Ave. (866–4230), with excellent pastries and breads at prices catering to the predominantly student clientele.

COFFEEHOUSES (CAFÉS). One of the pleasures of touring the Village is to stop into one of the numerous Italian-style coffeehouses for a cup of just about any sort of coffee or tea—in cooler weather—or some Italian ices in the summer. In the Continental tradition, these are places where you can sit . . . and sit . . . and sit. There are almost always tables outside on the sidewalk. You will probably stumble onto your own favorite, but just in case, here are a few good ones: **Caffè Reggio,** 119 MacDougal St.; **Café Figaro** at the corner of MacDougal and Bleecker Sts. (one of the best known, closed for a while and reopened a few years ago); **Caffè**

Borgia, across the street from Café Figaro; **Caffè Dante,** 79 MacDougal; **Bruno Bakery,** 506 W. Broadway, South of Bleecker, a bit off the main track; **Caffè Lucca,** at 228 Bleecker St. at Sixth Ave.; and **Café Sandolino,** 9 Jones St. (more of a student/seedy poet place, with light food, no outside tables). **Pane e Cioccolato,** 10 Waverly Place at Mercer St., is a hangout for New York University students (the university is all around it). The **Cornelia Street Café,** on Cornelia between Bleecker and W. Fourth St., is on a relatively quiet side street and so may be even more relaxing than these others.

Café de la Paix, a bar in the St. Moritz Hotel at Sixth Ave. and Central Park South (59th St.), is probably the nicest midtown people-viewing spot, though you may get tired of looking at the double-parked limousines.

NIGHTLIFE. When a Broadway baby says good night, it's usually early in the morning, as the song says. And there are plenty of ways to make it through the night in New York City, with bars and lounges permitted to stay open and serve liquor until 4 A.M. every night except Saturday (in reality Sunday morning), when closing time is 3 A.M. Increasingly, too, the big-name discos stay open considerably past that hour—consider that many don't even open until 11 P.M. or midnight—and over the last few years there has been a revival of semi-legal after-hours clubs. The latter either require an actual membership fee that can be used repeatedly, or *call* their fee at the door a membership fee, thus attempting to convince the authorities that they are private clubs (for which there are no restrictions on how late they can serve). The after-hours places actually do sometimes advertise discreetly in the *Village Voice,* catering to a young, high-paying, jet-setting crowd. And when there are the nightlife happenings you just come upon at an unlikely spot, such as not too long ago at a Thai restaurant-café where four young professionals were doing a concert version of *Oklahoma!*

But most New York nightlife is of a more traditional nature, even if the styles and venues have changed and the hours have gotten later. The classy old hotel nightclubs are gone—the Persian Room at the Plaza, the Empire Room at the Waldorf, the Maisonette at the St. Regis—as are the big, flashy comics-and-kickline places such as the Latin Quarter and the Copacabana (though the Copa has been reincarnated as a disco). The accent today is on discos, hip cabarets, trendy rock and roll clubs, and country-in-the-city real or fake honky-tonks. And while you can still find quality entertainment at a handful of hotels and other fashionably appointed addresses, most of New York's nightlife seems to be housed in converted theaters and movie houses, spruced up art deco ballrooms, onetime warehouses, and a onetime theater with a cavernous interior, banks of video screens, and some of the balcony seats left behind for sitting one out.

The rules as far as dress (and everything else—but we'll get to the rest in a moment) are concerned are probably what you'd expect—jackets and ties for men at the more traditionally-minded establishments, glitter and everything you've got at the big name discos, and casual-but-neat just about everywhere else. Admissions, cover charges and/or minimums, and show times vary from place to place, and sometimes from night to night at a given club depending on whether or not there is a live performer and on who that performer is. Call to check, and to find out what the policy is for reservations; some places will accept phone reservations, for others you may have to purchase tickets ahead. Such uncertainty is typical of the current nightlife scene, where the in spot one moment is closed the next; where the hot spot to see and be seen one night is forgotten by morning. Many clubs have a bar from which you can watch or at least hear the act without paying a cover or minimum; check. Some places stand out as the ones to go to if you have only a few nights on the town. We'll single them out first and then provide a longer but still *selective* list broken down into various categories—jazz, pop/rock, cabaret, disco dancing, country, floor shows, hotel rooms and piano bars, comedy/magic. Once in town, consult the *New Yorker* or *New York magazine* for comprehensive capsule listings of who's appearing where, for comprehensive capsule listings of who's appearing where, and the *Village Voice* for the most complete advertising section devoted to nightlife. While the outlying boroughs have their share of popular bars and entertainment, all the serious nightlife spots are centered in Manhattan, even for Brooklynites, a big night out involves a trip into "The City."

Key to credit card information following each listing:

AE = American Express
CB = Carte Blanche
DC = Diners Club
MC = MasterCard
V = Visa

Crème de la Crème

Bottom Line. 15 W. 4th St.; 228–6300. An intimate 400-seat club where rock-and-roll bands, jazz ensembles, folk and bluegrass musicians are the norm—but where classical flutist Jean-Pierre Rampal, modern dancer Laura Dean, and avant-garde composer/pianist Phillip Glass are also to be found. The club is a long black room with the stage plopped in the middle of one wall. The accoustics at the outer tables can be sketchy, so try to arrive in time to get a good seat. These days "graduates" sometimes return, but the emphasis remains firmly rooted in presenting the best new talent under the most professional circumstances. Salads, hamburgers, and pizza are available. Tickets generally range from $10–$12.50 with shows at 8 P.M. and 11 P.M. weekdays, 8:30 and 11:30 P.M. Fridays and Saturdays. No credit cards.

Café Carlyle. At the Carlyle Hotel, Madison Ave. and 76th St.; 570–7192. Bobby Short, considered the piano man's piano man for his mastery of the Broadway classics, appears October–December and April–June, alternating with other artists the rest of the year. Shows are at 10 P.M. and midnight, Thursday–Saturday. Cover charge is $30. No entertainment in July and August. All major credit cards.

Casey's. 1584 York Avenue at 84th St.; 570–5454. Once the old Zulu Lounge, but now completely revamped to a mahogany bar/dance club with brass touches, Casey's is host to a yuppie crowd. Besides a bigger dance floor and a DJ who spins Top 40 tunes, Casey's has a free admission every night before 10, after which it is $5 weeknights and $10 on Friday and Saturday. Open Tuesday–Saturday, 8:30 P.M. to 4 A.M. Wednesday is ladies night. All major credit cards.

Greene Street. 101 Greene St.; 925–2415. Greene Street will give you a taste of contemporary SoHo chic—a former truck garage, it is now a spacious restaurant and cabaret two stories high. With soaring walls, 10 skylights, fieldstone bar, tropical trees, pink and green mural, and no cover charge, the music ranges from classic to avant-garde jazz, with comedy upstairs. Open Tuesdays–Saturdays, 7 P.M.–2 A.M. All major credit cards.

Hors d'Oeuverie. 1 World Trade Center; 938–1111. With its breathtaking view, the Hors d'Oeuverie features a light jazz trio that alternates with a solo pianist beginning at 7:30 P.M. You *can* be entertained cheaply here—the music charge is a mere $2.95, and you can limit yourself to one drink ($3 to $4), but the temptation is to partake of the hors d'oeuvres, for which you are charged by the small plateful. Also, on weekends and during holiday seasons, get there early or you'll be subject to a long wait just to get into the elevator—a 107-story climb. All major credit cards.

King Cole Room. At the St. Regis Sheraton, Fifth Ave. and 55th St.; 872–6140. The only remaining old-style hotel-room nightclub with name entertainment in the city. During the week the King Cole Room offers live piano music. Saturday features dancing to the New Orleans Bourbon Street Jazz Band, beginning at 7 P.M. Consistently high-caliber, small-scale entertainment in a smartly gracious setting. All major credit cards. Food available.

The Palladium. 126 E. 14th St.; 473–7171. Another of Steve "Studio 54" Rubell's brainstorms. Names on their various guest lists are reportedly in the tens of thousands. These people waive the obligation to pay the $20 entrance fee, or the necessity of standing in line to be picked by the doorman. There is as gallery of photographs, prints, and other decorative items; commissioned art decorates the phone booths. It's so big, all the archetypes can mingle. Be sure not to miss the fun and fury downstairs. The Mike Todd Room behind the balcony seats is good for sitting and watching. AE, MC, V.

Rainbow Room. 30 Rockefeller Plaza; 632–5100. For a magical and romantic evening, dance atop the RCA Building to the Rainbow Room Orchestra and the Orchestra Carnaval. Both the Rainbow Room and the Rainbow Grill have been elegantly renovated and have spectacular views from the 65th floor.

The Surf Club. 415 E. 91st St.; 410–1360. Owned by the Beavers brothers, the Upper East Side stalking ground for the Nantucket and Wall Street crowd. Major credit cards.

Here then is a broader but still selective look at some of the better night spots in the Big Apple, broken down by category. "Inexpensive" refers to places where the cover and/or minimum total less than $5; elsewhere, figure on $10 *or more* per person.

Jazz

At jazz clubs in particular you can often sit at the bar and still have a full view of the stage, this can be a big savings when there are cover and/or minimum charges at the tables.

Angry Squire. 216 Seventh Ave. near 23rd St.; 242–9066. Pleasant nautical setting with small intimate booths. Barry Harris and Dakota Staton are regular vocalists. Music every night of the week. Food; $15 minimum. All major credit cards.

Bitter End. 147 Bleecker in the Village; 673–7030. New-talent rock usually, but appearances by the likes of Stephane Grappelli and others 'with some frequency. Music six days, comedy on Tuesdays. Sets usually begin at 8 P.M. No credit cards.

Blue Note. 131 W. 3rd St.; 475–8592. Same name, new club, with lots of mirrors and slatted wood and a stage accommodating trios and quartets most comfortably. A pleasant place to see some of your favorites up close, with shows at 9 and 11:30 nightly. with dinner served from 7 P.M. to 2 A.M. Admission varies; around $12. All major credit cards.

Bradleys. 70 University Pl.; 228–6440. Smokey and always crowded, it's the typical jazz bar, with the emphasis on reflective piano-bass combinations. Music from 9:45 nightly. Inexpensive. All major credit cards.

Crawdaddy. Vanderbilt and 45th St.; 687–1860. Music to go along with the New Orleans decor and food, special festivities always planned around Mardi Gras. All major credit cards.

Fat Tuesday's. 190 Third Ave. at 17th St.; 533–7902. Popular hangout (especially the bar and the street-level restaurant) with a cozy jazz club tucked away downstairs. Music seven nights, with sets at 8 and 10 P.M.. at 8, 10 and midnight Friday and Saturday, Les Paul every Monday at 8 and 10 P.M. downstairs. Dining. Cover, $10–$15; minimum, $7.50–$10. All major credit cards.

Jimmy Weston's. 131 E. 54th St.; 838–8384. The restaurant is popular hangout for spots celebrities, the bandstand in the far corner given over primarily to piano mainstream trios. AE, DC, CB.

Knickerbocker Bar and Grill. 33 University Pl.; 228–8490. The spirit of old Charlie Knickerbocker lives in atmospheric dining room where jazz wafts in from the bar. Noisy but comfortable with simple American fare. All major credit cards.

Michael's Pub. 211 E. 55th St. at Third Ave.; 758–2272. Atmospheric olde English roome with solid mainstream jazz and occasional jazz-based revues. Woody Allen and his Dixieland group on Mondays (including Oscar night). Continental food. A variable minimum, applicable to food or drinks; restaurant is moderate to expensive but highly respectable. All major credit cards.

Peacock Alley. Waldorf-Astoria, 301 Park Ave. at 50th St.; 872–4895. A cozy piano bar where the music plays from 7 P.M. to 1 A.M. and a nice spot for a bruch on Sundays with a harpist from 11 A.M. to 2:45 P.M. All major credit cards.

Red Blazer Too. 349 W. 46th St. at Eighth Ave.; 262–3112. Some say the big-band revival such as it is emanated from here thanks to regular weekday stands featuring a variety of local ensembles. It may be true. Large and always busy with a slightly touristy flavor, and Dixieland seven days. All major credit cards.

Saratoga. 995 Fifth Ave. (in Stanhope Hotel); 744–8714. Len Berge, pianist, is in residence in this classically stylish supper club. Sets at 10 and 11:30 P.M., no cover charge. Dinner and late night supper until 1 A.M. All major credit cards.

Sweet Basil. 88 Seventh Ave. S. just south of Christopher St. in the Village; 242–1785. Knotty pine walls adorned with jazz memorabilia and a wide range of mainstream and contemporary musicians make this one of the most consistently pleasing establishments around. Saturday brunch runs 2–6 P.M. and Sunday brunch features trumpeter Doc Cheatham from 3 to 7 P.M. Evening cover charge is $12 with a $6 minimum. Brunch is $6 minimum. All major credit cards.

Village Gate. 160 Bleecker St. in the Village; 475–5120. A mainstay on the jazz circuit, featuring name players. Music from about 9:30 P.M., seven days a week. Covers range from $12.50 to $25 depending on the act, or you can sip cocktails on the terrace where there is only a two-drink minimum after 10 P.M. and on weekends. All major credit cards.

Village Vanguard. 178 Seventh Ave. S. in the Village; 255–4037. The prototype jazz club—downstairs, smoky, with lousy sound system and cramped quarters. And everyone loves it just as it has been for 40 years. Proprietor Max Gordon can usually be spied napping at a center table. The Mel Lewis Big Band plays on Monday nights. All night sets are at 10, 11:30 P.M. and 1 A.M. $12 cover and $6 minimum weekdays. $12 cover and $6 minimum Fridays and Saturdays. No credit cards.

West End. 2911 Broadway at 114th St.; 666–9160. If you first discovered jazz while in college, you'll feel perfectly at home at this haunt frequented by Columbia and Barnard University students. Sets at 9, 10:30 P.M. and midnight with an additional set at 1:30 on weekends. Music Wednesday–Sunday with a $6 cover and $7.50 minimum. AC, MC, V. Inexpensive.

Zinno. 126 W. 13th St.; 924–5182. Italian restaurant with light mainstream entertainment nightly from 8 P.M. AE, MC, V.

Pop/Rock

Beacon Theatre. 2130 Broadway; 787–1100. This is one of the few actual *theatres* left that offers top-drawer rock, pop, blues, and Latin bands. You can sit in a comfy seat, close to the stage and enjoy good accoustics. Times and prices vary, so call. AE, MC, V.

Bitter End. 147 Bleecker St., in the Village; 673–7030. With the same owner as Kenny's Castaways, this is home for several well-known comedians and vocalists such as Joan Armatrading, Bill Cosby, Warren Zevon, and Steven Wright. This brick-walled, cozy club is also still noted for its share of "discoveries." Open from 8 P.M. to 4 A.M. every night. No credit cards.

CBGB & OMFUG. 315 Bowery near 3rd St.; 982–4052. New York punkers and New Wavers from Blondie to Talking Heads to whoever-the-rage-is-today all served their apprenticeship here. Loud, long, and narrow—and the going can get a mite tough. Always call for set times—but don't necessarily believe what they say. No credit cards.

China Club. Broadway at 75th St.; 877–1166. There's just a light above the door and a doorman behind the velvet rope to mark this club which is a hangout for music-biz types. This can be tiresome, except on those occasions when they bring their buddies like David Bowie to jam. Open seven days, 10 P.M.–4 A.M. AE, MC, V.

Eagle Tavern. 355 W. 14th St.; 924–0275. Traditional Irish music performed here on Mondays, Fridays and Saturdays; comedy on Thursdays. $4 cover weekdays, $5 weekends. No credit cards.

Home. 1748 Second Ave. at 91st St.; 427–3106. A neighborhood bar where the back room is given over to studio musicians and other pros who are working out new, mostly rock-oriented acts. MC, V.

J.P.'s. 1471 First Ave. at 76st St.; 288–1022. Popular record-business hangout with a handful of performers appearing on a rotating basis—and with major name concert acts dropping in after their shows to jam. All major credit cards.

Kenny's Castaways. 157 Bleecker St. in the Village; 473–9870. Folk-based rockers and old-time blues shouters are the mainstay with owner Pat Kenny's ever-jovial presence the place's biggest asset. No cover; two-drink minimum. Sets begin at 9 P.M. No credit cards.

Private Eyes. 12 West 21st St.; 206–7770. A video environment club with dancing from 10 P.M. to 4 A.M. Mondays-Saturdays. Cover $5 Mondays; $8 Tuesdays–Thursdays; $12 Fridays and Saturdays. AE.

Red Parrot. 617 W. 57th St.; 247–1530. Mostly a rock dance club but with a small stage and almost equally small area for the live audience. Still, some big names have appeared—from George Clinton to Cab Calloway. The action doesn't usually get started until 11 P.M. or after. Thursdays: N.Y. Latino, $12; Fridays and Saturdays: four Latin bands. Saturdays, pop headliners perform live. $10 covers Fridays, $15 Saturdays.

Pyramid Club. 101 Avenue A; 420–1590. This is the godfather of East Village clubs and manages to retain originality and spirit despite its venerable position. Entertainment ranges from serial drama to DJ dancing to comedy to drag shows. Sets begin very late and the joint is jumping until 4 A.M. Cover hovers between $7 and $10. No credit cards.

Ritz. 119 E. 11th St.; 254–2800. A 1935 ballroom (in an 1889 building) restored to its original Art Deco glamour and one of the most popular rock clubs in town. Video (on a 30' MX 30' screen) and dance music before and after shows—the latter featuring everything from rockabilly to jazz, new wave to reggae. Downstairs is all for dancing (only a few banquettes along the walls provide seating), and the balcony is usually reserved for visiting VIPs, so be prepared to stand and dance like a mad fiend. Cover varies, $10–$20. No credit cards.

S.O.B.'s. 204 Varick St., just south of the Village on the lower West Side; 243–4940. The initials stand for Sounds of Brazil—and the proprietor of this enormously popular TriBeCa live-music-and-dance emporium means it. The best Brazilian musicians in town are just about in residence here—and the line to get in, once the dinner hour has passed (6–10:30 P.M.), stretches around the block.

Speakeasy. 107 MacDougal St.; 598–9670. Run by the local community of folk musicians, Speakeasy's features current, high-caliber folk performers as well as some rock and acoustic sets. Suzanne Vega began here. Informal, inexpensive (usually $4 and up.) Open seven days a week. Monday night is "Open–Mike" night. Sets are 8:30 and 10 P.M. and 11 P.M. on weekends. All major credit cards.

1018. 515 W. 18th St. at 10th Ave.; 645–5156. This place has gone through various metamorphoses, most recently as a roller rink and hip-hop club. Now it's a large dance space with the latest in sound and vision. Open Wed.–Sat., Cover $10 or $15. No credit cards.

Tramps. 125 E. 15th St.; 777–5077. The one spot in the city regularly featuring traditional blues artists such as Otis Rush and Big Joe Turner. Entertainment seven nights 9:30–midnight. Cover weekdays $5–$7, $7 to $12 on weekends.

Cabaret

The Ballroom. 253 West 28th St.; 244–3005. Tapas (Spanish appetizers) bar and restaurant featuring performers like Blossom Dearie. Sets at 6:30, 9 and 11. All major credit cards.

Broadway Baby. 407 Amsterdam Ave.; 724–6868. Open 7 days from 8 P.M.–4 A.M. Piano bar; waiters and waitressses are sometime Broadway performers, and diners are invited to sing along or take the stage if they show exceptional talent. AE, MC, V.

The Duplex. 55 Grove St. near Seventh Ave. in the Village; 255–5438. A split-level West Village club popular among latter-day torch singers who try to turn their sets into mini-revues. No credit cards.

Freddy's Supper Club. 308 E. 49th St.; 888–1633. Christine Jorgensen made a "come-back" here, and that sort of explains the tone of the place. Entertainment Tuesdays–Saturdays, usually jazz and show tunes.

Greene St. See *Crème de la Crème* above.

Palsson's. 158 W. 72nd St.; 362–2590. Attractive second-floor room that seats about 60 people, with some additional space at the bar. Revues used to change every few weeks, but if a hit revue comes along, it may play for months. Reservations a *must.* The kitchen stays open until last call at 4 A.M. The show performs Monday to Friday, 8 and 10 P.M.; Saturday 7 and 10 P.M.; Sunday 5:30, 8, and 10 P.M. Cover charge at tables *and* bar. All major credit cards.

Sweetwater's. 170 Amsterdam Ave. near 67th St., north of Lincoln Center; 873–4100. Mostly singers of jazz and pop music—and a pleasant stop-off following Lincoln Center performances. Sets are at 9 and 11 P.M. weekdays, 9 P.M. and midnight weekends. Cover is $10 weekdays, $15 Fridays and Saturdays. All major credit cards.

Floor Shows

The days of extravagant Las Vegas and Parisian-style floor shows in New York, once available at the Latin Quarter and Copacabana, are gone. The few that remain are not very good attempts at scaled-down versions of those lavish spectacles, and cater almost exclusively to tourists. For those who insist, we list them herewith, but given the prices most such establishments charge, we suggest that Broadway's *42nd Street,* or something comparable, will be far more satisfying.

Bianchi & Margherita. 186 W. 4th St., Village; 242–2756. Not the usual type of floor show at all—instead, you hear live opera, show tunes, and multilingual melodies performed while you savor your veal piccata. The food's only fair, but the experience is fun. Music is performed Monday–Saturday starting at 7:30 P.M. and Sunday at 6 P.M. No cover. All major credit cards.

Café Versailles. 151 E. 50th St.; 753–3429. Probably the closest you'll come to a Paris-style revue, complete with partial nudity, feathered costumes, and kicking chorus line. Show and dinner are $45 per person plus drinks and tips on weekdays, higher on weekends; the show alone is a $12 cover with a two-drink minimum. Same premises as Club Ibis. (**Note:** closed for renovation, will re–open in July.)

Club Ibis. 151 E. 50th St.; 753–3429. Continental restaurant with exotic decor—but you can't eat decor. The 9 and 11 P.M. and 1 A.M. shows (Saturday 10 and 11:30 P.M., and 1 and 3 A.M.) help take your mind off the food when the Ibis girls are in good form. Upstairs room features belly dancers, Middle Eastern musicians, etc., from 10:30 P.M. $4 cover with a $15 minimum. $6 cover on weekends with a $15 minimum. AE.

Disco/Dancing

Adam's Apple. 1117 First Ave. near 61st St.; 371–8650. Three floors for dining and dancing. American and Italian cuisine. New outdoor café, bar, lounge, and interior café. Open seven days till 4 A.M. All major credit cards.

The Baja. 246 Columbus Ave. at 72nd St.; 724–8890. Opened in 1986 by young Wall Street entrepreneurs, this club resembles a playful, decadent Venice Beach. With free-form, neon art decorating the walls of the Big Pacific room, the Baja also has a dance floor (once a 1940s bowling alley) that's large enough to move around on—a rare treat in NYC! Tuesday is ladies' night. Admission Tuesday–Wednesday, $5; Thursday–Saturday, $10. All major credit cards.

The Cat Club. 76 E. 13th St.; 505–0090. This sometimes seems like a club in search of an identity. It probably *has* had nine lives. Currently they are featuring live New Wave bands on weekends. Open seven days. Cover during the week is $10; Fridays and Saturdays, $15. Things usually get going around 11 P.M. and on occasion, the Cat Club Dancers will appear at 1 A.M.

Copacabana. 10 E. 60th St.; 755–6010. Minus chorus girls but retaining some of its old glamour. The Copa is making a comeback as a disco. Open Tuesday, Friday, and Saturday from 10 P.M. to 5 A.M. Disco music on Fridays, disco, Latin music, and live bands on Saturdays, and Tuesdays. All major credit cards.

Limelight. 660 Sixth Ave. at 20th St.; 807–7850. Housed in a former church; complete with rock videos, church organ, and nooks and crannies to explore. Open seven days 10 P.M.– 4 A.M. Admission $18 Friday and Saturdays. Wednesday is the "Contraversy Club," admission $15, and Sunday is "Rock & Roll Church," admission $15. AE.

Le Onde. 160 E. 48th St.; 752–0200. Split-level supper club with good international food and piano music for listening/dancing from 8 nightly except Sunday. All major credit cards.

Nell's. 246 West 14th St.; 675–1567. Going to Nell's is like going to someone's home, that is if your friends regularly entertain Sting, Jagger, etc. Upstairs is a dining area in back, plush Victorian couches in front; and a DJ-dance floor downstairs. Oh yes, and a phalanx of extremely rude doorkeepers out front. Cover Sundays–Thursdays $5, Fridays and Saturdays $10. AE.

Rainbow Room and Grill. See *Crème de la Crème*.

Régine's. 502 Park Ave. at 59th St.; 826–0990. Mirrors reflect subdued lighting in this playpen for beautiful people with a good (if overpriced) restaurant open Monday–Saturday 7:30 to 12:30. Disco action from 10:30 P.M. to 4 A.M. Closed Sunday. A prix-fixe dinner is $54.50 and includes admission to the dance floor; otherwise cover is $15 weekdays, $25 Fridays and Saturdays. All major credit cards.

Ritz. Rockers, break-dancers, slam dancing—all the latest in full regalia. Young crowd, but it moves. See *Pop/Rock*.

Roma di Notte. 137 E. 55th St.; 832–1128. Dine on Italian food in a private cave, dance to music from 7:30 to 1:30. Closed Sunday. AE, DC.

Roseland. 239 W. 52nd St.; 247–0200. New York's largest dance hall features two live orchestras for continuous dancing nightly Thursday to

Sunday, with matinees Thursday, Saturday, and Sunday and disco nightly from midnight Thursday to Saturday. Has 700-seat restaurant/bar, featuring American cuisine, but no one goes for the food. Admission varies. AE, V, MC.

Stringfellows. 35 E. 21st St.; 254–2444. An import from Britain, this is an upscale stomping ground. Restaurant and nightclub with DJ dancing beginning at 11 P.M. Cover Mondays–Thursdays $15; Fridays $20, Saturdays $25. Closed Sundays. All major credit cards.

37th St. Hideaway. 32 W. 37th St.; 947–8940. Dining/dancing Monday–Thursday at 7 P.M.; Friday at 7:30 P.M.; Saturday at 8 P.M. in actor John Barrymore's former townhouse, with performers usually including singer, trio. Closed Sunday. All major credit cards.

The Tunnel. 220 Twelfth Ave.; 244–6444. This cavernous club is housed in an old subway tunnel, some of which has been left "in the raw"—tracks and all—as a sort of "before" picture. The "after" picture is a wild and funky place open seven nights, 10 P.M. to 4 A.M. Cover is $15 during the week, $20 on weekends. No credit cards.

Wednesdays. 210 E. 86th St.; 535–8500. Disco/bar/restaurant complex that resembles underground European street festival in the form of a block-long underground village and sidewalk cafés, bistros, wine-and-cheese shops, gaslights, trees, huge drinks, American food and all kinds of nightlife entertainment. Closed Sunday and Monday. $5 cover charge after 9 P.M. All major credit cards.

Country

Lone Star Café. 61 Fifth Ave. at 13th St.; 242–1664. The official Texas embassy in New York City, though the bands veer to blues and rock as often as to country. Still, the food and ambience are as close to Southernfried as two New York owners are ever likely to make it. Great chili, ribs, and salads, too. Music from about 9:15 seven nights a week. Average cover, $10–$15. All major credit cards.

O'Lunney's. 915 Second Ave. at 48th St.; 751–5470. The first New York country bar has the most genuinely Western feel to it—the sort of place where women in beehive hairdos and men in ten-gallon hats feel right at home. Live music that's always good for dancing from 9 P.M. Closed Sundays. $3. cover.—sometimes on two floors. All major credit cards.

Also check **Bottom Line, Other End,** and **Ritz.** All sometimes present name country acts.

Comedy/Magic

Caroline's. 332 Eighth Ave. at 26th St.; 924–3499. Also at 89 South Street Seaport; 233–4900. An unlikely neighborhood but a popular restaurant/cabaret where the microcphone is given over to headliners who are somewhere between local favorites and nationally recognized. Shows Tuesdays–Sundays. Shows Fridays at 8 and 11 and Saturdays at 8 and 10:30 Cover and minimum. AE, MC, V.

Catch a Rising Star. 1487 First Ave. near 78th St.; 794–1906. See young new comedians the same time Johnny Carson's talent scouts do—with bigname graduates frequently dropping in to test new material. Some singers change the pace, with the festivities beginning about 7:30 P.M. and the cream of the crop usually going on between 11 and 1. Kevin Nealon from Saturday Night Live frequently appears. Always a fun night, no matter how bad the acts get. $7–$12 cover and two-drink minimum. AE.

Comic Strip. 1568 Second Ave. near 82nd St.; 861–9386. Essentially same format as Catch—nonstop parade of up-and-comers—and frequently with the same acts shuttling between these clubs and the West Side's Improvisation. The fun begins about 9 P.M. Cover and minimum. AE, MC, V.

Dangerfield's. 1118 First Ave. near 61st St.; 593–1650. The "Can't get no respect" man does a stint himself several months out of the year, but mostly the stage is given over to promising newcomers—and Dangerfield has demonstrated a good ear for laugh-provoking talent over the years. Sets from 9:15 Sundays–Thursdays; Fridays at 9 and 12 and Saturdays at 8, 10:30, and 12:30. Sundays–Thursdays, $10 cover and $7 minimum; Fridays and Saturdays, $12.50 cover and $7 minimum. All major credit cards.

Improvisation. 358 W. 44th St.; 765–8268. Before there was Catch or the Comic Strip, the Improv, as it is fondly known, was giving birth to the careers of Richard Pryor, Robert Klein, David Steinberg, and others. They all return to see who the latest finds are as well as to tell their latest stories. Still the most Bohemian of the comedy rooms, and popular for after-theater entertainment and snacking. No credit cards.

Mostly Magic. 53 Carmine St. in the Village; 924–1472. Magic and comedy are paired with audience participation Saturdays at 2 P.M. for children, with periodic special programs for adults. Reservations necessary. Tuesdays–Thursdays, 9:30 P.M.; Fridays and Saturdays 9 and 11 P.M. All major credit cards.

Hotel Rooms and Piano Bars

Algonquin Oak Room. 59 W. 44th St.; 840–6800. Outstanding cabaret performers such as Steve Ross recreate the spirit of the '30s, '40s, and '50s from 9:15 P.M. Tuesday to Saturday and from 5:30 P.M. Sunday. Reservations suggested; $15 cover, $20 on Fridays and Saturdays. All major credit cards.

American Stanhope. See Saratoga Room, under Jazz.

Beekman Tower. 3 Mitchell Place at 49th St. and First Ave.; 355–7300. Great East River and UN views, and sweepingly gentle piano music to go with them, 9 P.M. Tuesdays–Saturdays. No cover, two-drink minimum. All major credit cards.

Bemelmans Bar. Hotel Carlyle, Madison Ave. at 76th St.; 744–1600. Romantically private, usually featuring Barbara Carroll's equally intimate piano playing. 10 P.M.–1 A.M. Tuesdays–Saturdays. All major credit cards.

Burgundy. 467 Amsterdam Ave.; 787–8300. This pleasant Upper West Side café/gallery serves up good food and jazz piano (often with a vocalist) seven nights from 9 P.M. to 1 A.M. $7.50 minimum at the tables on weekend evenings.

Chelsea Place. 147 Eighth Ave. at W. 17th St.; 924–8413. The Alex Room is an intimate retreat from the bustling singles scene at the main-floor bar or the pleasant if undistinguished downstairs restaurant. 5 P.M.–4 A.M. Cover after 8 P.M., Fridays and Saturdays, $10. All major credit cards.

L'Etoile. (The Star). 160 E. 48th St.; 752–0200. Newly opened, this piano bar/restaurant serves true Continental and Italian/American cuisine and hosts cheek-to-cheek dancing Friday and Saturday nights. L'Etoile's piano bar is open 4 P.M.–1 A.M., with a happy hour 5–7 P.M. Two pianists entertain on a lovely baby grand piano. All major credit cards.

Gramercy Park Hotel. 2 Lexington Ave.; 475–4320. A relaxing, calm piano bar overlooking Gramercy Park. Mondays–Fridays, 8 P.M. to midnight. All major credit cards.

Grand Hyatt of New York. Park Ave. at 42nd St.; 883–1234. Piano music for dining at **Trumpet's** restaurant. All major credit cards. 5:30 P.M. to 1 A.M.

Harry's Bar. 212 E. 42nd St.; 490–8900. Pianist performing from 5 P.M. to 1 A.M. All major credit cards.

Monkey Bar. 60 E. 54th St. in the Hotel Élysée; 753–1066. Johnny Andrews has been at the piano here Monday to Friday from 5:30 to 7:30 P.M. since 1941. Enough said. All major credit cards.

Novotel. 226 W. 52nd St.; 315–0100. Perched above Broadway with a smashing view of the lights and action is the *Wine Bistro.* Piano music 6 P.M.–1 A.M. The terrace is open when the weather warms up. Try a crispy French-bread tartine sandwich to accompany your wine. All major credit cards.

Omni Park Central. 870 Seventh Ave. at 55th St.; 247–8000. Disco dancing in the *Notes Bar.* Sunday–Thursday 5 P.M.–1 P.M. Friday and Saturday 5 P.M.–2 A.M. All major credit cards.

Parker-Meridien. 118 W. 57th St.; 245–5000. Piano players Monday–Saturday, 5 P.M.–1 P.M. at the **Montparnasse Bar.** All major credit cards.

Pierre Hotel. Fifth Ave. at 61st St.; 940–8185. Piano music filters through the conversation at the *Café Pierre* for listening, dining, drinking, and dancing from 8 P.M.–1 A.M. Mondays–Saturdays and 7 P.M.–midnight on Sundays. All major credit cards.

Plaza Hotel. Fifth Ave. at 59th St.; 759–3000. The Grand Dame of New York hotels has a trio for dancing in the stately **Edwardian Room** Tuesday to Saturday from 7:30 P.M. to 11:30 P.M. and piano and violin in the classic **Palm Court** from 4 to 12:30 P.M. Sunday until 11:30 P.M. All major credit cards.

Regency Bar. Regency Hotel, Park Ave. at 61st St.; 759–4100. A bit stuffy, perhaps, but intimate and with international overtones in the repertoire of the alternating pianists. Nightly from 6 P.M. All major credit cards.

St. Moritz Hotel. 50 Central Park South; 755–5800. Piano music at the **Café de la Paix** Wednesday–Saturday from 6 P.M.; Sundays at noon and 6 P.M. All major credit cards.

Sheraton Centre. 52nd St. and Seventh Ave.; 581–1000. Piano in **Caffè Fontana** seven-night cabaret with videos and dancing, Fridays and Saturdays 8 P.M.–2 A.M. in **La Ronde.** All major credit cards.

Spindletop. 254 W. 47th St.; 719–2870. Broadway-area restaurant serving Continental food and background piano music from 5 P.M. All major credit cards.

UN Plaza. 44th St. and First Ave.; 355–3400. Various pianists play from 6 P.M. to 12:30 A.M. in a mirrored maze with muted lights called—

what else? —the **Ambassador Lounge.** Mondays–Saturdays, 5:30 P.M.–midnight. All major credit cards.

La Vert Galant. 109 W. 46th St.; 382–0022. Excellent French restaurant with pianist-singer in the lounge Tuesday to Saturday from 7:30 P.M.–midnight. All major credit cards.

Village Corner. Bleecker St. at La Guardia Pl.; 473–9762. Interesting, intimate Village spot where the entertainment is nowhere near as tacky as the surroundings might suggest. Piano music from 8 P.M. nightly, featuring a pianist Friday and Saturday at 9 P.M. and on Sunday, a Jazz Trio from 3–6 P.M. and a pianist at 9 P.M. No credit cards.

Village Green. 531 Hudson St. at Charles St. in the West Village; 255–1650. Piano music from 5:30 P.M. in the upstars bar/lounge—the second flior of a tastefully appointed Greenwich Village restaurant. Closed Mondays. AE, MC, V.

Vista International. 3 World Trade Center; 938–9100. The **Vista Lounge** just above the lobby is where the piano is situated, though the music carries to the front reaches of the Greenhouse and American Harvest restaurants. Music from 7:30–11:30 P.M. Friday and Saturday nights. All major credit cards.

Waldorf-Astoria. Park Ave. and 50th St.; 872–4895. **Peacock Alley;** see *Jazz.* Also, piano bar in the Cocktail Terrace 7 P.M.–1 A.M. All major credit cards.

BARS. No one can drink in every one of Manhattan's bars—and live. Even if someone were to try, the number of places going into business and out of business would soon make the attempt meaningless. What we now offer the visitor to New York City is a *selection* of Manhattan bars, with an attempt to differentiate them by their qualities and their locations.

But we can take no responsibility for the results. Bars, even more than restaurants, are a very personal matter—especially to New Yorkers. Two seemingly similar bars, side by side, will each have its regular customers who will express disdain for the other place. Our descriptions, too, must be subjective to a great degree; "lively," for example, may mean different things to a football player than to a librarian.

Those who like well-appointed drinking places, where most of the clientele are well dressed, behave in a dignified manner, and have generally arrived at a comfortable station (or age) in life, would be well off at the good midtown hotel bars, many of which have been mentioned in the *Nightlife* section, above. These are in the Plaza Hotel *Oak Bar* class. Piano bars, which tend to be restrained, are covered there, too. At the (almost) other end of the scale are the neighborhood bars, with names like Dottie's Pub and McGowan's Tavern. These are where the doormen and cab drivers drink, and where you will be 100 percent certain of getting into a conversation, whether you want to or not. In this group are the chains—*Martin's, Blarney Stone,* and others—where you will also find quite good and *cheap* food counters, with hot pastrami and the like.

That leaves all the rest in the middle. With the exception of a few ethnic bars, we have chosen to cover our selection of bars by geographical area, and to give you some idea of where each place fits in the spectrum.

Now to the subject of Manhattan's famous (infamous?) singles bars. Is it possible for men and women to meet in, say, a commuter bar in Grand Central Station? The phrase "singles bar" seems to belong to a mysterious group of places where everyone eyes each other knowing he or she is single. Beyond that we can say nothing more definite, and can only mention which ones are clearly "singles"—though there are numerous borderline bars. By far the majority of the purely singles bars are on the Upper East Side. And in some parts of town the night of the week is important. Monday is usually the slowest day—Thursdays and of course, the weekends, are the hottest. Peak hours vary, too, much too irregularly to be given here. Also, the character of the clientele may change radically from, say, early evening to the late evening. There is also a belief in some quarters that singles bars wax and wane like the moon. Not true. Most of the places we'll mention here have been doing business for over a decade.

New York bars may stay open, legally, until 4 A.M. every night except Saturday (Sunday morning), when they must close at 3 A.M. Many places, however, close earlier; ask. At some places, when there is a particularly enjoyable crowd at closing time, the bartender will lock the doors and keep serving.

For a little amusement, ask any New York bartender about what happens here when the moon is full.

Enjoy some or all of the emporia below, but a word on New York street sense: Don't stumble unsteadily out of a bar late at night and stroll off into a quiet side street; you'll make yourself a mark. And don't think there is necessarily safety in numbers, unless the numbers are in the vicinity of double digit. Better take a cab and be safe, until you develop your own street sense.

Tipping the bartender has unfortunately become an established custom here at most middle- and upper-class bars, so leave something in some proportion to all your drinks, but not necessarily 15%.

Keep in mind that most New York bartenders put a lot more than the standard Continental shot (measure) into their concoctions, often serving what would be a double or even a triple. But beware of Bloody Marys and other concoctions with strong mixers; all too often, and even in "nice" places, these are light on the liquor.

In almost all of the bars below you can also eat, if not London broil, at least hamburgers and sandwiches. If the food is of special note, we'll say so. Remember, too, that New York likes to eat *late*.

Wall Street Area

This area pretty much empties out of people after work hours—but not entirely. Some stay to drink and socialize. *Harry's at Hanover Square,* 1 Hanover Square (a block south of Wall on Pearl St.) gets a very big crowd after work. *Pig 'n' Whistle South,* at 15 Trinity Place near Morris St., Bowling Green, is another crowded spot, as are *Rosie O'Grady's South,* at 211 Pearl St. north of Maiden Lane, and *Jim Brady's,* 75 Maiden Lane near William St. The latter two may have Irish music later in the evening. At Beaver near Wall St. is a famous name from the history of New York: *Delmonico's,* an upscale place for a quiet drink at the bar. Just a bit north, *Roeblings,* 11 Fulton St., helps brighten up the night scene at the South Street Seaport area as does *Flutie's,* on Pier 17, (owned by Doug Flutie). *Let's Make a Daiquiri,* also on Pier 17, serves delicious daiquiris and frozen drinks, which can be enjoyed on the deck overlooking the East River.

TriBeCa/SoHo

TriBeCa (TRIangle BElow CAnal St.) comes as close as any area south of 110th St. to being Manhattan's *terra incognita*, though if things take their usual course the artists and designers who now enjoy the lower rents and large loft spaces here, will soon be displaced by well-heeled dilettantes seeking an artsy ambience. Coats and ties and dresses and high heels are distinctly uncommon in bars here (and, to a lesser degree, in SoHo). Things usually don't liven up till well after 9 P.M.

Begin your TriBeCa bar tour at a typical TriBeCan place: *Raccoon Lodge,* 59 Warren St. east of West Broadway, where there is an excellent juke box, a pool table, and where you can drink your beer right out of the bottle, country style—though the bartender is likely to be a punk lady with a red dress and orange and green hair. Don't go before 11 P.M. *Morgan's Old New York Grill,* Reade St. near Hudson, has outdoor tables that are very pleasant at sunset in the summer. The bar inside, however, smells like the burial chamber of the Cheops Pyramid. If there is a pool game going on at *Barnabus Rex,* 155 Duane St., and if you don't have a seat at the bar, you may find yourself doing a lot of moving to keep out of the shooting line. Continuing north more or less along the Hudson St. axis—which will eventually bring you right up into SoHo, if you turn east and then go north on West Broadway—you come to *Puffy's,* 81 Hudson St., a bar in the Raccoon Lodge vein, but friendlier. Up the street from Puffy's at 99 Hudson is the *Sporting Club*—catch the game on their giant screens or video monitors. Great crowd on Monday nights and all weekend long. At 145 West Broadway is the *Odeon,* where uptown people come to eat their meat and fish with kiwis. Continuing up West Broadway, don't miss *El Internacional,* an incredibly popular tapas (Spanish appetizers) restaurant and wine bar. The decor is new wave/bizarre, and the clientele is an interesting mix of contemporary New Yorkers.

Cross Canal St. on West Broadway and you are in SoHo (South of Houston St.), which with its tight concentration of lofts, restaurants, bars, clubs, art galleries, and boutiques, is much more on the beaten path than TriBeCa. Your first stop should be at *The Manhattan Brewing Company Tap Room and Restaurant* on Broome St. just west of West Broadway. Ale (light, amber, and porter) is being brewed here for the first time in Manhattan in many a moon. The space is wonderful with the foamy stuff being downed next to beautiful copper brewing vats. A collegiate crowd. The *Broome Street Bar,* at the corner of West Broadway, is probably the best-known SoHo bar, though you'll come out smelling like a hamburger. The slick *Spring Street Bar,* corner of West Broadway, objectifies the soul of today's SoHo; glossy and tense, yet striving to be laid back. Other recommended stops are *I Tre Merli,* 463 West Broadway; *Central Falls,* 478 West Broadway; and the *Wine Bar,* 422 West Broadway. Most of these bars have a special SoHo feeling that comes mostly from the architecture of the old commercial buildings that house them.

This is not true, however, of *Frank Dowd's Rozinante Tavern,* corner of Sullivan and Spring sts., which is more of a mix between the new SoHo and the old Little Italy. (Across the intersection from Dowd's is an excellent pizzeria, Napoli Pizza, which has tables outside for eating and drinking in good weather.) The bar at *Raoul's,* 180 Prince Street, though little more than a passage through the restaurant's front room, affords a price-less sight of SoHo's punk *demimondaines* mixing with Wall Street lawyers. The bar on the southeast corner of Prince and Thompson-it has no legible sign—is one of the raunchiest, seediest joints in the area; you're on your own here.

Greenwich Village/Chelsea

Whereas SoHo's bars seem centered on one relatively small stretch of one street, West Broadway, the Village bars are nicely spread out, both in geography and in the type of clientele. The oldest is probably *McSorley's Old Ale House,* 15 E. 7th St., which banned women from its seedy delights until the 1970s. Go here, if for no other reason than to see what saloons looked like in New York a hundred years ago. This used to be a hangout for Village wise men; there was even a book written just about the place. Have the cheese and Bermuda-onion slices with your beer.

More in the middle of the Village, we recommend a stop at *Kettle of Fish,* 131 West Third St., where you will find a dart board and a usually satisfactory mix of genuine Village residents and NYU grad students. *Knickerbocker Saloon,* University Place at 9th St., has an older crowd, with jazz combo evenings. On Waverly Place near Greene St., *Garvin's* is a pleasant, open bar in a pretty good restaurant. *One Fifth Avenue's* bar (actually two bars) at 2 East 8th St. east of Fifth features conversation that seems to have been written by Woody Allen. The food here is some-what more pretentious than at most places in the neighborhood; live music in the front room later in the evening. A prime hangout for neighborhood lip artists is the *Cedar Tavern,* 82 University Place at 11th St. (The Cedar used to be a real artist's hangout when it existed in a couple of other loca-tions to the west.) At Fifth Ave. and 13th St. is the *Lone Star Café* ("Too Much Ain't Enough," says the banner across the facade), Texas' challenge to Manhattan.

Moving toward the so-called West Village: at 159 W. 10th St. is *Julius,* probably New York's oldest overt gay bar. At or near Sheridan Square (Seventh Ave. at Christopher and W. 4th Sts.) are the *Lion's Head,* 59 Christopher, and the nearby *55 Christopher Street;* both are dingy outposts of the local literati. The *Duplex,* 55 Grove off Seventh Ave. at Sheridan Square, has great sing-alongs later in the evening, in a semi-gay environ-ment. *Jimmy Day's,* right on Sheridan Square, is a good place for people-watching. They boast an impressive bevy of beers on tap, serve pretty good bar-type grub, and most important have tables on the sidewalk during the balmy months. Down Barrow St., near the corner of Bedford St., is a wooden-slatted door that gives into a little courtyard. At the other side of the yard is a door with a little barred window in it. This is the back entrance to *Chumley's,* an old Village hangout, and, on Sundays, often the site of poetry readings. The "front" entrance, with no sign, is just as hard to find.

If you like the Cedar Tavern, the Lion's Head, and Kettle of Fish, try the *Corner Bistro,* at 331 W. 4th St., near Abingdon Square, where Eighth Ave. starts off Hudson St. On Hudson St., at 11th St., is the *White Horse Tavern,* one of Dylan Thomas' favorite saloons— now expanded and with tables outside in good weather. We recommend a stop at the *Peculiar Pub,* 182 W 4th St., a place with lots of character and a menu listing beer from all around the world. *Café Iguana,* 19th St. and Park Ave. S., features Tex–Mex cuisine, music nightly, and an energetic, artsy/yuppie crowd. Don't miss *Chevy's,* on W. 20th St. between 5th and 6th, a dance/diner with a buffet Monday–Friday 5–8 P.M., dancing waiters and waitresses, and special events such as beach parties and lip synch contests. $5 cover weekdays, $10 on weekends.

Midtown and Vicinity

The midtown area has the widest variety of bars of any one part of the city; our review simply starts at the south and works north.

Pete's Tavern, Irving Place at 18th, was probably one of O. Henry's drinking spots. The bar itself is a work of art; tables outside in good weather. *Cadillac Bar,* 15 W 21st St., the waitresses carry tequilla "shooters" in their holsters, and customers write on the walls. *23rd Street Bar and Grill* at 158 E. 23rd, with a soothing green decor, is a congenial stop-in spot for beers or burgers. *Brew's* is a sawdust-on-the-floor emporium on 34th St. between Lexington and Third aves. Upon a plaza on the west side of Third Ave. at 38th is *Rio Grande,* two very lively Mexican restaurants, each with its own bar; the one on the north side, "Texas," seems more active and convivial earlier in the evening. We have mentioned the very good hotel bars. One of the coziest is the little bar—the Blue Bar—just inside the entrance to the *Algonquin Hotel,* around to the right. Throughout the midtown area, you will find that bars near the big companies' offices will be filled with—surprise!—people from those companies. For example, find the bars nearest the CBS building on Sixth Avenue and you'll find broadcasting people. Some bars attract all sorts of hotshots, such as *Charley O's* at 33 W. 48th St. (plus good eats), very convivial at night. Other places: *Maude's,* Lexington Ave. at 51st St. (a slightly younger ad crowd); *Fonda la Paloma,* 256 E. 49th St., the most comfortable, friendly, and generous Mexican-restaurant bar in New York, with Orlando serving; and the king of them all, *P.J. Clarke's,* 915 Third Avenue at 55th St. (Get some chili from the little grill near the front door.)

Charlie Brown's, in the Pan Am Building at the top of the escalators from Grand Central, has some singles action after work (all ages, it seems), as does *Houlihan's,* at 42nd and Lexington and 56th and Lexington. Happy hour with half-price appetizers 4–7 P.M. Or try *Ryan McFadden's,* 2nd Avenue at 42nd St. D.J. Wednesday–Saturday 5 P.M.–3 A.M. Young, business crowd. *Knicker's,* on Second Ave.,near 49th St., features facilities for chess and backgammon, all comers. *The Landmark Tavern,* Eleventh Ave. at the corner of 46th St., is in a somewhat grim neighborhood, but the bar is, in fact, a landmark, is well kept up, and is fun. Try it for Sunday brunch if you aren't otherwise adventuresome. *Mimi's,* 984 Second Ave. at 52nd St., is probably the best place in town for grown-up folks to mingle and have a good time. It's even busy on Mondays, with a sing-along piano bar. *O'Neal's at 57th Street* (Sixth Ave.) is a very tight fit, but the bar sometimes sees discreet single action. Nearby, the *Carnegie Tavern,* in and behind Carnegie Hall at Seventh Avenue and 56th St., is a very pleasant place for a pre- or post-concert toddy; live music too. If you're in the Times Square area and have a thirst and like actors, try the *Century Cafe,* 43rd St. east of Broadway.

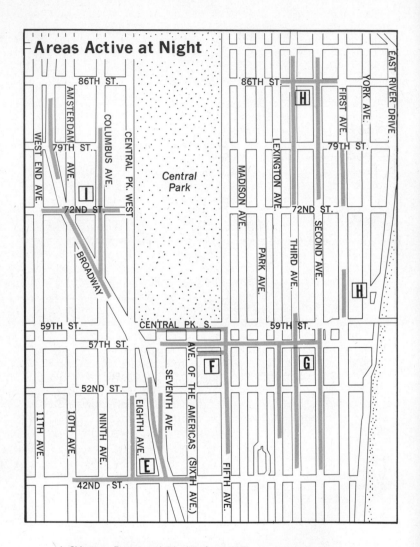

Areas Active at Night

(Map labels:) 86TH ST., AMSTERDAM AVE., COLUMBUS AVE., CENTRAL PK. WEST, WEST END AVE., 79TH ST., 72ND ST., BROADWAY, 59TH ST., 57TH ST., 52ND ST., 42ND ST., 11TH AVE., 10TH AVE., NINTH AVE., EIGHTH AVE., SEVENTH AVE., AVE. OF THE AMERICAS (SIXTH AVE.), CENTRAL PK. S., Central Park, MADISON AVE., PARK AVE., LEXINGTON AVE., THIRD AVE., SECOND AVE., FIRST AVE., YORK AVE., EAST RIVER DRIVE, FIFTH AVE., 86TH ST., 79TH ST., 72ND ST., 59TH ST.

A **Chinatown.** Few bars and clubs, lots of restaurants.
B **Little Italy.** Some bars, lots of cafes and restaurants.
C **SoHo.** Bars, restaurants, cafes, street happenings.
D **Greenwich Village.** You name it, they've got it here, on and off the streets.
E **Times Square Area.** Theaters, movie houses, both straight and porn; bars, restaurants; drug sales on the street. Sleazy and dangerous, especially along 42nd St. and after theaters close.
F **Midtown.** Centered on Fifth Ave. and 57th and 59th Streets. A place for strolling in the early and middle evening; look at shop windows and the other people. A fairly

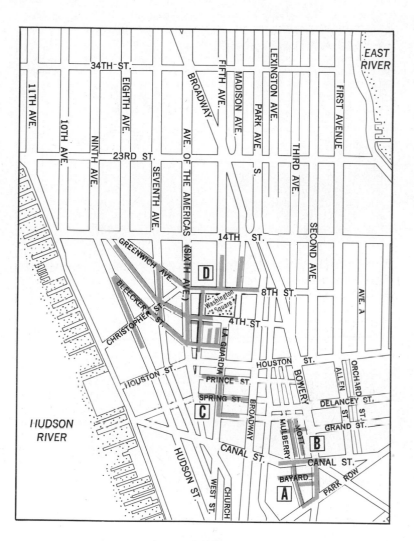

well-heeled group of strollers. 56th St. between Fifth and Sixth Aves. is "Restaurant Row." Some bars, lots of restaurants in entire area. Some street activity.

G **Midtown East.** Second, Third and Lexington Aves. Lots of restaurants. Lots and lots of bars. Nightclubs here, too, and discos.

H **Upper East Side.** The three singles streets: First, Second and Third Aves. Restaurants, bars, clubs, discos.

I **Lincoln Center.** Also part of the Upper West Side. Bars, restaurants, clubs, discos, particularly on Columbus Ave. Lots of street life and mummery.

Lincoln Center Area

O'Neals Baloon, is right across the street from Lincoln Center at 63rd St. The drinks are expensive but the place is busy and interesting. The name was originally to have been O'Neal's Saloon, but some city department objected, so to save money—and annoy the city—the owners merely exchanged a *B* for the offending *S.* Now there are lots of "saloons," such as *The Saloon* at Broadway and 64th St., a barn of a place. The bar has all the character of a baggage pick-up area in an airport. *The Ginger Man,* a small bar in a pleasant restaurant, is around the corner a few steps east on 64h St.

Going up Columbus Avenue from Lincoln Center, the bars come fast and usually furious. To single out just a few: *Columbus,* 69th and Columbus, is crowded with stars and stargazers; limos line the avenue in front and well-dressed bouncers keep out what they consider the "riffraff" and those under 25. At Columbus and 74th, *Il Cantone* has a "wine cellar" in the basement. *Palsson's,* 72nd St. between Broadway and Columbus—nice restaurant at back, too, as well as a modest cabaret upstairs. After 10:30 P.M. it attracts show-business types. *Memphis,* Columbus between 75th and 76th, owned by actor Al Corley (Stephen Carrington of TV's *Dynasty*) is currently *the* hot spot; beautifully designed, Cajun food, live jazz, lively bar. *Ernie's,* on Broadway near 75th St. is large, noisy, and usually jammed after 9 P.M. The waiters are all unregenerate preppies and the crowd a bit self-conscious, but it *is* hopping. The menu is 15 miles long and tends to be pricey, as are the daily specials. If you just want some munchies to go with your drink, try the pizzas. The *Museum Café,* at Columbus and 77th St., is well situated, across the street from the Museum of Natural History grounds.

Upper West Side

The *All-State,* on 72nd St. just east of West End Ave., is cozy, friendly, and very cheap, patronized by the younger working people of the neighborhood. On the corner of Amsterdam and 76th is the relatively tranquil West Side branch of *J. G. Melon,* a nice old-style-bar setting. *Amsterdam's Bar and Rotisserie,* on Amsterdam at 80th St., enjoy a frosty Rolling Rock and munch on their infamous chicken. *Lucy's Bar/Restaurant* and surf joint on Columbus at 84th St, is cacaphony in a very young, good-natured way, so grab a Dos Equis and enjoy. Two popular newcomers at Broadway and 89th are *Dock's* (west side) and *Ichabod's* (east side). The former is brass and tile floor with a great cold seafood bar. The latter is potted palms and neon; seats spill out onto the sidewalk in summer. *Hard Rock Cafe,* 57th St., between Broadway and 7th Ave., a touristy atmosphere, worth the wait to get in. Classic Rock played constantly with music memorabilia adorning every wall. *Brat's* at 2662 Broadway is near the Metro and Thalia cinemas and caters to the pleasanter neighbors. *Hanratty's,* Amsterdam and 95th St., is on a less-than-good block, but somehow its pleasant character attracts Upper West Side literary folks. *The Abbey Tavern,* off Broadway on 105th St., is a long-time spot for Columbia hangers-on; and the *West End,* 2911 Broadway almost opposite Columbia University, is the headquarters for the college's drinking class. There is live jazz in the back in the evenings.

Upper East Side

Now we are in Bar-Hopping Country. The bars that are pure-and-simple meeting places we will label as such, but up here the scenes are really where you find them. Many of the latest "in" spots aren't listed here: too new. But follow the crowds and you spot them. Note that some of these places actually charge admission on certain days, usually weekends; we do not attempt to list which charge, or when, or to tell you why you should pay such a charge anyway—we don't know why. First Ave. is "youngest," Second Ave. only a bit "older" in flavor (for late 20s, maybe), and Third is for fogies over 30.

First Avenue

The most well-worn strip is on First Ave. between 61st and 65th sts. The first and one of the most well known of all is *Thank God It's Friday*, in its bright blue building at 63rd St., now a rather staid place. A block south is *Adam's Apple*.

Skipping ten blocks to the north, there is a whole string of bars, has its own discrete atmosphere and devoted clientele. *Finnegan's Wake* (73rd St.); *Wilson's*, at 75th, has newly reopened and is currently popular; *JP's*, between 76th and 77th, features live rock music. *Petaluma's*, (at 73rd), a trendy bar/restaurant on the Upper East Side; and *Samantha's* (78th) for somewhat more mature clientele.

Second Avenue

Hudson Bay at 76th is a pleasant, quiet neighborhood place. *Mad Hatter*, between 77th and 78th sts., is less quiet, for the slicker East Sider, is a favorite jock hangout, especially for rugby players. *Mumbles*, at 78th, is very trendy and dressy—as if it has lost its way from Third Ave. *Olde New York* is a pleasant saloon between 81st and 82nd on the west side of Second. *Drake's Drum* (between 84th and 85th streets) has been a solid neighborhood standby for years.

On 84th St. between Second and Third aves. is *Brandy's*, a seedy-looking dive that is another survivor, with music nightly. Brandy's, with its gay overtones and extremely casual, nonthreatening atmosphere, comes close to being a European-style *boite*, and is a welcome relief from the affected cool so common on the Upper East Side. *Pedro's*, 251 E. 85th between Second and Third, looks even more downscale than Brandy's, but turns out to be quite a meeting place for Manhattan's Deep South contingent.

In the vicinity of the corner of Second Ave. and 88th St. stands three bars of special note. *Tuba City Truckstop*, at 88th and 2nd Ave., is a southwestern diner with an active and attractive crowd. *Elaine's*, across Second Ave., is fun if you are a nationally famous figure in the arts or politics. Otherwise, you'll be a lot happier across Second Ave. at *Rathbone's*, a rather jockish place run by a former British professional soccer player; nice food at reasonable prices, which is why the bar is unfortunately mostly turnover business from folks waiting for a table.

Third Avenue

This is the Champs-Élysées of the Upper East Side bar circuit. *Rusty's* at 73rd St., and *Churchill's*, a few doors to the north, are both for the over-

30s. *J.G. Melon,* at 74th St., is likewise a nice but hardly madcap place. *Harper,* between 74th and 75th sts., is mostly a restaurant, but the bar scene is considered attractive by the sort of young or used-to-be young people who read *Vogue* or *GQ* magazines. And if Harper isn't smug enough for you, do try *Jim McMullen* between 76th and 77th for the ultimate in nervous Third Avenue quasi-chic. *Ravelled Sleave,* between 78th and 79th, is a long-established preserve for preppies of all ages; and a very pleasant place withal. Definitely stop at *Ciao Bella,* at 75th St. and 3rd Ave. and have a "Bellini" (champagne and strawberries). Host and co-owner Enrico will greet you with a friendly "ciao." Very chic, Euro crowd.

Martell's, on the corner of 83rd St., is one of the most comfortable all-purpose bars on the Upper East Side. There is a large restaurant as well, and tables outside in good weather. For sports fans, a visit to *Polo Grounds* on 3rd Ave. at 83rd St. is a must. Watch your favorite game on wide screen televisions while sampling their vast assortment of beer.

Other Upper East Side bars are: *Beekman Tower Bar,* First Ave. at 49th St., a wonderful—and romantic—place for viewing the city at night indoors or out on the deck. For a taste of what's "down under," venture up 3rd Ave to 93rd St. and "blow the froth" of a Foster's lager at *Outback,* an Australian bar/restaurant. Up First Ave. a bit, at 53rd St., is the *Mayfair,* a gathering place for the executives who make their homes in this very affluent part of the city. For a look at famous people and not-so-famous people with money in the bank, have a drink at the bar at *Mortimer's,* Lexington at 75; this unfancy place passes for the Beautiful People's neighborhood burger joint.

Ethnic Bars

The ones we recommend happen to be mostly of the Irish persuasion. *The Green Derby,* 994 Second Ave. near 52nd St. and 1725 2nd Ave. at 89th St., makes an attempt to serve Guinness on tap—the right way. *The Eagle Tavern,* 355 W. 14th St., has country and Western, Irish and Scottish music on Monday and weekend evenings, and, every Thursday evening, a comedy session. *John Barleycorn,* 209 E. 45th St., has Irish music. *Jim Brady's* and *Rosie O'Grady's* we've mentioned in the *Wall Street* section.

Chances are that the bar you end up liking best isn't even listed by us. That's the way it is with New York City. Enjoy.

Index

General Information
for New York City

Auto clubs, 2
Auto travel & driving laws, 5–6
British Commonwealth visitors
    information, 2–3
Climate, 1, 4
Conversion tables, 9–10
Costs, 4–5
    food, 5
    hotels & motels, 4–5
Credit cards, 2
Drinking laws, 6
Emergencies, 8
Ethnic make-up, vii
Handicapped travelers, 8
Holidays, 6–7
Hotels & motels. *See under* New York
    City *for details*
Hours of business, 6–7
Information sources, 3. *See also* New
    York City
Local time, 6
Mail, 7
Metric conversion charts, 9–10
Package tours, 1–2
Packing & clothing, 3–4
Pets, 4
Religious worship, 6
Restaurants. *See under* New York City
    for details
Seasonal events. *See under* New York
    City
Senior Citizen discounts, 2, 8
Sports. *See under* New York City
Student discounts, 2, 8
Tipping, 7–8
Travel agents, 1
Traveler's checks, 2
Trip planning, 1–2

New York City

A & S Plaza, 202
Abigail Adams Smith Museum, 154–155,
    184
Abyssinian Baptist Church, 86
Addresses, key to, 119
Afro Arts Cultural Center, Inc., 184
Alexander's, 203
Algonquin Hotel, 69, 108
Alice Tully Hall, 80, 191, 192
Alternative Museum, 184
Altman's, 202, 204
American Academy of Arts and Letters,
    85, 184
American Ballet Theatre, 195
American Broadcasting Co. & Bldg., 70
American Craft Museum, 159
American Indian-Heye Museum &
    Foundation, 85, 178
American Institute of Graphic Arts, 184
American Museum of Immigration,
    38–39, 184
American Museum of Natural History,
    80–81, 141, 159–162
    plan of, 160–161
American Numismatic Society, 85, 162
American Stock Exchange, 102
Americas Society, 184
Apollo Theater, 86
Aquarium, 34, 95, 139, 142–143
Aqueduct race track, 97
Art galleries, 23, 82
Asia Society, 162–163
Astroland, 34, 139, 144
Atlantic Avenue (Brooklyn), 15, 33, 93
Atlantic City, 103
Aunt Len's Doll and Toy Museum, 184
Avenue of the Americas, 20, 68–72
Avery Fisher Hall, 80, 191, 192

Babysitting services, 140–141
Baker Field, 88
Bars, 295–299, 302–304
 ethnic, 304
 Greenwich Village/Chelsea, 298–299
 Lincoln Center area, 302
 Midtown, 299
 TriBeCa/SoHo, 297–298
 Upper East Side, 303–304
 Upper West Side, 302
 Wall Street area, 296
Bartow Mansion, 100, 187
Baseball (college), 150–151
Baseball (pro), 148
Basketball (college), 150–151
Basketball (pro), 149
Battery Park, 36, 39–40, 135, 151, 152
Battery Park City, 40
Beaches, 139–140
Bedford Street, 57
Beekman Place, 75
Bergdorf Goodman, 202, 204
Bethesda Fountain, 77, 135
Bible House, 185
Bicycling, 144–145
Billiard academies, 146
Billopp Conference House, 90
Bleeker Street, 56–57, 58
Bloomingdale's, 66, 201, 203
Boat Basin Marina (79th St.), 85
Bonwit Teller, 202
Boorman House, 53, 154
Botanic Garden (Brooklyn), 33, 94, 138
Botanical Garden (Bronx), 33, 35, 99, 136, 137–138
Botanical Gardens (Queens), 139
Bowery, The, 31, 50
Bowling alleys, 146
Bowling Green, 36, 40, 152
Bowne House, 96, 156, 188
Boxing, 149–150
Brazilian Row, 69
Brighton Beach, 15, 95
Broadway, 21, 66–68
 theater, 196–197
Bronx, The, 14, 15, 34–35, 97–100
Bronx Museum of the Arts, 187
Bronx Park, 99
Bronx Terminal Market, 97–98
Brooklyn, 33–34, 88–89, 92–95
Brooklyn Academy of Music, 33, 193, 196
Brooklyn Bridge, 15, 32, 34, 47
Brooklyn Children's Museum, 142, 188
Brooklyn Heights, 32, 33, 93, 155
Brooklyn Historical Society, 188
Brooklyn Museum, 33, 94, 163–164
 plan of, 166–167
Bryant Park, 68–69
Buchanan Apt. Bldg. Courtyard, 76

Cabarets & floor shows, 289–290
Cafés & coffeehouses, 283–284
Canal Street, 51

Carnegie Hall, 70, 191, 192
Castle Clinton National Monument, 39, 152
Castleton, 90
Caswell-Massey, 76, 203
Central Park, 76–77, 135
 map of, 134
Century Club, 69
Channel Gardens (Rockefeller Center), 71
Chelsea, 31, 61–63
Chelsea Hotel, 61, 114
Cherry Lane Theatre, 57
Chess & backgammon, 146
Children's activities, 141–144
 circus, 144
 fun & games, 142
 museums, 141–142
 other suggestions, 143–144
 sightseeing, 143
 zoos, 99, 137, 142–143
Children's Museum of Manhattan, 185
China House Gallery, 164
Chinatown, 30, 47–50
Chinese Museum, 48
Christmas window decorations, 144
Christopher Street, 58
Chrysler Building, 14, 75
Churches & synagogues, 102. See also individual listings
Circle-in-the-Square Theatre, 56–57
Circle Line cruises, 32, 88, 131
Circuses, 144
Citicorp Center, 76
City Center, The, 70, 195
City Hall Bldg. & Park, 46–47, 154
City Island, 35, 98, 100
Clam bars, 51
Cloisters, The, 33, 88, 164
 plan of, 168
Clove Lake Park, 136
Columbia Broadcasting System & Bldg., 70
Columbia University, 85, 88
Columbus Avenue, 21, 80
Columbus Circle, 35, 70
Comedy/magic, 292–293
Commerce Street, 57
Coney Island, 15, 34, 139–140
Conference House Association, 189
Connecticut (nearby), 103
Conservatory Gardens, 139
Convention & Visitors Bureau, 35, 102, 124
Cooper-Hewitt Museum (Andrew Carnegie Mansion), 84, 164–165
Corona, 97
Country music, 292
Cruises (one-day), 102
Customs House, 40, 152

Daily News Bldg., 75, 125
Dance, 23, 194–196
Delacorte Geyser, 32, 75

Delacorte Shakespeare Theatre, 77, 135, 200
Diamond Center district, 69
Discos, 291–292
Donnell Library, 157
Downtown West Side, 31
Drawing Center, 185
Dyckman House, 88, 155

East Harlem, 31
East River, 32
East Side, Lower, 31, 50–51
East Side, Upper, 31
East Village, 31, 59–60
Eighth Avenue, 21
8th Street, 52, 59
Eleventh Avenue, 21
Ellis Island, 39, 152
Empire State Bldg., 14, 66, 100, 143
Equitable Life Assurance Bldg., 40
Ethnic make-up, vii, 15
Excursions from New York City, 102–103
Exxon Building, 69–70

Fashion Institute of Technology, 185
Father Demo Square, 57
Federal Hall National Memorial, 44, 153, 185
Federal Hall Memorial Museum, 44
Federal Reserve, 44
Ferrara's Coffee Shop, 51
Fifth Avenue, 20, 63, 66
Fifty-Ninth St. Bridge. *See* Queensboro Bridge
Fire Island, 102
First Avenue, 19
Fishing, 147
Flatiron Bldg., 14
Flushing, 96
Flushing Meadows/Corona Park, 97, 136
Football (college), 150–151
Football (pro), 149
Ford Foundation Bldg., 75, 139
Fort Tryon Park, 86, 88, 135
Fort Wadsworth, 136
Fort Washington Park, 33, 85
Fraunces Tavern, 42–43, 152
Free events, 129–131
Frick Collection, The, 81, 165
  plan of, 169
Fulton Ferry, 33
Fulton Market Bldg., 43
Fulton St. Fish Market, 43, 203

Gambling, 151
Gardens, 137–139
Garment District, 31
Gateway National Park, 34, 140
Gay Street, 58
General Theological Seminary, 62
"Genius Row," 52
George Washington Bridge, 33
Goethe House, 185
Golf courses, 146–147

Golf tournaments, 150
Gracie Mansion, 32
Graham Galleries, 82
Gramercy Park, 31, 60
Grand Army Plaza, 94
Grand Central Terminal, 75
Grand Concourse, 35
Grand Hyatt Hotel, 75, 108–109
Grand Street, 51
Grant's Tomb, 33, 85, 155
Graveyard of Revolutionary Heroes, 86
Greenwich Avenue, 59
Greenwich Village, 18, 31, 52–59, 101, 154
Grey Art Gallery, 185
Grolier Club, 185–186
Grove Court, 57
Grove Street, 57–58
Guggenheim Bandshell, 80, 191
Guggenheim Museum, 82, 84, 165, 170
Guyon-Lake-Tysen House, 92

Hall of Fame for Great Americans, 33, 187
Hall of Science of The City of New York, 34, 97, 188
Hamptons, The, 102–103
Harbor Defense Museum, 170
Harlem, 31, 85–86
Harvard Club, 69
Haupt Conservatory, 99
Hayden Planetarium, 81, 141, 162
  laser shows, 141
"Hell's Kitchen," 62
Hemlock Forest, 35
Henri Bendel, 202–203
Henry Hudson Bridge, 33
Hispanic Society of America Museum, 85, 170
Historic sites, 151–156. *See also individual listings*
Historical Society, 80, 182
History & background, 27–32, 88–90, 92–93, 96–98
Hockey, 149
Holy Family Church, 76
Horseback riding, 148
Horse carriages, 132
Horse racing, 150
Hotels & motels, 105–116
  entertainment, 293–295
  general information, 105–107
  Manhattan, 107–116
    airports, 116
    deluxe, 108–111
    first class, 111–113
    inexpensive, 114–116
    moderate, 113–114
    super deluxe, 107–108
Hudson River, 36, 88
Hudson Street, 57
Hyde Park, 103

Ice-skating, 147

Information sources, 124–125
Institute of Fine Arts of New York
    University (Duke Mansion), 82
Interchurch Center, 186
International Center of Photography, 170
Intrepid Sea-Air Space Museum, 186
Introduction to New York City, 11–26
Inwood Park, 33

Jacob J. Javits Convention Center, 32, 63
Jacob Riis Park, 136, 140
Jacques Marchais Center of Tibetan
    Arts, 92, 189
Jamaica, 96
Jamaica Bay Wildlife Refuge, 95, 143
Japan House, 76, 138–139
Japan Society, 170
Jazz, 286–288
Jefferson Market Courthouse, 58, 154
Jersey shore, 103
Jewish Immigrant Memorial, 151
Jewish Museum (Warburg Mansion), 84,
    170–171
J.M. Mossman Collection of Locks, 186
Joffrey Ballet, 195
Jogging & running, 144–145
John F. Kennedy Airport, 34
Jones Beach, 140
Julliard School for the Performing Arts,
    80, 191, 192

Kitchen, The, 186

Lady of Lebanon Church, 155
La Guardia Airport, 34
Lefferts Homestead, 94–95, 155
Lexington Avenue, 20
Liberty Island, 36, 39
Libraries, 156–159. *See also individual
    listings*
    special-interest, 158–159
Library and Museum of the Performing
    Arts, 80, 156–157, 171, 191, 193
Library for the Blind and Physically
    Handicapped, 157
Lincoln Center, 31, 80, 101, 191
    area, 31
"Little Church Around the Corner," 58,
    61
Little Italy, 31, 51, 52
Little Red Schoolhouse, 34
Lord & Taylor, 202, 204
Lotteries, 151
Louis Armstrong Stadium, 97
Lower East Side, 31, 50–51

MacDougal Alley, 56
MacDougal Street, 56
Macy's, 201–202
    Thanksgiving Day Parade, 129
Madison Avenue, 20
Madison Square Garden, 149, 194
Manhattan, 11–14, 35–88
    key to street numbers, 119

Manhattan Bridge, 32
Manhattan Plaza, 68
Manhattan's Children's Museum, 142
Maps
    Central Park, 134
    Chinatown, 49
    Greenwich Village, 54–55
    Harlem, 87
    Lincoln Center, 78
    Little Italy, 49
    Lower Manhattan, 41
    Manhattan orientation, 30–31
    Midtown Manhattan, 64–65
    Morningside Heights, 87
    nightlife areas, 300–301
    Public Library, 157
    points of interest (Manhattan), 24–25
    shopping areas, 206–207, 216–217
    SoHo, 49
    subway, back cover
    United Nations, 74
    Upper East Side, 83
    Upper Manhattan, 87
    Upper West Side, 79
Marble Collegiate Church, 61
Marine Memorial, 39
Marriott Marquis (hotel/theater complex),
    68, 109
McBurney YMCA, 62
McSorley's Ale House, 298
Metropolitan Club, 69
Metropolitan Museum of Art, 82,
    171–173
    plans of, 174–177
Metropolitan Opera House, 77, 80, 192,
    194
Mid-Manhattan Library, 156
Midtown Manhattan, 31, 63–76
Minetta Brook, 56
Monsanto Bldg., 69
Morgan Bank Bldg., 44
Morningside Heights, 31, 85
Morris-Jumel Mansion, 86, 155
Morton Street, 57
Mott Haven Historic District, 35
Mott Street, 51
Movies, 189–190
Mulberry Street, 51
Municipal Bldg., 47
Murray Hill, 31
Museo Del Barrio, 186
Museum of American Folk Art, 178
Museum of Broadcasting, 141, 186
Museum of Holography, 141, 186
Museum of Modern Art, 70, 178–181
Museum of American Indian-Heye
    Foundation, 85, 178
Museum of the City of New York, 84,
    178
Museums, 23, 102, 159–189. *See also
    individual entries*
Music, 23, 190–194. *See also* Nightlife
    classical, 190–193
    popular, 194

Narrows, The, 36
Nathan Hale Statue, 154
National Academy of Design, 182
National Arts Club, 61
National Broadcasting Co. & Bldg., 70
Neighborhoods of New York, 101
New Brighton, 90
New Museum, 186
New York Aquarium, 34
New York City Ballet, 80, 194
New York City Center, 70
New York City Opera, 80, 192
New York Experience Theater, 69, 131
New York Fire Museum, 186–187
New York Historical Society, 80, 182
New York Magazine, 125
New York Mets, 34, 97
New York Newsday, 125
New York Philharmonic, 77, 80, 191
New York Post, 125
New York Shakespeare Festival Public
    Theater, 77, 200
New York State Theater, 80, 191, 192,
    194
New York Stock Exchange, 44, 102
New York Times, 67, 125
New York University, 56
New York Yacht Club, 69
New Yorker Magazine, 125
Newspapers & magazines, 125
Nightlife, 284–295
    cabaret, 289–290
    comedy/magic, 292–293
    country, 292
    crème de la crème, 285–286
    disco/dancing, 291–292
    floor shows, 290
    hotel rooms/ piano bars, 293–295
    jazz, 286–288
    map, 300–301
    pop/rock, 288–289
92nd Street YM-YWHA, 192
Ninth Avenue, 21

Off-Broadway theaters, 199–200
Off-Off Broadway theaters, 199–200
Old Merchant's House, 154
Opera, 192
Orchard Beach, 35, 99–100, 140
Orchard Street, 51
Our Lady of Pompeii Church, 57

Palisades, 33, 88
Pan Am Bldg., 75
Park Avenue, 20
Parking, 117
Parks, 133, 135–136. *See also individual
    listings*
Passenger ships piers & terminal, 68
Patchin Place, 58
Pelham Bay Park, 35, 98, 99, 136
Pen and Brush, 187
Piano & hotel bars, 293–295
Pierpont Morgan Library, 173, 178

Pier 17, 43
Player's Club, 60–61
Playland, 144
Plymouth Church, 93–94
Poe Cottage, 98–99, 155
Pop/rock music, 288–289. *See also* Music
Population, 14
Princeton University, 103
Prospect Park, 94, 136, 143
Provincetown Playhouse, 56, 199
Public Library, 156–157, 182–183
    42nd St. Library—main branch,
        156–157, 182–183
    map of, 157

Quaker Meeting House, 96
Queens, 14, 15, 34, 96–97
Queensboro Bridge, 32
Queens Museum, 34, 188

Radio City Music Hall, 70, 72, 143–144
Rainbow Room, 72, 233
RCA Building, 72, 143
Recommended reading, 125–126
Restaurants, 22–23, 229–284
    general information, 229–232, 234
    Manhattan, 234–279
    American-international, 234–240
        deluxe, 235–236
        expensive, 236–238
        inexpensive, 239–240
        moderate, 238–239
        super deluxe, 234–235
    Brazilian, 247–248
    British, 248–249
    Brunch, 233
    cafeterias, 232
    Cambodian, 249
    chains, 232
    Chinese, 249–252
    coffeehouses, 283–284
    Czechoslovakian, 252
    dairy, 245
    delicatessen, 245–246
    desserts, 233, 282–283
    fast food, 232
    French, 253–258
    German, 258–259
    Greek, 259
    Hawaiian, 259
    health food, 246–247
    Hungarian, 259–260
    Indian/Bangladesh, 260–262
    Irish, 262
    Italian, 263–270
    Jamaican, 270–271
    Japanese, 271–273
    Jewish/Kosher, 273–274
    Korean, 274
    Middle Eastern, 230, 274
    other boroughs, 279–282
    pizza, 232
    places with a view, 233
    Russian, 274–275

Restaurants (*continued*)
  Scandinavian, 275
  seafood, 243–245
  southern, 247
  Spanish, 275–276
  steak houses, 240–242
  Swiss, 276
  Tex-Mex, 276–277
  Thai, 278
  twenty-four hour restaurants, 232–233
  Ukrainian, 278
  Yugoslavian, 278–279
Richmond (Staten Island), 90
Richmondtown, 91
Richmondtown Restoration/Staten Island
  Historical Museum, 34, 91–92, 189
Riis Park, 136, 140
Riverdale, 35, 100
Riverside Church, 33, 85
Riverside Drive, 85
Riverside Park, 85, 135
Rockefeller Center, 70–72, 101
Roller skating, 145, 147
Roosevelt Island, 32, 73, 143

St. Anthony's Festival, 51
St. George (Staten Island), 90
St. John the Divine, 85
St. Luke's Chapel, 57
St. Luke's Place, 57
St. Mark's-in-the-Bouwerie, 60, 153
St. Mark's Place, 51, 59
St. Patrick's Cathedral, 72
St. Paul's Chapel, 45, 153
St. Peter's Church (Citicorp Center), 76
St. Peter's Episcopal Church, 62
Saks Fifth Avenue, 202, 204
San Gennaro Festival, 51
Sardi's Restaurant, 198, 235
Schermerhorn Row, 43
Schomburg Center for Research in Black
  Culture, 86
Science Museum. *See* Hall of Science of
  the City of New York
Seaport Museum, 43
Seasonal events, 126–129
Second Avenue, 19, 51
Seventh Avenue, 20–21, 63
Shea Stadium, 15, 97
Sheepshead Bay, 95
Sheridan Square, 58
Shopping, 23, 26, 200–228
  antiques, 218–221
  art & craft supplies, 225
  art galleries, 215, 218
  bargain shopping, 208
  beauty salons, 212–213
  books, 221–223
  children's clothing, 209–210
  cosmetics & toiletries, 212
  department stores, 144, 200–203, 210
  general information, 200–203
  gourmet food & equipment, 213–215
  jewelry, 211–212

leather & luggage, 212
maps of shopping areas, 206–207,
  216–217
men's clothing, 208–209
music & musical instruments, 223–224
photographic equipment, 224–225
records & tapes, 223
South Street Seaport, 203
specialty stores, 226–228
sporting goods, 225–226
tobacco, 215
toys, 213
women's clothing, 204–205, 208
Shrine of St. Elizabeth Ann Seton, 151
Shubert Alley, 198
Sightseeing checklist, 100–102
Sixth Avenue. *See* Avenue of the
  Americas
Sleepy Hollow, 103
Snug Harbor Cultural Center, 34, 92
Society of Illustrators Museum of
  American Illustration, 187
SoHo, 18, 31, 51–52
Soldiers & Sailors Monument, 33, 85
South Street Seaport, 102, 141–142, 153,
  183, 194
Special interest sightseeing, 131–133
Sports, 102, 144–151. *See also specific
  sports*
Spuyten Duyvil, 33, 88
Squash, 148
Stapleton, 90
Staten Island, 15, 34, 89–92
  ferry, 34, 90–91, 123
Staten Island Children's Museum, 142
Staten Island Historical Society Museum,
  91, 188–189
Staten Island Museum, 188–189
Statue of Liberty, 32, 36–39, 100, 143,
  152
Stock Exchange, 44, 102
Stone Street, 153
Store Front Museum, 188
Street life, 35–36
Studio Museum in Harlem, 183
Stuyvesant Park and Town, 153
Subways, 35, 116–117
  map, back cover
Sullivan Street, 57
Swimming pools, 143

Taxis, 18. *See also under* Transportation
Telephones, 105
Tennis, 150
Tennis courts, 147–148
Tenth Avenue, 21
Theater, 23, 196–200
  district, 31, 67
  ticket information, 196–198. *See also*
    TKTS booths
Theater Row, 199
Theodore Roosevelt Birthplace &
  Museum, 61, 154, 187
Third Avenue, 19–20

Thompson Street, 57
Tiffany's, 76
Times Square, 66–68, 102
Times Tower (Allied Chemical Bldg.), 67, 68
TKTS booths, 67–68, 125, 196, 197
  information, 125
Todt Hill, 34, 89
Tompkins Square, 60
Tompkinsville, 34
Tourist information services, 124–125
Tours, 131–133
Transportation, 35
  in New York, 116–124
    airports, 123
    auto, 35, 117–120
    information, 116
    bus, 35, 122–123
    ferries, 123
    limousines, 124
    subway, 35, 116–117
    taxis, 123–124
    walking, 35, 124
  to New York, 104–105
Treasure House, 92
TriBeCa, 31, 48, 101
Triboro Bridge, 32
Trinity Church, 44–45, 153
Trump Tower, 76, 203
Tudor City, 31, 75
Turtle Bay, 75–76
Twelfth Avenue, 21
21 Club, 234

Union Theological Seminary, 85
United Nations, 72–73, 74, 101
University Club, 69
Upper East Side, 31
Upper West Side, 31, 84–85
Urban Center, 187

Valentine-Varian Museum of Bronx History, 187–188
Van Cortlandt Park & House, 35, 99, 136, 155
Verrazano-Narrows Bridge, 36, 89, 90
Verrazano Statue, 152

Vietnam Veterans Memorial, 43
Village Square, 58–59
Village Voice (newspaper), 125
Vivian Beaumont Theater, 80, 191
Voorlezer's House, 34, 91

Wall Street, 18, 30, 43–44, 151, 153
Washington Arch, 53, 154
Washington Heights, 85
Washington Mews, 56
Washington Square & Park, 52, 53, 56, 135, 154
Wave Hill Center for Environmental Studies, 35, 100, 139, 143
Waverly Place, 58
West Broadway, 52
West End Avenue, 21
West Point, 103
West Side, Lower, 31
West Side, Upper, 31, 84–85
Westbeth, 58
White Horse Tavern, 58, 298
Whitney Museum of American Art, 82, 183–184
Wildenstein Gallery, 82
Williamsburg Bridge, 32
Willow Street, 93
Windows on the World Restaurant, 46, 101, 233
Wolfe's Pond Park, 140
Wollman Memorial Rink, 77
Woodstock, 103
Woolworth Building, 14, 40
World Trade Center, 14, 32, 46, 101, 143
World's Fair (site & bldgs.), 34, 97

Yale Club, 69
Yankee Stadium, 15, 32, 35, 97
YMCAs/YWCAs, 146
YMHAs/YWHAs, 146
Yorkville, 31, 84

Zabars, 84
Zoos,
  Bronx, 34–35, 99, 137, 142
  Central Park, 77, 137, 142
  others, 97, 137, 143

Fodor's Travel Guides

U.S. Guides

Alaska
American Cities
The American South
Arizona
Atlantic City & the
  New Jersey Shore
Boston
California
Cape Cod
Carolinas & the
  Georgia Coast
Chesapeake
Chicago
Colorado
Dallas & Fort Worth
Disney World & the
  Orlando Area

The Far West
Florida
Greater Miami,
  Fort Lauderdale,
  Palm Beach
Hawaii
Hawaii *(Great Travel
  Values)*
Houston & Galveston
I-10: California to
  Florida
I-55: Chicago to New
  Orleans
I-75: Michigan to
  Florida
I-80: San Francisco to
  New York

I-95: Maine to Miami
Las Vegas
Los Angeles, Orange
  County, Palm Springs
Maui
New England
New Mexico
New Orleans
New Orleans *(Pocket
  Guide)*
New York City
New York City *(Pocket
  Guide)*
New York State
Pacific North Coast
Philadelphia
Puerto Rico *(Fun in)*

Rockies
San Diego
San Francisco
San Francisco *(Pocket
  Guide)*
Texas
United States of
  America
Virgin Islands
  (U.S. & British)
Virginia
Waikiki
Washington, DC
Williamsburg,
  Jamestown &
  Yorktown

Foreign Guides

Acapulco
Amsterdam
Australia, New Zealand
  & the South Pacific
Austria
The Bahamas
The Bahamas *(Pocket
  Guide)*
Barbados *(Fun in)*
Beijing, Guangzhou &
  Shanghai
Belgium & Luxembourg
Bermuda
Brazil
Britain *(Great Travel
  Values)*
Canada
Canada *(Great Travel
  Values)*
Canada's Maritime
  Provinces
Cancún, Cozumel,
  Mérida, The
  Yucatán
Caribbean
Caribbean *(Great
  Travel Values)*

Central America
Copenhagen,
  Stockholm, Oslo,
  Helsinki, Reykjavik
Eastern Europe
Egypt
Europe
Europe *(Budget)*
Florence & Venice
France
France *(Great Travel
  Values)*
Germany
Germany *(Great Travel
  Values)*
Great Britain
Greece
Holland
Hong Kong & Macau
Hungary
India
Ireland
Israel
Italy
Italy *(Great Travel
  Values)*
Jamaica *(Fun in)*

Japan
Japan *(Great Travel
  Values)*
Jordan & the Holy Land
Kenya
Korea
Lisbon
Loire Valley
London
London *(Pocket Guide)*
London *(Great Travel
  Values)*
Madrid
Mexico
Mexico *(Great Travel
  Values)*
Mexico City & Acapulco
Mexico's Baja & Puerto
  Vallarta, Mazatlán,
  Manzanillo, Copper
  Canyon
Montreal
Munich
New Zealand
North Africa
Paris
Paris *(Pocket Guide)*

People's Republic of
  China
Portugal
Province of Quebec
Rio de Janeiro
The Riviera *(Fun on)*
Rome
St. Martin/St. Maarten
Scandinavia
Scotland
Singapore
South America
South Pacific
Southeast Asia
Soviet Union
Spain
Spain *(Great Travel
  Values)*
Sweden
Switzerland
Sydney
Tokyo
Toronto
Turkey
Vienna
Yugoslavia

Special-Interest Guides

Bed & Breakfast
  Guide: North America
  1936...On the
  Continent

Royalty Watching
Selected Hotels of
  Europe

Selected Resorts
  and Hotels of the U.S.
Ski Resorts of North
  America

Views to Dine by
  around the World